Software Product Line Engineering

Klaus Pohl · Günter Böckle
Frank van der Linden

Software Product Line Engineering

Foundations, Principles, and Techniques

With 150 Figures and 10 Tables

 Springer

Klaus Pohl
Institut für Informatik
und Wirtschaftsinformatik
Universität Duisburg-Essen
Schützenbahn 70
45127 Essen, Germany
pohl@sse.uni-essen.de

Günter Böckle
Siemens AG
Zentralabteilung Technik
Otto-Hahn-Ring 6
81730 München, Germany
guenter.boeckle@siemens.com

Frank van der Linden
Philips Medical Systems
Veenpluis 4–6
5684 PC Best, The Netherlands
frank.van.der.linden@philips.com

http://www.software-productline.com/SPLE-Book

Library of Congress Control Number: 2005929629

ACM Computing Classification (1998):
D.2.1, D.2.9, D.2.10, D.2.11, D.2.13, K.6.3

ISBN-10 3-540-24372-0 Springer Berlin Heidelberg New York
ISBN-13 978-3-540-24372-4 Springer Berlin Heidelberg New York

Springer is a part of Springer Science+Business Media
springeronline.com

© Springer-Verlag Berlin Heidelberg 2005
Printed in Germany

Cover design: KünkelLopka, Heidelberg
Typesetting: Camera-ready by the authors
Printed on acid-free paper   45/3142 YL   –   5 4 3 2 1 0

Preface

I. Software Product Line Engineering

Are you interested in producing software products or software-intensive systems at lower costs, in shorter time, and with higher quality? If so, you are holding the right book in your hands.

Software product line engineering has proven to be the methodology for developing a diversity of software products and software-intensive systems at lower costs, in shorter time, and with higher quality. Numerous reports document the significant achievements and experience gained by introducing software product lines in the software industry. Chapter 21 of this book summarises several cases.

Higher quality, lower cost, and shorter development times

Concerning the terminology, there is an almost synonymous use of the terms "software product family" and "software product line". Whereas in Europe the term software product family is used more often, in North America the term software product line is used more frequently. This is, among other things, reflected in the names of the two former conference series (the software product line conference series, started in 2000 in the USA, and the product family engineering (PFE) workshop series, started in 1996 in Europe) which were merged in 2004 to form the leading software product line conference (SPLC) series.

Software product line vs. software product family

In this book, we use the term *software product line*.

II. Readers of the Book

The book is for those people who are interested in the principles of software product line engineering. It elaborates on the foundations of software product line engineering and provides experience-based knowledge about the two key processes and the definition and management of variability.

Intended readership

We have written the book for practitioners, product line researchers, and students alike.

III. Book Overview

Framework for product line engineering

The book is organised according to our framework for software product line engineering, which has been developed based on our experience in product line engineering gained over the last eight years. The framework stresses the key differences of software product line engineering in comparison with single software-system development:

Two processes

a) *The need for two distinct development processes*: domain engineering and application engineering. The aim of the *domain engineering* process is to define and realise the commonality and the variability of the software product line. The aim of the *application engineering* process is to derive specific applications by exploiting the variability of the software product line.

Variability

b) *The need to explicitly define and manage variability*: During domain engineering, variability is introduced in all domain engineering artefacts (requirements, architecture, components, test cases, etc.). It is exploited during application engineering to derive applications tailored to the specific needs of different customers.

Among others, the book provides answers to the following questions:

- How can we save development costs and development time and at the same time increase the quality of software?
- How can we establish proactive reuse in software development?
- What is the variability of a software product line?
- What are the key activities and aims of the domain and application engineering processes?
- How can we document and manage the variability of a product line?
- How can we ensure consistency of the variability defined in different development artefacts like requirements, architecture, and test cases?
- How can we exploit variability during application engineering and thereby derive specific products from a common core?

Part structure

The book is divided into six parts:

Part I:	Introduction
Part II:	Product Line Variability
Part III:	Domain Engineering
Part IV:	Application Engineering
Part V:	Organisation Aspects
Part VI:	Experience and Future Research

Part I, Introduction, motivates the software product line engineering para-   *Introduction*
digm, introduces our software product line engineering framework, and provides an introduction into the example domain used throughout the book.

Chapter 1 outlines the basic principles of product line engineering
and its roots in traditional engineering.

Chapter 2 introduces our software product line engineering framework. It defines the key sub-processes of the domain engineering
and application engineering process as well as the artefacts produced and used in these processes.

Chapter 3 provides a brief introduction to the smart homes domain
from which examples are drawn throughout the book for explaining
the introduced principles and concepts.

Part II, Product Line Variability, defines the principles of the variability of a   *Variability*
software product line and introduces notations to document variability in all
software development artefacts.

Chapter 4 defines the principles of variability of software product
line engineering and introduces our orthogonal variability model,
which we use throughout this book to document variability in the
various software development artefacts clearly and unambiguously.

Chapter 5 defines how to document variability in requirements artefacts, namely textual requirements, features, scenarios, use cases,
statecharts, and class diagrams.

Chapter 6 defines how to document variability in architectural artefacts, namely in the development view, the process view, and the
code view of a software architecture.

Chapter 7 defines how to document the variability of component
interfaces and the variability within the internal structure of components.

Chapter 8 defines how to document the variability in test artefacts
such as test cases, test case scenarios, and test case scenario steps.

Part III, Domain Engineering, defines the key sub-processes of the domain   *Domain*
engineering process. For each of the sub-processes we define the construc-   *engineering*
tion of the common (invariant) product line artefacts as well as the variability of the software product line.

Chapter 9 introduces the principles of the product management sub-
process within the domain engineering process. This sub-process
mainly deals with topics related to economics and, in particular, to
product portfolio management.

Chapter 10 defines the principles of the requirements engineering sub-process. It defines and illustrates the identification and documentation of common and variable features and requirements for the software product line.

Chapter 11 deals with the definition of a reference architecture for the software product line. It shows how product line commonality and variability are incorporated in the reference architecture.

Chapter 12 deals with the detailed design of reusable software components. It defines how the commonality and variability defined in the reference architecture is mapped onto components.

Chapter 13 discusses the influence of variability on the different test levels and presents and analyses test strategies with regard to their applicability in software product line engineering. The main focus is on establishing a systematic reuse of test artefacts in product line test activities.

Chapter 14 presents a technique for selecting commercial off-the-shelf (COTS) components, which takes into account the variability of the software product line. We consider components that provide a significant fraction of the overall functionality, the so-called high-level components.

Application engineering Part IV, Application Engineering, defines the key sub-processes of the application engineering process. It shows how the orthogonal definition of variability established during domain engineering supports the exploitation and consistent binding of variability during application engineering – and thereby facilitates proactive reuse.

Chapter 15 defines the application requirements engineering sub-process. It tackles the problem of exploiting the common and variable artefacts of the software product line when defining an application. The chapter demonstrates how the orthogonal variability model supports the reuse of product line artefacts during application requirements engineering.

Chapter 16 deals with the application design sub-process which derives an application architecture from the reference architecture. By binding the variability according to the application requirements the required variants are selected and integrated into the application architecture. The sub-process also adapts the design according to application-specific requirements.

Chapter 17 deals with the realisation of a specific software product line application. Ideally, the realisation is achieved through a configuration of reusable domain components and application-specific ones by exploiting the commonality and variability of the components and their interfaces.

Chapter 18 deals with application testing. It shows how the variability – integrated into the domain test artefacts – supports the reuse of test case designs in application engineering. Consequently the effort of developing test cases for the different product line applications is significantly reduced.

Part V, Organisation Aspects, elaborates on two key aspects to be considered when introducing a software product line into an organisation: the organisation structure and the transition strategies.

Organisation aspects

Chapter 19 discusses the benefits and drawbacks of different organisation structures for software product line engineering.

Chapter 20 outlines transition strategies for moving from a single software production to a software product line. It discusses when to apply which strategy depending on the current situation within the organisation.

Part VI, Experience and Future Research, reports on the experience with product lines and briefly describes several essential topics for future research.

Experience and future research

Chapter 21 summarises experience reports about the application of the software product line engineering paradigm in several organisations. It also provides an annotated literature reference list as a guide for further reading.

Chapter 22 outlines key challenges for future research in the area of software product line engineering.

In addition, we provide at the end of the book:

End of the book

- Information about the *authors*

- The *literature references* used throughout the book

- A *glossary* for software product line engineering

- The *index*

IV. Share Your Experience!

We are interested in your feedback. If you have any suggestions for improvements, or if you have detected an error or an important issue that the book does not cover, please do not hesitate to contact us at:

Feedback

SPLE-Book@software-productline.com

or visit the book web page:

www.software-productline.com/SPLE-Book

V. Acknowledgements

Eureka/ITEA, public authorities

We would like to thank Eureka/ITEA, BMBF (Germany), NOVEM/ SENTER (Netherlands), and all the other national public authorities for funding the projects ESAPS (1999–2001), CAFÉ (2001–2003), and FAMILIES (2003–2005). Most of the results presented in this book have been researched and validated in these projects.

Layout and consistency

Our special thanks go to Ernst Sikora who helped us significantly in improving the consistency and the layout of the book, and to Silja Recknagel for her support in polishing the English.

Publisher

We thank Ralf Gerstner, Ronan Nugent, and Ulrike Stricker from Springer-Verlag, Heidelberg, for their support in getting this book to market!

Collaborators and colleagues

Last but not least, our thanks go to our collaborators within industry and universities, at both the national and the international level. Without the insight gained in numerous discussions, this book would never have been possible.

Klaus Pohl   University of Duisburg-Essen, Germany
Günter Böckle   Siemens Corporate Technology, Germany
Frank van der Linden   Philips Medical Systems, The Netherlands

May, 2005

Guidelines for Teaching

Many companies implement the software product line engineering (SPLE) principles for developing embedded software-intensive systems as well as information systems. Solid knowledge about SPLE will be crucial for employees in the future. The book has been designed to provide basic reading material that can serve for a 14-week course on SPLE as well as to accompany lectures embedded in an advanced course on software engineering.

Education of software engineers

Lectures on SPLE can be organised by taking our framework for SPLE as a basis. The framework stresses the key differences between SPLE and single-system development: the need to distinguish between two types of development processes (domain and application engineering) and the need to explicitly define and manage variability.

Framework

Under the assumption that a single lecture takes two hours, the material covered in this book can, amongst others, be used for the following teaching courses and modules:

a) A *14-lecture course on SPLE* which covers almost all the topics presented in this book (Section I).

14-lecture course

b) A *two-lecture module on SPLE* in an advanced software engineering course which introduces the key concepts of SPLE (Section II).

2-lecture module

c) A *four-lecture module on SPLE* in an advanced software engineering course which introduces the key concepts of SPLE and illustrates these concepts on a particular process phase of domain and application engineering, for instance using the domain and application requirements engineering sub-processes, or the domain and application design sub-processes (Section III).

4-lecture module

d) A *one-lecture module on the selection of COTS systems* which could be part of an advanced software engineering course. This lecture introduces the challenges and a technique for selecting a COTS (commercial of the shelf) component or system for a software product line (Section IV).

Lecture on COTS

e) A *three-lecture module on testing in SPLE* which could be part of a software quality assurance course or an advanced software engineering course. The module introduces the key concepts of SPLE and teaches

3-lecture module on testing

the challenges and basic solutions for testing domain and application artefacts (Section V).

In addition, we recommend a three-lecture module on:

Requirements engineering module

- requirements engineering for software product lines that could be part of an advanced requirements engineering course, and

Software design module

- software design for software product lines that could be part of an advanced software architecture or design course.

I. Fourteen-Lecture Course on SPLE

This course provides a good overview of SPLE. It teaches the important aspects of SPLE and is organised around the framework proposed in this book. Students attending the lectures should have basic knowledge of software engineering. After passing the course they will be familiar with the principles of SPLE: namely, variability management and the domain and application engineering processes.

For the 14-lecture course, we suggest the following structure:[1]

Basic principles and framework

➢ Two lectures for introducing the principles and a framework for SPLE:

    (1) SPLE principles (Chapter 1); SPLE experiences (Chapter 21)

    (2) Key differences between single-system development and SPLE; SPLE framework (Chapter 2)

Documentation of variability

➢ Four lectures on the principles of variability and the documentation of variability with special emphasis on the consistent definition of variability across the various development artefacts:

    (3) Principles of product line variability illustrated by examples; basic concepts (Chapter 4)

    (4) Concepts of the orthogonal variability meta model illustrated by examples (Chapter 4); documenting requirements artefacts (Chapter 5)

    (5) Documenting variability in requirements artefacts illustrated by a comprehensive example (Chapter 5); interrelations to design (Chapters 5 and 6)

---

[1] The number in brackets indicates the lecture in the course sequence, followed by the key contents of the lecture.

(6) Documenting variability in design, realisation, and test artefacts based on the orthogonal variability model (Chapters 6, 7, and 8)

➤ Five lectures on the domain engineering sub-processes with special emphasis on the differences between SPLE and development of single software systems: *Domain engineering*

(7) Introduction to product management; product portfolio definition; scoping (Chapter 9)

(8) Domain requirements engineering sub-process; defining variability, commonality and variability analysis; modelling requirements variability (Chapter 10)

(9) Domain design sub-process; refining requirements variability into design variability; defining the reference architecture/ platform (Chapter 11)

(10) Domain realisation; mapping design variability onto components (Chapter 12); COTS selection in high-level design; COTS selection technique (Chapter 14)

(11) Domain tests; strategies for domain testing; defining variability in test artefacts under the consideration of requirements, design, and realisation variability (Chapter 13)

➤ Two lectures on the derivation of application artefacts from domain artefacts through the binding of predefined variability: *Application engineering*

(12) Application requirements engineering and application design sub-processes; defining requirements for product line applications; binding variability defined in domain requirements and design artefacts; deriving the design of an application (Chapters 15 and 16)

(13) Application realisation and application test sub-processes; deriving the application realisation; deriving application test artefacts from domain test artefacts based on the variability binding established during application requirements engineering and application design (Chapters 17 and 18)

➤ One lecture on organisational aspects with an emphasis on the organisational consequences encountered with, when introducing SPLE in an organisation: *Organisation and transition*

(14) Influence of the organisation structure on SPLE; estimations for determining the ROI of SPLE; basic transition strategies for introducing SPLE in an organisation (Chapters 19 and 20)

Alternative
course structure   An alternative course outline could be based on organising the domain and
application engineering sub-process in such a way that each domain engineering sub-process is followed by the corresponding application engineering sub-process, i.e. domain requirements engineering, application requirements engineering, domain design, application design, etc. Teaching the topics in this sequence gives the advantage to emphasise the differences between domain engineering and application engineering activities as well as their interrelations. It has the disadvantage that the relations between the sub-processes in domain engineering as well as the relations between the application engineering sub-processes cannot be emphasised equally well as in the standard course outline.

II. Two-Lecture Module on SPLE

The two-lecture SPLE module provides an introduction to SPLE. It is designed to fit in an advanced software engineering course. In the two lectures the students learn the key motivations for introducing the SPLE paradigm in an organisation as well as the key differences from the development of single software systems. We suggest the following contents for the two lectures:

(1) Motivation and principles of SPLE (Chapter 1) including one or two experiences (Chapter 21); key differences between SPLE and the development of single systems (Chapter 2)

(2) The SPLE framework (Chapter 2); principles of software product line variability; overview of variability modelling (Chapter 4)

III. Four-Lecture Module on SPLE

The four-lecture SPLE module provides a comprehensive introduction to basic principles of SPLE and the differences between SPLE and the development of single software systems. We recommend the four-lecture module for an introduction to SPLE if time constraints permit it:

Motivation   (1) Motivation and principles of SPLE (Chapter 1) including one or two experiences (Chapter 21); key differences between SPLE and the development of single systems (Chapter 2)

Framework   (2) The SPLE framework (Chapter 2); principles of software product line variability; overview of variability modelling (Chapter 4)

(3)	Orthogonal variability meta model (Chapter 4); example of docu-menting variability in requirements or in design (depending on the phase chosen for this module in the next lecture)

Orthogonal variability model

(4)	Specifics of the domain and application engineering processes; we recommend the selection of a particular phase of domain and appli-cation engineering to illustrate the specifics of the two processes; we also recommend either the domain and application requirements engineering sub-processes (Chapters 10 and 15) or the domain and application design sub-processes (Chapters 11 and 16)

Details of selected development phase

IV. One-Lecture Module on COTS Selection

This lecture focuses on the challenges of selecting COTS components for a software product line during high-level design. In addition, our technique for selecting COTS components should be part of this lecture. This technique takes into account the domain requirements, the domain architecture, as well as the variability of the product line (Chapter 14).

COTS selection technique

V. Three-Lecture Module on Testing in SPLE

This three-lecture module provides a brief introduction to SPLE and focuses on the specifics of testing in the domain engineering and the application engineering sub-processes.

(1)	Motivation and principles of SPLE (Chapter 1); key differences between SPLE and development of single systems (Chapter 2); challenges for testing (Chapter 13)

Motivation

(2)	Principles of software product line variability; the orthogonal vari-ability meta model (Chapter 4); documenting variability in test arte-facts (Chapter 8)

Variability in test artefacts

(3)	Test strategies and evaluation criteria; preserving variability in test designs (Chapter 13); deriving application test cases from domain test cases; reuse of test artefacts (Chapter 18)

Test strategies

VI. Exercises

We recommend two types of exercises. The first type is an exercise which accompanies the lectures and aims at deepening the knowledge of the stu-dents of the principles of SPLE, variability modelling, and the domain and application engineering processes. The second type is an exercise after the lecture which, in addition to the first type, embeds practical exercises in extending the capability of a software product line. We recommend doing this by adding functional and non-functional features as well as deriving a product line application.

Paper-Based Exercises

For understanding the principles of SPLE and gaining experience with the orthogonal variability model as well as the various artefact models used in domain and application engineering, we recommend the following exercises:

Experience reports

(1) *Product line principles*: The students should become familiar with two to three experience reports (based on the annotated literature references in Chapter 21). They should summarise and compare the reported experiences and try to map the positive and negative experiences to product line principles. The results should be presented in a 20 minutes' talk and/or in written reports of about three to four pages.

Variability model

(2) *Defining variability*: Based on a natural language description of variability which has to be integrated into an existing software product line, the students should extend the orthogonal variability model (without considering the development artefacts).

Variability in requirements

(3) *Modelling variability in requirements artefacts*: The students are given an existing requirements document and a new variation to be integrated into the variability model as well as into the requirements artefacts. They have to consider variability dependencies and constraints during the integration. The example should be small in size.

Variability in design

(4) *Mapping variability in requirements artefacts to design artefacts*: The students are given a design document, a requirements document, and an orthogonal variability model for the product line. In the variability model and the requirements model, newly introduced extensions are marked. The students should map these extensions onto the software architecture of the product line considering variability constraints and dependencies as well as design constraints. The example should be small in size and, to avoid an unwanted focus, different from the example used in Exercise (3).

Optional: In addition, the students could be given the task to integrate internal design variability into the design. For example, they could be asked to make the architecture flexible so that the introduction of different types of middleware is facilitated, allowing the company to shift between different middleware providers.

(5) *Mapping variability in design artefacts to realisation artefacts*: The students are given a realisation document, a design document, a requirements document, and an orthogonal variability model for the product line. In the variability model and in the design models, newly introduced extensions are marked. The students should map these extensions to software components and their interfaces considering variability constraints and dependencies as well as realisation constraints. The example should be small in size and, to avoid an unwanted focus, different from the examples used in Exercises (3) and (4).

Variability in realisation

(6) *Defining domain test cases for system tests*: Based on a requirements document, a design document, and an orthogonal variability model, the students should design a set of test cases for some part of the requirements specification. The variability in the domain artefacts should be preserved, i.e. should be adequately introduced into the test case design.

Variability in test artefacts

(7) *Mapping application requirements to domain requirements artefacts*: Based on a list of application requirements artefacts (e.g. features and scenarios), the students have to identify the corresponding commonalities and the variability in the domain requirements artefacts. In addition, they have to suggest an appropriate binding of the variability defined in the domain requirements artefacts to realise the given application requirements.

Application requirements

(8) *Deriving an application design*: Based on the binding defined in the application requirements (documented in the orthogonal variability model and the application requirements artefacts), the students have to derive an application design that binds the domain design variability according to the application requirements.

Application design

(9) *Deriving system test case designs for an application*: Based on the variability bound in the orthogonal variability model, the students have to derive system test cases from the domain test cases to test a particular functional or quality feature of the given application.

Application test cases

(10) *Desirable tool support*: Based on their experiences gained during the exercise, the students should define a desirable tool support for product line engineering. Each student should focus on the support for a particular domain and application engineering sub-process, e.g. domain and application requirements engineering, or a cross-cutting aspect such as variability modelling or configuration support.

Tool support

(11) *Extending the variability meta model*: Based on their experience, the students should suggest extensions to the variability meta model in

Variability meta model

terms of a) specialisation of variation points and variants, b) relationships to and between domain artefacts, and c) relationships to and between application artefacts. The suggested extensions should be presented and discussed.

In addition, lecturers may add question-based exercises as appropriate.

Extending a Product Line and Deriving an Application

Example product line

A prerequisite for this exercise is the (partial) realisation of a software product line including up-to-date documentation of the features, the requirements, the design, the components, and the test cases of the software product line. This example product line may be based on the home automation example used in this book (Chapter 3).

Simulation of the two processes

The goal of this exercise is two-fold. The first phase aims at deepening the knowledge of SPLE by taking some of the exercises defined in Section V. In the second phase, domain and application engineering is practised by adding new features to an existing software product line as well as by deriving a product line application. This involves adaptations and additions to the models that are made in the first phase. Feedback between the steps in each of the two processes, and from application engineering to domain engineering, should be stimulated. When there is sufficient time, active rework should also follow from that. In contrast to the paper-based exercise, this is a more hands-on exercise, i.e. the extensions are made using tool support and a (partially) realised product line.

In the first phase, we recommend that the students are trained using a set of the paper-based exercises introduced above, e.g. Exercises (2), (3), (4), (7), and (8).

The second phase of the exercise consists of two parts:

Adding features

➤ *Integration of a new feature*: The students should add one or more functional and/or non-functional features or requirements which preferably affect the variability of an existing product line. If time permits it, we suggest:

(1) choosing a new feature which leads to an extension of existing variability and thereby letting the students experience that such an integration is typically easy to achieve due to the variation points, and

(2) choosing a feature that leads to the introduction of a new variation point – which is typically far more complex than the task described in (1).

The challenge in both cases is the coherent integration of the new feature in all product line artefacts, and, even more important, to consider the effects of the integration on the domain assets as well as on the existing applications. The students will experience the importance of traceability as well as of the orthogonal variability model if the extensions affect existing variations.

➢ *Derivation of a product line application*: The students are given a list of requirements artefacts (features, requirements, use cases, scenarios) for a new application. The challenge to derive the new application is two-fold. First, the students must map the application requirements to the product line requirements and decide which variability has to be bound to realise the given application requirements. Second, the students gain experience with the support for deriving an application based on the identified variability bindings in requirements, i.e. they experience how the orthogonal variability model supports the mapping of the variability bound during application requirements engineering onto the application design, the application realisation, and the application test designs. This exercise can be extended by giving the students the requirements for an application, which involve application-specific extensions of the application requirements artefacts (which should not be mixed up with extending the domain artefacts).

Derivation of product line application

Contents

22   Future Research   435

The Authors   439

References   445

Glossary   457

Index   461

Part I

Introduction

Part I

Introduction

Günter Böckle

1

Introduction to Software Product Line Engineering

In this chapter you will learn:

- o *The key principles of product line engineering for mechanical and electronic consumer products.*
- o *The key ideas of the software product line engineering paradigm.*
- o *The motivations and the prerequisites for adapting those principles to software engineering.*

1.1   Principles of Product Line Engineering

Production line

The way that goods are produced has changed significantly in the course of time. Formerly goods were handcrafted for individual customers. By and by, the number of people who could afford to buy various kinds of products increased. In the domain of automobiles this led to Ford's invention of the *production line*, which enabled production for a mass market much more cheaply than individual product creation on a handcrafted basis. However, the production line reduced the possibilities for diversification.

Individual and standard software

Roughly, both types of products, individual and mass produced ones can be identified in the software domain as well: they are denoted as individual software and standard software. Generally, each of these types of products has its drawbacks. Individual software products are rather expensive, while standard software products lack sufficient diversification.[2]

1.1.1   Mass Customisation

Individualised products

Customers were content with standardised mass products for a while – but not all people want the same kind of car for any purpose. Certain cars are used for travelling by a single person others for big families. Some cars are used by people living in cities, others mainly in the countryside. People want to have another car or a better one than their neighbours. Thus, industry was confronted with a rising demand for individualised products. This was the beginning of *mass customisation*, which meant taking into account the customers' requirements and giving them what they wanted (see Fig. 1-1).

We use the following definition of mass customisation:

> **Definition 1-1:** *Mass Customisation*
>
> Mass customisation is the large-scale production of goods tailored to individual customers' needs.
>
> [Davis 1987]

> **Example 1-1:** *Mass Customisation in Car Manufacturing*
>
> The four cars at the bottom of Fig. 1-1 are an example of mass customisation: different cars that meet individual customers' wishes, each produced in large numbers.

---

[2] See [Halmans and Pohl 2002] for a treatment of product line engineering for individual vs. mass-market software.

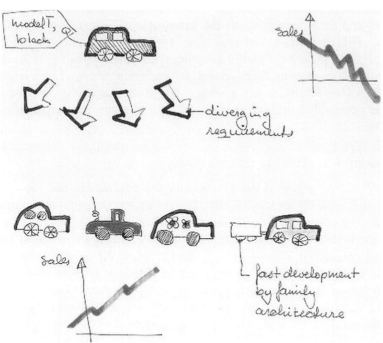

Not "one product fits all"

Fig. 1-1: Single product for all vs. individual products[3]

1.1.2 Platforms

For the customer mass customisation means the ability to have an individualised product. For the company mass customisation means higher technological investments which leads to higher prices for the individualised products and/or to lower profit margins for the company. Both effects are undesirable. Thus many companies, especially in the car industry, started to introduce *common platforms* for their different types of cars by planning beforehand which parts will be used in different car types.

Prerequisite for mass customisation

Originally, an automobile platform only consisted of floor panels, a suspension system, and rocker panels. Later more parts were added to the platform. The platform provided a structure for major components determining the body size and the size and type of the engine and transmission. The parts comprising the platform were usually the most expensive subsystem in terms of design and manufacturing preparation costs. The use of the platform for different car types typically led to a reduction in the production cost for a particular car type.

---

[3] Picture drawn by Loe Feijs.

Platform:
35% sales growth

The platform approach enabled car manufacturers to offer a larger variety of products and to reduce costs at the same time. The result was that within periods of three years (measured from 1980 to 1991 and averaged) those companies using the best platform strategy increased sales by 35%, whereas those companies starting from scratch for each new series of cars had a sales loss of 7% (for details, see [Cusumano and Nobeoka 1998]). The same pattern was observable in the camera industry and many others (Examples 1-2 and 1-3).

Example 1-2: *From the Camera World*

In 1987, Fuji released the Quicksnap, the first single-use camera. It caught Kodak by surprise: Kodak had no such product in a market that grew from then on by 50% annually, from 3 million in 1988 to 43 million in 1994. However, Kodak won back market share and in 1994, it had conquered 70% of the US market. How did Kodak achieve it? First, a series of clearly distinguishable, different camera models was built based on a common platform. Between April 1989 and July 1990, Kodak reconstructed its standard model and created three additional models, all with common components and the same manufacturing process. Thus, Kodak could develop the cameras faster and with lower costs. The different models appealed to different customer groups. Kodak soon had twice as many models as Fuji, conquered shelf space in the shops and finally won significant market share this way (for details see [Robertson and Ulrich 1999; Clark and Wheelwright 1995]).

Example 1-3: *Notion of Platform in Office Supplies*

The "Post-It" notes from 3M are considered a platform from which many individual products have been derived. For instance, "Post-it" notes with a company logo, or markers to select pages in books, etc. [Cooper et al. 2001].

Definition 1-2: *Platform*

A platform is any base of technologies on which other technologies or processes are built.

[TechTarget 2004]

"Platform" used in
various contexts

The term platform is used in various contexts as illustrated by Examples 1-1 to 1-3. A common definition of platform does not exist. For this book we use the definition given in Definition 1-2. Note that this definition encompasses all kinds of reusable artefacts as well as all kinds of technological capabilities.

1.1.3 Combining Platform-Based Development and Mass Customisation

The combination of mass customisation and a common platform allows us to reuse a common base of technology and, at the same time, to bring out products in close accordance with customers' wishes. The systematic combination of mass customisation and the use of a common platform for the development of software-intensive systems and software products is the key focus of this book. We call the resulting software development paradigm *software product line engineering*. In Section 1.2 we sketch the key implications of combining those approaches. The motivations behind the product line engineering paradigm are outlined in Section 1.3.

Platform and mass customisation

1.2 Engineering Customised Products

Combining platform and mass customisation in order to provide customised products has many implications for the development process as well as the developing organisation. We briefly sketch the three key influences.

1.2.1 Creating the Platform

In single-system engineering, products are regarded as independent, self-contained items. In the example presented in Fig. 1-1 (bottom), this means having four distinct projects for developing four distinct products. Developing these four types of cars by product line engineering requires the creation of a platform that suits all of them. This platform comprises all common parts, for instance a gear box that can be applied in all or most of the cars (in so far, the platform extends the original meaning of a car platform as described in Section 1.1.2). Furthermore, the platform determines the specifics that distinguish not only the four cars but also how to accommodate the customers' wishes for more individualised products. Briefly, creating the platform implies preparing for mass customisation. For our example, this means having four basic types of cars, each with numerous customisable features.

Preparing for mass customisation

The strategy that we have intuitively followed in the above example is, first, to focus on what is common to all products, and next, to focus on what is different. In the first step, artefacts are provided that can be reused for all products. These artefacts may be built from scratch or derived from another platform or earlier systems. Built-in flexibility makes it possible to reuse these artefacts in different applications, providing mass customisation. Cre-

Commonality first, differences later

ating this flexibility requires some effort. Therefore, in the automobile industry, the platform is usually developed by a distinct project. Several other projects are commissioned to develop the single cars or, more frequently, groups of cars, each group encompassing a subset of the product line's products.

1.2.2 Introducing Flexibility

Flexibility is the key

To facilitate mass customisation, the artefacts used in different products have to be sufficiently adaptable to fit into the different systems produced in the product line. This means that throughout the development process we have to identify and describe where the products of the product line may differ in terms of the features they provide, the requirements they fulfil, or even in terms of the underlying architecture etc. We thus have to provide flexibility in all those artefacts to support mass customisation.

Different cars of the same product line may for instance have different windshield wipers and washers. We design the cars in a way that allows a common approach to support the different motors for these different windshield wipers/washers, their different sizes, etc. Such flexibility comes with a set of constraints. If you drive a convertible, you would not want a rear window washer splashing water onto the seats! Therefore, the selection of a convertible car means the flexibility that the availability of the windshield wipers and washers is restricted, so that the rear window washer is disabled when the car roof is open.

This flexibility is a precondition for mass customisation; it also means that we can predefine what possible realisations shall be developed (there are only a certain number of windshield wiper configurations conceivable). In addition, it means that we define exactly the places where the products can differ so that they can have as much in common as possible.

Variability

The flexibility described here is called "variability" in the software product-line context. This variability is the basis for mass customisation. Variability is introduced and defined in detail in Part II of this book.

Sharing platforms between product lines

In the automotive industry, cars sharing the same platform and exhibiting similar features were called a *product line* or a *product family*. At this stage, the relation between a platform and a product line was straightforward. A manageable set of cars belonged to one product line that was based on a single platform. But soon, in the history of automobile development, platforms were shared across different product lines. New product lines used platforms of earlier product lines etc. Thus, the simple relation between platform and product line vanished. Consequently, it became necessary to manage carefully the trace information from a platform to the products derived from it. Without such trace information, it is barely possible to find out which parts of the platform have been used in which product. Thus, for example, the estimation of the impact of changes becomes difficult.

1.2.3 Reorganising the Company

Migrating from single-system engineering to a platform approach has far-reaching consequences. The products derived from platform artefacts can no longer be treated as being independent. They are related through the underlying technology. This also has to be reflected in the *organisation structure* of a company: it may be necessary to establish additional *organisation units*, e.g. one unit responsible for the platform, or by setting up additional communication paths between formerly independent units. Basically, the platform approach leads to *standardisation* of procedures, workflows, and the technology employed within an organisation or even across organisations.

A platform leads to standardisation

1.3 Motivations for Product Line Engineering

We already conveyed a first idea of the goals that product line engineering pursues: to provide customised products at reasonable costs. In this section, we briefly outline the key motivations for developing software under the product line engineering paradigm.

1.3.1 Reduction of Development Costs

A far-reaching change of engineering practices is usually not initiated without sound economical justification. An essential reason for introducing product line engineering is the reduction of costs. When artefacts from the platform are reused in several different kinds of systems, this implies a cost reduction for each system. Before the artefacts can be reused, investments are necessary for creating them. In addition the way in which they shall be reused has to be planned beforehand to provide managed reuse. This means that the company has to make an up-front investment to create the platform before it can reduce the costs per product by reusing platform artefacts.

Up-front investment

Figure 1-2 shows the *accumulated costs* needed to develop *n* different systems. The solid line sketches the costs of developing the systems independently, while the dashed line shows the costs for product line engineering. In the case of a few systems, the costs for product line engineering are relatively high, whereas they are significantly lower for larger quantities. The location at which both curves intersect marks the *break-even point*. At this point, the costs are the same for developing the systems separately as for developing them by product line engineering. Empirical investigations revealed that,

Pay-off around three systems

for software, the break-even point is already reached around three systems.[4] A similar figure is shown in [Weiss and Lai 1999], where the break-even point is located between three and four systems. The precise location of the break-even point depends on various characteristics of the organisation and the market it has envisaged, such as the customer base, the expertise, and the range and kinds of products. The strategy that is used to initiate a product line also influences the break-even point significantly [McGregor et al. 2002]. Chapter 20 elaborates on the initiation of product lines.

Lower development cost

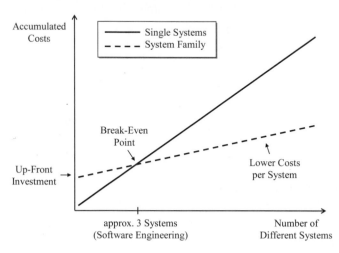

Fig. 1-2:   Costs for developing n kinds of systems as single systems compared to product line engineering

1.3.2   Enhancement of Quality

Improved quality through reuse

The artefacts in the platform are reviewed and tested in many products. They have to prove their proper functioning in more than one kind of product. The extensive quality assurance implies a significantly higher chance of detecting faults and correcting them, thereby increasing the quality of all products.

1.3.3   Reduction of Time to Market

Shorter development cycles

Often, a very critical success factor for a product is the time to market. For single-product development, we assume it is roughly constant,[5] mostly comprising the time to develop the product. For product line engineering, the time to market indeed is initially higher, as the common artefacts have to be built first. Yet, after having passed this hurdle, the time to market is consid-

---

[4]   [Clements and Northrop 2001]: The sidebar on p. 226, "It Takes Two", provides a closer examination of the break-even point for software product lines.

[5]   In practice, this number varies, but for showing the effect of single-system vs. product line engineering this assumption is sufficiently accurate.

erably shortened as many artefacts can be reused for each new product (see Fig. 1-3).

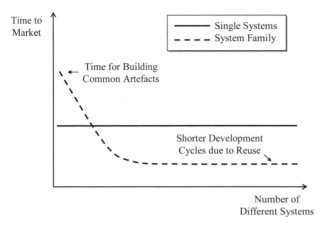

Fig. 1-3:   Time to market with and without product line engineering

1.3.4   Additional Motivations

In this section, we briefly outline additional motivations for introducing a software product line engineering paradigm. An overview of further motivations (and also key principles and solutions) can be found in [Pohl et al. 2001b].

1.3.4.1   *Reduction of Maintenance Effort*

Whenever an artefact from the platform is changed, e.g. for the purpose of error correction, the changes can be propagated to all products in which the artefact is being used. This may be exploited to reduce maintenance effort. At best, maintenance staff do not need to know all specific products and their parts, thus also reducing learning effort. However, given the fact that platform artefacts are changed, testing the products is still unavoidable. Yet, the reuse of test procedures is within the focus of product line engineering as well and helps reduce maintenance effort. The techniques used in product line engineering make a system better maintainable as stated in [Coplien 1998]: "The same design techniques that lead to good reuse also lead to extensibility and maintainability over time." *Propagation of error corrections*

1.3.4.2   *Coping with Evolution*

The introduction of a new artefact into the platform (or the change of an existing one) gives the opportunity for the evolution of all kinds of products derived from the platform. Similarly, developers who want to introduce a trend towards certain product features may do so by adding specific artefacts *Organised evolution* to the platform. Thus, it is possible to better organise development for evolution of the product range and reduce the effort compared to single-system engineering.

1.3.4.3   Coping with Complexity

Complexity by size increase

Due to the increased number of customers' wishes, the complexity of products increases. This holds especially for software, where code size and complexity sometimes increase beyond being manageable. The reason for this trend is that more and more functionality is put into software.

> **Example 1-4:** *Size of the Windows Operating System*
>
> In 1991 the size of Windows NT PDK 2 was 1.8 million SLOC,[6] see [Cusumano and Selby 1998] – Windows XP has about 45 million SLOC.

Complexity by hardware–software migration

In embedded systems, the complexity increase was further aggravated by moving functionality from hardware to software. This was done for several reasons, mostly because software provides more flexibility than hardware as well as a higher level of abstraction. Software enables complex interactions between functionality, and allows for distribution over a network. This causes a significant increase in the complexity of the system, making it difficult for developers to conceive the whole functionality. If no adequate measures are taken, high complexity leads to rapidly increasing error rates, long development cycles, and a higher time to market – influencing our key motivations.

Platform reduces complexity

The fact that the common parts are reused throughout the product line reduces complexity significantly. The platform provides a structure that determines which components can be reused at what places by defining variability at distinct locations; this reduces complexity. The reuse of common parts from the platform reduces the error rate and the development time.

1.3.4.4   Improving Cost Estimation

Platform simplifies cost estimation

The development organisation can focus its marketing efforts on those products that it can easily produce within the product line. Nevertheless, it can allow extensions not covered by the platform. Products that do need such extensions can be sold for higher prices than those products built by reusing platform artefacts only. Furthermore, calculating prices for products realised within the product line is relatively straightforward and does not include much risk. Consequently, the platform provides a sound basis for cost estimation.

---

[6]   SLOC = Source Lines of Code, the number of non-comment lines of code in a source program.

1.3.4.5 *Benefits for the Customers*

Customers get products adapted to their needs and wishes. This is just what they ask for – previously, users had to adapt their own way of working to the software. In the past, it often happened that customers had to get used to a different user interface and a different installation procedure with each new product. This annoyed them, in particular as it even happened when replacing one version of a product by the next version. So customers began to ask for improved software ergonomics. Accordingly, software packages were developed to support common user interfaces and common installation procedures. The use of such packages contributed to the proliferation of the idea of platforms. Moreover, customers can purchase these products at a reasonable price as product line engineering helps to reduce the production costs. Additionally, customers get higher quality products since the reusable components and their configurations have been tested in many products developed earlier and proved dependable. Moreover, many requirements are reviewed more often, not only in domain engineering but also in application engineering, and the architecture review for application architectures helps to find problems in the domain architecture, too.

Customers get higher quality for lower prices

Despite possessing individual features, the products of a product line have a lot in common due to the artefacts reused from the platform. Similar or the same user interfaces and similar major functionality make it easy for the customer to switch from one product to another. The customer does not have to learn new ways of using another product derived from the same platform.

Common look and feel

1.4 Software Product Line Engineering

Until recently software, especially embedded software was relatively small[7] and each product variant got its own variant of software. Software was a way to easily implement on the same hardware individual product variants that originally required individual hardware variants. Compared to hardware, software is easy and cheap to copy, transport, and replace. This fact was exploited by employing software flexibly and adapting it at very late stages of development, thus easing many problems of system developers. Not much thought was spent on how software was produced. Outside the embedded system world, software was typically not regarded as being variable. Either a customer could buy a software system including all possible features one might ever need, or software was produced for a single purpose by order of a single customer.

Past situation on software market

---

[7] See the introduction of [V. Ommering 2004], where it is shown how TV-set software grew from 1 kB in 1978 to 100 kB in 1990 and to 10,000 kB in 2004.

Demand for product line engineering

However, the situation in software engineering has changed. Almost all systems of a certain complexity contain software. Many systems in our environment are becoming software-intensive systems, not only because variability can be implemented more flexibly than in pure hardware, but also because of the fact that software allows the introduction of new functionality that could not easily be achieved without it. The amount of embedded software is growing, and the amount of variability is growing even faster. In many systems, this amount is now many times larger than before software came into play. Therefore, presently a strong need for adopting product line engineering can be observed in the software domain, especially when size and complexity exceed the limits of what is feasible with traditional approaches.

1.4.1 Definition

We define the term software product line engineering as follows:

> ***Definition 1-3:*** *Software Product Line Engineering*
>
> Software product line engineering is a paradigm to develop software applications (software-intensive systems and software products) using platforms and mass customisation.

Pure and embedded software

Our definition covers the development of pure software products or systems as well as the development of software that is embedded into a software-intensive system, i.e. a system that closely integrates hardware and software. Being an integral part of many everyday products, embedded software constitutes a great proportion of the total amount of software being developed and sold. With respect to this book, it is valid to consider both kinds of software, as the principles of product line engineering are the same for them.

Managed variability

Developing applications using *platforms* means to plan proactively for reuse, to build reusable parts, and to reuse what has been built for reuse. Building applications for *mass customisation* means employing the concept of *managed variability*, i.e. the commonalities and the differences in the applications (in terms of requirements, architecture, components, and test artefacts) of the product line have to be modelled in a common way. The definition of the commonalities and the variability, the documentation, the subsequent deployment, and the management are key focuses of this book.

Constraining adaptations

Managed variability has a great impact on the way software is developed, extended, and maintained. Usually, for those who understand how a piece of software works, it is also easy to change it and adapt it to suit a new purpose. However, such changes often corrupt the original structure of the software and hamper quality aspects like understandability or maintainability. In order to be able to deal with adaptations in a managed way, they have to be accomplished in a reproducible manner. The abundance of possibilities for adapting a piece of software has to be restricted to those places where it makes sense to do so. More than other engineering disciplines, software product line engineering deals with ways to restrict variation in a manageable way.

1.4.2 Software Platform

Definition 1-3 makes use of the term platform. In the software industry, this term is often used to denote the underlying computer system on which application programs can run. This may be the hardware used, e.g. the processor, or, more often, the combination of hardware and operating system (see Example 1-5).

Classic computer platform

Example 1-5: *Symbian as a Platform*

The Symbian operating system is used by several companies as a platform for some of their product lines of mobile phones, including Nokia, Siemens, and Motorola.

In software architecture the term platform is used slightly differently but still in line with the classic meaning. A software architecture usually consists of multiple layers. From the viewpoint of one layer, its underlying layer is called its platform.

Platforms in software architecture

Though the above interpretations of platform are quite common in software engineering, they do not reflect what makes up a platform in software product line engineering. This kind of software platform must enable the creation of entire products from reusable parts. Therefore, we use the definition given in Definition 1-4.

Meaning of platform in this book

Definition 1-4: *Software Platform*

A software platform is a set of software subsystems and interfaces that form a common structure from which a set of derivative products can be efficiently developed and produced.

[Meyer and Lehnerd 1997]

The subsystems belonging to a software platform encompass not just code but also requirements, architecture, and other artefacts of the development process.

1.4.3 Prerequisites

The fact that product line engineering entered the software engineering domain much later[8] than other domains was due to several reasons. Past barriers for adapting the product line engineering paradigm to software development have been partly overcome but can still complicate the adoption of software product line engineering if not taken carefully into consideration. To overcome these barriers, certain *prerequisites* are necessary for adopting software product line engineering.

1.4.3.1 Enabling Technologies

Implementation technology

For a long time, an important barrier to adopting software product line engineering was the lack of adequate technology for applying the principles of product line engineering in an easy way. In addition, part of the technology available was not used in practice. The development of such enabling technology supported the introduction of software product line engineering. Actually, the implementation technologies of standard software engineering are used for product line engineering, no new ones are introduced. Coplien states that "many software families are naturally expressed by existing programming language constructs" [Coplien 1998].

Object-oriented programming

Object-oriented programming is a major enabling technology. Many programs were (and still are) written in procedural programming languages. These languages make encapsulation and information hiding hard to put into practice. Yet, encapsulation is a prerequisite for realising managed variability. Object-oriented modelling and programming concepts mitigated this barrier by supporting approved design principles in a more natural way.

Component technology

Another important achievement is the introduction of component technology. Component technology enables developers to package software as loosely coupled parts. Components can be developed, compiled, linked and loaded separately. Only at run-time are they combined into a working system. This helps developers to focus on a particular component and thus to cope with complexity. Besides, component technology limits the scope where variation is possible and thus supports the realisation of managed variability.

Binding techniques

Late-binding techniques, especially installation and run-time dynamic binding, allow for late configuration choices. By applying late binding, variability can be designed and implemented in a uniform way without bothering about how the actual variants look. This facilitates the implementation of platforms and provides an easy way to realise mass customisation.

---

[8] However, the basic ideas had already been proposed in the 1970s by Dijkstra [Dijkstra 1972] and Parnas [Parnas 1976].

The quasi-standardisation of middleware, interoperability, and interface descriptions supports late binding. It also speeds up the configuration of applications enormously and helps in defining the platform and its boundaries. Software from different origins can be used to work together inside an application. Middleware facilitates the development of loosely coupled components, thus contributing to reduced complexity and easing managed reuse.

Middleware

Configuration management is another important prerequisite for being able to cope with the complexity of large applications consisting of many parts in different versions. Therefore, sophisticated configuration management is necessary to succeed in software product line engineering.

Configuration management

1.4.3.2   Process Maturity

Lacking maturity in software engineering can affect the success of software product line engineering even more seriously than technological matters.

For a long time, software development processes were unstructured, hardly well defined, and also not well understood. The increasing application of assessments, e.g. postulated by CMMI· led to better software development processes. Process models such as CMMI help to identify the weak parts of software development processes, thus driving their improvement and fostering the use of sound engineering principles in software practice.

Process models

The CHAOS report [Standish Group 1995] showed that inadequate requirements engineering is a major cause of problems in software projects. Consequently, thorough requirements engineering comprising the identification of commonality and variability is a major prerequisite for software product line engineering.

Requirements engineering

The history of software and system development shows that abstraction plays a major role in making the complexity manageable. Although modelling techniques were available, they were often not used or people used different techniques, mostly on an ad hoc basis. The major driver for using modelling techniques was the foundation of UML [OMG 2003], which has become an industrial standard. This standardisation of modelling notations helps engineers to become aware of methods for modelling variability, too.

Modelling techniques

1.4.3.3   Domain Characteristics and Expertise

Another major prerequisite for software product line engineering is sufficient domain expertise. Only people who know their markets and/or customers can identify commonalities and variability in an adequate way for developing platforms and variability.

Software is flexible and all sorts of variability can be added to it. Wrong choices are, however, costly. The introduction of variability that is not used leads to additional costs for developing it and, at a later stage, removing it

Domain knowledge

again. Failing to introduce the required variability leads to additional costs for realising common and even variable parts in each product. Moreover, it is important to use an appropriate level of abstraction to define the variability of a product line. Ideally, the variability abstractions match the commonly used domain abstractions. Domain-related abstractions are known to the customers and developers and thus help them to understand the variability of the product line. Not knowing the domain leads to incorrect abstractions with the danger that they are not perceived by the stakeholders, and thus cause wrong choices, which have to be repaired afterwards.

The better you know the domain and the more experience you have with your products, the more likely it is that you can successfully introduce a software product line.

Domain stability
The stability of the domain is also an important factor for the successful introduction of software product line engineering. If everything changes every half-year in an unpredictable way, the investment costs never pay off. This situation is similar to not understanding the domain well: variability is added that is not needed and the variability that is actually required is not available.

Günter Böckle
Klaus Pohl
Frank van der Linden

2

A Framework for Software Product Line Engineering

In this chapter you will learn:

- ○ *The principles of software product line engineering subsumed by our software product line engineering framework.*
- ○ *The difference between domain engineering and application engineering, which are the two key processes of software product line engineering.*
- ○ *Where variability of the product line is defined and where it is exploited.*
- ○ *The structure of this book, which is derived from the framework.*

2.1   Introduction

Our framework for software product line engineering incorporates the central concepts of traditional product line engineering, namely the use of platforms and the ability to provide mass customisation.

Platform artefacts

A platform is, in the software context, a collection of reusable artefacts (Definition 1-4). These artefacts have to be reused in a consistent and systematic way in order to build applications. Reusable artefacts encompass all types of software development artefacts such as requirements models, architectural models, software components, test plans, and test designs.

Planning for reuse

The experience from reuse projects in the 1990s shows that without proper planning the costs for reuse may be higher than for developing the artefacts from scratch. It is therefore crucial to plan beforehand the products for which reuse is sensible, together with the features that characterise these products. The planning for reuse continues throughout the whole development process.

Mass customisation through variability

To facilitate mass customisation (Definition 1-1) the platform must provide the means to satisfy different stakeholder requirements. For this purpose the concept of variability is introduced in the platform. As a consequence of applying this concept, the artefacts that can differ in the applications of the product line are modelled using variability.

The following sections outline our software product line engineering framework.

2.2   Two Development Processes

The software product line engineering paradigm separates two processes:

The software product line engineering paradigm separates two processes (see e.g. [Weiss and Lai 1999; Boeckle et al. 2004b; Pohl et al. 2001b, V.d. Linden 2002]):

Establishing the platform

- *Domain engineering*: This process is responsible for establishing the reusable platform and thus for defining the commonality and the variability of the product line (Definition 2-1). The platform consists of all types of software artefacts (requirements, design, realisation, tests, etc.). Traceability links between these artefacts facilitate systematic and consistent reuse.

Deriving applications

- *Application engineering*: This process is responsible for deriving product line applications from the platform established in domain engineering; see Definition 2-2. It exploits the variability of the product line and ensures the correct binding of the variability according to the applications' specific needs.

The advantage of this split is that there is a separation of the two concerns, to build a robust platform and to build customer-specific applications in a short time. To be effective, the two processes must interact in a manner that is beneficial to both. For example, the platform must be designed in such a way that it is of use for application development, and application development must be aided in using the platform.

Separation of concerns

The separation into two processes also indicates a separation of concerns with respect to variability. Domain engineering is responsible for ensuring that the available variability is appropriate for producing the applications. This involves common mechanisms for deriving a specific application. The platform is defined with the right amount of flexibility in many reusable artefacts. A large part of application engineering consists of reusing the platform and binding the variability as required for the different applications.

Flexibility and variability

> **Definition 2-1:** *Domain Engineering*
>
> Domain engineering is the process of software product line engineering in which the commonality and the variability of the product line are defined and realised.

> **Definition 2-2:** *Application Engineering*
>
> Application engineering is the process of software product line engineering in which the applications of the product line are built by reusing domain artefacts and exploiting the product line variability.

2.3   Overview of the Framework

Our software product line engineering framework has its roots in the ITEA projects ESAPS, CAFÉ, and FAMILIES [V.d. Linden 2002; Boeckle et al. 2004b; CAFÉ 2004] and is based on the differentiation between the domain and application engineering processes proposed by Weiss and Lai [Weiss and Lai 1999]. The framework is depicted in Fig. 2-1.

ITEA projects

The *domain engineering process* (depicted in the upper part of Fig. 2-1) is composed of five key sub-processes: product management, domain requirements engineering, domain design, domain realisation, and domain testing. The domain engineering process produces the platform including the commonality of the applications and the variability to support mass customi-

Domain engineering

sation. We briefly describe the domain engineering process and its sub-processes in Section 2.4.

Application engineering

The *application engineering process* (depicted in the lower part of Fig. 2-1) is composed of the sub-processes application requirements engineering, application design, application realisation, and application testing. We briefly describe the application engineering process and its sub-processes in Section 2.6.

Domain and application artefacts

The framework differentiates between different kinds of development artefacts (Definition 2-3): domain artefacts and applications artefacts. The *domain artefacts* (Definition 2-4) subsume the platform of the software product line. We briefly characterise the various artefacts in Section 2.5. The *application artefacts* (Definition 2-5) represent all kinds of development artefacts of specific applications. We briefly characterise these artefacts in Section 2.7. As the platform is used to derive more than one application, application engineering has to maintain the application-specific artefacts for each application separately. This is indicated in the lower part of Fig. 2-1.

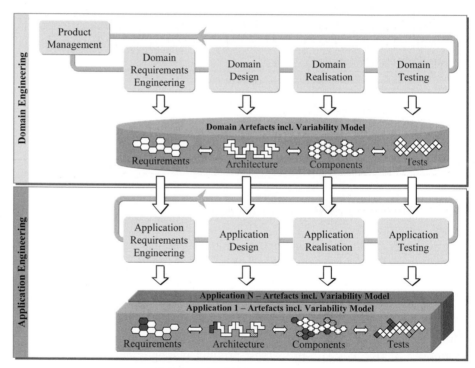

Fig. 2-1:   The software product line engineering framework

Note that neither the sub-processes of the domain and application engineering processes, nor their activities, have to be performed in a sequential order. We have indicated this by a loop with an arrow in Fig. 2-1 for each process.

No sequential order implied

In this book, we define the key activities that have to be part of each product line engineering process. The order in which they are performed depends on the particular process that is established in an organisation. Thus, the sub-processes and their activities described in this book can be combined with existing development methods such as RUP (Rational Unified Process, see [Kruchten 2000]), the spiral model [Boehm 1988], or other development processes.

Combination with existing processes

When the domain engineering process and the application engineering process are embedded into other processes of an organisation, each sub-process depicted in Fig. 2-1 gets an organisation-specific internal structure. Nevertheless, the activities presented in this book have to be present. An example of an organisation-specific process is the FAST process presented in [Weiss and Lai 1999].

Organisation-specific adaptation

> **Definition 2-3:** *Development Artefact*
>
> A development artefact is the output of a sub-process of domain or application engineering. Development artefacts encompass requirements, architecture, components, and tests.

> **Definition 2-4:** *Domain Artefacts*
>
> Domain artefacts are reusable development artefacts created in the sub-processes of domain engineering.

> **Definition 2-5:** *Application Artefacts*
>
> Application artefacts are the development artefacts of specific product line applications.

2.4   Domain Engineering

The key goals of the domain engineering process are to:

Main goals

- Define the commonality and the variability of the software product line.
- Define the set of applications the software product line is planned for, i.e. define the scope of the software product line.

- Define and construct reusable artefacts that accomplish the desired variability.

The goals of domain engineering are accomplished by the domain engineering sub-process. Each of them has to:

- Detail and refine the variability determined by the preceding sub-process.

- Provide feedback about the feasibility of realising the required variability to the preceding sub-process.

Five sub-processes The domain engineering part of the software product line engineering framework is highlighted in Fig. 2-2. We briefly explain the domain engineering sub-processes in this section, whereas domain artefacts are explained separately in Section 2.5.

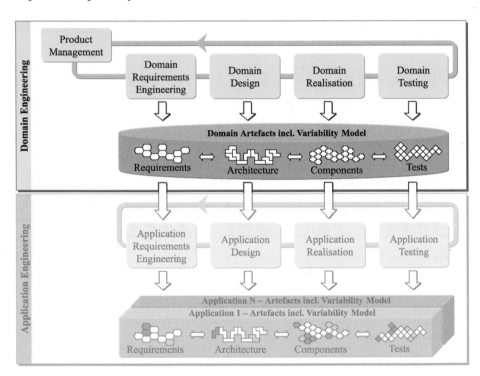

Fig. 2-2:   The domain engineering process

2.4.1 Product Management

Scope of the product line Product management deals with the economic aspects of the software product line and in particular with the market strategy. Its main concern is the management of the product portfolio of the company or business unit. In product line engineering, product management employs scoping techniques to define what is within the scope of the product line and what is outside.

The *input* for product management consists of the company goals defined by top management. The *output* of product management is a product roadmap that determines the major common and variable features[9] of future products as well as a schedule with their planned release dates. In addition, product management provides a list of existing products and/or development artefacts that can be reused for establishing the platform.

Input and output

Product management for software product lines differs from product management for single systems for the following reasons:

Differences from single-system engineering

- The platform has an essential strategic meaning for the company. The introduction and elimination of an entire platform have a strong influence on entrepreneurial success.

- A major strength of software product line engineering is the generation of a multitude of product variants at reasonable cost.

- The products in the product portfolio are closely related as they are based on a common platform.

- Product management anticipates prospective changes in features, legal constraints, and standards for the future applications of the software product line and formulates (models) the features accordingly. This means that the evolution of market needs, of technology, and of constraints for future applications is taken into account.

We deal with the principles of product management, activities, and artefacts in Chapter 9.

2.4.2 Domain Requirements Engineering

The domain requirements engineering sub-process encompasses all activities for eliciting and documenting the common and variable requirements of the product line.

Elicitation and documentation

The *input* for this sub-process consists of the product roadmap. The *output* comprises reusable, textual and model-based requirements and, in particular, the variability model of the product line. Hence, the output does not include the requirements specification of a particular application, but the common and variable requirements for all foreseeable applications of the product line.

Input and output

---

[9] A feature is an abstract requirement (see Definition 5-4 for the definition of "feature" by Kang et al.).

Differences from single-system engineering

Domain requirements engineering differs from requirements engineering for single systems because:

- The requirements are analysed to identify those that are common to all applications and those that are specific for particular applications (i.e. that differ among several applications).

- The possible choices with regard to requirements are explicitly documented in the variability model, which is an abstraction of the variability of the domain requirements.

- Based on the input from product management, domain requirements engineering anticipates prospective changes in requirements, such as laws, standards, technology changes, and market needs for future applications.

The artefacts and activities of domain requirements engineering are described in detail in Chapter 5 and Chapter 10.

2.4.3 Domain Design

Definition of reference architecture

The domain design sub-process encompasses all activities for defining the reference architecture of the product line. The reference architecture provides a common, high-level structure for all product line applications.

Input and output

The *input* for this sub-process consists of the domain requirements and the variability model from domain requirements engineering. The *output* encompasses the reference architecture and a refined variability model that includes so-called internal variability (e.g. variability that is necessary for technical reasons).

Differences from single-system engineering

Domain design differs from design for single systems because:

- Domain design incorporates configuration mechanisms into the reference architecture to support the variability of the product line.

- Domain design considers flexibility from the very first, so that the reference architecture can be adapted to the requirements of future applications.

- Domain design defines common rules for the development of specific applications based on the reference architecture.

- Domain design designates reusable parts, which are developed and tested in domain engineering, as well as application-specific parts, which are developed and tested in application engineering.

The artefacts and activities of domain design are described in detail in Chapter 6 and Chapter 11.

2.4.4 Domain Realisation

The domain realisation sub-process deals with the detailed design and the implementation of reusable software components.

Detailed design and implementation

The *input* for this sub-process consists of the reference architecture including a list of reusable software artefacts to be developed in domain realisation. The *output* of domain realisation encompasses the detailed design and implementation assets of reusable software components.

Input and output

Domain realisation differs from the realisation of single systems because:

Differences from single-system engineering

- The result of domain realisation consists of loosely coupled, configurable components, not of a running application.

- Each component is planned, designed, and implemented for the reuse in different contexts, i.e. the applications of the product line. The interface of a reusable component has to support the different contexts.

- Domain realisation incorporates configuration mechanisms into the components (as defined by the reference architecture) to realise the variability of the software product line.

The artefacts and activities of domain realisation are described in detail in Chapter 7 and Chapter 12.

2.4.5 Domain Testing

Domain testing is responsible for the validation and verification of reusable components. Domain testing tests the components against their specification, i.e. requirements, architecture, and design artefacts. In addition, domain testing develops reusable test artefacts to reduce the effort for application testing.

Validation of reusable components

The *input* for domain testing comprises domain requirements, the reference architecture, component and interface designs, and the implemented reusable components. The *output* encompasses the test results of the tests performed in domain testing as well as reusable test artefacts.

Input and output

Domain testing differs from testing in single-system engineering, because:

Differences from single-system engineering

- There is no running application to be tested in domain testing. Indeed, product management defines such applications, but the applications are available only in application testing. At first glance, only single components and integrated chunks composed of common parts can be tested in domain testing.

- Domain testing can embark on different strategies with regard to testing integrated chunks that contain variable parts. It is possible to create a sample application, to predefine variable test artefacts and apply them in application testing, or to apply a mixture of the former two strategies.

We describe the artefacts produced by domain testing in Chapter 8 and deal with product line test strategies and techniques in Chapter 13.

2.4.6 Other Software Quality Assurance Techniques

Inspections, reviews, and walkthroughs

Besides testing, other software quality assurance techniques are also applicable to software product line engineering, most notably inspections, reviews, and walkthroughs. These techniques have to be integrated into the domain and application engineering processes.

Techniques for single systems

To our knowledge, specialised techniques for software product line inspections, reviews, or walkthroughs have not been proposed. There is also a lack of experience reports identifying required adaptations of inspection, review, and walkthrough techniques known from the development of single software systems. We thus refer the interested reader to the standard literature on software inspections, reviews, and walkthroughs such as [Fagan 1976; Fagan 1986; Freedman and Weinberg 1990; Gilb and Graham 1993; Yourdon 1989].

2.5 Domain Artefacts

Common platform

Domain artefacts (or domain assets; see Definition 2-4) compose the platform of the software product line and are stored in a common repository. They are produced by the sub-processes described in Section 2.4. The artefacts are interrelated by traceability links to ensure the consistent definition of the commonality and the variability of the software product line throughout all artefacts. In the following, we briefly characterise each kind of artefact including the variability model.

2.5.1 Product Roadmap

Major features of all applications

The product roadmap describes the features of all applications of the software product line and categorises the feature into common features that are part of each application and variable features that are only part of some applications. In addition, the roadmap defines a schedule for market introduction. The product roadmap is a plan for the future development of the product portfolio. Its role in domain engineering is to outline the scope of the platform and to sketch the required variability of the product line. Its role in application engineering is to capture the feature mix of each planned application.

Note that the output of product management (the product roadmap) is not contained in the framework picture. The main reason for this is that the product roadmap is not a software development artefact in the common sense. Moreover, it guides both domain and application engineering, and is not an artefact to be reused in application engineering. In domain engineering, it guides the definition of the commonality and the variability of the software product line. In application engineering it guides the development of the specific products. We thus decided to define the product roadmap neither as a domain nor as an application artefact. We deal with the essential techniques for defining the product roadmap in Chapter 9.

Product roadmap not in framework picture

2.5.2 Domain Variability Model

The domain variability model defines the variability of the software product line. It defines what can vary, i.e. it introduces variation points for the product line. It also defines the types of variation offered for a particular variation point, i.e. it defines the variants offered by the product line. Moreover, the domain variability model defines variability dependencies and variability constraints which have to be considered when deriving product line applications. Last but not least, the domain variability model interrelates the variability that exists in the various development artefacts such as variability in requirements artefacts, variability in design artefacts, variability in components, and variability in test artefacts. It thus supports the consistent definition of variability in all domain artefacts.

Product line variability

We describe the variability model in greater detail in Chapter 4. To distinguish our variability model from the definition of variability within other development artefacts, we call it the "orthogonal variability model".

Orthogonal variability model

2.5.3 Domain Requirements

Domain requirements encompass requirements that are common to all applications of the software product line as well as variable requirements that enable the derivation of customised requirements for different applications. Requirements are documented in natural language (textual requirements) or by conceptual models (model-based requirements). Variability occurs in functional as well as in quality requirements. In Chapter 5, we elaborate on modelling variability in requirements using the orthogonal variability model.

Reusable requirements artefacts

2.5.4 Domain Architecture

The domain architecture or *reference architecture* determines the structure and the texture of the applications in the software product line. The structure determines the static and dynamic decomposition that is valid for all appli-

Core structure and common texture

cations of the product line. The texture is the collection of common rules guiding the design and realisation of the parts, and how they are combined to form applications. Variability in the architecture is documented by refining the orthogonal variability model and adding internal variability (i.e. variability that is only visible to the engineers). The architectural texture defines common ways to deal with variability in domain realisation as well as in application design and application realisation. Chapter 6 elaborates on the documentation of variability in design artefacts using the orthogonal variability model.

2.5.5 Domain Realisation Artefacts

Detailed design and implementation

Domain realisation artefacts comprise the design and implementation artefacts of reusable software components and interfaces. The design artefacts encompass different kinds of models that capture the static and the dynamic structure of each component. The implementation artefacts include source code files, configuration files, and makefiles. Components realise variability by providing suitable configuration parameters in their interface. In addition to being configurable, each component may exist in different variants to realise large differences in functionality and/or quality. We elaborate on variability in domain realisation artefacts in Chapter 7.

2.5.6 Domain Test Artefacts

Reusable test designs

Domain test artefacts include the domain test plan, the domain test cases, and the domain test case scenarios. The domain test plan defines the test strategy for domain testing, the test artefacts to be created, and the test cases to be executed. It also defines the schedule and the allocation of resources for domain test activities. The test cases and test case scenarios provide detailed instructions for the test engineer who performs a test and thus make testing traceable and repeatable. We include variability definitions in domain test artefacts to enable the large-scale reuse of test artefacts in application testing. We deal with the documentation of variability in test artefacts in Chapter 8.

2.6   Application Engineering

Main goals

The key goals of the application engineering process are to:

- Achieve an as high as possible reuse of the domain assets when defining and developing a product line application.
- Exploit the commonality and the variability of the software product line during the development of a product line application.

- Document the application artefacts, i.e. application requirements, architecture, components, and tests, and relate them to the domain artefacts.

- Bind the variability according to the application needs from requirements over architecture, to components, and test cases.

- Estimate the impacts of the differences between application and domain requirements on architecture, components, and tests.

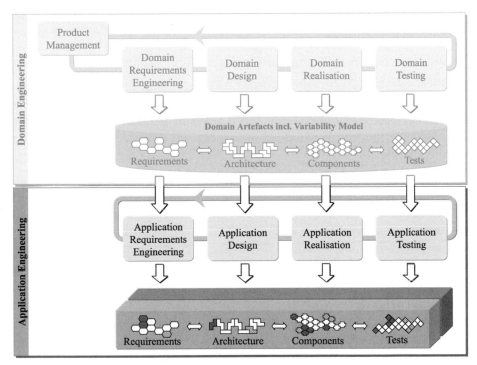

Fig. 2-3:   Application engineering

The framework introduces four application engineering sub-processes: application requirements engineering, application design, application realisation, and application test. Each of the sub-processes uses domain artefacts and produces application artefacts. Figure 2-3 highlights the application engineering part of the software product line engineering framework. We characterise the application engineering sub-processes in this section. Application artefacts are described in Section 2.7.

Four sub-processes

2.6.1 Application Requirements Engineering

The application requirements engineering sub-process encompasses all activities for developing the application requirements specification. The achievable amount of domain artefact reuse depends heavily on the applica-

Specification of applications

tion requirements. Hence, a major concern of application requirements engineering is the detection of deltas between application requirements and the available capabilities of the platform.

Input and output

The *input* to this sub-process comprises the domain requirements and the product roadmap with the major features of the corresponding application. Additionally, there may be specific requirements (e.g. from a customer) for the particular application that have not been captured during domain requirements engineering. The *output* is the requirements specification for the particular application.

Differences from single-system engineering

Application requirements engineering differs from requirements engineering for single systems for the following reasons:

- Requirements elicitation is based on the *communication of the available commonality and variability* of the software product line. Most of the requirements are not elicited anew, but are derived from the domain requirements.

- During elicitation, *deltas* between application requirements and domain requirements must be detected, evaluated with regard to the required adaptation effort, and documented suitably. If the required adaptation effort is known early, *trade-off decisions* concerning the application requirements are possible to reduce the effort and to increase the amount of domain artefact reuse.

We deal with the specific activities of application requirements engineering in Chapter 15.

2.6.2 Application Design

Specialisation of reference architecture

The application design sub-process encompasses the activities for producing the application architecture. Application design uses the reference architecture to instantiate the application architecture. It selects and configures the required parts of the reference architecture and incorporates application-specific adaptations. The variability bound in application design relates to the overall structure of the considered system (e.g. the specific hardware devices available in the system).

Input and output

The *input* for application design consists of the reference architecture and the application requirements specification. The *output* comprises the application architecture for the application at hand.

Differences from single-system engineering

Application design differs from the design process for single systems for the following reasons:

- Application design does not develop the application architecture from scratch, but derives it from the reference architecture by binding variability, i.e. making specific choices at places where the reference architecture offers different variants to choose from.

- Application design has to comply with the rules defined in the texture of the reference architecture. The rules cover the binding of variability as well as the incorporation of application-specific adaptations.

- Application design must evaluate the realisation effort for each required adaptation and may reject structural changes that would require a similar effort as for developing the application from scratch.

We elaborate on the key problems and solutions of application design in Chapter 16.

2.6.3 Application Realisation

The application realisation sub-process creates the considered application. The main concerns are the selection and configuration of reusable software components as well as the realisation of application-specific assets. Reusable and application-specific assets are assembled to form the application.

Component configuration and development

The *input* consists of the application architecture and the reusable realisation artefacts from the platform. The *output* consists of a running application together with the detailed design artefacts.

Input and output

Application realisation differs from the realisation of single systems because.

Differences from single-system engineering

- Many components, interfaces, and other software assets are not created anew. Instead, they are derived from the platform by binding variability. Variability is bound, e.g. by providing specific values for component-internal configuration parameters.

- Application-specific realisations must fit into the overall structure, e.g. they must conform to the reusable interfaces. Many detailed design options are predetermined by the architectural texture. Application-specific components can often be realised as variants of existing components that are already contained in the platform.

We deal with the challenges of application realisation in Chapter 17.

2.6.4 Application Testing

The application testing sub-process comprises the activities necessary to validate and verify an application against its specification.

Complete application test

Input and output

The *input* for application testing comprises all kinds of application artefacts to be used as a test reference,[10] the implemented application, and the reusable test artefacts provided by domain testing. The *output* comprises a test report with the results of all tests that have been performed. Additionally, the detected defects are documented in more detail in problem reports.

Differences from single-system engineering

The major differences from single-system testing are:

- Many test artefacts are not created anew, but are derived from the platform. Where necessary, variability is bound by selecting the appropriate variants.

- Application testing performs additional tests in order to detect defective configurations and to ensure that exactly the specified variants have been bound.

- To determine the achieved test coverage, application testing must take into account the reused common and variable parts of the application as well as newly developed application-specific parts.

We elaborate on the specific challenges and the activities of application testing in Chapter 18.

2.7   Application Artefacts

Traceability between application artefacts

Application artefacts (or application assets) comprise all development artefacts of a specific application including the configured and tested application itself. They are produced by the sub-processes described in Section 2.6. The application artefacts are interrelated by traceability links. The links between different application artefacts are required, for instance, to ensure the correct binding of variability throughout all application artefacts.

Traceability between domain and application

Many application artefacts are specific instances of reusable domain artefacts. The orthogonal variability model is used to bind variability in domain artefacts consistently in the entire application. Traceability links between application artefacts and the underlying domain artefacts are captured to support the various activities of the application engineering sub-processes. These links also support the consistent evolution of the product line. For example, if a domain artefact changes, the application artefacts affected by this change can be easily determined. In the following, we briefly characterise each kind of application artefact.

---

[10] The artefacts used as a test reference comprise the application requirements specification, the application architecture, and the component and interface designs.

2.7.1   Application Variability Model

The application variability model documents, for a particular application, the *Variability bindings*
binding of the variability, together with the rationales for selecting those *for applications*
bindings. It is restricted by the variability dependencies and constraints
defined in the domain variability model. Moreover, the application variability model documents extensions to the domain variability model that have
been made for the application. For example, it documents if a new variant
has been introduced for the application. It also documents if existing variants
have been adapted to match the application requirements better and if new
variation points have been introduced for the application. Briefly, the application variability model documents the variability bindings made and all
extensions and changes made for a particular application. Note that, similar
to other application artefacts, a separate application variability model is
introduced for each product line application. We deal with the definition of
the application variability model in Chapter 15.

2.7.2   Application Requirements

Application requirements constitute the complete requirements specification *Complete*
of a particular application. They comprise reused requirements as well as *specification*
application-specific requirements. The reuse of domain requirements
involves the use of the orthogonal variability model to bind the available
variability. Application-specific requirements are either newly developed
requirements or reused requirements that have been adapted. Chapter 15
elaborates on how to define the application requirements specification.

2.7.3   Application Architecture

The application architecture determines the overall structure of the consid- *Specific instance of*
ered application. It is a specific instance of the reference architecture. For the *reference architecture*
success of a product line, it is essential to reuse the reference architecture for
all applications. Its built-in variability and flexibility should support the
entire range of application architectures. The application architecture is
derived by binding the variability of the reference architecture that is documented in the orthogonal variability model. If application-specific requirements make it necessary to adapt the reference architecture, the stakeholders
must carefully weigh up the cost and benefit against each other. We deal
with the development of the application architecture based on application
requirements and the reference architecture in Chapter 16.

2.7.4   Application Realisation Artefacts

Application realisation artefacts encompass the component and interface *Configuration*
designs of a specific application as well as the configured, executable appli- *parameters*
cation itself. The required values for configuration parameters can be pro-

vided, for example, via configuration files. These parameter values are evaluated, for example, by makefiles or the run-time system. The values can be derived from the application variability model.

Application-specific realisation

Many application realisation artefacts are created by reusing domain artefacts and binding the available variability. However, part of the realisation artefacts usually has to be developed in the application realisation sub-process for the specific application. Chapter 17 deals with the development of an application based on reusable components.

2.7.5 Application Test Artefacts

Complete test documentation

Application test artefacts comprise the test documentation for a specific application. This documentation makes application testing traceable and repeatable. Many application test artefacts can be created by binding the variability of domain test artefacts which is captured in the orthogonal variability model. Moreover, detailed test instructions such as the particular input values to be used must be supplemented. For application-specific developments, additional test artefacts must be created. We deal with the development of application test artefacts in Chapter 18.

2.8   Role of the Framework in the Book

Two processes and variability

The book is organised according to the two key differences between software product line engineering and single-system development:

- The need for *two distinct development processes*, namcly thc domain engineering process and the application engineering process.

- The need to explicitly define and manage *variability*.

Part II chapters

Part II elaborates on the definition of variability, which is the central concept for realising mass customisation in software product line engineering. The part consists of five chapters:

- Principles of Variability (Chapter 4)

- Documenting Variability in Requirements Artefacts (Chapter 5)

- Documenting Variability in Design Artefacts (Chapter 6)

- Documenting Variability in Realisation Artefacts (Chapter 7)

- Documenting Variability in Test Artefacts (Chapter 8)

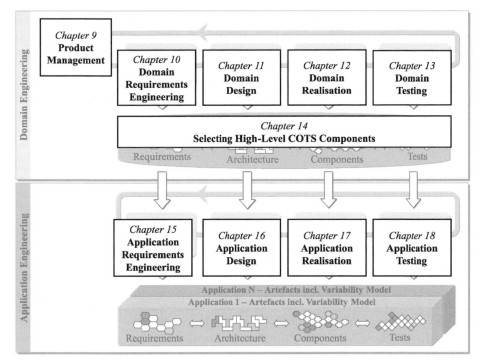

Fig. 2-4:   Structure of Parts III and IV

Part III elaborates on the creation of the platform and thus on the definition of the commonality and the variability of the software product line. The chapters are shown in the upper half of Fig. 2-4. Each of the first five chapters of Part III elaborates on one of the sub-processes of domain engineering (as shown in the upper part of Fig. 2-4). The last chapter of Part III deals with the specific problem of selecting off-the-shelf components in domain engineering. The chapters of Part III are:

Part III chapters

- Product Management (Chapter 9)
- Domain Requirements Engineering (Chapter 10)
- Domain Design (Chapter 11)
- Domain Realisation (Chapter 12)
- Domain Testing (Chapter 13)
- Selecting High-Level COTS[11] Components (Chapter 14)

---

[11] COTS is the acronym for Commercial Off-The-Shelf. A high-level COTS component provides a significant fraction of the functionality of a software product line.

Part IV
chapters

Part IV elaborates on the use of the platform to derive specific product line applications. It shows how product line variability is exploited to develop different applications. Each chapter explains one of the four application engineering sub-processes (shown in the lower half of Fig. 2-4):

- Application Requirements Engineering (Chapter 15)

- Application Design (Chapter 16)

- Application Realisation (Chapter 17)

- Application Testing (Chapter 18)

Part V
chapters

Part V deals with the institutionalisation of software product line engineering in an organisation. Its focus is on the separation between the domain and application engineering processes. The chapters of Part V are:

- Organisation (Chapter 19)

- Transition Process (Chapter 20).

Part VI
chapters

Part VI presents experiences with software product line engineering gained in 15 organisations and briefly characterises essential fields for future research. Whenever possible, we employ the terminology introduced in our framework to make clear the relationships between the topics considered in Part VI and our framework. The chapters of Part VI are:

- Experiences with Software Product Line Engineering (Chapter 21)

- Future Research (Chapter 22)

Klaus Pohl
Ernst Sikora

3

Overview of the Example Domain: Home Automation

In this chapter you will learn:

- o *Basic domain knowledge about the home automation domain, from which most of the examples in this book have been taken.*
- o *Examples of goals, functions, and variability in the home automation domain.*
- o *The key building blocks of a home automation system illustrated by an example.*

3.1   Smart Home Fundamentals

Major
characteristics

In recent times, smart homes have moved into the focus of scientific and technological research and development. Most everyday-life technical devices are controlled by microprocessors. Home automation integrates such devices into a network. The network allows the devices to coordinate their behaviour in order to fulfil complex tasks without human intervention. Intuitive user interfaces allow easy access to the functionality of a smart home.

Related
domains

A variety of domains contribute to the evolution of smart homes. An overview is given in Fig. 3-1. The relation between home automation and these domains becomes clearer in the course of this chapter. For example, 'web technology' allows to access home functions remotely through the Internet.

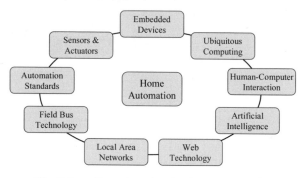

Fig. 3-1:   Domains related to home automation

3.1.1   Goals

Comfort, security,
safety, low cost

The home automation domain tackles four major goals: comfort, security, life safety, and low costs. Smart home technology addresses these goals in different ways. Comfort is increased by automating tedious tasks and by an intuitive and well-designed user interface. Security is addressed by identification mechanisms and surveillance equipment like outdoor cameras. Notification mechanisms additionally contribute to security by allowing for immediate reaction, e.g. in the case of an attempted burglary. A similar reasoning holds for life safety. Here, sensors detect danger to life – for example, caused by fire or electricity. Another aspect of life safety is health monitoring, which can be part of a smart home as well. The fourth goal of home automation, namely low costs, has two facets. First, expenses for purchasing and installing the system should be low. Second, home automation helps to reduce running costs by smart energy management, which prevents unnecessary heating, lighting, and other kinds of energy consumption. For example, when a resident opens a window, heating can be turned down automatically for that room.

3.1.2 Stakeholders

Various stakeholders are involved in the development, installation, and usage process of a home automation system. When dealing with home automation, the interests of these stakeholders have to be accounted for. The interest of the residents of the home defines a large part of the requirements that a smart home must satisfy. Residents are not necessarily identical with the building owner who invests money for the installation of the system. Thus, the building owner has own interests as well. In many cases, a caretaker may also be involved, who is responsible for the administration of the house and for accounting tasks. Managers of the company developing the home automation system and bringing it to market have a strong interest in the features of their products as well. Regarding the development process, the installation, and technical maintenance of the smart home, three more stakeholders can be identified: developers, installers, and maintenance personnel (technicians). This non-exhaustive list of stakeholders is depicted in Fig. 3-2.

Viewpoints

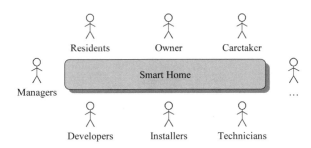

Fig. 3-2: Examples of stakeholders in the smart home domain.

3.1.3 Smart Homes vs. Conventional Homes

Regarding technical equipment in homes as it is today reveals that in most cases only few functions are automated. For example, the residents of a conventional home switch lights on and off manually when entering or leaving a room. Similarly, they check whether windows are closed by walking from room to room, for instance when a storm is expected, or for security reasons. Often, there are already some automated functions in a conventional home such as alarm equipment, sensor-controlled roller shutters or programmable timers for power outlets. But in contrast to smart homes these devices do not cooperate. A typical situation that shows the drawbacks of isolated devices is when the heating is on and some windows are open at the same time.

Conventionally low automation

Window sensors belonging to the alarm equipment would not remind the residents to adjust heating or notify the heating system about open windows.

Software control in smart homes Smart homes are characterised by a high degree of automation. Their devices are integrated into a home network. So, the smart home constitutes an entire system that is made up of individual *subsystems* and whose behaviour is determined by the software controlling it. Thus, it is possible to coordinate the functions provided by different subsystems.

Common user interface A major advantage that comes along with networking and software control is the facility to provide a unified management layer for the whole system. In order to interact with a particular device of a smart home, the residents do not have to frequent this device and operate its individual user interface. Instead the user can access all devices via a common *user interface* such as a touch screen. The consequence is for example that residents do not need to walk from room to room in order to check if some window is open, because they can get this information from a centralised user interface.

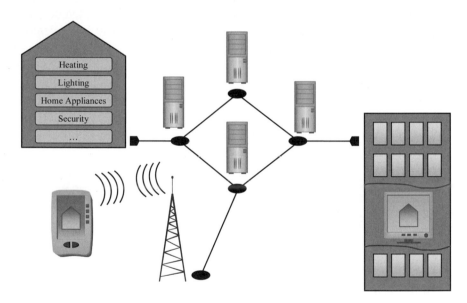

Fig. 3-3:   Remote access to the smart home

Remote access In fact, the residents can use Internet applications and mobile computers to control their home from any place. Figure 3-3 illustrates the possibility to control home functions remotely via the Internet, e.g. from the home owner's work place (right side of the picture) or via a wireless, handheld PC (bottom left). A simple scenario that shows the value of remote access is checking whether an electric iron has been switched off, after already having left on a vacation trip.

3.2   Building Blocks of a Home Automation System

In this section, we take a more technical viewpoint on home automation in order to elaborate on typical components that a smart home contains.

3.2.1   Sensors and Actuators

Sensors and actuators are mechanical or electronic components that measure and respectively influence physical values of their environment. *Sensors* gather information from the physical environment and make it available to the system. For example, infrared sensors can be used to detect the presence of a person in a room. Likewise, the system can act on its environment by means of *actuators*. An example is a light actuator that is capable of switching on or off or of dimming one or more electric lights.

Measuring and influencing the environment

3.2.2   Smart Control Devices

Smart control devices read data from sensors, process this data, and activate actuators, if necessary. A single control device is responsible only for a fraction of the total functionality of the smart home, such as the lighting of one room. For many control and automation tasks a smart control device can act autonomously, i.e. without control by a central server. But there are also tasks that demand communication among different control devices or with the home gateway (see next section).

Control automation

Example 3-1: *Electronic Door Locks*

Later in the book, we use examples that deal with door locks, which provide different kinds of authentication such as fingerprint-based authentication. The technical realisation of an electronic door lock employs actuators for locking and unlocking a door, and possibly sensors that detect the state of a door (e.g. open or closed). The sensors and actuators are connected to a control device that is responsible for a particular door and has to communicate with other devices, e.g. to access a database with fingerprint data of authorised persons. As this book is about software product line engineering, we do not consider the hardware configuration in our examples but the software necessary to provide the door lock functionality. We assume that this software is somehow deployed on the home automation hardware.

There are two major types of control devices: devices that are produced to be flexibly adaptable to a wide range of tasks, and devices that are dedicated to a special purpose. The former type are able to execute custom software and connect different kinds of sensors and actuators. The latter type often come together with sensors and actuators necessary for the given purpose. The

General and special purpose devices

examples used in this book do not explicitly distinguish between the two types. However, we assume that some kind of software is necessary to provide the functionality of the control device. Example 3-1 illustrates the role of control devices in the examples in this book.

3.2.3 The Home Gateway

Configuring and monitoring

The home gateway is the central server of a smart home. It offers the processing and data storage capabilities required for complex applications. Users such as residents or technicians can access the services offered by the home gateway via different front-ends that interact with the home gateway and provide the user interface. The services offered by the home gateway mostly pertain to overall system management functionality such as the configuration, monitoring, and control of the subsystems and their devices, or the detection of failures.

Database

User management is a necessary component of the home gateway software. Each individual user has different access rights and different preferences with regard to the system functions. This kind of information is stored in the database of the home gateway and can be accessed by other devices such as electronic door locks (see Example 3-1). Moreover, the home gateway stores a model of the home automation system. This model captures the types, physical and logical locations, configuration parameters, etc., of all devices in the home automation system.

Workflows

As stated above, smart control devices can operate autonomously. For example, the application program of a lighting control device can handle an event, caused by a resident operating a light switch, without involving the home gateway. However, in a home automation system various events can occur that may demand complex reactions or a multitude of processing steps from the system. Different events and reactions can be combined to workflows. The management and processing of workflows is within the responsibility of the home gateway. Example 3-2 illustrates such a workflow.

Other functions

The home gateway may also support other functions, such as audio and video entertainment, Internet access, e-shopping, or email (see for example [InHouse 2004]).

> **Example 3-2:** *An Example Workflow for Fire Detection*
>
> On the detection of fire, the home gateway shuts all windows, closes gas valves, deactivates power outlets, switches on emergency lights, unlocks doors, activates the alarm, and informs the fire station. Each of these steps may involve several sub-steps and additional events. Moreover, the event of detecting fire may coincide with other events such as the detection of glass breakage, which otherwise indicates an attempted burglary. The different events may demand reactions that are in conflict with each other, e.g. unlocking doors on the detection of fire and locking doors on the detection of glass breakage. Rules are necessary how to deal with the coincidence of different events.

3.2.4 Networking

Like conventional computer networks, the network of a smart home can be based on various communication media, e.g. twisted pair cable. To avoid additional cabling, power-line communication or wireless communication can be used. A realistic home automation system is inclined to employ a *heterogeneous* network made up of various network standards and various communication media. *Network interfaces* are devices that allow for integrating diverse types of networks and communication media into the home network. Apart from the internal network that links devices inside the home, external networks such as the public Internet, ISDN, and mobile phone networks can be integrated as well.

Heterogeneous network

It is not just that network technology comes in many different forms; the devices connected to the home network can also differ greatly with respect to their functionality and their software and hardware. As a consequence, the software architecture of a smart home must be able to cope with all kinds of networks and technical devices. This aspect is characteristic of many distributed systems.

Software architecture supporting heterogeneity

3.2.5 Standards in the Home Automation Domain

Technological standards simplify the development of complex technical systems and help to achieve compatibility between devices developed by different manufacturers. In the home automation domain, standards are used for instance with regard to network technology. Typically, the networking of a smart home is based on field bus technology such as the European Installation Bus (EIB, see [EIBA 2004]) and the Local Operating Network (LON, LonWorks, see [Echelon 1999; LonMark 2004]), or on local area network technology (e.g. Ethernet or wireless LAN).

Network standards

Software frameworks Certain aspects of the software architecture are standardised. A well-known framework employed in the home automation domain is the OSGi framework (Open Service Gateway Initiative, see [OSGi 2003]). Apart from the OSGi standard, other vendor-specific software frameworks are also available.

3.3   An Example

In order to follow the examples presented in this book, it is useful to examine some simple example models of a home automation system before going into software engineering details.

3.3.1   System Functionality

Figure 3-4 contains a schematic picture of a smart home with some networked devices from the following subsystems: lighting control, door and window control, and home appliances control. In the following, these subsystems are described in more detail.

Smart lighting The lighting control subsystem comprises switches, lights and sensors. A smart home is expected to adapt lighting based on a number of factors. The overall intensity of light in a room and the presence of persons are two basic factors lighting control should take into account. However, the favoured lighting can also depend on the current activity of the residents and on individual habits. For example, different lighting would be desired for a dinner party than for reading a book. Moreover, a smart home can offer an elaborate vacation mode that uses lighting control and other subsystems to let the house appear occupied.

Doors and windows The door and window control subsystem monitors the state of doors and windows. Endowed with the information about all doors and windows, i.e. whether they are open, closed, locked, or unlocked, the smart home can for example remind the residents to shut some windows in certain situations. Outer doors can be unlocked electronically based on some kind of identification mechanism (see Example 3-1).

Roller shutters Window control also encompasses electric roller shutters. However, opening and closing roller shutters affects lighting. Hence, the door and window control subsystem and the lighting control subsystem have to interact with each other. For example, when roller shutters are closed, lighting control can switch on a lamp without the residents having to intervene or to operate both subsystems individually.

Home appliances The basic function of home appliances control is to monitor and control power outlets. This allows the residents to monitor power consumption and switch off individual power outlets. In recent times, microprocessor-controlled home appliances have become available that provide sophisticated device interfaces enabling a tight integration into the smart home. This kind of integration allows, for example, monitoring and operating a washing machine at the user interface of the home automation system.

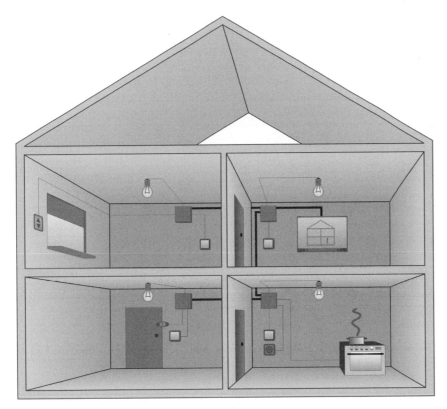

Fig. 3-4:   Schematic picture of a smart home with lighting, door and window, and home appliances control

Smart homes contain more subsystems, such as heating, fire and smoke detection, access control, audio and video equipment, Internet access, etc. However, the previous considerations suffice to give a general understanding of typical smart home applications. *Other subsystems*

The value of home automation becomes obvious if we consider that all the functions so far mentioned are available at the same user interface. In addition, being equipped with an Internet or ISDN connection, the smart home can offer remote access functionality (see Fig. 3-3). The user interface itself may be realised in different ways. It is possible to employ a TV set, a wall-mounted touch screen, a handheld PC or some other device. The user inter- *Different user interfaces* face software can provide a graphical user interface but may also offer a speech interface or – as sometimes suggested by human–computer interaction research – a human-like embodied character. The following, brief scenario gives an idea of the prospects home automation can provide:

Example 3-3: *Remote Access to the Smart Home*

The residents are going on holiday. On the motorway they doubt whether they have shut all the windows and locked the door in their hurry. They access their home using a handheld PC with mobile Internet connectivity. After ascertaining themselves that everything is all right, they activate the vacation mode for their home in order to save energy and protect it from burglars.

3.3.2   A Simple System Configuration

Light control   In the following, we briefly sketch a system configuration that facilitates lighting control as depicted in Fig. 3-5. This system consists of a home gateway and two control devices, all of which are connected to a common network. One of the control devices is responsible for monitoring the state of light switches. The other one controls the lights attached to it.

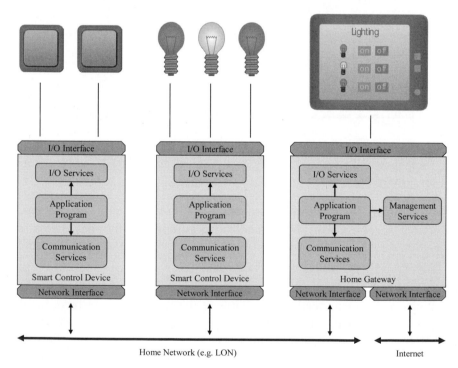

Fig. 3-5:   Example configuration of a home automation system

The application programs that run on the control devices determine the reaction of the system to the activation of a light switch. The application programs use I/O services provided by the lighting control devices that monitor the switches and control the lights. The communication services provided by the control devices enable the exchange of messages among the application programs.

Control devices

The software of the home gateway comprises a server application that can interact with various front-ends. The front-end shown in Fig. 3-5 provides a touch screen as user interface. Moreover the home gateway enables Internet access to the smart home through an additional network interface

Home gateway

3.3.3 System Component Interaction

To portray the dynamics of a home automation system, we consider an example scenario describing internal system interactions. The scenario in Fig. 3-6 assumes that the system is equipped with sensors that are able to detect water intrusion, e.g. in the basement of the house.

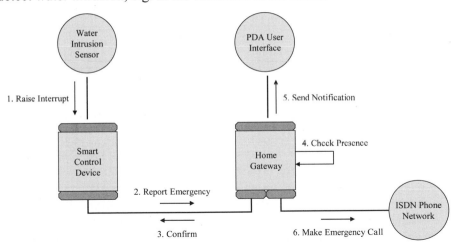

Fig. 3-6: Scenario with internal system interactions

When a sensor detects water intrusion, the smart control device reports this emergency event to the home gateway, which holds the knowledge about the workflow that deals with this event. The home gateway acknowledges receipt of the emergency message with a confirmation message. Having received the confirmation, the smart control device leaves further processing to the home gateway. The home gateway enquires of the security subsystem whether any residents are in the house. Failing to identify any residents, the home gateway sends a notification to the PDA user interface and waits for further instructions from a resident. After some period of time has elapsed

Water intrusion scenario

without an answer from the mobile user interface, the home gateway calls an emergency phone number that has been chosen by the residents for the case of water intrusion. This action marks the end of the depicted workflow.

3.4   Software Variability in Smart Home Applications

The reason for dealing with home automation systems was to get insight into a domain in which applying product line engineering is almost imperative. The following examination demonstrates variability that is inherent to a home automation system.

3.4.1   Examples of Variability

Choice of variants

Variability allows choosing between different options, which we call variants. By a different choice of variants, one home automation system can differ from another. In the following we present some examples of variability in a home automation system:

Different remote and local user interfaces

- *User interface variability*: One aspect of smart homes, where variability is easy to identify, is the user interface. Various realisations of local and remote user interfaces have been discussed or hinted at throughout the chapter. Part of them constitute alternatives, others tend to coexist in the same system. A typical set of variants might for example comprise a graphical TV interface, a web-based interface, and a PDA interface. Software variability is necessary to support different kinds of user interfaces for the home automation system.

Different control algorithms

- *Available sensors*: The kinds of sensors installed in the home automation system influence the possible realisations of control tasks. A simple example is the task of roller shade control. When timer control and luminance sensors are available, the rules for opening and closing roller shades depend on the current time and on the amount of daylight. When weather sensors are additionally available, roller shades can be opened in case of strong wind in order to prevent damage. Software variability allows the provision of different control algorithms according to the available sensors in the home automation system.

Different levels of fail-safety

- *Fail-safety*: The home automation system may support different levels of fail-safety. For example, the basic level can provide self-tests and failure reports. Higher levels can include redundant system components for the most important functions. Software variability is needed to support different levels of fail-safety. For example, the software of a redundant system has to detect malfunctions, deactivate defective components and relocate tasks to back up components.

- *Assistance for older and handicapped people*: Home automation systems must fulfil additional requirements when they are used by older and handicapped people. These users may have difficulties with everyday activities and in the operation of the normal user interface. The additional requirements, which only apply for a certain group of customers, are realised by certain variants of the software.

Different kinds of assistance

The essence of the above examples is that the support of different options leads to variability in the software of the smart home. This is the most important observation with regard to the use of the examples in the book.

Software variability

3.4.2 Causes of Variability

In this section we analyse the reasons for software variability such as the variability presented in the examples of the previous section.

In order to make the system work, each individual configuration of hardware devices must be supplied with appropriate software. Hardware and software have to be compatible with each other. The support of different hardware configurations demands software variability. This is the software engineers' point of view on variability as software engineers have to deal with the different technologies that are supported or used by the home automation system. The technical point of view is typically a minor concern for the customer, who is mostly interested in the functionality of the home automation system.

Customer wishes and technical constraints

The interrelation between customer wishes, hardware, and software is illustrated in Fig. 3-7. The customer demands certain functionality and certain quality. The home automation system has to satisfy the required functionality and quality. It consists of a specific hardware configuration and a software configuration that depend on each other.

Functionality and quality

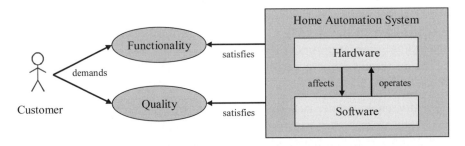

Fig. 3-7:   Interrelations between customer needs, hardware, and software

Different customers have different demands with respect to the overall level of automation as well as to the specific functions of their home automation

Different customer needs

system. In addition, customers have different demands with regard to the quality of the system. Both required functionality and required quality affect the price of the home automation system. The differences in customer needs are a reason for variability.

Example 3-4: *Variability Caused by Customer Needs*

It may be the case that one customer wants to have electronically controlled door locks with fingerprint authentication while another customer does not want to have electronic door locks at all for cost reasons. In order to be able to provide both customers with applications that satisfy their individual wishes, the home automation system has to support variability in door locks.

Hardware

Not only differences in customer needs but also technical reasons cause variability as illustrated in Example 3-5.

Example 3-5: *Variability Caused by Differences in Hardware*

The home automation system supports fingerprint sensors from two different manufacturers, which differ in the resolution of the scanned fingerprints. Hence, the software of the home automation system has to support variability in the resolution of fingerprint images.

3.5   Role of the Home Automation Domain in the Book

Commonality and variability

The remaining chapters of this book make use of the example domain in order to explain software product line engineering techniques. The example domain is used to illustrate the commonality as well as possible variability among the applications of a product line. Requirements engineers, architects, programmers, and test engineers have to deal with the commonality and variability when developing a platform of reusable software artefacts, e.g. for a home automation system. Such a platform allows the creation of a variety of customised home automation applications by reusing the platform artefacts.

Independent examples

Typically, each chapter uses only a fragment of the smart home, whereas the purpose of this chapter was to provide a coherent overall picture. Moreover, each chapter uses the home automation example in a slightly different way depending on the main focus of the chapter. Though some examples are closely related, in general, the examples are independent of each other. They are not meant to depict a single, consistent model of a home automation software product line.

Part II

Product Line Variability

Part II: Overview

Documenting and managing variability is one of the two key properties character-ising software product line engineering. The explicit definition and management of variability distinguishes software product line engineering from both single-system development and software reuse.

In this part you will learn:

- *The principles of software product line variability.*

- *How to document explicitly the variability of a software product line in require-ments, design, realisation, and test artefacts.*

- *How to facilitate the consistent management of variability across the various domain artefacts.*

The documentation of the commonalities and the variability in all artefacts is illus-trated using examples from the home automation domain.

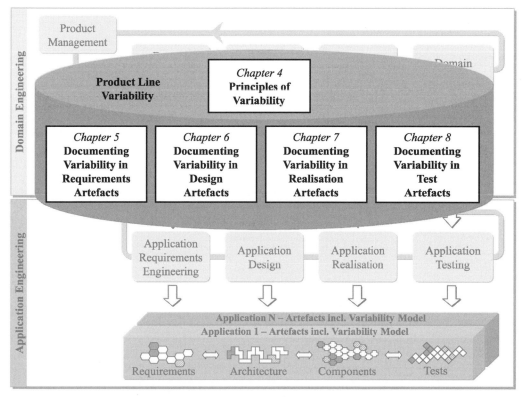

Fig. II-1: Chapter overview of Part II

Kim Lauenroth
Klaus Pohl

4

Principles of Variability

In this chapter you will learn:

- ○ *Basic knowledge about the variability of a software product line.*
- ○ *The difference between external and internal software product line variability.*
- ○ *The basic concepts for modelling variability: variation points, variants, and their interrelation.*
- ○ *An orthogonal variability model used throughout this book to define variability across all software development artefacts.*

4.1   Introduction

Variability in domain artefacts

We introduce variability modelling in order to support the development and the reuse of variable development artefacts. In software product line engineering, variability is an essential property of domain artefacts. Hence, we use variability modelling in this book to capture the variability of domain requirements, architecture, components, and tests (the artefacts highlighted in Fig. 4-1).

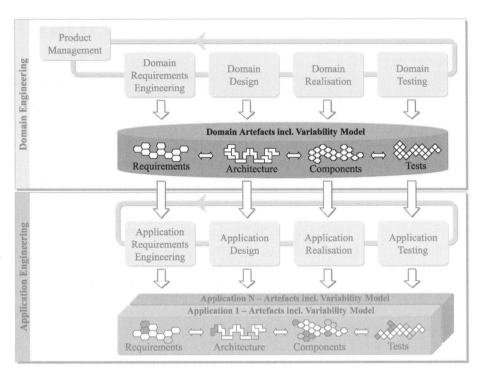

Fig. 4-1:   Focus of variability modelling

Abstraction levels

Variability is introduced during the product management sub-process when common and variable features of the software product line applications are identified. As domain requirements detail the features defined in product management, variability is carried over to domain requirements. Similarly, this holds for design, realisation, and testing. Requirements engineering, design, and realisation deal with models of a system at different levels of abstraction. At each level, variability from the previous level is refined and additional variability is introduced, which is not a result of refinement. For instance, it may be necessary to introduce variability at the architectural level in order to make a component compatible with different versions of a standard component library. Variability at different abstraction levels is considered in more detail in Section 4.5.4.

We refer to the sum of all activities concerned with the identification and documentation of variability as *defining variability*. Variability is defined during domain engineering. It is exploited during application engineering by binding the appropriate variants.

Defining and exploiting variability

Defining and exploiting variability throughout the different life cycle stages of a software product line is supported by the concept of *managed variability*. This concept basically encompasses the following issues:

Managed variability

- Supporting activities concerned with defining variability.

- Managing variable artefacts.

- Supporting activities concerned with resolving variability.

- Collecting, storing, and managing trace information necessary to fulfil these tasks.

Each sub-process in application engineering binds variability introduced by the corresponding sub-process in domain engineering. This has to be done in a consistent way to ensure that the required variant is built correctly. The moment of variability resolution in realisation is often called the *binding time* of the variability. The binding time is not within the focus of variability modelling. To increase flexibility, the design may demand moving the binding time to a rather late phase in the realisation, for instance during the building of the actual system. There is a trend to decide very late on the binding time, and thus make the binding time variable; see [V. Ommering 2004]. For further reading on variability management; see [Bosch et al. 2002; Bachmann et al. 2003].

Binding time

4.2   Variability Subject and Variability Object

In common language use, the term variability refers to the ability or the tendency to change. To be more precise, the kind of variability we are interested in does not occur by chance but is brought about on purpose. We illustrate variability in the real world with a few examples:

"Variability" in common language

- An electric bulb can be lit or unlit.

- A software application can support different languages.

- Chewing gum can be sweet or sour.

- A triple band mobile phone supports three different network standards.

Three questions

It might be a good exercise for the reader to search for variability in his or her surroundings. In order to characterise variability in more detail, we formulate three questions that are helpful in defining product line variability.

What does vary?

The first essential question is "what does vary?" Answering this question means identifying precisely the variable item or property of the real world. The question leads us to the definition of the term *variability subject*.

> **Definition 4-1:** *Variability Subject*
>
> A variability subject is a variable item of the real world or a variable property of such an item.

Why does it vary?

The second question is "why does it vary?" There are different reasons for an item or property to vary: different stakeholder needs, different country laws, technical reasons, etc. Moreover, in the case of interdependent items, the reason for an item to vary can be the variation of another item.

How does it vary?

The third question is "how does it vary?" This question deals with the different shapes a variability subject can take. To identify the different shapes of a variability subject we define the term *variability object*.

> **Definition 4-2:** *Variability Object*
>
> A variability object is a particular instance of a variability subject.

Consciousness of variability

A vital effect of regarding the three questions is a shift in the way of thinking about variability. Being aware of variability and dealing with it consciously is an important prerequisite of variability modelling. In order to provide a better understanding of variability subject and variability object, we give some examples from different domains (Examples 4-1 to 4-3). Note that the variability space, i.e. the available options, may be very large or even infinite, such as the number of possible colours in Example 4-1.

> **Example 4-1:** *Variability Subject and Objects for "Colour"*
>
> The variability subject "colour" identifies a property of real-world items. Examples of variability objects for this variability subject are red, green, and blue.

> **Example 4-2:** *Variability Subject and Objects for "Payment Method"*
>
> Payment method is a variability subject and payment by credit card, payment by cash card, payment by bill, and payment by cash are examples of variability objects.

Example 4-3: *Variability Subject and Objects for "Identification Mechanism"*

The identification mechanism of a home security system is a variability subject, keypad and fingerprint scanner are examples of variability objects.

The reasons for the variability subject to vary can be for instance different security standards or different customer needs. Changing the identification mechanism of an electronic door lock also leads to changes in other system components like the database that stores the keys:

a) Keypad: The database for this identification mechanism stores numerical keys.

b) Fingerprint scanner: In this case, the database stores graphical information, i.e. the characteristics of a fingerprint.

In this example, changing the identification mechanism of a door lock from keypads to fingerprint scanners causes variability in the key database.

4.3   Variability in Software Product Line Engineering

In this section, we define the central concepts for variability in software product line engineering.

4.3.1   Variation Point

In software product line engineering, variability subjects and the corresponding variability objects are embedded into the context of a software product line. They represent a subset of all possible variability subjects and a subset of all possible variability objects from the real world, which are necessary to realise a particular software product line. We reflect this transition in our terminology and define the term *variation point*[12] (Definition 4-3) accordingly.

Variability in product line context

The definition applies to all kinds of development artefacts, i.e. requirements, architecture, design, code, and tests. Contextual information of a variation point encompasses the details about the embedding of the variability subject into the software product line, such as the reason why the variation

Contextual information

---

[12] Jacobson et al. define variation point as "one or more locations at which the variation will occur" [Jacobson et al. 1997]. This definition is similar to the definition presented in this book, but Jacobson et al. focus on UML models, whereas this chapter takes a more general view on variability by linking variability in the real world and variability in software product lines. Furthermore, our definition emphasises that a variation point exists in a certain context.

point was introduced. Examples of such reasons are the specifics of different countries in which the software product line applications are sold, different stakeholder needs, or different marketing strategies for the applications.

Definition 4-3: *Variation Point*

A variation point is a representation of a variability subject within domain artefacts enriched by contextual information.

4.3.2   Variant

Variability object representation

We define the term *variant*, which is a representation of a variability object, in analogy to the term variation point (Definition 4-4). We illustrate the transition from variability subjects to variation points, and from variability objects to variants in Example 4-4.

Self-contained entities

It is important to recognise that variation points and variants are self-contained entities that are distinct from artefacts like requirements, architecture, etc. A variant identifies a single option of a variation point and can be associated with other artefacts to indicate that those artefacts correspond to a particular option. Yet, for the sake of simplicity, in cases in which there is no danger of confusion, the artefacts associated to a variant are referred to as variants themselves (Section 4.6.9 deals with such terminology issues in more detail).

Definition 4-4: *Variant*

A variant is a representation of a variability object within domain artefacts.

Example 4-4: *Colour of a Car as Variation Point*

The variability subject 'colour'[13] shown on the left of Fig. 4-2 has several variability objects ('red', 'blue', 'green', 'yellow', etc.). An automotive company wants to build cars in different colours, therefore a variation point "colour of a car" (car is the context of the variation point) is defined.

An example automotive company builds red and green cars, therefore only the variants 'red (car)' and 'green (car)' are defined on the right of Fig. 4-2. Other variability objects ('yellow', etc.) are not considered as variants for the automotive company, e.g. for marketing reasons.

---

[13] We use single quotes when we refer to the elements of a figure, such as 'colour' in Fig. 4-2.

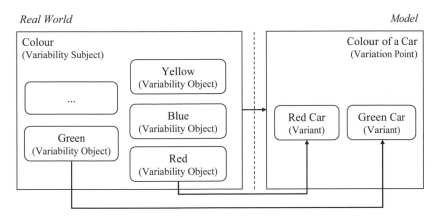

Fig. 4-2:   Relation between variability in the real world and in a model of the real world

4.3.3   Defining Variation Points and Variants

Variation points and variants are used to define the variability of a software product line. Thus, it is essential to be able to identify variation points and variants in a systematic manner. In the following, we provide three basic steps for accomplishing this task.

Three steps

The first step is to identify the item of the real world that varies, i.e. identifying the variability subject (Example 4-5).

Identify variability subject

The second step is to define a variation point within the context of the software product line. This step is necessary as there is a difference between variability in the real world (represented by variability subjects) and variability in a software product line (represented by variation points). For instance, a variation point only offers an excerpt of the possible variability in the real world. A variation point becomes part of the model of the system under consideration and affects this model in different ways. For example, a variation point can mean that there are different requirements to choose from and that there will be different applications, which result from a particular choice model.

Define variation point

In the third step, the variants are defined. For this purpose, it is necessary to select variability objects of the identified variability subject and define them as variants of the variation point. Adding the variants supplements the information provided by the variation point by specific instances. However, the variation point still captures unique information not represented by the variants. For example, the variants do not capture the variability subject. Moreover, the set of variants is likely to change over time, while the variation point tends to remain constant.

Define variants

> **Example 4-5:** *Identifying the Variability Subject*
>
> The engineers of a home automation software product line suggest different ways of communication between system components, e.g. cabled LAN, wireless LAN, Bluetooth, or power line. The engineers' suggestions yield the variability subject "kind of network".

> **Example 4-6:** *Creating a Variation Point*
>
> Example 4-5 defined the variability subject "kind of network". The resulting variation point for the home automation system is "home automation system network". The variation point indicates that the home automation product line has to support different kinds of networks, yet without stating which ones. The development artefacts to be developed are already affected by the existence of the variation point. For example, it may be necessary to introduce an architectural layer that provides a common view of different types of networks.

> **Example 4-7:** *Defining Variants*
>
> Example 4-5 already mentioned possible variability objects for the variability subject "type of network". The engineers select cabled LAN and wireless LAN and define them as variants of the variation point "home automation system network". The variants make clear that the software to be developed has to support cabled LAN as well as wireless LAN. This allows engineers to develop the software far more efficiently than would be possible knowing only that there are different kinds of networks. Still the engineers have to prepare for future changes in the set of variants, i.e. the addition of other kinds of networks.

4.3.4   Variability of a Software Product Line

Customised applications enabled

Variability of a software product line is variability that is modelled to enable the development of customised applications by reusing predefined, adjustable artefacts. Hence, variability of a software product line distinguishes different applications of the product line. Example 4-8 illustrates what we mean by the variability of a software product line.

Decision: variability or commonality

Commonality denotes features that are part of each application in exactly the same form. Example 4-9 illustrates what we mean by commonality. In software product line engineering, one can often decide whether a feature is variable for the software product line (Example 4-8) or whether it is common to all software product applications and thus adds to the commonality (Example 4-9).

> **Example 4-8:** *Variability in the User Interface Language*
>
> The customers of a home automation system can decide on the language of the user interface before the system is installed. Moreover, for an additional charge, a multilingual version is offered that allows selecting the user's favourite language at any time (e.g. by selecting a flag symbol on a touch screen).

> **Example 4-9:** *User Interface Language as Commonality*
>
> The user interface of a home automation system offers users a choice of their preferred language. This feature is part of each home automation system sold to any customer.

4.4 Variability in Time vs. Variability in Space

There is a fundamental distinction between variability in time and variability in space that is essential for software product line engineering (see [Bosch et al. 2002; Coplien 1998]). We define variability in time as follows:

> **Definition 4-5:** *Variability in Time*
>
> Variability in time is the existence of different versions of an artefact that are valid at different times.

An unavoidable fact in software engineering is that development artefacts evolve over time, e.g. when they have to be adapted due to technological progress. This kind of change is denoted as evolution or as variability in time. Variability in time applies to single-system engineering as well as to software product line engineering. Configuration management is a common technique used to manage different versions of development artefacts that are valid at different times.

Configuration management

Yet, there is an important difference between single systems and software product lines with regard to variability in time. In the domain artefacts of a software product line, there are predefined locations, identified by variation points, at which it is relatively easy to introduce changes. If the required change pertains to such a variation point, engineers have already recognised the need for change with respect to a certain variability subject. The following example illustrates this situation:

Evolution supported by variation points

> **Example 4-10:** *Evolution in a Software Product Line*
>
> The engineers of a home automation system expect technological progress in identification mechanisms. Therefore they define a variation point "door lock identification mechanism" with just one variant "magnetic card". Later, when sufficiently reliable fingerprint scanners appear on the market, the engineers replace the variant "magnetic card" by the variant "fingerprint scanner".

Predetermined locations for changes

Hence, variation points help to keep the impact of changes small by providing guidance for software engineers who can then enforce separation of concerns for the variable aspect. The necessary changes tend to have only local impact. Thus, less effort is necessary to add a new variant than to realise arbitrary changes. However, in our example it could also have happened that the engineers were not aware of future variability in identification mechanisms. In this case the amount of rework for replacing the old identification mechanism would probably be much higher as there would be no predetermined locations in the development artefacts to introduce such a change. This might even cause the engineers to argue for keeping the old mechanism instead of integrating the new one.

Next, we define variability in space:

> **Definition 4-6:** *Variability in Space*
>
> Variability in space is the existence of an artefact in different shapes at the same time.

Variants assigned to variation point

We associate the different shapes of a variable artefact with variants and assign these variants to the same variation point (see Section 4.6).

> **Example 4-11:** *Variability in Space*
>
> A home automation system offers the variation point "system access by" with four variants: web browser, mobile phone (SMS), telephone call (computer voice), and secure shell client (SSH). These variants are associated, for instance, with requirements artefacts of the software product line.

Differences from variability in time

Variability in space is quite different from variability in time. The time dimension covers the change of a variable artefact over time. The space dimension covers the simultaneous use of a variable artefact in different shapes by different products. The time dimension of variability is synonymous with software evolution, whereas the space dimension of variability is a younger field of research.

Single-system engineering does not provide the means to deal with variability in space in an adequate manner, whereas the goal of software product line engineering is to build similar products that differ within a defined scope. These products are normally offered at the same time and therefore – in contrast to single software system development – understanding and handling variability in space is an important issue of software product line engineering. Hence a major goal of this book is to provide the reader with sufficient information on variability in space. When speaking of variability we mostly mean variability in space. If necessary, we use the complete terms variability in time and variability in space to avoid confusion.

Our focus: variability in space

Development artefacts vary in time as well as in space. In addition, the categorisation of the occurrence of variability in a development artefact as variability in time or variability in space can change over time. Figure 4-3 illustrates the usage of keypads, magnetic cards, and fingerprint scanners in an 'economy line' and a 'professional line' of a home automation system. Magnetic cards on the one hand and keypads or fingerprint scanners on the other hand are clearly examples of variability in space. Yet, there is a small area that marks the transition from keypads to fingerprint scanners (indicated by small waves). This area expresses that the transition from keypads to fingerprint scanners is a smooth one. During the time period highlighted by the waves (Fig. 4-3), both versions of electronic door locks are used in the professional line of home automation systems. According to Definition 4-6 the coexistence of both variants is considered as variability in space.

Change of variability over time

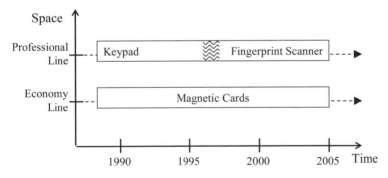

Fig. 4-3:   Variability in time and space

4.5   Internal and External Variability

Customer view

Different stakeholders perceive differently what is variable: customers want applications customised to their individual needs. This entails that customers must be aware of at least a part of the variability of a software product line (Fig. 4-4).

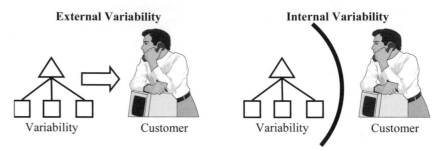

External Variability   **Internal Variability**

Variability   Customer   Variability   Customer

Fig. 4-4:   Internal and External Variability

Developer view

On the other hand, variability is an integral part of domain artefacts and thus a major concern of the organisation that develops the software product line. In order to be able to differentiate between these two views we define the terms *external variability* and *internal variability*:

> **Definition 4-7:** *External Variability*
>
> External variability is the variability of *domain artefacts* that is visible to customers.

External variability

As external variability is visible to customers, they can choose the variants they need. This can happen either directly or indirectly. In the former case, customers decide for each variant whether they need it or not. In the latter case product management selects the variants thereby defining a set of different applications among which the customers can choose. The two cases can also be combined, i.e. product management defines a set of applications but only binds a part of the external variability. Thus the customers are able to decide about the unbound variants themselves.

> **Definition 4-8:** *Internal Variability*
>
> Internal variability is the variability of domain artefacts that is hidden from customers.

Internal variability

All decisions that concern defining and resolving internal variability are within the responsibility of the stakeholders representing the provider of a software product line. The customer does not have to take internal variability into account when deciding about variants.

Example 4-12: *External Variability*

The customers of a home automation system can choose between three electronic door lock identification mechanisms: keypad, magnetic card, and fingerprint scanners.

Example 4-13: *Internal Variability*

The communication protocol of a home automation system network offers two different modes: one is optimised for high bandwidth, the other for error correction. The installers measure the quality of the available communication medium and choose the mode based on the measurement results.

4.5.1 Causes of External Variability

External variability directly contributes to customer satisfaction as customers are aware of this kind of variability and can select those options that serve their needs best. Thus, different stakeholder needs are a cause of external variability.

Stakeholder needs

Yet, there are more causes. External variability can for example be introduced because of differences in laws that apply to the domain of the software product line (e.g. the medical domain or the home automation domain). Similarly, different standards that have to be fulfilled by the applications of a software product line can be the reason for external variability.

Laws and standards

Example 4-14: *Different Standards Causing External Variability*

A home automation product line supports two security standards, which are officially imposed by a home automation association, namely basic security and high security. The basic security standard demands that the front door is secured by a numeric keypad. The high security standard demands a numeric keypad and additionally a biometric identification mechanism. Only homes compliant with the latter standard receive an official security certificate.

4.5.2 Causes of Internal Variability

Internal variability often emerges when refining or realising external variability. The realisation of each option offered to the customer typically demands several fine-grained options at a lower abstraction level. The

Refinement of external variability

customer is usually interested in high-level decisions, not in those at a fine-grained level. Therefore, the different realisation alternatives need not be communicated to the customer.

Refinement of internal variability

Similarly, the realisation or refinement of internal variability can lead to more internal variability at a lower abstraction level. The relation between variable artefacts at different abstraction levels is a complex one. For instance, a variable requirement can relate to a couple of variable artefacts at the architecture level. Conversely, it is possible that one variable artefact at the architecture level is influenced by a couple of variable requirements. Thus there is an *n-to-m* relation between artefacts at different abstraction levels.

Technical reasons

Finally, technical issues that do not have to be considered by the customer can be the cause of internal variability. Typical examples of such technical reasons are testing, implementation, installation, or maintenance issues or matters of scalability, portability, etc.

> **Example 4-15:** *Technical Issues as Causes of Internal Variability*
>
> The fingerprint scanner door lock in a home automation system can use two different ways of storing fingerprint images, compressed and uncompressed. The uncompressed algorithm is used during system maintenance and development to enable fine-tuning and testing of the algorithm. Compressed image storage is used during the normal system operation to save database capacity.

4.5.3 Deciding between Internal and External Variability

Different considerations have to be weighed up to declare whether variability is internal or external. For instance, customer interest, business strategy, and marketing issues have to be considered.

Reduced complexity

Hiding variability from the customer (internal variability) leads to *reduced complexity* to be considered by the customer. Being faced with all possible decisions necessary to derive an application from domain artefacts, the customer would be overwhelmed with the number of possible decisions and their interrelations. Hence, restricting the customer's view by hiding internal variability makes the decision process more convenient and thereby attracts more customers.

Business strategy

In addition, declaring variability as being internal can contribute to protecting company secrets from competitors and thus hinder them from imitating innovative ideas too early. This illustrates that also *business strategy* influences the differentiation between internal and external variability.

> **Example 4-16:** *Internal Variability as a Part of Business Strategy*
>
> The use of a LAN as an alternative to the EIB (European Installation Bus; see Chapter 3) in a home automation system might be a competitive advantage for the company, since it allows the use of low-cost components. It might be wise not to draw competitors' attention to this feature too early.

Finally, marketing is a crucial aspect to consider when declaring variability as internal or external. Being able to choose between several variants can significantly increase the customer's perceived value of a product. Yet, there may be other cases in which the variability of a new software product line interferes with older applications that still generate high profits for the company. Then, it might be advisable not to offer this variability to customers until sales of the other applications drop. Hence, marketing people have to consider carefully the pros and cons of making variability visible to customers.

Marketing reasons

4.5.4 The Variability Pyramid

Variability is defined at some abstraction level of domain artefacts and refined at lower abstraction levels. When creating application artefacts, the variability of domain artefacts is considered again in order to bind the required variants.[14] The *variability pyramid* in Fig. 4-5 illustrates the amount of variability[15] that has to be considered at each abstraction level.

Defining and binding variability

Stakeholder needs, laws, and standards make up the top of the pyramid. The growth of the pyramid represents the typical increase of the complexity of variability from higher to lower abstraction levels:

Increase of variability complexity

- Requirements variability usually leads to a larger amount of variability in architecture. For example, a requirement is typically mapped to more than one design element. Consequently, the variability in a requirement leads to variability in several design elements and thus to an increase of the variability definitions. Similarly, variability in design is refined into variability in components which again increases the variability complexity. Finally, software testing also has to take into account the variability defined in requirements, in design, and in components. The variability must, for example, be considered in test cases but, equally, in test environments, test mock-ups, and simulators. Therefore, the complexity of the variability is again increased.

---

[14] Svahnberg et al. deal with resolving variability at different stages of software product line engineering in [Svahnberg et al. 2001].

[15] The amount of variability is introduced as an abstract entity here. The reader can think of the amount of variability as a measure based on the number of variation points, variants and variable artefacts.

- The complexity of variability also increases due to the introduction of additional internal variability. The introduction of internal variability is represented in Fig. 4-5 by the arrows leading from outside the pyramid to its interior (see Section 4.5.2 for examples of internal variability).

Increase of interrelations

With the increase of variability definitions, the number of variants and variation points increases together with an increase of the interrelations between variants, variation points, and development artefacts, i.e. the complexity of the variability increases.

External variability

External variability is represented as a grey area at the core of the pyramid, shrinking in size from top to bottom. This represents the decrease of external variability from higher to lower abstraction levels. The reason for this decrease is that the customer is primarily interested in the features or requirements of an application but usually less interested in the internal realisation. A customer may have to decide on specific aspects of the architecture but probably does not want to deal with implementation issues. Curved arrows in Fig. 4-5 leading from the core of the pyramid to its outer regions represent external variability causing internal variability.

The large amount and high complexity of variability inherent in the variability pyramid can only be handled by means of managed variability. The first step towards managed variability is a common notation for variability as introduced in the following section.

Variability pyramid

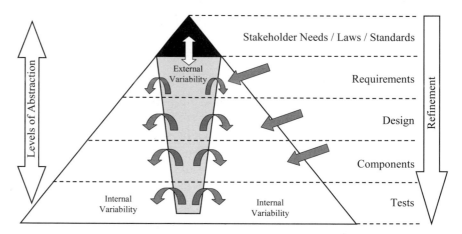

Fig. 4-5:   Amount of variability at different abstraction levels

4.6   Orthogonal Variability Model

In this section we introduce the meta model and the graphical notation of our orthogonal variability model.

4.6.1   Explicit Documentation of Variability

An adequate documentation of variability information should at least include all the information needed to answer the following questions:

Required variability information

- *What varies?* To be able to answer this question the variable properties of the different development artefacts have to be explicitly defined and documented by variation points. For documenting the variability in requirements one has to take into account textual requirements, features, scenarios, and traditional requirements models (Chapter 5). Variability in the product line architecture may affect the system structure, behaviour, or the deployment of software to hardware (Chapter 6). Variability in realisation artefacts includes variability in components and interfaces as well as variability implementation mechanisms, such as aspect-oriented programming or pre-compiler macros (Chapter 7).

  What?

- *Why does it vary?* This question was analysed in Section 4.5 for internal and external variability. The causes of external variability are, for instance, stakeholder needs, laws, and standards, or simply product management decisions. The causes of internal variability include the realisation of external variability, realisation of other internal variability, as well as technical variability. We capture the causes of variability in textual annotations of variation points and variants.

  Why?

- *How does it vary?* Answering this question means explicitly documenting the available variants and linking them to domain model elements that correspond to these variants by trace links. We call the links "artefact dependencies".

  How?

- *For whom is it documented?* The distinction between internal and external variability defines the audience of a variation point and/or its variants. This distinction is based on the fact that, for instance, variability documentation for customers is different from variability documentation for software test engineers. The separation in presenting internal and external variability can be achieved in different ways, e.g. by using different documents for different stakeholders. We record the separation by distinguishing between internal and external variation points.

  Documented for whom?

The explicit documentation of variability has significant advantages as mentioned in the previous sections. The three key advantages are the improvement of making decisions, communication, and traceability. We briefly characterise each of these aspects:

Advantages of explicit documentation

- Explicitly documented variability improves decision making by forcing engineers to document the rationales for introducing a certain variation point or a certain variant. The documentation of rationales can be used for example by customers (external variability) in their choice of a cer-

  Decision making

tain variant or by engineers in their task of defining or binding variability.

Communication
- Explicit variability modelling improves communication about the variability of a software product line by providing a high-level abstraction of variable artefacts. For instance, communicating variability to customers benefits from the existence of an explicit variability model. The explicit documentation of variability subjects as variation points enables customers to pinpoint the decisions to be made. The explicit documentation of variability objects as variants allows customers to consider the available options for each decision.

Traceability
- Explicitly documented variability allows for improved traceability of variability, for instance between its sources and the corresponding variable artefacts. This type of link is necessary, for example, to perform application requirements engineering efficiently (Chapter 15). In addition, traceability links facilitate the implementation of changes, e.g. with respect to a variation point. Thus, the variability model of a software product line provides an entry point to navigate through all kinds of development artefacts.

Example 4-17: *Improved Customer Communication*

The customers of a home automation system are interested in remote access to the system. A brochure on the home describes the variation point 'remote access by' with the variants 'dial-up isdn access' and 'internet-based access'. This tells the customers that the home automation system supports two different ways of satisfying their needs.

4.6.2 Orthogonal Variability Definition

Variability in artefact models
Variability can be defined either as an integral part of development artefacts or in a separate variability model. Many research contributions have suggested the integration of variability in traditional software development diagrams or models such as use case models, feature models, message sequence diagrams, and class diagrams. Kang et al. and Fey et al. use feature models to represent variability [Kang et al. 2002; Fey et al. 2002]. Halmans and Pohl and von der Maßen and Lichter introduce variability in use case models [Bühne et al. 2003; Halmans and Pohl 2003; V.d. Maßen and Lichter 2002]. Bosch et al. and Svahnberg et al. deal with variability in implementation structures [Bosch et al. 2002; Svahnberg et al. 2001].

Shortcomings of integrated variability
Modelling variability within the traditional software development models has some significant shortcomings. First, if variability information is spread across different models it is almost impossible to keep the information con-

sistent. Second, it is hard to determine, for instance, which variability information in requirements has influenced which variability information in design, realisation, or test artefacts. Third, the software development models (e.g. feature models) are already complex, and they get overloaded by adding the variability information. Fourth, the concepts used to define variability differ between the different kinds of software development models. Consequently, the variability defined in different models does not integrate well into an overall picture of the software variability. Yet, such an overall picture turns out to be essential for software product line engineering. Fifth, the definition of the variability information within a single development model often leads to ambiguous definitions of the variability contained in development artefacts (we provide an example of such an ambiguous definition in Section 5.4.1).

For these and other reasons (for instance, those described in [Bachmann et al. 2003; Geyer and Becker 2002; Muthig and Atkinson 2002; Bühne et al. 2004b; Bühne et al. 2005]), approaches have been proposed that suggest defining the variability information in a separate model. We call such a model an "orthogonal variability model" (Definition 4-9). The variability model presented in this chapter is such a model.

Orthogonal variability modelling

> **Definition 4-9:** *Orthogonal Variability Model*
>
> An orthogonal variability model is a model that defines the variability of a software product line. It relates the variability defined to other software development models such as feature models, use case models, design models, component models, and test models.

An orthogonal variability model provides a cross-sectional view of the variability across all software development artefacts. In the following subsections we incrementally introduce the elements of our orthogonal variability model. For each element we define a graphical notation. We use the orthogonal variability model throughout the book for the definition of the variability of a software product line across all development artefacts.

Variability meta model

4.6.3 Variation Points, Variants, and Variability Dependencies

The basic elements of our orthogonal variability model are defined in the meta model in Fig. 4-6 using UML 2 notation. The two central elements of the variability meta model are the 'variation point' and 'variant' classes (Definitions 4-3 and 4-4).

Basic elements

The 'variation point' class is an abstract class (indicated by the italic font in Fig. 4-6) and is specialised into the two classes 'internal variation point' and 'external variation point'. This specialisation is complete and disjoint. Con-

Internal and external variation points

sequently, every variation point is either of the class 'internal variation point' or 'external variation point'. The two classes have different semantics. The 'internal variation point' has associated variants that are only visible to developers but not to customers. The 'external variation point' has associated variants that are visible to developers and customers.

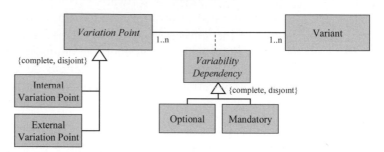

Fig. 4-6:   Variation point, variant, and the variability dependency in the variability meta model

Textual annotations

Each model element depicted in Fig. 4-6 has an attribute called textual annotation that allows us, for instance, to record the rationales for introducing the element. For the sake of simplicity, the attributes are shown neither in Fig. 4-6 nor in the other models in this chapter.

Variability dependency

A variability dependency is the association class of an association between the 'variation point' and the 'variant' classes. The association states that a variation point offers a certain variant. The multiplicities of the association enforce the following conditions:

- Each variation point must be associated with at least one variant.

- Each variant must be associated with at least one variation point.

- A variation point can offer more than one variant.

- A variant can be associated with different variation points.

The variability dependency is defined as an abstract class (indicated by the italic font). We specialise the variability dependency relationship into a mandatory and an optional relationship (Fig. 4-6). The specialisation is defined as complete and disjoint.

Optional variability dependency

The optional variability dependency states that a variant related to the variation point can be a part of a particular product line application but does not need to be a part of it (Definition 4-10).

> **Definition 4-10:** *Optional Variability Dependency*
>
> The optional variability dependency states that a variant can (but does not need to) be a part of a product line application.

> **Example 4-18:** *Optional Variability Dependency*
>
> Defining three identification mechanisms, 'keypad', 'magnetic card', and 'fingerprint scanner', as optional variants allows the customer to choose any combination of variants. The customer can decide to have none of the identification mechanisms, only one, any combination of two mechanisms, or all of them as a part of the home security system.

The mandatory variability dependency states that a variant is required for a variation point to which it is related. This does not imply that the variant has to be included in all applications of the software product line. A mandatory variant is only part of an application if the related variation point is part of it.

Mandatory variability dependency

> **Definition 4-11:** *Mandatory Variability Dependency*
>
> The mandatory variability dependency defines that a variant must be selected for an application if and only if the associated variation point is part of the application.

> **Example 4-19:** *Mandatory Variability Dependency*
>
> A home automation system offers different key lengths for encrypted remote communication (128 bits to 1024 bits). The software product line engineer wants to state that 128 bit encryption is required for minimal data protection and that it must be available in each application that offers remote access. Therefore, the engineer defines the 128 bit encryption as a mandatory variant and 256 bit, 512 bit, and 1024 bit encryption as optional variants. The 128 bit encryption is, however, only part of applications which include remote communication.

4.6.4 Alternative Choice

A variability model must offer the facility to define the minimum and the maximum number of optional variants to be selected from a given group of variants. Consequently, we define a modelling element that allows us to group optional variants and to define multiplicities for each group (Definition 4-12).

Selectable amount of variants

> **Definition 4-12:** *Alternative Choice*
>
> The alternative choice groups a set of variants that are related through an optional variability dependency to the same variation point and defines the range for the amount of optional variants to be selected for this group.

Alternative choice

Figure 4-7 shows the necessary extensions of the variability meta model. Newly introduced elements are depicted in dark grey, whereas previously introduced elements are depicted in light grey. The meta model contains an additional class 'alternative choice'. The class is associated with the 'optional' class by a 'part of' association. The multiplicities of the 'part of' association enforce the following conditions:

- The alternative choice groups at least two optional variability dependencies.

- Each optional variability dependency may be part of at most one alternative choice but does not have to be part of one.

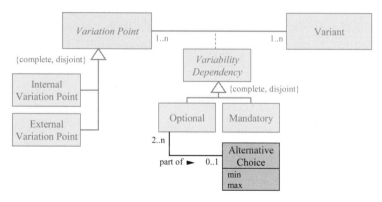

Fig. 4-7:   'Alternative choice' in the variability meta model

> **Example 4-20:** *Alternative Choice*
>
> By declaring the optional variants 'keypad', 'magnetic card', and 'fingerprint scanner' as alternative choices with 'min' taking the value "1" and 'max' taking the value "2", the variability model states that at least one and at most two of the variants can be selected.

'Alternative choice' meta class

The 'alternative choice' class contains two attributes, 'min' and 'max'. They are needed to specify the range for the permissible numbers of variants to be selected from the group. Additionally, the 'alternative choice' class has the constraint (which is not clear from Fig. 4-7) that the optional variability dependencies that are part of a group must refer to the same variation point.

4.6.5 Variability Constraints

The variability meta model described so far does, amongst other things, not support the documentation of relationships between variants that belong to different variation points. Yet such restrictions are required in variability modelling, for instance in the following cases:

Additional restrictions required

- The modeller wants to state that a variant V_1 requires a variant V_2 to function correctly. Consequently, if V_1 is selected for an application, V_2 also has to be selected.

- The modeller wants to state that if variant V_1 is selected, variant V_2 must not be selected.

- The modeller wants to state that a variation point must be part of an application depending on the selection of a particular variant made for another variation point.

The first two cases describe relationships between a variant and another variant. We call the first relationship a "requires" dependency and the second one an "excludes" dependency. The third case describes a "requires" dependency between a variant and a variation point. Similarly, there may be "requires" and "excludes" relationships between variation points. To model these kinds of relationships we extend the variability meta model by three types of constraint dependencies (Fig. 4-8). A constraint dependency documents a restriction that exists between two variants (Definition 4-13), between a variation point and a variant (Definition 4-14), or between two variations points (Definition 4-15). Each restriction is either of the type "requires" or "excludes".

Constraint dependency types

The meta model in Fig. 4-8 represents the variant constraint dependency (Definition 4-13) by the abstract association class 'variant constraint dependency' which is specialised into a 'requires_V_V' class and an 'excludes_V_V' class. The specialisation in the meta model is defined as complete and disjoint. The multiplicity at both ends of the 'constrains' association is '0..n', because a variant can (but need not) be constrained by an arbitrary number of other variants and a variant can (but need not) constrain an arbitrary number of other variants.

Variant to variant constraints

Definition 4-13: *Variant Constraint Dependency*

A variant constraint dependency describes a relationship between two variants, which may be of one of two types:

a) *Variant requires variant* (requires_V_V): The selection of a variant V_1 requires the selection of another variant V_2 independent of the variation points the variants are associated with.

b) *Variant excludes variant* (excludes_V_V): The selection of a variant V_1 excludes the selection of the related variant V_2 independent of the variation points the variants are associated with.

Example 4-21: *Variant Requires Variant*

A home automation system provides a variation point 'wireless communication' with two variants 'WLAN' and 'Bluetooth' and a variation point 'secure connection' with two variants 'VPN' (Virtual Private Network) and 'SSH' (Secure Shell). The selection of 'WLAN' requires the selection of 'VPN' as a secure connection. This is documented by introducing a requires_V_V relationship between the 'WLAN' and the 'VPN' variants.

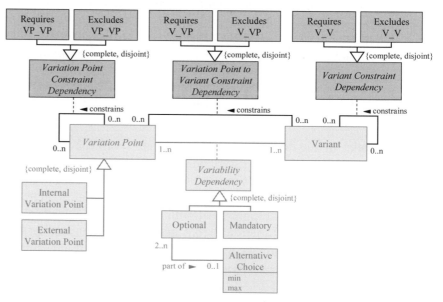

Fig. 4-8:   The constraint dependency in the variability meta model

---

Example 4-22: *Variant Excludes Variant*

A home automation system provides a variation point 'wireless communication' with two variants 'WLAN' and 'Bluetooth' and another variation point 'motion detection' with two variants 'optical sensors' and 'radar-based sensors'. It is not possible to combine the variant 'WLAN' with the variant 'radar-based sensors' because both use similar frequencies and interfere with each other. This is documented by introducing an excludes_V_V dependency between the variants 'WLAN' and 'radar-based sensors'.

The extensions required in the meta model for including the variant to variation point constraint dependency (Definition 4-14) are similar to those made for the variant constraint dependency, i.e. an association with multiplicities, an abstract class, and two concrete sub-classes (Fig. 4-8).

Variant to variation point constraints

Definition 4-14: *Variant to Variation Point Constraint Dependency*

The variant to variation point constraint dependency describes a relationship between a variant and a variation point, which may be of one of the two types:

a) *Variant requires variation point* (requires_V_VP): The selection of a variant V_1 requires the consideration of a variation point VP_2.

b) *Variant excludes variation point* (excludes_V_VP): The selection of a variant V_1 excludes the consideration of a variation point VP_2.

Example 4-23: *Variant Requires Variation Point*

Wireless LAN provides different standards with different transfer speeds. Hence, the variant 'WLAN' requires a variation point 'LAN Standard' that is related to variants representing the different standards of wireless LAN communication (e.g. IEEE 802.11a, b, and g). This is represented by introducing a requires_V_VP relation between the variant 'WLAN' and the variation point 'LAN-Standard'.

Example 4-24: *Variant Excludes Variation Point*

If only one LAN type can be selected, the selection of cabled LAN makes the selection of different antennas for wireless communication unnecessary. This is represented by introducing an excludes_V_VP relation between the variant 'cabled LAN' and the variation point 'antenna for wireless communication'.

Variation point constraints

To include the variation point constraint dependency (Definition 4-15), the meta model is extended in a similar way as for the former two dependencies (an association with multiplicities, an abstract class, and two concrete subclasses; see Fig. 4-8). The variation point constraint dependency affects the variants that are assigned to a variation point. If a variation point is excluded its variants are also excluded. The modeller should therefore handle variation point dependencies with care.

Definition 4-15: *Variation Point Constraint Dependency*

A variation point constraint dependency describes a relationship between two variation points, which may be of one of two types:

a) *Variation point requires variation point* (requires_VP_VP): A variation point requires the consideration of another variation point in order to be realised.

b) *Variation point excludes variation point* (excludes_VP_VP): The consideration of a variation point excludes the consideration of another variation point.

Example 4-25: *Variation Point Requires Variation Point*

Any selection of a variant at the variation point 'wireless communication' requires the selection of some variant at the variation point 'antenna for wireless communication'. This is represented by introducing a requires_VP_VP relation between the variation point 'wireless communication' and the variation point 'antenna for wireless communication'.

Example 4-26: *Variation Point Excludes Variation Point*

The home automation system does not support combining wireless communication and cabled communication. Hence the variation points 'wireless communication' and 'cabled communication' exclude each other – represented by an excludes_VP_VP relation between those two variation points.

4.6.6 Traceability between Variability Model and Other Development Artefacts

Variability in software artefacts

Modelling variation points, variants, and their relationships is only part of the work when modelling the variability of software product line artefacts. Developers also have to relate the variability defined in the variability model to software artefacts specified in other models, textual documents, and code

(Fig. 4-9). The means to document such relationships is to define traceability links between the variability model and other development artefacts.

The arrows depicted in Fig. 4-9 relate the variability definitions or, to be more precise, the variants in the variability model with software artefacts, such as requirements, design, realisation, and test artefacts, that document the refinement and/or realisation of the variability at the different development stages. Basically, variants may be related to artefacts of an arbitrary granularity, e.g. to an entire use case or to a single step of a use case scenario (Chapter 5).

Relating artefacts to variants

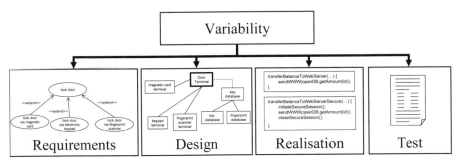

Fig. 4-9: Relating variants and development artefacts

To be able to relate variability definitions to other software artefacts we extend the variability meta model (Fig. 4-10) by a relationship which we call "artefact dependency".

Artefact dependency

The meta model depicted in Fig. 4-10 contains an additional class 'development artefact' that represents any kind of development artefact. Particular development artefacts are sub-classes of the 'development artefact' class. The 'realised by' association relates the 'variant' class with the newly introduced 'development artefact' class. The artefact dependency is realised as an association class of the 'realised by' association. The multiplicities of the association define the following conditions:

Variant realisation

- A development artefact can but does not have to be related to one or several variants (multiplicity '0..n').

- A variant must be related to at least one development artefact and may be related to more than one development artefact (multiplicity '1..n').

There are cases in which a development artefact needs to represent a variation point. For instance, in design, an abstract class may realise the common behaviour of several variants. In other cases, developers may want to anticipate that there are variants, which are not yet defined. These situations are covered by introducing an artefact dependency between a variation point and

Variation point representation

a development artefact. The variability meta model is extended by a 'represented by' association, which relates the 'variation point' class with the 'development artefact' class. This artefact dependency is realised as an association class of the 'represented by' association. The multiplicities of the association define the following conditions:

- A development artefact can but does not have to be related to one or several variation points (multiplicity '0..n').

- A variation point can but does not have to be related to one or more development artefacts (multiplicity '0..n').

Specialisation of artefact dependency
The artefact dependency can be further specialised, for example to capture domain-specific dependencies. Such a specialisation is, however, not within the scope of this book.

4.6.7   Graphical Notation

To be able to graphically represent the variability information defined under the meta model introduced in the previous sections, we associate each concrete class in the meta model with a graphical notation as depicted in Fig. 4-11.

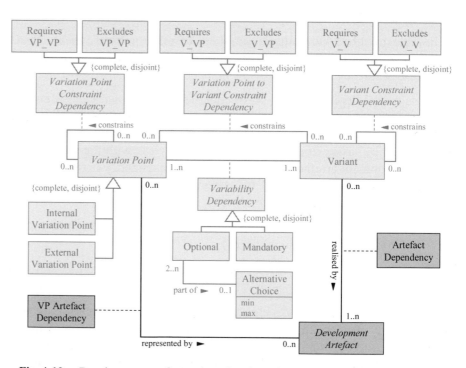

Fig. 4-10:   Development artefact and artefact dependency in the variability meta model

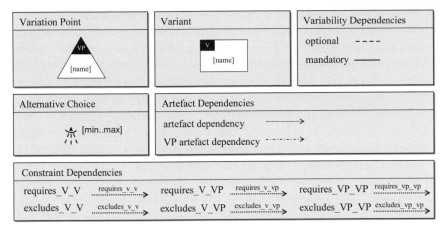

Fig. 4-11:   Graphical notation for variability models

The graphical notation for the alternative choice shows the permissible range [min..max] in square brackets. The default range is [1..1]. In the diagrams of this book we omit the range if it is the default range.

Default range of alternative choice

4.6.8   An Example

Figure 4-12 illustrates a simple example of orthogonal variability modelling. The use case diagram contains a single use case 'open front door' of the actor 'inhabitant'. This use case includes two other use cases, 'unlock door by keypad' and 'unlock door by fingerprint'. The variability diagram defines a single variation point 'door lock' with two variants 'keypad' and 'fingerprint scanner', related to the variation point by an alternative choice with the default range [1..1]. Each variant is associated with the corresponding use case by an artefact dependency.

Orthogonal variability modelling

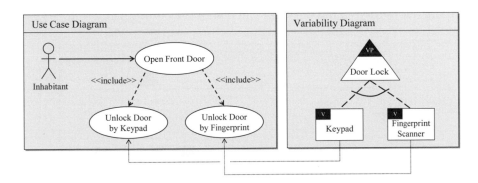

Fig. 4-12:   Example of orthogonal variability modelling

*Representing
variability in
use case diagram*

Using the graphical notation proposed by Halmans and Pohl [Halmans and Pohl 2003], Fig. 4-13 depicts the variability defined in Fig. 4-12 within the use case diagram. Based on the artefact dependencies between the variants in the orthogonal variability model and the use cases, the two use cases 'unlock door by keypad' and 'unlock door by fingerprint' have been stereotyped as variants (depicted by the black 'V'). In addition, the two use cases are related to an explicit representation of the variation point within the use case model (as suggested in [Halmans and Pohl 2003]), which is related by an 'includes' relationship to the use case 'open front door'. Note that for representing this information within the use case diagram, no additional information is required other than the information contained in the orthogonal variability model. The representation of the variability information within the use case diagram is deduced from the orthogonal variability model and the artefact dependencies depicted in Fig. 4-12. Similarly, variability can also be highlighted in other conceptual models or even textual documents based on the orthogonal variability and its relations to the artefacts.

4.6.9 Terminology Issues

*Artefacts representing
variation points*

Despite being a self-contained entity of the variability model, a variation point is also an abstraction of development artefacts that represent variability (e.g. interface definitions). In order to allow simpler wording, these development artefacts are sometimes also referred to as *variation points*, though, strictly speaking, they are representations of a variation point defined in the variability model.

*Artefacts realising
variants*

A similar statement holds for variants. Artefacts which are associated to a variant are frequently referred to as *variants* themselves, though, strictly speaking, they merely realise a certain aspect of a variant. The strict form corresponds to the orthogonal view of variability as illustrated by the example in Fig. 4-12, whereas the short form hints at the possibility of representing variability within development artefacts as illustrated in Fig. 4-13.

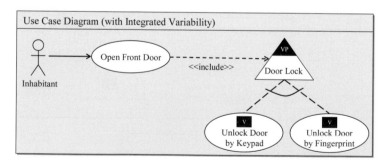

Fig. 4-13:   Representing variability in a use case diagram

4.7   Handling Complexity in Variability Models

An orthogonal variability model can easily become very complex. For example, a variability model for automotive software easily offers more than a thousand variation points and several thousand variants. A typical way of dealing with the complexity is to introduce abstract variation points which combine concrete variation points and predefine the bindings of their variants. For example, the automotive industry offers equipment packages for cars like a business package or a family package. By choosing one of those packages several variations are chosen, i.e. if a customer selects a business package, implicitly several variants are selected, e.g. automatic air-conditioning, a mobile phone, and a navigation system.

Complexity of variability models

The orthogonal variability meta model facilitates the packaging of variation points and variants. The different packages are represented by a variation point. Each package is represented as a variant of this variation point. A variant representing a package is linked to the variants that are included in the package via 'requires_v_v' dependencies. Note that a variant that is included in a package can include other variants that represent other packages. We illustrate the use of packaging in Example 4-27.

Package definition

Example 4-27: *Packaged Variants*

The variability model in Fig. 4-14 includes the variation point 'security package' and the two alternative variants 'basic' and 'advanced'. These variants represent packages. Selecting the 'basic' package also selects the variant 'motion sensors' of the variation point 'intrusion detection' and the variant 'keypad' of the variation point 'door locks'. If the 'advanced' package (variant) is selected, the variants 'camera surveillance' and 'fingerprint scanner' are chosen.

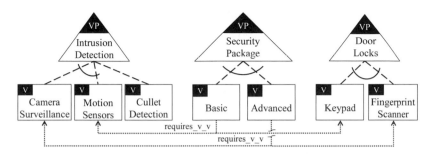

Fig. 4-14:   Example of packages realised by abstract variants

4.8   Differences from Single-System Engineering

Variability documented explicitly

Single-system engineering deals with variability in time and employs configuration management to manage different versions of development artefacts. Software product line engineering has to deal with variability in time as well as variability in space. The presence of variability in space means that the same set of development artefacts is used to derive multiple applications with different features. The shift to software product line engineering has far-reaching consequences on the development process and artefacts created by this process. Therefore variability has to be explicitly defined. This makes variability a first-class subject.

Variation point and variant

- Variation points and variants provide a high-level abstraction of variable development artefacts that significantly improves the management of these parts.

Dependencies and constraints

- Variability modelling restricts the set of variants that can be chosen together by introducing different kinds of dependencies between variation points and variants. Therefore, amongst other things, the consistent definition of applications is eased.

- Variability modelling supports the communication of the variability of the product line, e.g. to customers.

4.9   Summary

Separate model for variability

Variability modelling is a central technique required to put software product line engineering into practice. The variability of a software product line is specified in a separate model consisting of variation points, variants, and their relationships. In domain engineering, variants are linked to domain artefacts realising the variability of the software product line. Variation points and variants can be introduced at each abstraction level of domain artefacts and refined at lower abstraction levels.

Internal and external variability

Variability modelling, as an integral part of software product line engineering, focuses on the explicit documentation of the variability of a software product line. Variability enables the derivation of distinguishable product line applications. The importance of being able to communicate the available variability of a software product line to customers entails the distinction between internal and external variability.

Tool support

Establishing tool support for modelling variability and managing it across different development artefacts is still a research challenge (see Section 22.6). The focus of the PRIME project [PRIME 2005] is the development of a variability management tool.

Klaus Pohl
Thorsten Weyer

5

Documenting Variability in Requirements Artefacts

In this chapter you will learn:

- o *About the documentation of requirements for a software product line.*
- o *How to document requirements variability using the orthogonal variability model.*
- o *How to document variability in textual requirements, use cases, and scenarios as well as in requirements models such as feature models, class diagrams, data flow diagrams, and state machine diagrams.*

5.1   Introduction

Variability in domain requirements

We describe the way of documenting variability in different kinds of requirements artefacts in order to provide the reader with the basic knowledge that is necessary to document requirements variability in the domain artefacts of a software product line. The sub-processes and artefacts closely related to documenting variability in domain requirements are highlighted in Fig. 5-1.

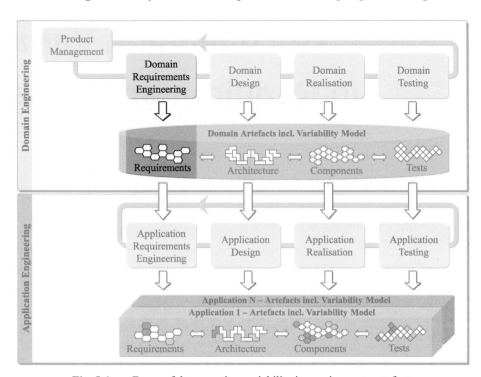

Fig. 5-1:   Focus of documenting variability in requirements artefacts

Embedding in the framework

Domain requirements are created in the domain requirements engineering sub-process. They encompass requirements common to all applications of the software product line as well as variable requirements enabling the creation of different applications. Domain requirements artefacts are the input for the domain design sub-process, which is concerned with developing the domain architecture. Domain testing uses domain requirements artefacts to provide reusable test artefacts for the software product line. Application requirements artefacts are created in the application engineering sub-process by exploiting the common and variable domain requirements artefacts.

Requirements

The IEEE defines the term requirement as follows:

> **Definition 5-1:** *Requirement*
>
> A requirement is:
>
> (1) A condition or capability needed by a user to solve a problem or achieve an objective.
>
> (2) A condition or capability that must be met or possessed by a system or system component to satisfy a contract, standard, specification, or other formally imposed document.
>
> (3) A documented representation of a condition or capability as in (1) or (2).
>
> [IEEE 1990]

When we refer to requirements in this book, we consider a requirement as an object with a unique identifier imposing a prescriptive, self-contained statement about the properties of the system under consideration.

5.2   Documenting Requirements

Requirements are documented using natural language text (textual requirements documentation) or using a requirements modelling language such as data models, behavioural models, or functional models (see e.g. [Davis 1993; Wieringa 1996]).

5.2.1   Model-Based vs. Textual Requirements Documentation

A textual requirements specification, on the one hand, does not limit the expressiveness of the specified requirements. On the other hand, the use of natural language introduces the danger of ambiguity, i.e. textual requirements specifications typically allow more than one interpretation and are thus often a source for misunderstanding.

Textual requirements

Model-based requirements have an underlying model, which defines the set of permissible language elements, the set of composition rules, and, if the modelling language is a formal language, the formal semantics. An example of a modelling language is a finite state automaton, which allows system behaviour to be documented in terms of states, inputs, outputs, and state transitions. Model-based requirements have a restricted expressiveness in contrast to natural language.

Model-based requirements

A model defines an abstraction of a system at a chosen level of detail from a particular viewpoint (which is typically determined by the purpose of the

Model vs. diagram

model). In contrast, a diagram is a graphical presentation of a collection of model elements [Rumbaugh et al. 2003].

5.2.2   Requirements Artefacts

Text and *models*

Requirements artefacts support the documentation of requirements in terms of text and various kinds of models. We define the term requirements artefacts as follows:

> **Definition 5-2:** *Requirements Artefacts*
>
> Requirements artefacts are products of the requirements engineering process specified using natural language and/or requirements models.

Examples of requirements artefacts are textual requirements, goals, features, use cases, and scenarios as well as behavioural, functional, and data models.

5.2.3   Goals and Features

Stakeholder intent, *system characteristics*

Goals describe the intent of a stakeholder with respect to the system under consideration, whereas features describe the characteristics that a system offers to its customer. This leads to the following definitions:

> **Definition 5-3:** *Goal*
>
> A goal is an objective the system under consideration should achieve.
>
> [V. Lamsweerde 2001]

> **Definition 5-4:** *Feature*
>
> A feature is an end-user visible characteristic of a system.
>
> [Kang et al. 1990]

Overlap of goal and *feature definitions*

There is an overlap between the goal and feature definitions. In most cases, feature and goal models define similar information. Goal models have been introduced by the requirements engineering community to express high-level intentions regarding the system, which are refined into more concrete requirements. Feature models have been introduced by the software design community to abstract from a given high-level architectural design, i.e. to express the high-level requirements of an architecture. To express the intentions of a system, goal models as well as feature models can be used. For example, unlocking the front door of a home electronically can be both a goal as well as a feature. In this chapter, we describe the documentation of variability in feature models. Yet, the proposed notation can also be used to define variability in goal models.

5.2.4 Scenarios and Use Cases

Customers and users typically prefer talking about concrete sequences of actions that describe system usage rather than talking about abstract models of a system (see e.g. [Carroll 2000; Weidenhaupt et al. 1998]). For this reason, *scenarios* are widely used in requirements engineering. Scenarios describe concrete sequences of actions related to the intended application. Scenarios can be documented in different representation formats, such as natural language, tabular notation, or sequence diagrams. A scenario is defined as follows:

Concrete sequence of actions

> **Definition 5-5:** *Scenario*
>
> A scenario is a concrete description of system usage which provides a clear benefit for the actor of the system.

Pohl and Haumer distinguish between three types of scenarios [Pohl and Haumer 1997]:

Three kinds of scenarios

- *System internal scenarios* focus on the system itself, i.e. they do not consider the context in which the system is embedded. System internal scenarios are used, for example, to represent interactions between system components or subsystems.

- *Interaction scenarios* focus on the interaction of the system with stakeholders and/or other systems.

- *Contextual scenarios* additionally represent information about the context of the system itself. For example, business goals are stated and related to the services provided by a system, relationships between stakeholders external to the system are represented, the use of information obtained from the system is expressed, or organisational policies are stated. Consequently, contextual scenarios extend interaction scenarios.

Scenarios are well suited for capturing the context of a system, developing innovative requirements, and establishing traceability, e.g. to goal models (see e.g. [Pohl and Haumer 1997; Haumer et al. 1999; Rolland et al. 1998; Carroll 1995]).

Scenario usage in development practice

To cope with the complexity of distributed, heavily interacting (embedded) systems, it is necessary to refine scenarios hierarchically and thereby capture requirements at different levels of abstraction (e.g. system level, subsystem level, etc.; see [Pohl and Sikora 2005]).

Scenario abstraction levels

*System
interactions*

A *use case* represents an interaction of one ore more actors (user and/or system) with the considered system, which offers a concrete benefit to these actors. The concrete interactions between the actors and the system are described in terms of scenarios, the so-called use case scenarios. Use case scenarios typically focus on the actor–system interactions, but also provide contextual information such as the goals behind an interaction. Thus, a use case scenario typically defines a certain way of achieving a given goal. Usually, there are several use case scenarios representing alternatives of accomplishing the same goal or failing to accomplish it, e.g. due to unexpected events. Consequently, a use case comprises a number of positive and negative use case scenarios. Moreover, use cases provide information about the system state before and after the execution of the use case scenarios in terms of pre- and post-conditions. We define the term use case as follows (see also [Rumbaugh et al. 2003]):

> ***Definition 5-6:*** *Use Case*
>
> A use case is a description of system behaviour in terms of scenarios illustrating different ways to succeed or fail in attaining one or more goals.

*Structured use
case definition*

A *use case template* is a tabular structure consisting of so-called slots. Each slot represents a different type of information necessary to define a use case. The use case name, the use case goal, its primary actors, its preconditions, and the initiator of the use case are examples of such slots. The use case template guides the documentation of a use case (see e.g. [Halmans and Pohl 2003; Cockburn 2000; Schneider and Winters 2001; Kulak and Guiney 2003]). We define a use case template as follows:

> ***Definition 5-7:*** *Use Case Template*
>
> A use case template is a tabular structure guiding the textual documentation of use cases.

*Overview of
system use cases*

A *use case diagram* is a graphical notation that provides an overview of the use cases of a system.[16] It shows the relationship between actors and use cases as well as the interrelations among use cases themselves. Use cases can be related by "extend", "include", and by generalisation relationships.

---

[16] Large systems are typically subdivided into several abstraction levels, such as system level, subsystem level, and component level. The use case diagram can be used to provide an overview of the use cases at any abstraction level, i.e. of the system use cases as well as the subsystem and component use cases.

A *use case model* captures the functionality of a system. To document a use case model, at least the following three components are necessary [Larman 2002]:

Use case model

- The template-based description of all use cases.

- The adequate documentation of all use case scenarios.

- One or more use case diagrams providing an overview of all use cases.

5.2.5 Traditional Requirements Models

There are three kinds of traditional models, namely models of function, data, and behaviour (see e.g. [Davis 1993; Wieringa 1996] for examples of such models).

Functional analysis is based on decomposing the system under consideration into a set of functions and their interrelations. For example, the *data flow diagram* (DFD) is used in structured analysis [DeMarco 1979]. It documents graphically:

Structured analysis

- The data flows of a system.

- The manipulation of data (functions or processes).

- The location of persistent data (data stores).

- The data sources and sinks outside the context of the system.

Data flow diagrams describe a system at different levels of abstraction. The data flow diagrams at a coarse-grained level are refined by those at finer grained levels. Data flow diagrams are supplemented by so-called *mini-specs*, which define the atomic functions, and by a *data dictionary*, which defines all terms used (see [DeMarco 1979; McMenamin and Palmer 1984] for details).

Data flow diagram refinement

Data modelling focuses on the data processed and stored in a system as well as the relations between the data. A popular data modelling approach is the entity relationship model [Chen 1976]. UML 2 (Unified Modelling Language [OMG 2003]) introduces the *class diagram* to define the data, or more generally, the static structure of a system.

Stored/processed data of a system

In requirements engineering, class diagrams document the essential entities of the system under consideration.[17] Relationships between classes represent relationships between concrete or abstract real world items that are essential for the system. The class diagram provides different kinds of relationships

UML class diagram

---

[17] The class diagram is also used at other stages of software development. We use it in domain realisation to describe the internal structure of components. Similar statements hold for the state machine diagram also described in this section.

such as associations and generalisations. Class diagrams are at the so-called type layer, which means that a class diagram defines a set of valid instances. An instance of a class diagram consists of objects, i.e. instances of classes, and links between objects, i.e. instances of associations. Multiplicities determine the admissible lower and upper bounds for the number of instances that can participate in an association. Associations may carry association names and roles. In addition, attributes and operations can be defined for a class. Such details are considered particularly in detailed design (Chapter 7). The class diagram notation itself can be extended and thereby adapted to different modelling purposes. The UML 2 enables extensibility for example by means of stereotypes, which allow the semantics of model elements to be enriched. For more details, see e.g. [OMG 2003; Rumbaugh et al. 2003; Booch et al. 1999].

State-dependent system behaviour   The third kind of traditional requirements models focuses on the behaviour of a system. Behavioural requirements can be modelled in different ways, e.g. in terms of actions, interactions or state transitions. The state machine model is a popular example of behavioural modelling. Its basic elements are states and state transitions. A state transition is triggered by an external stimulus. Guard conditions restrict the permissible state changes. A state change can only happen when the guard condition is satisfied. A state machine can additionally initiate actions that are executed within a state or during a state transition. Statecharts [Harel 1987] are a popular state machine notation. UML 2 incorporates them in terms of the *state machine diagram*:

Definition 5-8: *State Machine Diagram*

A state machine diagram depicts discrete behaviour modelled through finite state-transition systems. In particular, it specifies the sequences of states that an object or an interaction goes through during its life in response to events, together with its responses and actions.

[OMG 2003]

5.3   Variability in Textual Requirements

Ambiguity in natural language   Textual requirements express variability by certain keywords or phrases. Yet, documenting requirements variability in this way leaves room for ambiguity. Additionally, it suffers from other shortcomings (Section 5.2).

Example 5-1: *Variability in Textual Requirements*

The home security system shall be equipped with *either* black and white *or* colour cameras capable of taking infrared pictures.

In Example 5-1 it is not clear whether only colour cameras or both types of cameras must be capable of infrared shooting. Requirements variability has to be documented in an unambiguous systematic way that also supports traceability between different kinds of artefacts. Therefore, either explicit variability modelling has to be enabled for textual requirements, or developers have to use model-based requirements. The former solution is presented in this section.

Clear variability documentation

5.3.1 Defining Variability in Textual Requirements

Figure 5-2 illustrates a text fragment, in which requirements variability has been made explicit by highlighting the variation point and its variants thus adding more accuracy to Example 5-1.

Explicit variability in textual documentation

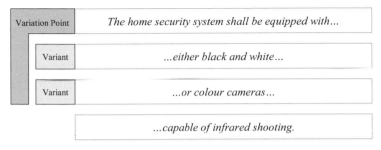

Fig. 5-2: Variability in textual requirements

In fact, the variation point in this example is the 'type of camera of the home security system'. Yet, this cannot be expressed without rewriting the text. Moreover, the effects of a variation point are not necessarily restricted to a single part of the textual requirements specification.

It is possible that the selection of a variant has an influence on several different parts of the document. The orthogonal variability model circumvents these problems. Figure 5-3 illustrates the use of orthogonal variability modelling in a slightly extended version of Example 5-1. The orthogonal variability model allows the selection of a chunk of text corresponding to the selected variant. The variant 'colour cameras' influences two different parts of the document, namely the requirements concerning the installed cameras and the requirements concerning the required storage system.

Orthogonal variability definition

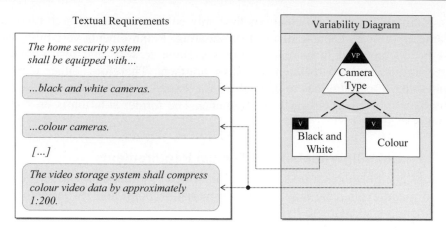

Fig. 5-3:   Orthogonal variability modelling in textual requirements

5.3.2   Documenting Variability Using XML

XML and
XSLT

Text can be augmented in different ways in order to improve the documentation of variability, e.g. by using tabular structures, different kinds of markup structures, or hyper-references. In Internet applications, XML (eXtensible Markup Language, [Laurent and Cerami 1999]) and XSLT (eXtensible Stylesheet Language Transformation, [Kay and Houser 2001]) are commonly used for exchanging and processing text-based documents.

XML-based
variability
documentation

XML and XSLT can also be applied to enable the explicit documentation of variability in textual requirements. XML provides the means to document variability and XSLT provides the capability of processing XML documents, e.g. in order to generate a document for a specific selection of variants (see Fig. 5-4). Thus, the XML-based approach is able to cope with defining as well as with binding variability.

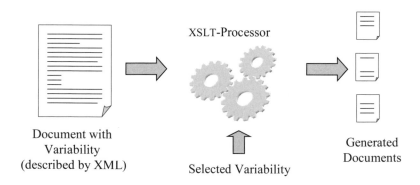

Fig. 5-4:   Variability in textual requirements documentation with XML and XSLT

Yet, the approach implies adding structural information to natural language text in terms of XML tags. For example, it is possible to enclose text fragments by XML tags, include unique identifiers in the tags and thus enable establishing links from the orthogonal variability model to the textual requirements document. The notation used in Example 5-2 employs tags to mark text fragments. It provides an identifier of the corresponding variant for each fragment. Consequently, it is possible to select the text fragments that belong to specific variants. However, requirements documents of this kind are more difficult to write, and their readability is restricted unless they are processed, for example, as outlined in Fig. 5-4. For more details on XML-based variability documentation, we refer to [John and Muthig 2002].

XML tags
for variants

Example 5-2: *Text Enriched by XML Tags*

The home security system shall be equipped with

*<text-fragment variant-id="v1">*black and white cameras.*</text-fragment>*

*<text-fragment variant-id="v2">*colour cameras.*</text-fragment>*

[...]

<text-fragment variant-id="v2">

The video storage system shall compress colour video data by approximately 1:200.

</text-fragment>

5.4   Variability in Requirements Models

Model-based requirements encompass features (or goals), use case models, and traditional requirements models – i.e. functional models, data models, and behavioural models. In their basic forms, these models are mostly not able to document variability as required by software product line engineering. Therefore, diverse extensions of model-based requirements artefacts have been proposed by research and industry such as the use of stereotypes in UML diagrams. Yet, these approaches integrate variability modelling into requirements models. The orthogonal variability model allows variability to be documented in a common way across different models without modifying the existing notations.

Approaches
using extended
requirements models

5.4.1   Variability in Feature Models

Features describe the functional as well as the quality characteristics of the system under consideration. The feature modelling approach allows a hierarchical decomposition of features which yields a feature tree:

Functionality
and quality

> **Definition 5-9:** *Feature Tree*
>
> A feature tree hierarchically structures the set of features of a system. A feature can be decomposed into several sub-features that are mandatory, optional, or alternative.

Optional and alternative features

Figure 5-5 presents an example feature tree for a home security system. Besides the features of the system, feature trees typically also define part of the variability of the system since they define:

- *Optional features*, which can be selected or left out at will and

- *Alternative features*, which allow the choice of one feature out of a given set.

Graphical notation

The typical notation used for representing mandatory, optional, and alternative features is similar to the notation used in our orthogonal variability model (Section 4.6.7).

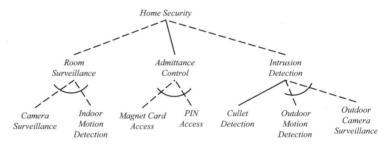

Fig. 5-5:   Feature tree of a home security software product line

Ambiguous variability definition

A shortcoming of the feature tree is its inability to distinguish between alternative features that are common to all applications (and therefore should be denoted as a commonality of the software product line) and alternative features that can be selected separately for a specific application.

Lack of grouping mechanism

Modelling variability in a feature model may lead to misinterpretations (Example 5-3). Moreover, the feature tree lacks a grouping mechanism that would allow arbitrary features to be assigned to some variant.

Variability model provides clarity

Defining the variability of a feature tree with the orthogonal variability model enhances the expressive capabilities (compared to representing the variability within the feature tree). It leads to clearer variability definitions and avoids misinterpretations.

Example 5-3: *Ambiguity in a Feature Tree for Home Security*

Figure 5-5 contains two alternative features that are related to 'admittance control': 'magnet card access' and 'PIN access'. 'Admittance control' itself is a mandatory feature of the 'home security' system. This part of the feature tree allows different interpretations:

a) Each application shall support exactly one of the two types of admittance control.

b) Each application shall support both types of admittance control. The users are allowed to choose whether they use magnet card access or PIN access.

c) An application shall support either one of the two types of admittance control or both types and allow the users to decide which one to use.

The interpretations a) and c) indicate that the feature tree foresees variability which is, however, different in a) and c). According to these interpretations, it is possible to build at least two home security systems which differ in the realisation of admittance control. In contrast, interpretation b) indicates that the admittance control is invariant for all applications and thus represents a commonality.

Example 5-4: *Grouping Features of the Home Security System*

The developing organisation might want to offer two variants, 'camera surveillance' and 'motion detection', that apply to 'room surveillance' as well as to 'intrusion detection'. The features that belong to each of the variants are split across different branches of the feature tree in Fig. 5-5. Restructuring the feature tree according to the grouping is not always a viable solution as the original decomposition of the system is then lost. Moreover, some other variant might require a different structure which is in conflict with the structure imposed by 'camera surveillance' and 'motion detection'.

Example 5-5: *Use of the Orthogonal Variability Model*

Figure 5-6 depicts a part of the variability contained in the feature tree in Fig. 5-5 using the orthogonal variability model. The variability diagram consists of the variation point 'home security by' with two alternative variants, 'camera surveillance' and 'motion detection'. The variants are linked to the corresponding subsets of the feature tree by artefact dependencies.

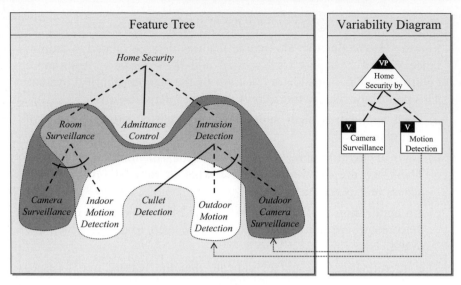

Fig. 5-6:   Feature tree of a home security system

Variant   The variability model enables the selection of parts of the feature tree by
selection   selecting variants in the variability model. Figure 5-7 illustrates the effects of
selecting the variant 'camera surveillance' in Example 5-5.

A more detailed comparison of modelling software product line variability
using the orthogonal variability model vs. using a feature tree is given in
[Bühne et al. 2004b] and [Bühne et al. 2004c].

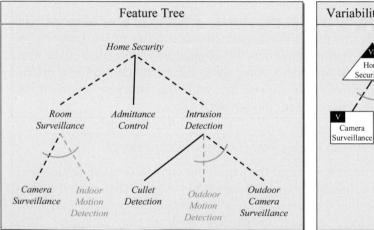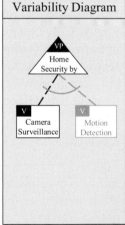

Fig. 5-7:   Effects of selecting the variant 'camera surveillance'

5.4.2 Variability in Use Case Models

A use case is typically documented using template-based use case descriptions, use case scenarios, and/or use case diagrams. In each of these documentations variability can occur. We elaborate on the documentation of variability in those documentations. We further illustrate how the orthogonal variability model glues together the variability expressed in the different types of documentations.

5.4.2.1 Template-Based Use Case Descriptions

Textual use case descriptions are typically structured using use case templates (see [Halmans and Pohl 2003] for an example). In principle, each use case slot (such as Primary Actor, Precondition or Main-Scenario) can be used to express variability of the product line. The documentation of the variability within the slots is in textual form and thus the guidelines for documenting textual requirements hold (see Section 5.3). In addition, the variability defined in a use case template has obvious relations with the other use case documentations like use case diagrams or use case scenarios. Those interrelations can be managed via the orthogonal variability model as illustrated in Chapter 4.

Variability within use case slots

5.4.2.2 Use Case Scenarios

As scenarios document sequences of interactions between two or more actors, basically, they are able to describe variability by varying the interactions as well as the constellation of actors.

Variability in interactions

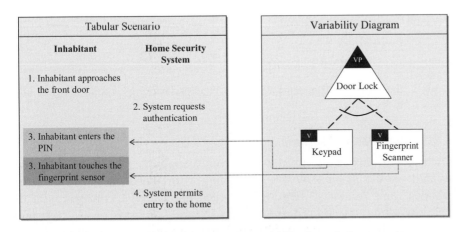

Fig. 5-8: Example of documenting variability in a tabular scenario

A common way to document scenarios is to use a tabular notation as illustrated in Fig. 5-8. The scenario in Fig. 5-8 contains the basic steps that are necessary to unlock the front door of the intelligent home. As there are two

Tabular notation

variants for authenticating to the system, namely 'keypad' and 'fingerprint scanner', the scenario contains a variable step. The variants are linked to the corresponding scenario steps by artefact dependencies. When a variant is selected, only those parts remain in the scenario description that are related to this variant. As before, variants can be linked to multiple steps even in different scenarios.

Sequence diagram   Another way of documenting scenarios is the use of sequence diagrams, e.g. as defined by the UML 2 standard. In general, a sequence diagram can be of two different types: the generic type documents all conceivable scenarios in one sequence diagram, whereas the instance type documents a single scenario [Booch et al. 1999]. Documenting variability in sequence diagrams implies using the generic type. Figure 5-9 exemplifies the documentation of variability scenarios using sequence diagram notation.

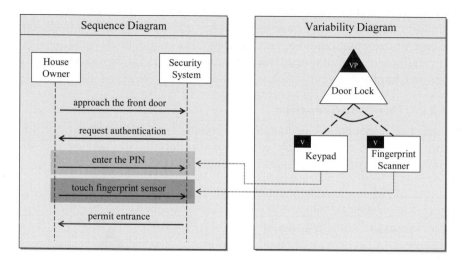

Fig. 5-9:   Example of documenting variability in scenarios using sequence diagram notation

5.4.2.3   Use Case Diagrams

Common and variable use cases   Use case diagrams can be used to document variability in terms of use cases provided by the system, actors interacting with those use cases, and the "includes" and "extends" relations between use cases. Compared with the variability which can be represented in use case scenarios or use case templates, the variability which can be documented in use case diagrams is on a more abstract level. Figure 5-10 illustrates the documentation of variability in a use case diagram.

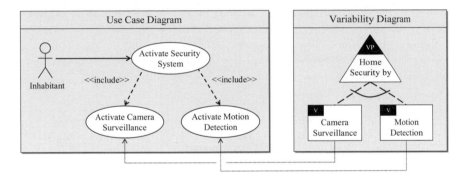

Fig. 5-10:   Example of documenting variability in a use case diagram

5.4.2.4   *Traceability between Variability Model and Use Case Model*

The definitions of variability in use case diagrams, use case scenarios, and use case templates can overlap. For example, an actor of the system is defined in all three types of use case documentations. If one introduces a variability of an actor in one type of documentation, e.g. in a use case diagram, this variability must be "propagated" to the other documentations, i.e. the three types of documentations must be kept consistent.

Overlapping information

In order to manage the overlapping and potentially different definitions of variability within the use case model, we use our orthogonal variability model. The orthogonal variability model allows to link a variant with the different definitions of variability within the use case model. Following the traceability links – or, to be more precise – the artefact dependencies (Section 4.6), the analyst can determine how a given variant is realised in the use case model and check if the different definitions of variability are consistent. In Fig. 5-11 the variant 'motion detection' is represented through the dark shaded areas of the use case model. Similarly, the variant 'camera surveillance' is depicted with light grey shading. Without the use of the orthogonal variability model it would be much harder or, in a large system, close to impossible, to relate the various documentations of the same kind of variability.

Related variability definitions

5.4.3   Variability in Traditional Requirements Models

Besides feature models and use case models, traditional requirements models still play an important role in requirements engineering for software product lines. Therefore, it is necessary to document variability in data flow models, class models, and state machine models.

Functions, data, behaviour

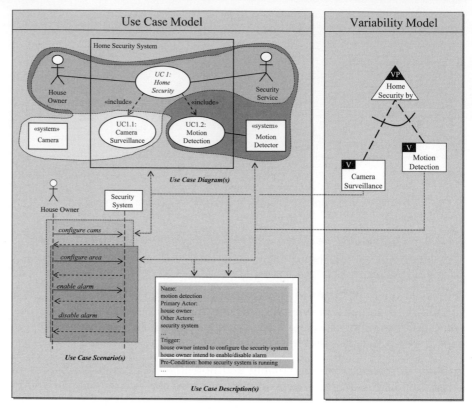

Fig. 5-11: Use of the orthogonal variability model to interrelate variability in a use case model

5.4.3.1 Variability in Data Flow Diagrams

Variable data flows and functions

Since a functional model describes the flow and manipulation of data in a system, it can be used to express variability in the flow of data and in the functions manipulating the data.

Example 5-6: *Data Flow Diagram for Home Security*

Figure 5-12 shows a data flow diagram describing example data flows for the two variants 'camera surveillance' and 'motion detection' of the variation point 'home security by'. The data flow diagram shows the functions, data stores, and data flows that are necessary to realise both variants. Two areas of different grey shading highlight the fragments of the data flow diagram corresponding to the variants 'camera surveillance' and 'motion detection'.

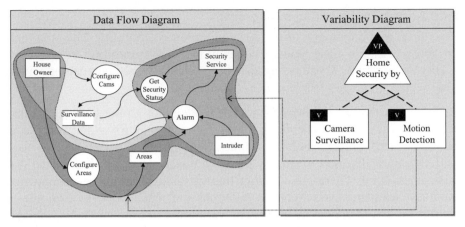

Fig. 5-12: Example of documenting variability in a data flow diagram

The graphical notation presented in Fig. 5-12 supports documenting variability within a single data flow diagram instead of having to provide multiple diagrams for different variants. Yet, fine-grained aspects, such as variability within a function, data flow, or data store not refined in a child data flow diagram, have to be documented in the corresponding mini-specs or in the data dictionary.

Fine-grained variability

> **Example 5-7:** *Selecting Variants*
>
> The selection of a variant within the variability model implies choosing the corresponding subset of diagram elements of the data flow diagram. Figure 5-13 shows the resulting data flow diagram after selecting the variant 'camera surveillance' (left) or the variant 'motion detection' (right) respectively.

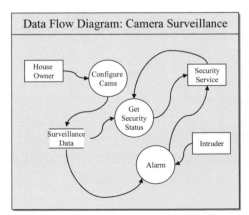
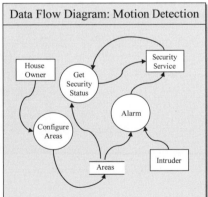

Fig. 5-13: Effects of selecting a variant

5.4.3.2   *Variability in Class Diagrams*

Structural variability

Class diagrams document structural requirements variability. The structural variability within a class model frequently involves variability in behaviour, quality, or function. These occurrences of variability are documented within other requirements models (e.g. use case models).

Standard class diagram insufficient

Basically, variability is inherent in class models due to the fact that a class model specifies a set of instances. These instances may for example differ in the number of objects and their links. The inherent variability of class models is typically used to specify the valid instances of the class model that exist at run-time. Therefore, product line variability cannot be documented using the standard class diagram notations and concepts. For example, a multiplicity could denote inherent class variability or product line variability. We thus propose to model product line variability in class diagrams using the orthogonal variability model. Thereby, we can clearly differentiate between product line variability (defined using the orthogonal variability model) and the inherent class variability. The relation between multiplicities and variability is discussed in detail in Chapter 7.

Coarse- and fine-grained variability

In this chapter, we focus on those aspects of variability in class diagrams necessary to document requirements variability. This means that we associate variants with coarse-grained subsets of classes. However, variability may have more fine-grained manifestations, which then requires variants to be associated with single elements of the class diagram. Figure 5-14 illustrates the representation of requirements variability within a class model using the orthogonal variability model.

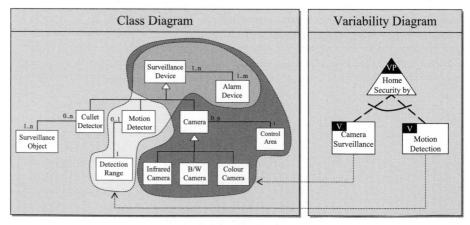

Fig. 5-14:   Example of documenting variability in a class diagram

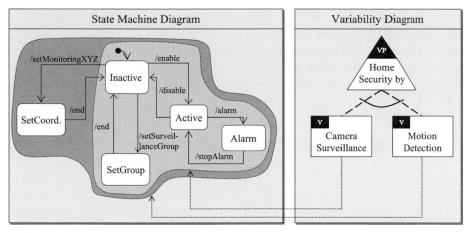

Fig. 5-15: Example of documenting variability in a state machine diagram

5.4.3.3 *Variability in State Machine Diagrams*

A state machine model documents requirements concerning the behaviour of the intended applications. We document requirements variability by linking variants to certain parts of a state machine diagram. Like data flow diagrams, state machine diagrams also support hierarchical refinement, which allows the introduction of variability at different levels of detail. Figure 5-15 provides an example of modelling the behavioural aspects of variants in a state machine diagram.

Behavioural variability

5.5 Traceability Between Variability Model and Requirements Artefacts

The orthogonal variability model documents the variability of a software product line and defines traceability links between variants and variation points and the corresponding definitions of the variability in requirements artefacts. Variability in requirements is expressed in different models such as:

- Feature models
- Textual requirements
- Use case descriptions
- Traditional requirements (data, function, and behaviour)

Orthogonal to those models, the variability model defines the variations of the software product line. Through the relationship between a variant of the orthogonal variability model and the associated development artefacts, it is possible to document the characteristics of the variant concerned from dif-

Variants and associated artefacts

ferent perspectives (e.g. data, function, behaviour, and quality). Furthermore, the relationships support the consistent implementation of changes. Starting from a changed development artefact, other artefacts affected by the change can be found by following the relation to the associated variant and from the variant to the other associated artefacts. This procedure is shown in Fig. 5-16.

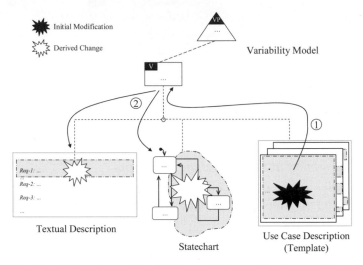

Fig. 5-16: Use of the orthogonal variability model for performing consistent changes

Traceability

The traceability between the variability model and the different types of requirements models is established through artefact dependencies. Figure 5-17 depicts the basic types of relationships between the variants defined in the orthogonal variability model and different types of requirements artefacts.

To features

- The relationship between the variability model and the feature model (① in Fig. 5-17) links the variants to the corresponding features. A feature can be linked to an arbitrary number of variants within the variability model and vice versa.

To textual requirements

- The relationship between the variability model and textual requirements (② in Fig. 5-17) marks aspects of variants that have to be expressed by textual descriptions (almost qualitative aspects, e.g. laws and standards).

To traditional requirements models

- The relationship between the variability model and traditional requirements models (③ in Fig. 5-17) marks aspects of variants that are expressed by traditional requirements artefacts (i.e. behavioural, structural, functional, and qualitative aspects).

- The relationship between the variability model and use case models (④ in Fig. 5-17) describes aspects of variants that are documented by use cases, use case scenarios, and template-based use case descriptions.

To use case models

We illustrate the usage of artefact dependencies in Example 5-8. For further reading on interrelating different kinds of requirements (at different levels of abstraction), we refer to [Bühne et al. 2004a].

Example 5-8: *Usage of the Artefact Dependencies*

Figure 5-18 exemplifies the documentation of the variant 'colour camera surveillance' through feature models, use case models, traditional requirements, and textual descriptions. The functional, behavioural, structural, and qualitative characteristics of the variant 'camera surveillance' are described through the associated artefacts. The variant 'colour camera surveillance' influences specific parts within each model. When the analyst, changes a use case related to 'colour camera surveillance', the traceability links indicate the parts of the textual description, the class diagram, etc. affected by the change.

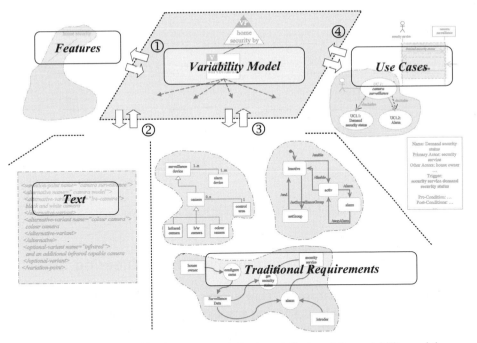

Fig. 5-17: Relationships between requirements artefacts and the variability model

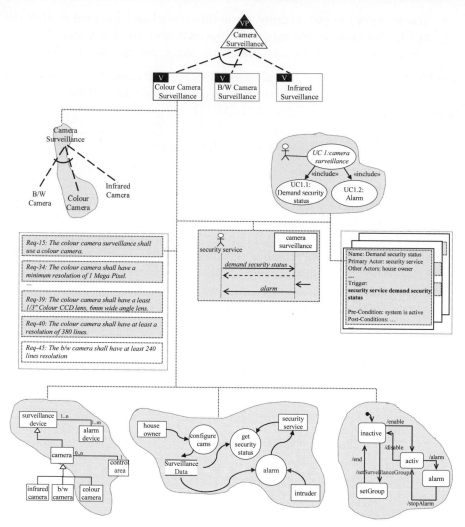

Fig. 5-18:   Example of interrelating a variant with different requirements artefacts

5.6   Differences from Single-System Engineering

Variability in requirements   In single-system engineering, requirements for each application are documented separately without keeping track of the commonalities and the differences of the applications. In software product line engineering, common requirements are documented together with all variable requirements. A separate variability model enables keeping track of the variability of different kinds of requirements artefacts. Requirements artefacts for a specific application can be derived from domain requirements by binding the variability.

Documenting requirements variability in an orthogonal variability model and relating this model to requirements artefacts facilitates the usage of the requirements documentation in design, realisation, and testing, as well as the refinement and realisation of the required variability.

Variability documentation

5.7 Summary

Software product line engineering implies documenting the variability of different kinds of requirements artefacts in a separate variability model. Each variant defined in the variability model is related to requirements artefacts that describe the implications of the variant on different requirements concerning the functionality, structure, behaviour, and quality of the system. The relations between variants and requirements artefacts are represented by artefact dependencies. Consequently the variability of requirements artefacts is documented clearly and unambiguously:

Common and variable requirements artefacts

- Feature models contain variability themselves. Nevertheless, the orthogonal variability model helps to unambiguously document product line variability.

Orthogonal variability model

- Use case models allow variability to be documented inside a slot of the use case template, inside a scenario, or in a use case diagram. In many cases, trade-off decisions are possible at which place variability should be documented. The orthogonal variability model relates the different places at which variability is defined to each other.

- Traditional requirements models allow the expression of variability mostly by selecting the subsets of diagram elements related to a specific variant. If hierarchical decomposition of the model is possible, variability can be modelled at different levels of abstraction.

- Documenting variability in textual requirements by means of the variability model is possible, but may hamper readability.

Finally, the variability model supports the developers in keeping the different views of variable requirements artefacts consistent. Likewise, in application requirements engineering the variability model is used to create a consistent set of application requirements artefacts.

Consistent variability definition and binding

Frank van der Linden

6

Documenting Variability
in Design Artefacts

In this chapter you will learn:

- o *The origins of the variability to be considered when defining an architecture.*
- o *How to define variability in different architectural views such as the development view, the process view, and the code view.*
- o *How the orthogonal variability model can be applied to document variability in the different views and to keep those views consistent.*

6.1   Introduction

Variability in reference architecture

Requirements have to be satisfied in applications to fulfil the users' wishes. Design is the next step towards applications. During design, it is determined how the applications are built in a technical sense. In software product line engineering, the domain architecture (or reference architecture; see Section 6.3) is valid for many applications. Hence, one of the main concerns of the domain architect is to design for flexibility. The orthogonal variability model enables the documentation of variability in design artefacts in a clear and understandable manner thus easing the reuse of these artefacts. The sub-processes and artefacts closely related to the documentation of variability in the reference architecture are highlighted in Fig. 6-1.

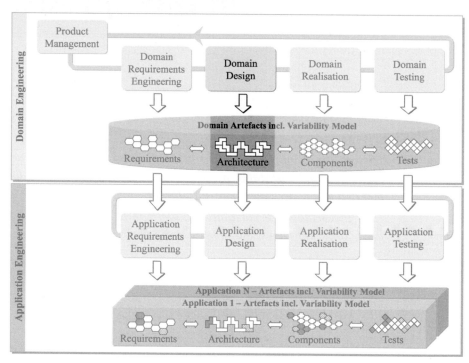

Fig. 6-1:   The reference architecture is the focus of documenting variability in architecture

High-level and low-level design

Software design consists of two phases: high-level design and low-level (or detailed) design.[18] The main result of high-level design is the architecture capturing the general design decisions including the main software structure.

---

[18] This is a matter of viewpoint. In fact, design is hierarchical. Each level of design sees itself as high-level design. It results in a decomposition of the system. For each of the parts, a separate detailed design is made. In this chapter, we take the viewpoint of the software architect.

Documenting variability in the architecture is the focus of this chapter. Software developers do detailed design and implement the different software components. They have to adhere to the architecture. From the perspective of the architecture, detailed design is part of the realisation. Chapter 7 is concerned with the variability issues of detailed design.

The domain design sub-process is responsible for creating common and variable design artefacts. Domain design gets its main input from domain requirements engineering. The reference architecture is used as an important guide during domain realisation and application design.

Relation to the framework

6.2 Architectural Artefacts

In this section, we briefly present the different kinds of artefacts used in software architecture. Jazayeri et al. define four main concerns which the architect has to deal with [Jazayeri et al. 2000] and which lead to the essential artefacts of architectural design. The first two concerns, namely *architecturally significant requirements* and *concepts*, make up the interface between requirements engineering and architecture. The former concern means that architects have to identify those requirements that have an essential impact on the architecture. The latter concern means that architects have to create a conceptual architecture prior to building structural models of the software. The other two concerns, namely *structure* and *texture*, are the main ingredients of the architecture.

Four architecture concerns

The most recognised aspect of the architecture is the structure of a software system:

Architectural structure

> **Definition 6-1:** *Architectural Structure*
>
> The architectural structure is the decomposition of a software system into parts and relationships.

In addition, the architecture defines the texture of the produced systems.[19] While the architectural structure determines which parts are built separately, the texture determines the general rules each of the parts has to obey.

Architectural texture

> **Definition 6-2:** *Architectural Texture*
>
> The architectural texture is the collection of common development rules for realising the system.

---

[19] This term is introduced in [Jazayeri et al. 2000] to give a single name to, and to emphasise the importance of, the common rules determined by the architecture.

Examples 6-1 and 6-2 illustrate the architectural structure and architectural texture for the home automation domain.

Example 6-1: *Structure in Home Automation*

The structure of the home automation applications depicted in Fig. 6-2 includes four layers (each of which has an internal structure consisting of subsystems and components; see Fig. 6-3). The layers can be characterised as follows:

- 'Basic control', for common computing platform infrastructure involving process, file, database, and communication infrastructure.
- 'Device control and management', which provides a basic domain-specific infrastructure, for the control and management of all kinds of devices. For instance, it controls specific actuators and sensors, such as door actuators and smoke sensors.
- 'Home functions', which provide management of basic domain-specific functions. They combine the control of several devices, such as the integrated control of opening and closing of doors.
- 'Integrated functions', which combine the home functions into integrated applications. For instance, a 'vacation function' involves lighting, heating, and door and window management.

Within each layer the variability is determined by the variation in the functionality provided, and by the variation in the functionality provided by the layer below it. For the basic control layer variability in the layer below is triggered by hardware variability.

Example 6-2: *Texture in Home Automation*

The texture of the home automation applications contains:

- The use of layering in the structure, as described in Example 6-1.
- The use of a hierarchy of layers, subsystems, and components as described in Example 6-1.
- The facade pattern [Gamma et al. 1995] that demands a single interface at subsystem level.
- The observer pattern, which decouples user interface issues from the data.
- The presence of an initialisation interface with a prescribed set of functions at each component.
- The use of high-priority processes for user interface handling and medium-priority processes for user functions.

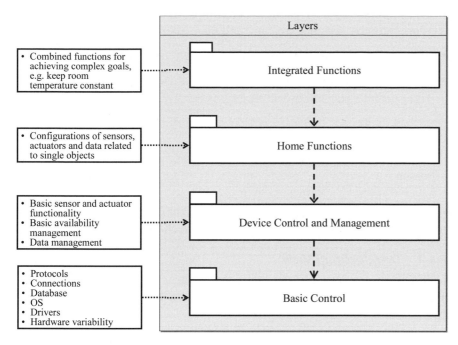

Fig. 6-2:   Layers of a home automation application

The texture consists of coding rules and general mechanisms, such as styles [Shaw and Garlan 1996] and design patterns [Gamma et al. 1995] to deal with the many situations that occur during realisation and coding. The texture has to be used everywhere in the design of the system. In many cases, the texture provides standard ways to deal with quality requirements, such as performance, maintainability, and many others. It prescribes detailed design issues to simplify the task for the developer by solving common problems only once and by determining the way the software infrastructure has to be used. As a consequence, it increases commonality and reusability of all design and realisation artefacts.

Styles and patterns

6.2.1 Architecture Views

The architectural structure is usually not documented as a single entity. In many cases, different views upon the architecture exist, which together determine the structure.[20] The views describe different aspects of the systems, but there is not a defined relationship between them, leaving some freedom for realisation. Important views are:

Four aspects of software architecture

- *Logical view*: This view incorporates the requirements models.

---

[20] Views are defined in [Kruchten 1995; Soni et al. 1995; Obbink et al. 2000] where different names are used for the same views. We use the terminology introduced in [Kruchten 1995].

- *Development view*: This view determines the decomposition of the software into components, objects, and their interfaces.

- *Process view*: This view determines the activities during execution.

- *Code view*. This view determines the distribution of the software over files, directories, and processing units.

> **Definition 6-3:** *Logical View*
>
> The logical view describes the applications in terms of the problem domain.

The logical view is typically expressed in terms of requirements artefacts. The remaining three views are the focus of this chapter.

6.2.1.1 Development View

Structural decomposition

The development view models the software structure in layers, subsystems, components, object classes, interfaces, and their different kinds of relationships.

> **Definition 6-4:** *Development View*
>
> The development view shows the (hierarchical) decomposition of the system into pieces, each of which is the subject of a separate detailed design.

Development view notations

Several notations exist for the development view, all describing the structural entities graphically with boxes, and their relationships with annotated lines, or actual containment of boxes in each other. For instance, object classes may be contained in components, which in turn may be part of a layer or a subsystem. UML 2 [OMG 2003] has several notations for the development view:

- *Package diagram* describes packages and their relationships. A package is a grouping of other diagrams, each with its own internal detailed design.

- *Component diagram* describes components and their relationships.

- *Class diagram* describes classes and their relationships. It is mainly used for detailed design of the internals of components and interfaces, and thus belongs to detailed design.

- *Object diagram* describes relationships between objects in a specific execution. It belongs to detailed design.

The *component diagram* is the most important diagram for the architecture. It is the main means to decompose the system according to the development view, incorporating the high-level decomposition of the software system into components and their relationships. Each component diagram is used to describe an internal design for a part of a layer or subsystem. Its design is mainly based upon experience and partially dependent on the set of requirements to be fulfilled. In addition, the architect takes into account the general principles of complexity management, resulting in layered abstractions, and of the divide-and-conquer strategy. To enable this, the architect needs representations for layers and subsystems. The *package diagram* is not specifically meant for this. Yet, since it is a means for clustering arbitrary elements, it is used to cluster components in subsystems and layers. An important quality characteristic of software engineering (and in particular of software product line engineering) is to design for flexibility, thereby enabling ease of adaptation. By putting similar functionality together in the same subsystem and component, changes are kept local, which is crucial for fast adaptations.

Subsystems and components

The other two diagrams are less important for architecture. The *class diagram* denotes the decomposition of the system into object classes, which is one level below the component structure in the decomposition hierarchy. The class diagram gives more details than the component diagram. Such a low level of detail obscures the architecture by too much complexity. This results in too little emphasis on the general principles and causes problems in later adaptations of the architecture. The architect determines only parts of the class diagrams to ensure compliance with architectural principles. The remainder is the topic of detailed design. The *object diagram* is less useful as it mainly depicts a specific moment in a specific execution of a specific application. However, it may be used for analysing difficult relationships, or specifying specific crucial parts of the system.

Class and object details

6.2.1.2 Process View

The process view describes the behaviour of the systems during actual execution. It models processes, threads, their interactions, and often resource usage.

System behaviour

Definition 6-5: *Process View*

The process view shows the decomposition of the running system into ordered activities and their relationships.

The architect uses the process view to model the processing behaviour of the system. Choices in this view have an influence upon speed, throughput, and reaction times. There are several notations for the process view. UML 2 provides the following diagrams for documenting the process view:

Process view notations

- *Interaction overview diagram*: This diagram describes relationships between different process view diagrams.

- *Timing diagram*: This diagram describes sequences of execution phases.

- *State machine diagram*: This diagram decomposes the system into state-charts [Harel 1987].

- *Activity diagram*: This diagram describes behaviour in terms of actions, control flows, and data flows in a Petri-net-like manner [Peterson 1981; Reisig 1985].

- *Communication diagram*: This diagram describes a specific sequence of interactions in a specific execution of a system focusing on how the internal structure corresponds with message passing.

- *Sequence diagram*: This diagram is another way to describe a specific sequence of interactions in a specific execution of a system, yet focusing on the order of messages.

Process diagrams for architecture

The most important diagrams for the architecture are those that enable abstraction from the details of the observable behaviour of a system. This holds for the interaction overview diagram, the timing diagram, and the state machine diagram. An *interaction overview diagram* is used to provide an overview of the control flow between interactions through a dialect of activity diagrams. The interactions themselves can be detailed later, e.g. during detailed design. The *timing diagram* describes the sequence(s) of phases that hold for a group of objects. For each phase, a different process view diagram may be determined, involving different activities, interactions, and relationships. Designing it correctly separates the concerns of different execution phases, which saves a lot of complexity of the behaviour. For instance, start-up, shut-down, or error-state behaviour may be completely different from the normal operational mode. The *state machine diagram* is able to capture the behaviour of the complete system in more or less detail. As long as the level of detail is not too low, the state machine diagram is very useful for architecture. Detailed design uses the state machine diagrams in more detail.

Process detail diagrams

The other three diagrams are less useful for the architect. The activity diagram is typically used to describe the behaviour of the system following one use case. Thus, it is preferably used in requirements engineering, although in certain situations the architect may use it to get a first idea of which activities take place in the system before going into more detail. The communication diagram and the sequence diagram are used during detailed design as they both depict mainly a specific part of an execution in a specific implementation. However, the architect uses them for analysing difficult relationships, or specifying specific crucial parts of the behaviour.

Alternatives for the process view exist in more formal approaches.[21] We do not consider these approaches, because they presently have a small impact, in particular due to insufficient scaling towards large systems. This certainly holds for the added complexity introduced by software product line engineering. However, formal methods play a role in detailed design. Several formal approaches exist that scale up better, and have proven themselves in the development of large embedded system product lines.[22] These approaches usually combine the development and the process views in such a way that the detailed design of the development view mainly involves processes and threads, i.e. elements of the process view. The combination of the threads into communicating processes and process scheduling is mainly dependent on a few predefined mechanisms and can be automated.

Formal approaches

6.2.1.3 Code View

The code view maps source code and executable code into files and directories, and their distribution over executable processing nodes.

Source code structure

> **Definition 6-6:** *Code View*
>
> The code view shows the decomposition of the executable code into files and an assignment of these files to processing units.

The mapping of executable code to processing units has to consider the roles of the different processing units. Example roles are clients, servers, and database processing. Each role is related to a certain set of executable code. Certain processing units may have more than one role. UML 2 provides a *deployment diagram* for this purpose.

Code view notation

The code view is a part of the architecture and should not be intermixed with detailed design and realisation, which is the subject of Chapter 7. The code view determines the interrelations between the software artefacts after development. Detailed design is part of development and produces the code, which has to obey the architecture, incorporating the code view.

Differences from detailed design

6.3 The Reference Architecture

All decisions on variability in design have to be communicated and documented for future use. As an important consequence, it is necessary to have clear representations for variation points, variants, and mechanisms to realise

One architecture for the product line

---

[21] There are many such formalisms; examples are: CCS [Hoare 1985], CSP [Milner 1980], LOTOS [Brinksma 1988], Petri nets [Reisig 1985], and process algebra [Bergstra and Klop 1984; Baeten et al. 1990].

[22] For instance, COLD [Feijs et al. 1994] and SDL [Belina et al. 1991; Bræk and Haugen 1993].

variability. The architecture developed during domain engineering is called the *reference architecture*. It is defined as follows:

> **Definition 6-7:** *Reference Architecture*
>
> The reference architecture is a core architecture that captures the high-level design for the applications of the software product line.

Variability included in architecture

The reference architecture includes the variation points and variants documented in the variability model. It provides limits for the architectures of the separate applications, i.e. the application architectures. It determines which components are reusable and thus have to be developed during domain realisation.

Documentation of variability

In software product line engineering, the structure of a collection of applications has to be captured, and this means that the structure itself should exhibit variability. In fact, architecture variability is mainly incorporated in the structure. The texture captures a common part of the product line. Most structure diagrams are able to express variation points and variants, although some are more suitable than others. The most important ways of expressing variability are discussed in this chapter.

In the following sections, we discuss the variability in the development, process, and code views of architecture. Variability in the logical view has been discussed in Chapter 5.

6.4   Variability in the Development View

The development view is the most important one to capture commonality and variability. In particular, a large part of architecture variability is captured in the component diagram.

6.4.1   Subsystems and Layers

High-level structure

Subsystems and layers are best described in the package diagram, which enables the architect to group similar components. The package diagram, in fact used as a subsystem diagram, denotes the high-level decomposition of the software system into subsystems and their relationships. The structure described in the package diagram itself is valid for the entire product line.

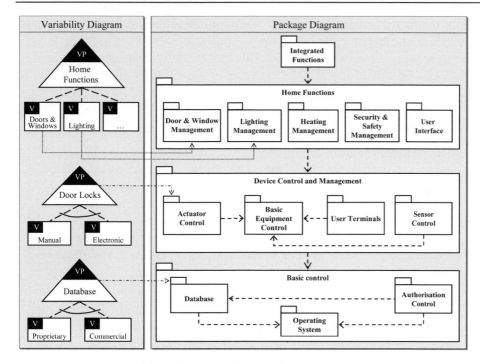

Fig. 6-3: Subsystem diagram for home automation

Figure 6-3 illustrates the documentation of variability in a package diagram that describes the layers and subsystems of a software product line. Basically, layers as well as subsystems may be variable (i.e. associated with variants). In a layered architecture, each subsystem is assigned to a layer matching the abstraction level of the involved functionality. This assignment is fixed for all applications of the product line. In order to design for flexibility, the architect typically determines subsystems in such a way that the required variability is encapsulated within subsystems. Consequently, the variable parts of the package diagram closely correlate with the elements of the variability model. Typically, the subsystems in the higher layers deal with external variability. They are only present when the customer needs them. The variation points realised by the lower level subsystems are caused either by detailing external variability or by internal variability. Most of the internal variants differ in the use of available technology and performance requirements. Usually all these subsystems are present in each application, with variants dealing with quality issues and technology choices of the specific application features.

Variable subsystems

The variability diagram in Fig. 6-3 contains artefact dependencies between variation points and architectural artefacts. Such a dependency indicates that the artefact at the target end has different instances. For example, it abstracts

Variation point artefact dependency

from the fact whether the variants of a variation point imply the variation of the entire artefact or variation in the internal structure of the artefact. Hence, the dependency can be used to hide this fact or to defer the decision about it. This may be due to the abstraction level of the considered model or due to notational limitations of the used diagram type.

Example 6-3: *Subsystems and Layers for Home Automation*

The package diagram in Fig. 6-3 shows the subsystems and layers of a home automation product line. The layers 'basic control', 'device control and management', 'home functions', and 'integrated functions' are present in each application. Variability becomes manifest in the subsystems. The subsystems in the 'home functions' layer deal with external variability. They are only present when the client requires them. So, a system without any door and window management has no 'door & window management' subsystem.

The architect introduces internal variability, e.g. by putting lower level functionality related to the actuation of door and window locks in the 'device control and management' layer. Thus, the internal structure of the 'actuator control' subsystem provides components for the variants 'manual' and 'electronic' of the variation point 'door locks'. The internal structure has to be documented in a component diagram.

The variation point associated with the 'database' subsystem of the 'basic control' layer declares two variants: 'proprietary' and 'commercial'. These variants differ mainly in quality issues and are decided on for example with regard to the size of the system.

6.4.2 Components

Component variability

A subsystem is decomposed into a collection of interacting components. UML 2 provides the component diagram for describing configurations of components. Figure 6-4 illustrates the documentation of variability in the component diagram. Each component may realise a variant and is thus only present in an application for which the corresponding variant has been bound. Variability in the internal structure of a component is primarily considered in detailed design.

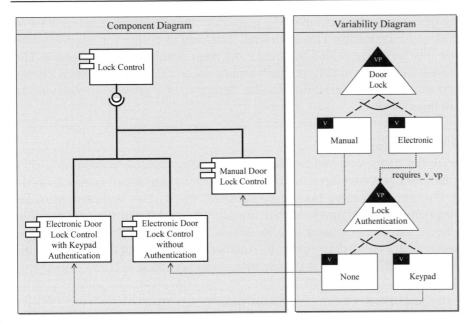

Fig. 6-4: Example components in the 'door & window management' subsystem

---

Example 6-4: *Components for Door and Window Management*

Figure 6-4 presents a part of the components of the 'door & window management' subsystem. The subsystem contains common components for door and window control such as 'lock control'. But there are also special components only for door or window control. The door lock components are shown in Fig. 6-4.

The variability model describes the external variability of door locks provided by the subsystem. The variation point 'door lock' offers an alternative choice with two variants, namely 'manual' and 'electronic'. The former variant is realised by the 'manual door lock control' component. The latter variant requires a decision for the 'lock authentication' variation point, i.e. one of the variants 'keypad' and 'none'. Each of them is realised by a separate component in the component diagram. All three door lock components use the generic door and window lock functionality available in the 'lock control' component.

6.4.3   The Role of Interfaces

Components are connected with each other through interfaces. An interface describes the functionality in a providing component that is required by another. Since the interface is an abstract description of the internal function-

Interfaces support flexibility

ality of the providing component, there may be several implementations of the same functionality. This is an important way to design for flexibility: the same interface is provided by several different designs of a component. The different designs typically realise variants of one or more variation points. Interfaces hide the variability in the design of the providing components from their clients.[23]

6.4.4 Configurations

Variable component configurations

Variability in the component view implies using *variable configurations* of components and interfaces. In many cases, configurations of components do not change arbitrarily, but in coordinated ways. The architect provides restrictions on configurations that are allowed and those that are not. For instance, the architect uses lists to denote which components are common and which are variable or optional. Another important tool for restricting the number of configurations is the use of a *component framework*.

> **Definition 6-8:** *Component Framework[24]*
>
> A component framework is a structure of components, or object classes, where *plug-in components* or object classes may be added at specified *plug-in locations*. To fit, each plug-in has to obey rules defined by the framework.

Component framework

The domain architect introduces frameworks to ease mass customisation. Variation points are represented by locations in the framework where plug-in components may be added. Variants are realised by specific choices of the plug-in. A component framework is part of the architectural texture. The texture usually also provides additional restrictions on the plug-in, e.g. by disallowing connections of the plug-in outside the specified plug-in location. This additionally eases the choices to be made by the developer of the plug-in and facilitates the configuration activity. Many frameworks for basic functionality are available commercially, e.g. J2EE [Alur et al. 2003]. The domain architect decides on their use. In addition, the architect may design additional frameworks for product line specific functionality.

> **Example 6-5:** *Home Automation Framework*
>
> A part of a framework for home automation is depicted in Fig. 6-5. The main structure of door lock control is shown here. The parts in solid lines compose the common part of the framework. Optional and

---

[23] Still, the different designs may vary in quality aspects, such as resource usage, which is in fact observable by the clients. Chapter 7 deals with this issue.

[24] This should not be confused with other frameworks introduced in this book. For a more extensive definition and treatment of component frameworks, see [Szyperski 1997].

variant parts are depicted by dotted lines. The framework determines the main structure and covers the generic management functions of the main parts, 'lock control', 'user interaction', and 'authentication', which have a fixed configuration, as shown in the figure. Plug-in components are marked by the use of 'plug-in' in their names. The plug-in locations are required interfaces. The plug-in components are connected to these locations through their own provided interfaces.

At the top right hand side, some plug-in components are depicted that are in the 'device control and management' layer: 'lock actuator plug-in' and 'open/close sensor plug-in'. They represent variable plug-in components to control different sensors and actuators. As can be seen from the solid connection, at least one 'lock actuator plug-in' component has to be present. However, the presence of an 'open/close sensor plug-in' component is optional, depicted by the dotted interface and connection.

The variable plug-in components for door lock control connect to an interface provided by the 'lock control' component. At least one of them has to be present. The 'electronic door lock plug-in' has an optional connection to an interface of the 'authentication manager' component. The 'authentication plug-in' represents components for different authentication mechanisms such as keypad authentication. The plug-in is optional. The 'authentication manager', which is part of the framework, always grants authentication in the case of absence of the 'authentication plug-in'. In this way, the framework can be used for all kinds of situations with more or less complex door control functionality, and the 'user control manager' is not bothered by the presence or absence of authentication.

Note that authentication variability is present at three places in the diagram: the presence of an 'authentication plug-in' component, the variable presence of an optional interface between the 'electronic door lock-plug-in' and the 'authentication manager' components, and the variability of the 'electronic door lock plug-in' component, which has variants with and without authentication. Thus the single external variation point of having authentication leads to many internal variation points in design, in both the involved components and the configuration itself. The addition to the variability model is shown in the new variation point on authentication algorithm. The component framework presented in Fig. 6-5 is considered in more detail in Chapter 11.

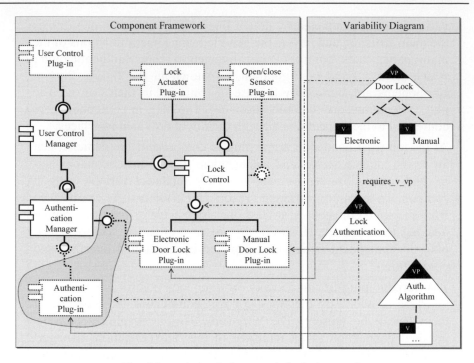

Fig. 6-5:   A simple framework for lock control

Plug-in components for variants   The architect assigns plug-in components as variants for certain variation points and delegates the binding of variability related to the plug-in components to the realisation sub-process. Several plug-in variants are built during realisation. Some of them have variability. The 'electronic door lock plug-in' component in Fig. 6-5 has variants with and without authentication. Domain realisation may build separate plug-in components for these different variants, or there may be variants capable of dealing with both situations, i.e. with and without authentication.

Plug-in registration   A component framework usually determines for each plug-in location a special *access interface* to be provided by the plug-in component. In addition, the framework itself has a *registration interface* to give the plug-in component access to the framework through the registration of the access interface. Through registration, the plug-in makes itself known to the framework, which afterwards is able to access the plug-in. In many cases, the combination of a required access interface and a provided registration interface makes up the plug-in location.[25] So, two-way communication between the framework and the plug-in is established without the developer of the framework (during domain engineering) having to know which plug-in com-

---

[25] More complex configurations of interfaces may be used for a single plug-in location. Alternatively, sometimes a single interface is enough.

ponents are available, since these are usually developed later than the framework itself, e.g. during application engineering. In Fig. 6-5 only the registration interfaces are depicted. This reduces the complexity of the picture. The access interfaces are only connected during run-time and not to be used by other components than the one the plug-in is bound to. Adding them to the picture may lead to erroneous connections that access the plug-in components directly, and not via the framework.

6.5   Variability in the Process View

The process view describes the behaviour of the applications during actual execution. It models processes, threads, their interactions, and often their resource usage.

Threads, processes, resource usage

Variability in the process view has different manifestations:

- Different groupings of threads to processes.

- Threads and processes, which may be optional, have multiple instances, or both.

- Different process scheduling mechanisms and process priorities.

- Different process communication mechanisms.

Each choice influences the processing behaviour of the applications, and has an influence on speed, throughput, and reaction time upon events. Within software product line engineering, variable requirements dealing with performance or other quality issues lead to different choices for the process view. In addition, internal variability may lead to variability in the process view, influenced by the hardware or basic infrastructure used.

Impact of variants

Many of the diagram types used in the process view do not have a notation for variability. Most of these diagrams only depict commonality. Apart from applying the variability model (this has been demonstrated in Chapter 5 for the state machine diagram) the architect has the option to rely upon indirect means by using a *process table*. This assigns processes to priorities and threads to processes. Threads are often assigned to components and vary together, i.e. each variant of the component has its own variant of the thread. If the component is optional, the thread is optional as well. If the component can have multiple variants in a single application, the threads have multiple instances as well.

Process table

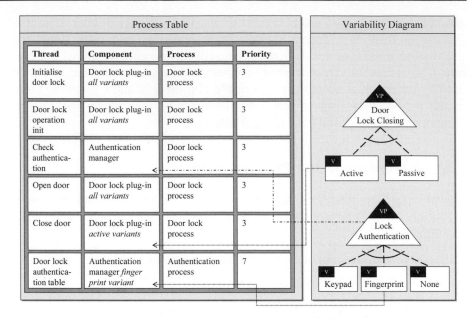

Fig. 6-6:   Example of documenting variability in the process view

---

Example 6-6: *Process Table*

Figure 6-6 shows an excerpt of the process table for home automation, related to door lock control. Almost all threads in this excerpt are part of the 'door lock process'. They are defined in the 'door lock plug-in' components. Not all variants define the same threads. Only the variant that closes the door automatically ('active' variant) defines a thread for closing the door. Moreover, the 'authentication manager' component has responsibility for defining the 'check authentication' thread, which has different implementations for different kinds of authentication. Finally the 'door lock authentication table' thread is defined in the 'authentication manager' component only for the 'fingerprint' variant as fingerprint authentication has higher computational requirements than the other variants. It is part of a separate low-priority process, the 'authentication process'.

6.6   Variability in the Code View

Files, directories,   The code view deals with the distribution of source code over files and di-
processing units   rectories and of executable code over processing units. Variability occurs in:

- the decomposition itself,

- the number and roles of the processing units, and
- the mapping of code to processing units.

The UML 2 deployment diagram does not provide notational elements for variable deployments. Thus, similarly as for the process view, the architect may resort to using lists. The drawback of this approach is that the list has to be updated for each separate application. Example 6-7 illustrates the documentation of variability in the deployment using the variability model.

Deployment diagram

Example 6-7: *Deployment for Home Automation*

A part of the code view of home automation for a specific application with fingerprint authentication is shown in Fig. 6-7 together with the corresponding part of the variability model. It shows where the executables related to the components of Fig. 6-5 are mapped on the hardware. In addition, it denotes the protocol that is used between the devices, namely RMI (Remote Method Invocation) between the 'authentication processor' and the 'central processor'. The 'authentication processor' and the connector '<<RMI>>' are only available for fingerprint authentication.

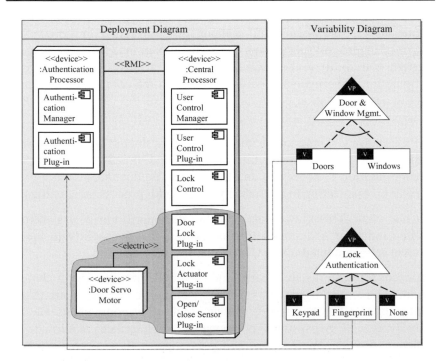

Fig. 6-7: Example of documenting variability in the code view

6.7   Differences from Single-System Engineering

*Design artefacts for
different applications*

Notations that are used to document software architecture in single-system engineering mostly do not provide sufficient means to express variability. Software product line engineering is concerned with documenting the reference architecture which is valid for all applications of the product line. Each application may imply a different set of subsystems and a different configuration of components within these subsystems. Consequently, each application may consist of a different set of processes and threads and also show a different deployment of executable code to processing units. Therefore, in contrast to single-system engineering, an additional variability model is necessary that clearly documents the available options and their effects on the different architecture views.

6.8   Summary

*Variability in
architecture views*

The architect has to provide a reference architecture that is flexible enough to cope with the required variability in the design. The variability model allows documenting variability in the development view, the process view, and the code view of the architecture:

- *Development view*: This view deals with the decomposition of a system into layers, subsystems, and components. Variability in the configuration of layers and subsystems is documented in the UML 2 package diagram. Variability in the internal structure of a subsystem, i.e. in the configuration of components, is documented in the component diagram. In both cases, variation points and/or variants of the variability model are associated with variable elements of development view diagrams.

- *Process view*: This view deals (among other things) with the decomposition of system behaviour into processes and threads. Variability in the configuration of processes and threads can be documented in a process table by associating the variability model with process table entries.

- *Code view*: This view deals with the decomposition of a system into files and their assignment to processing units. Variability in the code view is documented in the UML 2 deployment diagram.

*Component
frameworks*

Component frameworks are created and used to restrict the design choices in a product line and to cope with variability. Plug-in components are essential constituents of a flexible design. However, all other components may have variability as well. Subsystems, components, and interfaces at a low level of abstraction provide internal variability to support the external variability provided by the higher abstraction levels. At these higher abstraction levels variability is mainly influenced by requirements variability.

Frank van der Linden

7

Documenting Variability in Realisation Artefacts

In this chapter you will learn:

- ○ *How to document and realise variability defined by the domain design in software components.*
- ○ *About the mapping of product line variability onto component configurations and component interfaces, as well as the internal structure of components.*

7.1   Introduction

Variability in detailed design and code

As discussed in Chapter 6, we regard realisation from the viewpoint of the architect. We focus on variability in detailed design and on the techniques that enable the composition of the parts that are developed in domain realisation into different applications. The implementation of variability is crucial for software product line engineering. There are many ways to implement variability within programming languages and tools that support development. For realisation technology, the reader is referred to [Coplien 1998; Atkinson 2001; Muthig and Patzke 2003; Greenfield et al. 2004]. Realisation mechanisms are not within the scope of this book.

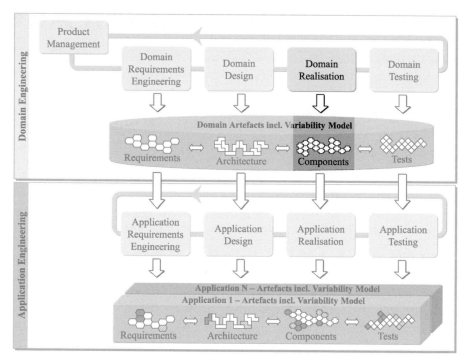

Fig. 7-1:   Domain components are the focus of documenting realisation variability

Components and interfaces

The sub-processes and artefacts closely related to the documentation of variability in domain realisation artefacts are highlighted in Fig. 7-1. Domain design provides the main input for domain realisation in terms of the architectural structure and the architectural texture. The structure determines the components and interfaces that have to be designed and implemented. Furthermore, it documents external as well as internal variability. The texture provides common guidelines that, among other things, specify common rules for dealing with variability in component and interface design and implementation. The domain realisation sub-process is concerned with creating common and variable realisation artefacts including the reusable components. Domain testing creates the test artefacts for the components and performs part of the testing (test activities are distributed over domain and application testing). The reusable components and interfaces are provided to the application realisation process, which is responsible for realising a specific application based on the application architecture. This is done mostly by assembling a suitable configuration of domain components and partially by developing application-specific components.

7.2   Detailed Design Artefacts

Detailed design deals with the design of components and interfaces, which are determined by the architecture. Figure 7-2 gives an overview of these main elements of detailed design. Components are the main pieces out of which the applications are built. Interfaces are the externally visible parts of the components and are used to connect components. The realisation of a single interface can usually not be assigned to the realisation of a single component, since many interfaces are provided and required by multiple components. Therefore, interfaces are separate entities, distinct from components; see Fig. 7-2. For the design, interfaces are of equal importance as components and therefore have to be designed carefully.

Components and interfaces

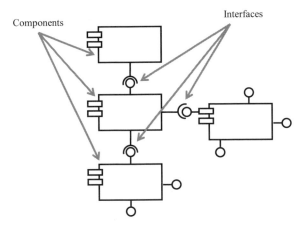

Fig. 7-2:   Elements of detailed design

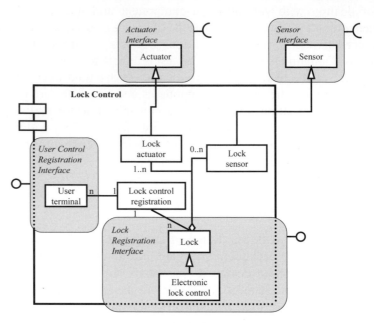

Fig. 7-3:   Component and interface structure

Architecture is the basis of realisation

The reference architecture is the most important input for the component and interface design. The designer of a component or an interface has to know the place and role of the component or interface in the architecture. If a component is part of the platform, it is used within many applications. A failure in such a component has widespread effects and thus has to be prevented by ensuring strict quality requirements.

Required and provided interface

Interfaces are the means for connecting components. Components provide functionality to other components via a *provided interface*. On the other hand, components use a *required interface* for accessing functionality provided by other components. A complete application is configured by connecting the required interface of each component to exactly one, matching[26] provided interface of another[27] component. For each involved component, all required interfaces, except possibly optional ones, should be connected.

Interface design precedes component design

The interfaces that a component requires or provides have to be designed before the actual internal design of the component can be done. The architect usually only determines what interfaces exist, what their role is, and which

---

[26] Matching does not always mean equality; there are cases where a "smaller" required interface may be connected to a "larger" provided interface, see e.g. [V. Ommering et al. 2000].

[27] Although we do not disallow the connection of two interfaces of the same component, this case seldom occurs in practice.

components should provide or require the interface. Each interface provides several elements, which may either be implemented by the providing component or subsequently be required via another interface.

> **Example 7-1:** *Interfaces for Lock Control*
>
> In Fig. 7-3 a class diagram of a home automation component for lock control is depicted. It has two provided interfaces, one for 'user control registration' and one for 'lock registration'. The first one contains a class 'User terminal' to inherit from, and to call methods of, in order to bind a specific user terminal to it, and to enable the user to interact with the 'Lock control'. The second one has two classes, 'Lock' and 'Electronic lock control', to inherit from and to enable the binding of several kinds of locks, and calling their methods. The required interfaces are those that define the classes 'Sensor' and 'Actuator' to inherit from. The actual implementations are the 'Lock actuator' and 'Lock sensor' classes that inherit from 'Sensor' and 'Actuator' respectively. The 'Lock control registration' class is not part of the component interface. It is used to connect classes that are registered via the provided interfaces to the 'Lock' class.

The internal structure of a component or an interface consists mainly of object classes and functions. The designer may use a UML 2 class diagram to document them. The design of an interface should preferably be self-contained, i.e. it should not refer to other designs. The design of a component incorporates the design of its required interface as a basis to build upon. The provided interfaces should be abstractions of the component designs. *Internal structure*

7.3 Component Interface Variability

Interfaces are important means to realise variability. Different components that provide the same interface can be bound to others that require them. This results in a large number of possible configurations of domain components in product line applications. A good and stable design of the interfaces is crucial for allowing flexible configurations. Interfaces may be variable, but that is usually to be avoided. If an interface is variable the components providing and requiring the interface have to agree upon the variant to use. Although this scheme is possible, its advantage of reducing development effort is usually too low with respect to the effort needed to select the proper variant consistently. *Stable interfaces*

The most important constraint on an interface is the variability in the different components that have to be connected. The substructure of the interface *Abstraction of variability* provides an abstract view of object classes and constants in the providing component. The following kinds of variability have effects on the design of an interface:

- The use of different algorithms or protocols

- Differences in resources provided

- Differences in application configuration

- Many providing components

7.3.1 Variability in Algorithms and Protocols

Abstraction from algorithms

The same functionality may be implemented in different ways which all have to be supported by a single interface. The interface has to provide an abstract view of this kind of variability. The interface carries functions or object class methods that execute the algorithm or protocol (Example 7-2). The argument and result types of these methods have to be chosen in such a way that each perceivable algorithm can deal with them. This may involve the introduction of additional classes that incorporate certain argument or result lists.

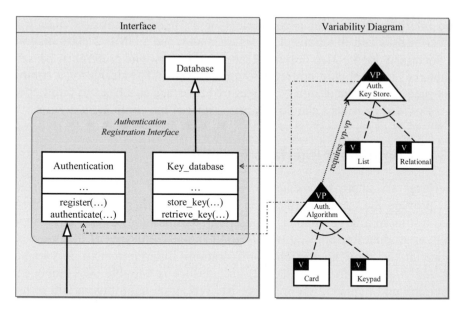

Fig. 7-4:   Interface for registering authentication objects

Example 7-2: *Authentication Registration Interface*

Figure 7-4 presents the interface provided by the 'authentication manager' component and required by the diverse 'authentication plug-in' components. Each plug-in component implements a different authentication algorithm. The 'authentication registration interface' allows the plug-in components to register at the 'authentication manager' component (Section 6.4).

The interface carries the class 'Authentication' with enough functionality for each class implementing an authentication algorithm. For instance, it carries an 'authenticate' method. In each 'authentication plug-in' component (Section 6.4), a sub-class has to be defined that performs the authentication according to its own algorithm. Moreover the 'Authentication' class contains a function to register objects of the class at the 'authentication manager'. This method is defined in the 'authentication manager' component itself to be reused by all 'authentication plug-in' components. The interface also carries the class 'Key_database', which is used by the authentication algorithm and has to be known by the 'authentication manager' for proper functioning.

Example 7-3: *Authentication Registration Interface with Resource Information*

In the interface diagram of Fig. 7-5 the interface of Fig. 7-4 is extended with resource information. If the authentication algorithm takes a lot of time, it needs a separate asynchronous process to finish. In the meantime it can perform necessary administration tasks, which otherwise would have to wait till authentication is finished and which keep the lock closed for too long. The interface thus makes a difference between having the additional asynchronous authentication process or not. This is manifested in an additional parameter 'sync' in the 'register' method of the 'Authentication' class. If a class is registered with 'sync' being false, the component providing the interface is able to deal with this situation in the additional process. The biometrical data, like an iris scan, can be collected, and processing starts before an actual authentication request is received. The actual request may arrive later because the doorknob has not been touched yet.

7.3.2 Variability in Resources

Different components deal with the same kind of functionality, but often provide (and/or use) different amounts of certain resources. Examples of such resources are memory size, processing time, screen space, bandwidth, and communication speed. In many cases the component requiring the inter-

Abstraction from resource variation

face needs at least some abstract information about the required resource size. This often is its value with respect to a given scale. The scale may be more or less abstract, such as the absolute screen size in pixels, or only just a distinction between large, medium, and small.

Parameters
for variants
The interface should carry functions, or parameters that distinguish between the actual values of the resource (Example 7-3). This enables run-time checking, e.g. if the provided resource is large enough. In addition, there should be (de-)allocation functions to be able to claim and free the resources.

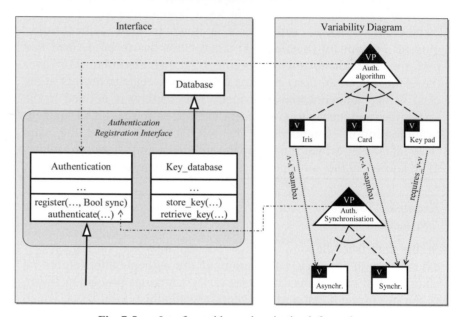

Fig. 7-5:   Interface with synchronisation information

7.3.3   Variability in Application Configuration

Abstraction from
configuration variants
In many cases variability is related to the application configuration, including differences in hardware and software. Such differences may be, for instance, different memory sizes or differences in the availability of certain software packages. Requiring components need an abstract view on the configuration. Consequently, the interface should carry functions, methods, or parameters that distinguish between the variants (Example 7-4). Differences in resources can be seen as a special case of differences in configuration. While resources are related to internal properties of hardware and software, configuration relates to all kinds of system properties.

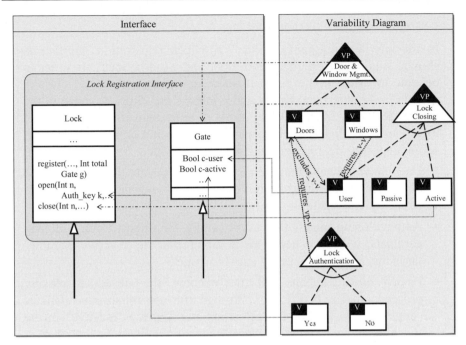

Fig. 7-6:   Lock registration interface

7.3.4 **Many Components Providing the Interface**

There may be many components providing the same interface. For instance, this occurs for system-wide aspects affecting all or most components, such as initialisation (Example 7-5), error handling, or software maintenance. The interface carries only a few object classes that have few methods which are usually very generic.

Generic interfaces

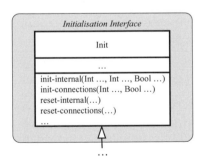

Fig. 7-7:   Initialisation interface

Example 7-4: *Lock Registration Interface*

In the interface diagram of Fig. 7-6 a lock registration interface is shown. It is used to register both door and window locks. In order to be able to differentiate between them, an additional 'Gate' class is present in the interface. Doors and windows are kinds of gates. In the future there may even be other kinds of gates as well, which have to be opened and closed, such as sunshades or water taps. Each gate has some properties dealing with the way it is closed:

- User closing means that the gate needs a separate user command to close. This is captured in the 'c-user' parameter in the 'Gate' class being equal to "true".

- Active closing means that after waiting for a short time, a closing command will be issued. This is captured in the 'c-active' parameter in the 'Gate' class being equal to "true".

- Passive closing means that after opening, the subsequent closing proceeds mechanically, e.g. through the use of springs. This is captured in both the 'c-user' parameter and the 'c-active' in the 'Gate' class being equal to "false".

The interface deals with all variability related to different numbers of gates and their way to close. The requirements are such that doors are never 'user closing' and windows are always 'user closing'. Each registering command is able to register more than one gate of a single kind. The interface deals with variability in the gates to be registered and controlled by the inclusion of the gate as a parameter. In this way lock control uses the parameters of the gate itself to know how to close. Many configurations of all kinds of gates can be controlled. To select the right gate in the configuration, the 'open' method requires an identifier of the gate to be opened and an authentication key, which has a default value in cases that do not require authentication. The 'close' method needs the identifier of the gate.

Example 7-5: *Initialisation Interface*

The initialisation interface is shown in the interface diagram of Fig. 7-7. The architectural texture demands that each component provides the interface. It is used for initialising and resetting components. The interface has generic functions for initialising or resetting the internal part of the component, and for initialising or resetting the connections to other components. For generic parameters, types like Int, Bool, or Char are used. These types are known by all components. Consequently, all components can use the functions.

7.4   Internal Component Variability

Realisation of components deals with the variability requests of the architect by using the following mechanisms, often in a mixture:

Realisation of variability

- Providing different variants of a component
- Providing variability within the component

Class diagrams are used to document the internal structure of components. This structure mainly consists of interacting object classes. Some of these classes are defined in provided and required interfaces. Therefore, classes in interfaces are usually also part of the class diagram (Example 7-6).

Documentation of internal structure

Example 7-6: *Variability in the Components*

Figure 7-8 shows a class diagram of a lock control component. The component has several provided and required interfaces. At the top of the figure, two classes are depicted that are required for the control of actuators and sensors. Through the required interfaces for 'Sensor' and 'Actuator', these classes are used for inheritance[28] to 'Lock sensor' and 'Lock actuator' in the lock control component. The provided interfaces carry classes for inheritance themselves. For instance, the generic 'Lock' class has a sub-class 'Electronic lock control' in the same interface, which is inherited through the 'lock registration interface'. In addition to these interfaces and their inheritance relationships, some other occurrences of variability can also be found in Fig. 7-8. The optional presence of a door lock sensor is modelled by defining the multiplicity of the 'Lock sensor' class as 0..n. Similarly the presence of more than one actuator is modelled through the multiplicity annotation 1..n. Finally, some variability in run-time instances is shown in this diagram. The 'Lock sensor' class has an attribute 'period' which describes the polling time in microseconds. This attribute is adapted at run-time according to the time of day and the particularities of the use of the door.

Inheritance, multiplicity annotations, and class attributes are the main ways to describe variability in class diagrams. In particular, inheritance is used to provide variants for abstract classes available in required interfaces. Part of the variability in the class diagram is variability that relates to the run-time instances of the class model. This kind of variability is not related to product line variability, which determines the differentiation between the different

Defining variability in class diagrams

---

[28] Note that these classes are depicted at the top of the figure, but appear in the lower level subsystems 'Device control and management'. This is a consequence of a flaw in the inheritance notation. The interested reader is referred to [Firesmith 1994] for a discussion on this topic.

applications. Only the latter one is of importance for software product line engineering. Therefore we use the orthogonal variability model to capture the variability of the product line.

Orthogonal variability definition

Care should be taken to determine what variability means during detailed design. As stated in Chapter 5, the variability in the class diagram can be used either for defining different run-time instances, for distinguishing between variants (Example 7-7), or even something in between, i.e. applications having a smaller range of variability than expressed in the diagram. In general the variability model should reflect the available range of permissible variants. In addition, the designer may resort to other means, e.g. explanatory text, to distinguish clearly between these cases.

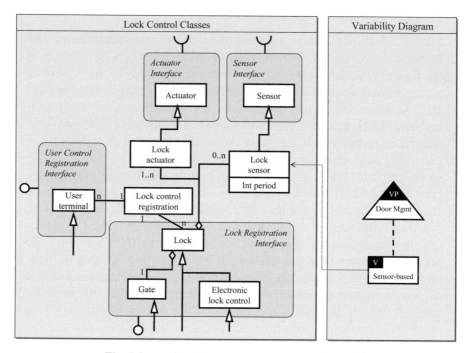

Fig. 7-8:   Class diagram of a 'Lock control plug-in'

Process view follows development view

So far, we have considered the development view (or the static view) of detailed design. The process view of detailed design may be documented for instance in terms of sequence charts or state machines. The documentation of variability in sequence charts and state machines has been covered in Chapter 6. However, typically the high level of detail in detailed design makes the documentation of variability more difficult than in requirements engineering. The designer usually follows the guidelines of the architect, assigning threads and processes to objects or object classes. This allocation adheres to the required variability. The consequence of this procedure is that process view variability and development view variability are closely related.

> **Example 7-7:** *Variability in the 'Lock Control Plug-in'*
>
> In Fig. 7-8 the relationship between the 'Lock' class and the 'Lock sensor' class shows that there may be zero, one, or many lock sensor objects available per lock. This specification allows applications in which exactly one such object is available. However, the diagram may also be interpreted as "it must be possible to configure the number of sensors at run-time in each application". Then, each application should possess the option of having any number of sensors available, including none. The exact number is determined at run-time. In this case the multiplicity in the diagram does not denote product line variability.

7.5   Differences from Single-System Engineering

The detailed design and the implementation of domain components basically have to rely on the notations and mechanisms that are also employed in single-system development. The main difference to normal software engineering is the presence of variability, which has to be incorporated in the design. The internal structure of a component may differ from application to application. The component interface has to be generic to support these differences. In order to support systematic development and reuse, the variability of the product line provided by the components has to be clearly documented in the variability model.

Generic interfaces, realised variability

In addition, the reference architecture is an important constraint, more so than the architecture of a single system. This is caused by the fact that the architecture governs the similarity of the design of the parts by means of the texture. The texture defines rules that guide the realisation and the documentation of component variability.

Realisation guided by texture

7.6   Summary

Developers have to create a detailed design for each component specified in the architecture. In doing so, they document the variability provided by each component in the variability model. The variability model provides a consistent view of the available component variability and supports the configuration of components. Interfaces provide a common view of variable components and an abstraction from their internal details. They are designed

Variability in components

Variability in interfaces

in such a way that each (variable) component requiring some interface can be coupled to each component providing this interface.

Variability documentation
The internal structure of each component is documented in the class diagram. As the class diagram does not distinguish between product line variability and the variability of run-time instances, product line variability of components has to be documented in terms of variation points and variants that are linked to the variable elements of the class model.

Klaus Pohl
Ernst Sikora

8

Documenting Variability in Test Artefacts

In this chapter you will learn:

- o *How to use the orthogonal variability model to document variability in test artefacts.*
- o *The differences between test artefacts in single-system engineering and in software product line engineering.*

8.1   Introduction

Variability in
test artefacts

Test artefacts contain the instructions for testers what to test, when to test, how to test, and how to document the test results. The test results themselves are test artefacts, too. Test artefacts enable repeatable and traceable tests. Testing is performed in domain engineering as well as in application engineering and thus test artefacts are created in both processes. A major task of domain testing is to develop test artefacts that can be reused efficiently in application testing. This is achieved with a clear and unambiguous documentation of variability in test artefacts. In this chapter, we focus on that documentation. We provide a brief description of important test artefacts and show how to employ the orthogonal variability model. The sub-processes and artefacts closely related to documenting variability in domain tests are highlighted in Fig. 8-1.

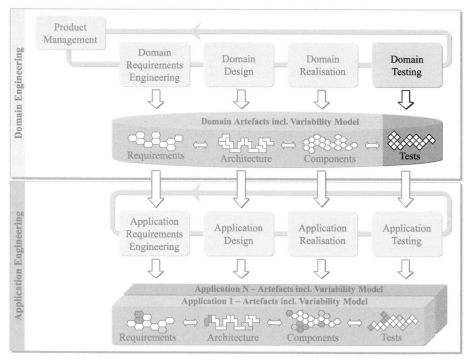

Fig. 8-1:   Focus of documenting variability in test artefacts

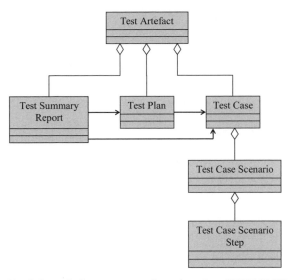

Fig. 8-2:   Software test artefacts, based on [IEEE 1998]

8.2   Test Artefacts

The constituents of test documentation known from single-system engineering are shown in Fig. 8-2. We refer to the test plan, test case, test case scenario, scenario step, and the test summary report as *test artefacts* (Definition
8-1), whereas the software artefact under test is called item under test or *test
item*.

*Main constituents of
test documentation*

> **Definition 8-1:** *Test Artefacts*
>
> Test artefacts are products of the test process containing plans, specifi-
> cations, and test results.

A comprehensive overview of test artefacts can be found, for example, in the
IEEE standard for software test documentation [IEEE 1998]. In the following, we briefly characterise the test artefacts from Fig. 8-2:

*Characteristics of the
test artefacts*

- *Test plan*: A test is conducted according to a test plan, which determines
  the test cases to be performed. The test plan also assigns priorities to the
  test cases, allocates the resources available for testing, and specifies the
  tools to be used.

*Resource
allocation*

- *Test case*: A test case defines the conditions, the input data, and the
  expected output data for a test. Each test case has a defined test goal and
  includes one or multiple test case scenarios, which describe different
  ways of achieving the goal. A test case also defines the required test

*Logical and
detailed test cases*

environment, information about how to execute the test, and the fail–pass criteria, i.e. the conditions that must be true for the test item to pass the test. There are two levels of abstraction at which a test case may be defined. Logical test cases describe the data, conditions, and actions in principle, yet without referring to details such as the particular data values to be entered within a scenario step (however, the data range may be specified). Detailed test cases provide all the details necessary to perform the test, leaving no room for interpretation.

Sequence of actions
- *Test case scenario*: A test case scenario describes a specific sequence of actions. The execution of this scenarios results in achieving the test goal. Each action is defined as a scenario step.

Instructions for tester
- *Test case scenario step*: A test case scenario step includes instructions for the tester to perform a specific action and, optionally, the expected result for the test step.

Results of test execution
- *Test summary report*: A test summary report provides an overview of the results of a specific test execution.

8.3 Variability in Test Artefacts

In software product line engineering, the test artefacts introduced in Section 8.2 have to include variability or at least refer to it.

8.3.1 Test Plan

Generic and specific test plans
The test plan is required for domain engineering as well as for application engineering. The test plan for domain engineering must unambiguously define the test activities to be performed in domain engineering and therefore it does not contain variability. Nonetheless, a generic test plan for future application test processes may be prepared. In the following, we characterise the

Effects of variability
impact of software product line engineering on the generic test plan:

Resource consumption
- To determine an appropriate allocation of resources, resource consumption must be estimated based on the variants and the common and variable requirements. At least a rough estimation of resource consumption for each common or variable requirement is necessary. Dependencies between variants may increase complexity and the required amount of resources.

Selection of variants
- The test plan must specify which common and variable test cases are to be performed. To perform variable test cases, the test plan must specify which variants to bind.

- The priority of a reusable test case is typically different in domain and application engineering. If tests are performed in domain engineering, the corresponding test cases have high priorities in domain engineering but low priorities in application engineering. The assignment of priorities can also depend on the selected variants, e.g. to indicate that a test case is of a high priority for a particular variant, but a low priority for other variants. *Priorities*

- The tool support defined in the test plan must deal with the question of how to model variability in test artefacts and how to bind variability in application testing. If the available tools do not provide adequate variability support, custom tags, textual notes, or other available constructs for instance may be used to denote variable elements. *Tool support*

The test plan is specified as a natural language document. Therefore, for the attributes of the test plan, we encourage the use of the same modelling techniques as for the natural language requirements (Section 5.3). Figure 8-3 presents an example of a generic test plan, which is related to a variability model. By binding variants in the variability model the related parts of the generic test plan are selected for a particular application. *Natural language documentation*

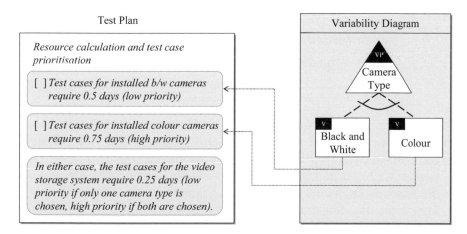

Fig. 8-3: Example of orthogonal variability modelling in a generic test plan

8.3.2 Test Case

Common and variable test cases are the most important test artefacts. The constituents of the test cases are affected by variability in the following ways: *Effects of variability*

- The test data to be used may be different for each selected set of variants. The test documentation must include the different test data and its relation to variants in the orthogonal variability model. *Test data*

Test environment
- Environmental needs impose restrictions on permissible hardware and software configurations in which the item under test is executed. Different variants of the test item may have different environmental needs. The test documentation must specify the different needs and relate them to the corresponding variants in the orthogonal variability model.

Fail–pass criteria
- The fail–pass criteria define in which cases the test item fails or passes the test. The test documentation must specify which fail–pass criteria have to be applied for a particular variant, for instance by defining which deviations from the test case scenarios of the considered variant are tolerable.

Structured natural language
The specification of test cases is contained in structured natural language documents and is therefore similar to natural language requirements and test plans.

8.3.3 Test Case Scenario

Three types of test case scenarios
A test case scenario contains the expected flow of actions that should emerge during test execution. It puts the included test case scenario steps in the right order. Product line variability leads to the following three types of scenarios:

- A scenario is common to all intended applications.

- A scenario is specific for one variant.

- A scenario is adaptable to two or more variants.

Example 8-1: *Adaptable Test Case Scenario*

The home security system has three different variants for the electronic door lock. The test case scenario shown in Fig. 8-4 contains common steps as well as variable steps for the particular variants. The step 'enter tester data as valid' ensures that a precondition is met, i.e. the tester is known to the system and authorised to unlock the door. The steps 'lay finger on scanner', 'enter PIN in keypad', and 'use magnetic card' describe the individual ways for each variant to authenticate to the system. The 'grant access' step includes the verification if the system identifies the tester correctly and permits entry. The way the verification is performed depends on the particular variant. It may, for example, involve checking the internal state of the fingerprint authentication component. The final step 'open door' is a common step as either variant allows the tester to open the door. Due to the common start-up and finalisation steps, this scenario falls within the category "adaptable scenario for two or more variants".

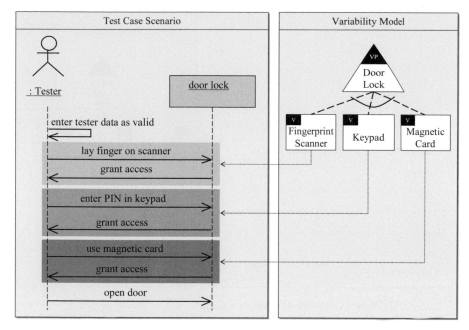

Fig. 8-4: Example of an adaptable test case scenario for three variants

The specification of test case scenarios is similar to scenarios used in requirements engineering (Section 5.4) and, thus, the notations are the same. However, the information in a test case scenario is more detailed than the information in a use case scenario.

Scenario notations

8.3.4 Test Case Scenario Step

The scenario steps are the constituents of a domain test case scenario. They are affected by variability in the following ways:

Effects of variability

- The input specification may be different for each variant as the selected variant can have an influence on the input data of the test item. The test documentation must include the different input specifications and their relation to variants in the orthogonal variability model.

Input

- The expected output of a scenario step depends on the chosen variants. The test documentation has to include the different output specifications and their relations to the variants in the orthogonal variability model.

Output

- Execution information gives individual guidance on how to perform the test case steps. The execution information details the story line down to actions like pushing a specific button, clicking the right mouse button, or browsing to a specific line in a log file. As the actions may depend on the selected variants, so does the execution information.

Execution information

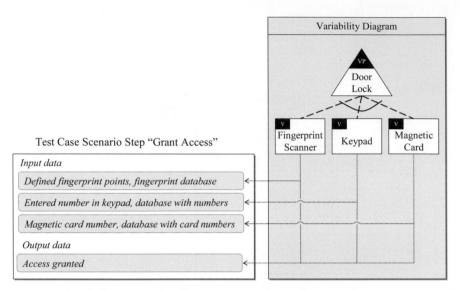

Fig. 8-5:   Example of a test case scenario step in natural language

Natural language,   Test case scenario steps and the variability therein may be specified with
sequence diagrams   natural language or within sequence diagrams. We provide an example of
modelling the variability of a test case scenario step in a structured textual
document in Fig. 8-5 and in a sequence diagram representation in Fig. 8-6.

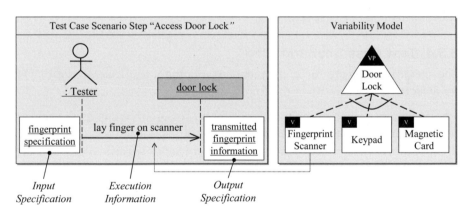

Fig. 8-6:   Example of a test case scenario step in a sequence diagram

8.3.5 Test Summary Report

Effects of   The test summary report refers to the tested system, the related test plan, and
variability   the executed test cases. It documents the results of the execution of each test
case and provides the overall summary of a test execution, which may

include, for instance, a classification of the detected defects. Variability affects the test summary report in the following ways:

- The description of the tested system also documents the incorporated variants.

- Each test case is described with the corresponding variants used in it.

- The classification of defects distinguishes between defects in domain artefacts and defects in application artefacts.

The test summary report has to refer to variants but does not contain variability itself. Consequently the test summary report can be documented in the same way as in single-system engineering but has to include some additional information.

Additional information

8.4 Differences from Single-System Engineering

In single-system engineering developers create test artefacts for a specific application and the artefacts are valid for this application only. In software product line engineering, test activities are distributed between the domain and the individual applications. As the components under test as well as the test references used (e.g. requirements) contain variability, the test artefacts also must consist of common and variable parts to be reusable. The test documentation is responsible for determining which of the variable parts to use for which configuration.

Test artefacts for different configurations

8.5 Summary

The variability contained in the specification of test artefacts leads to variability in the test artefacts. In particular, variability affects test cases, test case scenarios, test case scenario steps, as well as the test summary report. Moreover, to deal with software product line testing efficiently, domain test engineers define a generic test plan. The test plan is related to the available variants and is reused to derive test plans for specific applications. Using the orthogonal variability model, domain test engineers can document clearly which variants relate to which test artefacts.

Variability in test artefacts

Part III

Domain
Engineering

Part III: Overview

In domain engineering the commonality and the variability for a set of envisioned product line applications are identified, documented, and produced. The variability is explicitly documented in the orthogonal variability model in order to facilitate the reuse of product line assets during application engineering. In this part you will learn how the sub-processes highlighted in the figure below:

- *Construct reusable domain artefacts.*

- *Define the desired commonality and variability for the succeeding sub-process.*

- *Detail and refine commonality and variability established in the preceding sub-process.*

- *Provide feedback about the feasibility of realising variability to the preceding sub-process.*

Thereby we establish a seamless integration of variability throughout all domain engineering artefacts.

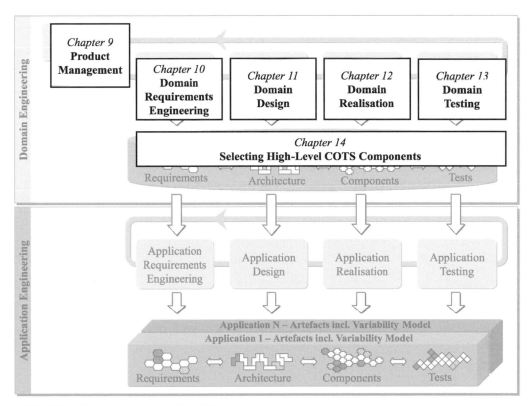

Fig. III-1: Chapter overview of Part III

Elisabeth Niehaus
Klaus Pohl
Günter Böckle

9

Product

Management

In this chapter you will learn:

- o *The economical background of product management.*
- o *The principles of designing a product portfolio and managing it over the lifetime of the software product line.*
- o *The relation between product management and product line scoping.*
- o *The challenges for product management in software product line engineering.*

9.1   Introduction

Goals of product management

The goal of product management is to make a major contribution to entrepreneurial success by integrating the development, production, and marketing of products that meet customer needs.[29] Product management is responsible for enforcing entrepreneurial goals throughout the software engineering process. Therefore it has an influence on requirements engineering, design, realisation, and testing. The sub-processes and artefacts closely related to product management are highlighted in Fig. 9-1.

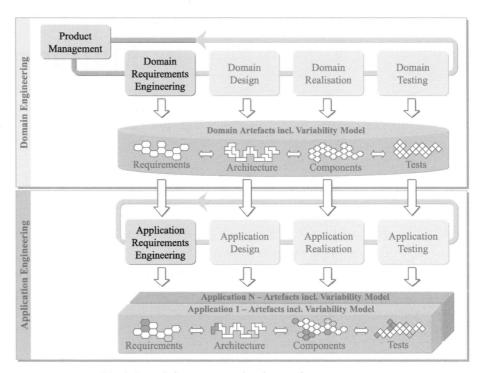

Fig. 9-1:   Sub-processes related to product management

Main results

The major result of product management with respect to the software product line framework is the *product roadmap*. Note that we did not include the product roadmap in the framework picture as it is no development artefact in the common sense (Section 2.5.1). The product roadmap outlines the product line as far as it is foreseeable at a given point in time. It defines the major common and variable features of all applications of the product line as well

---

[29] The definition of the term entrepreneurial success is not quite simple as it depends on the goals of the company. Besides measurable quantities like profit, earning power, shareholder value or product profitability, this term also covers qualitative factors such as the motivation of personnel.

as a schedule for delivering specific applications to customers or for bringing them to market. The features defined in the product roadmap directly affect domain and application requirements engineering.

Domain and application requirements engineering have to adhere to the features specified in the roadmap. While domain requirements engineering provides reusable requirements artefacts, application requirements engineering creates the requirements artefacts for specific applications, which are envisaged in the product roadmap. The following subsections elaborate on the basic information flows between product management and its related sub-processes as shown in Fig. 9-2.

Interrelations with other sub-processes

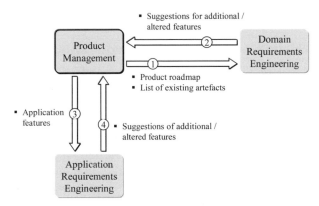

Fig. 9-2:   Information flows between product management and other sub-processes

9.1.1 Interrelation with Domain Requirements Engineering

The product management sub-process specifies a product roadmap, which outlines the scope for domain requirements engineering (first bullet of ① in Fig. 9-2). The roadmap implements the company's strategy for providing customers with what they need at the appropriate point in time. The schedule for bringing out applications is the result of strategic reasoning and effort estimation performed jointly by product managers and developers. In addition to the roadmap, product management provides a list of existing artefacts (second bullet of ① in Fig. 9-2) which could serve as a basis for deriving domain requirements. For example, product management could provide a set of previously developed products or applications that are relevant for the definition of requirements for the product line. These artefacts may be used as a basis for the development of domain artefacts.

Product roadmap, existing products

Domain requirements engineering is responsible for working out the requirements specification, which describes the problem that must be solved by the software architects, designers, and programmers. The insights gained

Feedback from domain requirements engineering

in domain requirements engineering with regard to the major features of the product line, especially its externally visible variability, are communicated back to product management as suggestions for additional and altered features (② in Fig. 9-2).

Adaptation of product roadmap

During the life cycle of the product line, product management has to react to various developments on the market: the change in customer needs, the appearance of new technologies, competitors coming up with new features, and shifts in demand and prices. These developments necessitate adaptations of the product roadmap, such as the introduction of new features or the elimination of outdated applications from the product portfolio. Hence the interaction between product management and domain requirements engineering is an ongoing task.

9.1.2   Interrelation with Application Requirements Engineering

Platform features

Product management specifies which applications should be derived in application requirements engineering (③ in Fig. 9-2) by prescribing the application features, i.e. which application should possess which of the common and variable features. In a steady state of the product line's lifetime many of these features are already accounted for by the requirements artefacts produced in domain requirements engineering. Application engineering exploits the available variability of domain requirements to derive application requirements artefacts according to the features prescribed by product management.

Application-specific features

In certain situations (e.g. customer-specific application development, pilot applications, etc.) the features determined by product management have to be realised by application engineering. Later, successful developments may be propagated to domain engineering.

Feedback from application engineers

Like domain requirements engineering, application requirements engineering provides feedback to product management in terms of suggestions for additional or altered features (④ in Fig. 9-2), which result from new insights gained in the requirements engineering process.

9.2   Terminology

Different kinds of products

The definition of the term *product* relates to goods or services offered in the market (Definition 9-1). The goods considered in software product line engineering are applications. The term application denotes both software and software-intensive systems (Section 1.4). Products may also be services or solutions offered to the customer. Companies offer a large variety of services such as the development and maintenance of customer-specific software, or the assembly of a system from configurable components. Complex products consisting of a number of goods and services such as a turnkey-ready industrial plant are called solutions. The kind of products (goods, services, or solutions) offered is interrelated with the business type of the company.

> **Definition 9-1:** *Product*
>
> Products are goods or services offered in the market, which are suitable by their functions and characteristics to satisfy concrete customer needs.
>
> [Sabisch 1996]

In Definition 9-2, we provide a definition of *product management* used in economics. As this definition is quite general, we provide a more specific definition of product management as a sub-process of software product line engineering in Definition 9-3.

Product management

> **Definition 9-2:** *Product Management (General Definition)*
>
> Planning, organising, executing, and controlling of all tasks, which aim at a successful conception, production, and marketing of the products offered by a company.

> **Definition 9-3:** *Product Management (In the Software Product Line Framework)*
>
> Product management is the sub-process of domain engineering for controlling the development, production, and marketing of the software product line and its applications.

Based on the observation of the market and the organisation itself, product management defines a product portfolio with a roadmap and the major common and variable features of the planned products of the product line.

Product roadmap

9.3 Traditional Product Management Activities

Basically, product management encompasses the following activities [Sabisch 1996]:

- *Market and product strategy definition*: This activity implies the concretisation of company objectives and strategies defined by corporate management.

  Concretisation of company objectives

- *Product definition*: This activity includes developing, rating, and choosing new ideas for products. Product ideas that have been selected

  Development of product ideas

for realisation are concretised by defining the major features of the envisioned product.

Conservation of potentials

- *Product support*: This activity deals with conserving and enhancing the potentials of products that have already been introduced in the market.

Identification of distribution channels

- *Market introduction*: This activity implies identifying suitable distribution channels and supplying them with new products as well as announcing the new products to potential customers.

Analysis of customers and competitors

- *Market observation*: This activity is concerned with monitoring and analysing customer groups, current or potential competitors, trends of prices, buying patterns, usage patterns, and technology, as well as barriers to market entry (e.g. legal restriction of permission or high initial investments) or market exit.

Process guidance

- *Product controlling*: This activity is concerned with monitoring and guiding the product management process, e.g. by observing the sales volume obtained for each product.

9.4 Portfolio Management

Product portfolio

An essential task of product management is the management of a company's *product portfolio*. In this section we focus on the strategic aspects of portfolio management and elaborate on the design of new products as well as on the management of existing products in the subsequent sections. The term product portfolio is defined as follows:

> **Definition 9-4:** *Product Portfolio*
>
> The set of product types[30] that are offered by a company is called the product portfolio of this company.

Management process

To decide which amount of resources is allocated to which project a *portfolio management* process is necessary (Definition 9-5).

> **Definition 9-5:** *Portfolio Management*
>
> Portfolio management is a dynamic decision process, whereby a business's list of active new product (and development) projects is constantly updated and revised.
>
> [Cooper 2001]

---

[30] Hence, the product portfolio typically contains classes of products, not all the individual products of a company.

In the portfolio management process, new projects are evaluated, selected, and prioritised, while existing projects may be accelerated, cancelled, or de-prioritised. The value of portfolio management techniques has been demonstrated by a study conducted by PRTM Management Consultants [PRTM 2004]. A survey among 120 companies, including for example Honeywell and IBM, revealed: "Companies with advanced product portfolio management capabilities have a 10% higher profitability than the industry average" and "companies with mature portfolio management practices grow over 50% faster than those with only project management expertise".

Benefits of portfolio management

9.4.1 IT Business Types

The kinds of products (goods, services, or solutions) offered by different IT companies show a large diversity. Within the IT industry, there are four main business types, which can be determined based on two main discriminating aspects:

Differentiating factors of business types

- The amount of time that customers need to make a purchase decision.

- The binding[31] of the customer by the purchase decision.

Figure 9-3 presents the two discriminating aspects and the resulting business types.

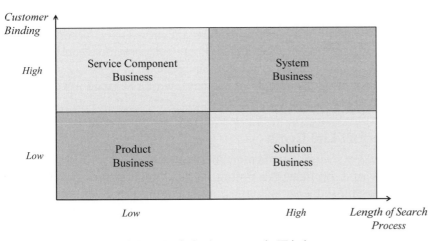

Fig. 9-3:   Main business types in IT industry

The four business types depicted in Fig. 9-3 can be characterised as follows:

- *Product business*: A prefabricated product or service is offered to the market. The customer can remain anonymous. The purchasing decision

Prefabricated mass product

---

[31] The customer may be bound to the vendor, to a product type or to a technology.

is typically quick and not connected to other purchasing decisions. The development and sale of standard software like MS Office is an example of product business.

Specific product or service

- *Solution business*: A specific product or service is offered to an individual customer. A service is performed on site or a product is installed on site. The purchasing decision is not connected to other purchasing decisions. The development and sale of a stand-alone, customer-specific solutions such as the software for a power plant or a postal distribution system are examples of solution business.

Set of prefabricated mass products

- *System business*: A prefabricated set of unspecific, related products and services is offered to the market. The purchase decision for one product is connected to purchase decisions of other products. The development and sale of a software-system consisting of an operating system and several integrated software applications is an example of system business.

Individualised product

- *Service component business*: A prefabricated but individualised product or service is offered to an individual customer. The purchase decision is connected with other purchase decisions of the same customer. An example is the development and sale of additional modules providing extra functionality for software already in use.

Business types in this chapter

The focus of this chapter is on product business and system business. As the customer can remain anonymous in these business types, product management is responsible for ensuring a match between customer requirements and product features. However, product management is also relevant for the solution and the service component business, yet it is shaped towards dealing with individual customers in these business types.

9.4.2 Product Life Cycle

Idealised sales and profit curves

The *product life cycle* describes an idealised progression of the profit and sales curves of a product. According to this life cycle, each product progresses through a sequence of stages: introduction, growth, maturity, saturation, and degeneration. Sales and profit can be described as a function of the life cycle stages as sketched in Fig. 9-4.

Product life cycle stages

The different life cycle stages are characterised as follows:

- *Introduction*: The product is rather unknown to potential customers. Hence the sales volume is low. High expenditures, e.g. for setting up distribution channels and increasing the popularity of the product, result in a negative profit.

- *Growth*: As the product becomes better known on the market, sales and profit increase quickly. Usually some competitors enter the market at this stage.

- *Maturity*: The rapid increase of sales diminishes. Prices have to be cut to win additional market share. Consequently, the profit declines slowly.

- *Saturation*: The sales volume is at its maximum. This stage is often characterised by hard competition for market share. The results are even further declining profits.

- *Degeneration*: Increasingly the product is substituted by new products. Demand and sales decrease further. Therefore profit also continues to decrease. In order to avoid losses the product must be taken off the market, or a product relaunch has to be initiated.

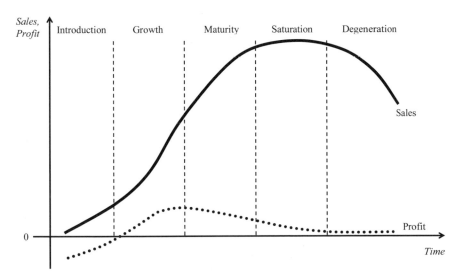

Fig. 9-4:   Product life cycle diagram

One problem of the product life cycle model is that it does not allow the prediction of the length of the individual stages [Sabisch 1996]. In addition, the profit and sales development of real products often differ substantially from the ideal curve. Nevertheless, the product life cycle model provides valuable support for the strategic decisions concerning a company's product portfolio.

Criticism of the product life cycle

Product management has to develop strategies to overcome the fundamental difficulties inherent in each stage of the product life cycle. An essential goal

Impact on product management

of product management is to reach the profitable life cycle stages and to avoid premature degeneration. The next section elaborates on this issue.

Technology life cycle A similar model as for the life cycle of a product also exists for technologies. Each technology progresses through a sequence of stages from future technology, through pacemaker technology, key technology, and basic technology, to replaced technology [Pepels 2003; Kleinaltenkamp and Plinke 1999]. The technology life cycle describes the competitive potential of a technology as an *S*-shaped function of the life cycle stages. The technology and the product life cycles are closely related as technologies are incorporated into products.

9.4.3 Product Portfolio Analysis

Resource allocation to projects *Portfolio analysis* allows a systematic evaluation of the product portfolio. During the analysis, each product (or product type) is rated according to two variables and thereby its location in a two-dimensional matrix is determined. The goal of portfolio analysis is to identify weaknesses in the product portfolio, to define improvement strategies, and above all to support decisions about resource allocation to the projects of a company.

Balance across life cycle stages A balanced product portfolio should contain a conducive mix of products across different life cycle stages. Products in the growth or maturity stage are necessary since these products yield high profits yet still demand investment until they reach the saturation stage. Products in the saturation stage yield profits that can be reinvested in products that are in the introduction or growth stage. Products in the introduction stage ensure future sales and profit. The market-growth/market-share portfolio of the Boston Consulting Group (BCG) assigns the products or product groups on the basis of market growth and market share to four main categories, each of which represents a certain stage in the product life cycle. The BCG portfolio is depicted in Fig. 9-5.

BCG matrix

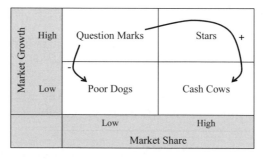

Fig. 9-5:   Product portfolio matrix of the Boston Consulting Group with a positive and a negative evolution path [Welge and Al-Laham 1999]

For each product, standard strategies can be derived due to the position of the product in the matrix:

- *Question marks*: These products have a high market growth and a low market share. Products in the introduction or early growth stage are assigned to this position in the product portfolio matrix. The standard strategy is to invest in these products in order to reach a high market share in the growing market so that the former question mark product will move to the stars quadrant. As resources are scarce it may not be possible to invest in all question marks. In this case it has to be analysed which products have the highest potential for evolving into stars. However, despite all efforts, question marks may not reach the stars quadrant but end up as poor dogs.

- *Stars*: Stars are characterised by a high market growth and a high market share. They are usually in the late growth or maturity stage. To protect the high market share in a growing market the increasing sales volume has to be reinvested in these products.

- *Cash cows*: Cash cows are products with a high market share but a low market growth. These circumstances usually apply for the saturation stage, in which the sales volume is at its maximum. As the market growth is low and is not expected to rise again, the standard strategy for cash cow products is to reduce investments to the degree that is necessary to keep these products in the cash cow quadrant as long as possible. Hence, cash cows are the products that yield profits for the company.

- *Poor dogs*: Products with a low market growth and a low market share are called poor dogs. Products in the late saturation or degeneration stage are usually located in this quadrant, for which product elimination is recommended.

The BCG method assumes that market growth and market share are the main criteria for a high success potential. This is often criticised, since a market with a high growth rate can be unattractive because of intensive competition or high market power of the customers. On the other hand, a small market share is not necessarily connected with little success potential. In addition, the factors market share and market growth always refer to a concrete market, whose definition is, however, subjective. Hence, although the standard strategies of the BCG method provide useful guidance, they should be applied with deliberation. For further details see for example [Welge and Al-Laham 1999].

9.4.4 Product Interdependences

Diversified portfolios

Formerly, product diversification was common in product portfolios of large companies. Product diversification became popular since the mid-1960s by the application of the BCG portfolio and was often realised by acquisition. The goal was to spread business risk by being present in several markets. Thus large conglomerates emerged. Yet, long-term studies revealed that these conglomerates are rarely successful. Profound knowledge of the acquired business units and the respective markets is crucial for effective management, since knowledge from one branch of industry cannot be implicitly applied to other branches. Hence, false investments are easily made [Plinke 2002].

Core competencies

Managers design the product portfolio of a company or business unit in such a way that managing the products jointly in a portfolio yields synergistic effects. Core competencies provide a potential area for gaining synergistic effects through a joint product management [Welge and Al-Laham 1999].

Product interdependences

Consequently, the product types in the product portfolio of a company or business unit are typically related. There are several kinds of *interdependences* by which the products in a product portfolio may be related:

- *Acquisition interdependence*: The products are placed together when they are sold or are part of a common sales promotion.

- *Usage interdependence*: The products are used complementarily. They provide a solution for a certain problem field.

- *Demand interdependence*: Customers buy these products during the same purchase process.

- *Selection interdependence*: The products can replace each other. They offer alternative buying solutions for the customer.

- *Engineering interdependence*: The products originate from the same engineering process.

Adding and deleting products

The effects caused by the different interdependences have to be considered especially when new products are added to the product portfolio or removed from it:

- When a new product is added, the product manager has to check, for example, whether there is usage interdependence with other products. These products should be added to the portfolio as well.

- When a product is removed from the portfolio and there is still some demand, the product manager must ensure that alternative solutions exist (i.e. products related by selection interdependence to the deleted product).

Interdependences can also be proactively designed into new products. For example, complementary features between different products cause a usage interdependence and induce customers to buy a combination of products instead of a single product.

Complementary features

9.4.5 Product Variants

Product management literature refers to different solutions for the same application problem as *product variants*. Product variants are typically related by *selection interdependence*. Particularly in stagnating and shrinking markets, a high increase of product variants can be observed. This happens for different reasons:

Motivations for product variants

- Retaining a high market share necessitates the adaptation of products to heterogeneous customer requirements.

- When internationalisation is sought to react to stagnating domestic demand, customisation of products is indispensable, since often different likings, technical standards, or legal restrictions exist.

In addition, there is a general trend towards increasing product individualisation and thus towards a higher amount of variants. To decide which variants are to be offered, the costs and benefits of the variants have to be determined. The *costs of flexibility* (in the view of product management) originating from generating variants are considerable. Thus reasonable *standardisation* (in the sense of increased commonality) is imperative for obtaining and conserving competitive advantages [Kleinaltenkamp and Plinke 1999]. Software product line engineering is a method of systematically developing variants in a standardised manner.

Standardisation

9.4.5.1 Costs of Flexibility

When quantifying the benefits of variants, it is crucial to know which product properties are important for the customer. Having a high number of variants provides the opportunity to address many customer groups. Furthermore, there are some product types for which the customer-perceived value is increased by the sheer variation (e.g. in the food industry). On the other hand, a high quantity of variants may confuse customers. For determining the cost effects of variants, all company sectors have to be examined. The following list shows examples of costs caused by a high quantity of variants for the different departments of a company:

Impact on the company

- *Research and development*: The development of customised variants of existing products displaces the development of new products.

- *Purchasing*: The task of the purchasing department is difficult. Instead of buying high quantities of a small number of input material types, small quantities of a high number of input material types are required. As a result, purchase conditions are bad.

- *Production*: The storage costs and the risk of shortages are high. Production techniques and configuration management are complicated.

- *Marketing and sales*: The complexity of marketing and sales activities is high. The company is faced with cannibalistic effects,[32] a high quantity of product descriptions, and extensive price boards.

- *Customer service*: Service staff have to be trained for a high quantity of variants and hence service performance is likely to be low.

Cost causation These cost effects may occur with a delay and a non-linear progression. Reducing the number of variants again may not reduce costs to the same extent. So-called *sunk costs*, such as the acquisition costs for a flexible production facility, still persist after the number of variants has been reduced. In spite of the cost increase caused by variants, traditional cost accounting unfairly privileges variants [Roever 1994]. In traditional cost accounting, overhead costs are apportioned to produced units by amount or weight of the units. Having a high number of variants causes a disproportional increase of overhead costs in many departments (e.g. marketing etc. as explained above). As cost accounting distributes overhead costs proportionally, this leads to a distortion of real cost causation that privileges variants with a small number of produced units.

9.4.5.2 *Reduction of Costs Caused by Variants*

Economical production The necessity to offer customised products is in conflict with the necessity of economical production. Herrmann and Seilheimer propose the following strategies to cope with this problem [Herrmann and Seilheimer 2000]:

- *Upgrading products by standard integration of formerly supplementary features*: Reducing complexity, which is caused by supplementary features, decreases production costs. The achieved cost reduction of integrating supplementary features into the platform might be high enough to offer them without an increase of prices.

- *Modular structure*: A modular structure allows for a high diversity of variants under the condition of a low increase of complexity (e.g. software with a base module and additional modules). If customer benefit is affected by variation, modularisation should be handled with caution. Variants with a high degree of modularisation tend to appear too similar to customers. In the software industry where customer benefit by variation used to be rare, modular structures are very common.

---

[32] One product displaces another product of the same company in the market.

- *Platforms*: The usage of platforms and non-variable parts lowers the diversity of parts and the production complexity. Each product includes the functions of the platform plus the functions of its variable components. The suitability of a platform concept is determined by the underlying product structure.

For product line engineering, we use platforms to produce variants based on planned reuse, but also managed variability to improve the suitability of the platform for mass customisation at reasonable cost. We deal with these aspects throughout the book.

Platform and managed variability

9.5 Extension of the Product Portfolio

Adding new products to the product portfolio allows the company to close strategic gaps within the product portfolio. Such gaps emerge if all or most existing products are in the saturation or degeneration stage of the product life cycle [Brockhoff 1999]. To extend the product portfolio, product managers can embark on a product innovation strategy or a product imitation strategy. Both strategies yield a set of product ideas, which has to be assessed and from which one or a few ideas are selected for realisation.

Product ideas

A product can be described by its functional and qualitative features. Product development has to ensure that customer needs are realised by the product features. There are different criteria for selecting an appropriate bundle of features. In this section, we focus on customer satisfaction, which is the main criterion of the classification scheme by Kano [Kano 1984]. In addition, we briefly deal with quality function deployment (QFD) and target costing, which incorporate other criteria such as product differentiation and costs.

Product definition

9.5.1 Product Innovation

A company that follows a product innovation strategy may for example want to appear as a pioneer in the market and establish a new brand. A major challenge for product innovation is to identify the correct innovation fields faster than competitors and to accommodate customer needs better and in a more economical way. Within the technical domain, the relevance of product innovation is enforced by the following developments:

Challenges of the innovation strategy

- The decreasing length of product life cycles.

- The decreasing length of technology life cycles.

- The increasing payoff time.

- The increasing occurrence of price erosion originating from the market to keep older product generations attractive compared to younger generations.

- The increasing importance of the utilisation frequency for market success (e.g. mobile phones).

Active and passive generation of ideas

The central topic with regard to product innovation is the generation of new product ideas and concepts. The company can either follow a passive identification strategy or perform an active search.

9.5.1.1 Passive Identification

Inexpensive, but limited effectiveness

Passive identification is based on the assumption that even without carrying out a systematic, goal-oriented search, sufficient product ideas are available from the company itself or its environment. The company just has to support the submission and collection of product ideas by suitable information and communication systems. On the one hand this procedure is relatively inexpensive. On the other hand, the amount and the degree of recentness of the obtained product ideas are rather limited. Thus, this procedure is only recommendable for slight strategic gaps in the product portfolio.

9.5.1.2 Active Search

Technology push and demand pull

The active search for new product ideas my be driven either by technology push or by demand pull [Pepels 2003]:

- *Technology push*: Refers to the active search for application and commercialisation possibilities of available technological knowledge.

- *Demand pull*: Describes the identification of a demand potential for a problem solution that has not yet been realised. Proper technologies are searched for in order to meet the identified demand potential.

Success of demand pull

Demand pull yields successful product ideas more frequently, whereas product ideas initiated by technology push bear a higher degree of recentness. However, the distinction between technology push and demand pull is sometimes criticised as it is difficult to distinguish for a new product idea whether it originates from technology push or demand pull [Brockhoff 1999].

Restriction of the search area

Observations indicate that an unrestricted search for new ideas is rarely effective [Brockhoff 1999]. The following topics may be used for an initial restriction of the search area:

- Unexpected successes and failures

- Demographic trends

- Shifts of opinion and attitude

- Changes of market and branch structure

- Dialogues at trade fares

- Evaluation of field service reports

- Encouragement of employee inventions

- Cooperation with a lead user

For further reading on product innovation, see e.g. [Cooper 2001].

9.5.2 Product Imitation

The term *product imitation* refers to the development of products that are similar to already existing products (with respect to possible uses). The imitation is usually stimulated by a successful product innovation of another company. Overcoming market entrance barriers such as patents, customer habits, obstructed distribution channels, and dominant competitors is the prerequisite of a successful product imitation. Moreover, the incentives of development departments often aim at the creation of product innovations. Especially in technically sophisticated sectors, it is therefore difficult to embark on an imitation strategy and not to drift into a (more risky) innovation of existing product ideas [Schewe 2000]. Companies that embark on an imitation strategy must possess the following capabilities:

Challenges of the imitation strategy

- *Analysis*: Successful product innovations have to be identified and the concerned market entrance barriers have to be assessed. The products of competitors have to be analysed thoroughly. Their special strengths and weaknesses have to be understood [Cooper 2001].

Required key capabilities

- *Technology*: In order to achieve a maintainable time to market and a high product quality at the same time, a high technological potential is required. The imitation is in competition with the products of the technologically more experienced innovator.

- *Marketing*: Customers and distribution channels have to be persuaded to switch to the new product.

- *Production*: Since the imitator enters the market in one of the later stages of the product life cycle, there is less time for expanding the company's production capacities according to the rapidly increasing demand.

9.5.3 Assessment of Product Ideas

Once product ideas have been identified (e.g. by innovation or imitation), product management has to assess the ideas and come to a decision about which products will be actually developed. This strategic decision requires at

Preliminary stage of product definition

least some knowledge about the intended features of the products. Hence, it is a preliminary stage of product definition (the product definition activity is outlined in Section 9.3). However, product definition employs more sophisticated techniques and is performed to elaborate the product ideas that have been chosen for development. Examples of such techniques are discussed in the subsequent subsections. The assessment of product ideas can be accomplished by the following steps:

Initial assessment

1. *Coarse screening*: All product ideas are initially tested for whether they fulfil certain knock-out criteria. The knock-out criteria are usually available in the form of yes or no questions that filter out a bigger part of the product ideas.

Detailed assessment

2. *Fine screening*: The objective of the fine screening is to evaluate to what extent the resources that are required for the realisation of the product idea are existent in the company. Scoring models are predominantly used for this purpose. Table 9-1 shows an example of such a scoring model. In this scoring model, each product idea is rated with the same set of resource-potential criteria (first column on the left side). The resource potential is rated with zero points if it is not usable or highly insufficient for the realisation of the product idea, whereas ten points mean that it is usable and completely sufficient. The multiplication of each rating with its relative weight and summation yield the final score. One point of criticism is that scoring models are a methodically naïve approach. Hence, the results of scoring models should not be used blindly. They are rather reference points among other information. Their advantage is the enforcement of a systematic procedure.

Product concept

3. *Concept trial*: The product concept is explained verbally, in writing, with images, or by a prototype to potential customers in order to examine whether the product concept is understandable and plausible. The goal of this step is to determine how important the product features are to potential customers.

Predicted cost and sales volumes

4. *Profitability analysis*: Product ideas that have passed the concept trial undergo a profitability analysis. In this context the initial purchases and repurchases are based on the forecast of the sales volumes as well as the costs for the individual stages of the product life cycle. The final decision on the realisation of the product idea is made by means of decision models (e.g. investing model) [Erichson 2000].

Table 9-1: Example of a scoring model used in fine screening

Resource Potential	Relative Weight (A)	Application for Product Idea (B)											Criteria Value (A*B)
		0	1	2	3	4	5	6	7	8	9	10	
Company Image	0.05					X							0.2
Financial Resources	0.2									X			1.6
Marketing Know-How	0.2								X				1.4
Production Capacities	0.1										X		0.9
Production Process	0.15									X			1.2
R&D Know-How	0.15								X				1.05
Staff Qualification	0.1					X							0.5
Sales Force	0.05							X					0.3
Total	1												7.15

9.5.4 Product Definition with the Kano Scheme

The Kano method [Kano 1984; Kano et al. 1996; Sauerwein 2000] allows choosing a set of product features that yield high customer satisfaction. The key element of this method is the classification scheme for customer requirements illustrated in Fig. 9-6. The four categories of the Kano classification scheme are characterised as follows:

Requirements categories

- *Basic requirements*: Absence of these requirements leads to high customer dissatisfaction, whereas their presence or further enhancement does not contribute to customer satisfaction. For example, in the home automation domain, high reliability is a basic requirement. If the home automation system fails several times a day, this causes strong customer dissatisfaction.

High dissatisfaction if absent

- *Satisfiers*: Customer satisfaction is proportional to the degree of implementation of these requirements. In the home automation domain, lighting, door, and window control are examples of satisfiers.

Proportional increase of satisfaction

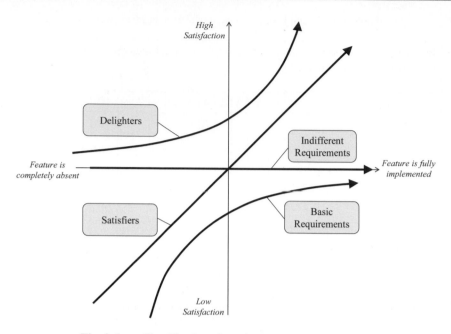

Fig. 9-6:   Classification of requirements according to Kano

Strong positive effect
- *Delighters*: Customer satisfaction levels off if these requirements are not realised. But if implemented, delighters have a strong, positive effect on customer satisfaction. This category mainly includes requirements whose implementations were neither expected nor claimed by customers, possibly because they thought them to be technically impossible. Customers are often willing to pay high prices for the implementation of delighters. In the home automation domain, audio and video control are examples of delighters.

No effect on satisfaction
- *Indifferent requirements*: The implementation or absence of these requirements has no effect on customer satisfaction. The database to be used in a home automation system is an example of an indifferent requirement as long as the database does not affect other requirements.

Five-step procedure
The definition of a product using the classification scheme consists of the following five steps:

1. Identify the customer requirements
2. Construct a questionnaire
3. Perform a survey
4. Analyse and interpret the collected data
5. Select the product features

The following subsections explain each of the five steps in more detail.

9.5.4.1 Identifying Requirements

First, those features that are crucial for product success have to be deter- *Interview*
mined. Customer requirements may be elicited for example by qualitative *topics*
interviews that cover the following four topics:

- What does the interviewee associate with the processes of buying and using this product?
- Which problems, difficulties, annoyances, and complaints exist in the context of the buying process and the usage?
- Which criteria does the customer take into consideration when choosing the product?
- What would the customer like to change? Which new product features could fulfil customer expectations even better?

According to empirical studies, 90 to 95% of the relevant customer require- *Empirical*
ments can be identified with approximately 20 to 30 interviews ([Griffin and *results*
Hauser 1993], quoted in [Herrmann 1998]). The elicited customer requirements correspond to one or more product features that can also be identified
by this procedure. For further details, see for example [Condon 2002].

9.5.4.2 Constructing the Questionnaire

Having identified the relevant requirements to be rated in the survey, market *Functional and*
researchers construct a questionnaire consisting of a functional and a dys- *dysfunctional*
functional question for each requirement. *questions*

> **Example 9-1:** *Functional and Dysfunctional Questions in the Home Automation Domain*
>
> For the feature "roller shade control" the functional and the dysfunctional questions can be formulated as follows:
>
> - *Functional question*: Suppose that your home automation system could open and close roller shades automatically, what would you think about that?
> - *Dysfunctional question*: Suppose that your home automation system would not be able to open and close roller shades automatically, what would you think about that?

The interviewee has five possible answers for each functional and dysfunc- *Five possible*
tional question (like, expected, don't care, can live with it, and dislike). *answers*
Answering both questions yields a location in Table 9-2.

Table 9-2: First table for data interpretation

		Dysfunctional Question				
		Like	Expected	Don't care	Can live with it	Dislike
Functional Question	Like	?	3	3	3	2
	Expected	5	4	4	4	1
	Don't care	5	4	4	4	1
	Can live with it	5	4	4	4	1
	Dislike	5	5	5	5	?

Relation to the categories The numbers in the table are used for interpreting the data. They refer to the following categories:

1. Basic requirements
2. Satisfiers
3. Delighters
4. Indifferent requirements
5. Undesired requirements

Classification not stable No requirement should fall into the "?"-category (Table 9-2). Otherwise it must be checked whether the customer misunderstood one of the questions. One problem with the classification scheme is that the classification is not stable. If requirements for a product are defined which is going to be launched a couple of years later, forecasting the proper category-assignment is difficult.

9.5.4.3   Arranging the Survey

Oral interviews For data collection, written as well as oral interviews are possible. The standardised oral interview is recommended due to its high rate of return and the possibility to intervene in the case of comprehension problems.

9.5.4.4 *Analysing and Interpreting the Data*

The collected data is analysed by determining the distribution of customer ratings over requirements classes for each requirement. The result of this analysis is a table like the one presented in Table 9-3.

Distribution of customer ratings

Table 9-3: Second table for data interpretation (adapted from [Herrmann 1998])

		Frequency of Occurrence of the Individual Requirements Classes						Total in %	Category
		1	2	3	4	5	?		
Customer Requirements	Heating Control	(51.3)	31.3	6	8.5	1.4	1.5	100	1
	Roller Shade Control	28.5	(47.1)	8.4	13.6	1.4	1.0	100	2
	Audio & Video	3.3	19.6	(66.8)	8.1	0.7	1.5	100	3
	...	...	...	...	...	...	...	...	...

A strong statistical spread of category assignments for one requirement is an indication that the interviewed customer group is not homogeneous. Technically versed users may for example rate requirements as basic, which are, however, satisfiers for technical laypersons. It may be sensible to offer product variants in order to address multiple customer groups.

Interpretation of analysis results

If even after market segmentation, requirements cannot be assigned to the above-mentioned categories unambiguously, the following rule is applied regarding the categories introduced above: 1>2>3>4.[33] If more than one category is eligible, a worst-case assumption is made with respect to the effect of the requirement being absent. For example, if the ratings are spread between basic requirement (category 1) and delighter (category 3) the requirement is assigned to the former category as the absence of a basic requirement would have strong negative effect.

Assignment rules

9.5.4.5 *Selecting Product Features*

Often it is not possible to satisfy all requirements in a single product. This may be due to technical restrictions, or it may aim at keeping development costs and time to market low. Thus a decision has to be made on which requirements should be realised by product features. To avoid low customer

Basic requirements, satisfiers, delighters

---

[33] A>B means: if the collected answers are distributed between categories A and B the requirement is assigned to category A.

satisfaction, all basic requirements and, after that, all satisfiers should be implemented at least at a medium level. By additionally including two or three delighters, high-performance products can be developed [Herrmann 1998].

9.5.5 Quality Function Deployment (QFD)

Sales focus, service focus

The QFD method of [Akao 1990] consists of four stages. During these stages customer requirements are elicited and refined to the level of directions for the development or production process. A speciality of the QFD method is the consideration of competitive products. By analysing customer requirements and competitive products, unique selling points for product differentiation can be determined (sales focus). Furthermore, problem areas with a negative effect on the product or company image can be detected (service focus). For further details, see for example [Schröder and Zenz 1996].

9.5.6 Target Costing

Cost and benefit

When deciding which requirements have to be implemented the costs arising have to be considered. The method of target costing allows product component costs only at the level at which the components contribute to customer benefit. For further reading, see for example [Herrmann 1998].

9.6 Management of Existing Products

Expansion and elimination

In this section, we consider the conservation and expansion of the potentials of existing products as well as the elimination of products from the product portfolio.

9.6.1 Conservation and Expansion of Potentials

Identifying potentials

The goal of conserving and expanding product potentials is to keep the product attractive in comparison to competing products and substitutes. Hence, in a first step, the potentials for improving the considered product have to be identified. Clues for improvement may be gained by observing changes regarding usage, customers, competitors, technology, and general conditions (e.g. social, legal). The following measures are examples of possibilities to conserve or extend existing product potentials [Huber and Kopsch 2000; Tomczak et al. 2000]:

- *Increase of the internal efficiency*: This increase is achieved by optimising the development processes, fixing bugs that have been discovered after market introduction, reducing costs, and enhancing quality.

- *Marginal modifications*: This measure aims at a slight improvement of the perceived value of existing products like rejuvenation of the product logo. The modification is made in order to extend the product life cycle.

- *Revitalisation*: Products at a later stage of the product life cycle are slightly modified and offered to the same customer group with the goal to reinitiate the product life cycle. The resource needs of a successful revitalisation are easily underestimated. The reasons why the present products are in the degeneration stage have to be identified and the new product concept has to be communicated to potential customers.

- *Bundling*: Several products are sold together. Benefits expected from bundling are lower costs (e.g. due to a simplification of the range of products), sales increase (e.g. due to decision anomalies of the customer regarding complex product offers), a better solution of customer problems achieved by a slight adjustment of the products, and the construction of market entrance barriers (e.g. the bundling of operating system software with computers).

9.6.2 Product Elimination

In general, products can only be marketed economically during a certain time period and have to be phased out subsequently. Since the future development of market and development conditions cannot be precisely forecast, this is a complex decision. In some cases, there is also an emotional relationship with formerly successful products, especially with those that the company was founded on. Companies tend to offer a multitude of new products without phasing out old ones. Thus products involving loss are carried along and are only phased out during a crisis. In order to counter this bias, processes should be implemented to assure a regular, structured decision about the elimination or continuation of the offered products. In addition to a lack of profitability, legal restraints (e.g. in the sectors of health or environmental protection) may necessitate the elimination of products. Another reason why products are eliminated is the wish to focus the product programme on certain core sectors to avoid growing complexity. For product line engineering, product elimination has to consider the platform. Whenever a product is eliminated it has to be determined if platform assets that are part of this product can be removed from the platform. This reduces platform complexity and the effort for a managed platform evolution. For platform assets, maintenance contracts play a significant role for their evolution and potential removal from the platform – an asset for which maintenance has to be provided must not be removed from the platform, or other assets must be determined to replace the former one so that the maintenance offer can be continued.

Reasons for phasing out products

Phasing-out process

Products can be eliminated immediately by sale or closure and scrapping of the related facilities. In some cases longer phasing-out processes are necessary because of existing contracts, the necessity to stock spare parts, or dependencies with other products of the company [Brockhoff 1999; Herrmann 1998].

9.7   Scoping

Scope of a software product line

Product management activities for product lines are sometimes called *product line scoping*. Kruchten describes the formulation of the scope of a project in the inception phase as "capturing the context and the most important requirements and constraints so that you can derive acceptance criteria for the end product" [Kruchten 2000]. This is similar to the descriptions of product line scoping, for instance, in [Clements and Northrop 2001]. An example of a method that supports product line scoping is PuLSE-Eco [DeBaud and Schmid 1999; Schmid 2002].

Three kinds of scoping

The main goal of scoping methods is to identify the products that will belong to the product line as well as to define their major features. According to [Bosch 2000b] there are at least three different forms of scoping:

- Product portfolio scoping

- Domain scoping

- Asset scoping

Product portfolio scoping aims at defining the products that should be developed as well as their key features. Domain scoping aims at defining the boundaries of a domain and closely corresponds to the classical project scoping. Asset scoping aims at identifying particular components to be developed for reuse.

Commonality and variability

Commonality and variability analysis is a basic part of product line scoping that has been described in many places, e.g. in [Ardis and Weiss 1997] and [Coplien et al. 1998] where it is traced back to Dijkstra [Dijkstra 1972] and Parnas [Parnas 1976], to domain engineering in IBM's 360 mainframe series, and to even earlier sources from general engineering. Slightly different definitions of the terms commonality and variability can be found in the product line scoping literature (see Section 4.3 for our definition commonality and variability). Weiss defines commonality as "a list of assumptions that are true for all family members" [Weiss 1998], which is also compliant with our usage of the word. Weiss describes variability through "variabilities define how family members may vary" and "variabilities define the scope of the family by predicting what decisions about family members are likely to change over the lifetime of the family". Whereas this implies only feature variability, we consider variability in all kinds of artefacts in this book. Coplien et al. define commonality as "an assumption held uniformly across a given set of objects" and variability as "the variations among those products" [Coplien et al. 1998], where "those" refers to the products of the product line.

The product line scoping literature focuses on product definition and on certain aspects of product portfolio management. Other major activities of product management such as market and product strategy definition, product definition, product support, market introduction, market observation, and product controlling (Section 9.3) are mostly neglected in the scoping literature.[34]

Focus on product definition and portfolio management

9.8 Differences from Single-System Engineering

In software product line engineering, the fundamentals of product management described in this chapter also apply. Yet, as multiple applications are derived from the same platform, the applications are interrelated by engineering interdependence (see Section 9.4.4 for a description of product interdependences). The generation of variants is a major strength of product line engineering (Section 9.4.5 describes the economic impact of product variants). Hence, a company applying product line engineering can manage the additional complexity more easily and thus reap the benefits of product variants.

Product variants

In portfolio analysis, the product line might be regarded as a single product type in the product portfolio but is typically divided into multiple product types as illustrated in Example 9-2.

Portfolio analysis

Example 9-2: *Product Portfolio for a Home Automation Product Line*

The home automation product line comprises different product types, which can be used in combination:

- Home security system
- Lighting control system
- Remote access extensions
- Wireless control extensions
- etc.

---

[34] Clements and Northrop mention that the "market analysis" practices drive the definition of the scope of a software product line but do not provide details [Clements and Northrop 2001].

9.8.1 Strategic Role of the Platform

Platform and application life cycles

Product management has to consider the life cycle of the platform as well as the life cycles of individual applications. The life cycle of the platform is longer than the life cycles of individual applications. The development and market introduction of the platform require a large amount of resources. Consequently the platform has a considerable strategic relevance for the company.

Flexibility of the platform

- *Preparation for future products*: Before new product types can be integrated into the product portfolio, product managers have to make sure that the new product can be efficiently developed within the product line. In order not to restrict future product ideas too much, the platform must be flexible enough to accomplish the demands of future applications.

New features

- *Expansion*: The expansion of product potentials can be performed in an economical manner for all products by implementing new features in the platform. To minimise risk, new features can first be realised in a lead product and then made available in the platform.

Avoiding early elimination

- *Elimination*: The elimination of a product line is a major step, which is mostly done with the intention to substitute a product line by another product line. Having to eliminate a product line too early (e.g. due to insufficient demand) must be prevented by carrying out soundings of market needs, e.g. by pilot applications.

Platform offered in the market

- *Platforms as products*: Platforms may even become products themselves. In this case customers are enabled to derive applications from the platform and offer them to the market or use them as an integral part of their own products.

9.8.2 Product Definition

Identification of variability

In product definition, product managers are concerned with the definition of the major common and variable features of the product line, i.e. the features of multiple applications. Variability has to be taken into account in each step of product definition. For the application of the Kano classification, this means for example:

- The designers of the questionnaire used for customer interviews should put a strong emphasis on identifying variability in customer needs.

- A high statistical spread in customer ratings for a certain customer requirement indicates the necessity to introduce variability in product features.

- The basic requirements should be implemented as common domain artefacts since basic requirements have to be met by each application.

- Delighters need not be part of the domain artefacts, e.g. if they are based on a fast-changing technology.

We provide more details of applying the Kano classification scheme in software product line engineering in Chapter 10.

9.8.3 Output

Product management has to provide a product roadmap that is used by domain engineering to create a requirements specification for the product line. The product roadmap contains the features identified by the product definition activity and a schedule for market introduction. The features in the roadmap comprise common as well as variable features. The product roadmap is a plan for the future development of the product portfolio. Hence, it is the result of strategic planning.

Roadmap

Domain engineers need the roadmap to build reusable domain artefacts. Application engineers need the roadmap to select the appropriate domain artefacts, configure specific applications, and develop application-specific artefacts.

Domain and application engineering

In addition to the roadmap, product management provides a list of previous products of the organisation that may be reused for the product line. This list contains also partial products, components, and other assets. The decisions about what earlier assets may be reused for the domain artefacts of the software product line and what features should be realised by the product line are mostly made either by product managers or by a group that encompasses product managers, platform managers, and architects.

Reuse of existing assets

9.9 Summary

The goal of product management is to make a major contribution to entrepreneurial success by integrating the development, production, and marketing of products that meet customer needs. Based on the global and very abstract company goals, strategic decisions have to be made.

Enforcement of company goals

The portfolio management technique enables well-founded decision making about the existing and planned products of a company or business unit. In their decisions, product managers have to consider thoroughly the various interdependences between products, such as the usage interdependence which exists between complementary products. Many companies are faced with stagnating or even shrinking markets. In order to win market share, companies have to accommodate individual customer wishes by product

Portfolio management

variants. Yet, variants make up a major challenge for various divisions of the company, such as research and development or marketing.

Kano classification   A product can be defined as a bundle of features. The Kano method enables the optimisation of the choice of features with respect to customer satisfaction. It classifies customer requirements into basic requirements, satisfiers, delighters, and indifferent requirements. In software product line engineering the Kano classification can help in identifying common and variable features.

Scoping   In software product line engineering, product management activities, in particular, product definition and certain aspects of portfolio management, are subsumed under the term product line scoping. Commonality and variability analysis is a fundamental technique used in product line scoping.

Stan Bühne
Klaus Pohl

10

Domain Requirements Engineering

In this chapter you will learn:

- o *The challenges of domain requirements engineering.*
- o *About the interrelations between the domain requirements engineering sub-process and the product management, domain design, and application requirements engineering sub-processes.*
- o *How to identify common and variable product line requirements.*
- o *How to document the identified commonalities and the variability in the various requirements artefacts using the orthogonal variability model.*

In addition, a comprehensive example illustrates the definition of variability in requirements artefacts for a software product line.

10.1   Introduction

Goals of domain requirements engineering

The main goals of domain requirements engineering are the development of common and variable domain requirements and their precise documentation. Domain requirements engineering is a continuous process of proactively defining the requirements for all foreseeable applications to be developed in the software product line. A particular issue for domain requirements engineering is to identify and explicitly document the external variability. The sub-processes and artefacts closely related to the domain requirements engineering sub-process are highlighted in Fig. 10-1.

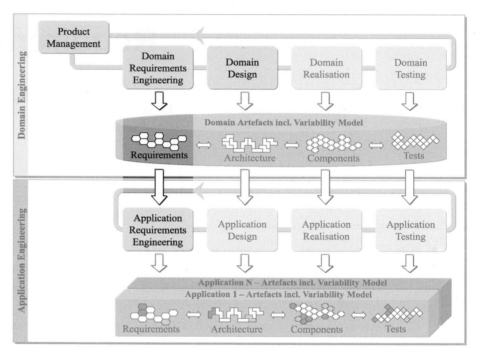

Fig. 10-1:   Sub-processes and artefacts related to domain requirements engineering

Related sub-processes

Domain requirements engineering has to adhere to the specification of the product line's major features provided by product management. Based on these features, it creates detailed common and variable requirements sufficient to guide domain design (and thereby also realisation as well as testing). In addition, domain requirements engineering provides the input for the application requirements engineering sub-process, which is concerned with creating application-specific requirements artefacts.

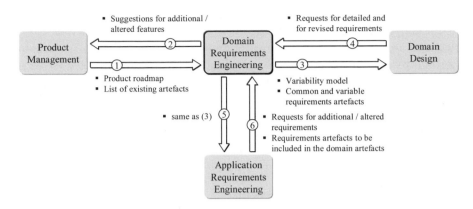

Fig. 10-2: Information flows between domain requirements engineering and other sub-processes

In the remainder of this section, we elaborate on the interrelations between the sub-processes highlighted in Fig. 10-1. The basic information flows between these sub-processes are depicted in Fig. 10-2.

Artefact flows

10.1.1 Interrelation with Product Management

The key input for the domain requirements engineering process is the product roadmap from product management (first bullet ① in Fig. 10-2). This roadmap includes an initial set of intended products for the product line as well as their intended commonalities and variability. It further defines the product line with respect to the envisaged applications and a schedule for bringing out marketable products. In addition, product management identifies existing artefacts that have been developed in previous projects and which should be considered when defining the domain requirements (second bullet of ① in Fig. 10-2).

Product roadmap, existing products

The domain requirements engineering sub-process provides suggestions on additional and altered features as well as feature refinements (② in Fig. 10-2) to product management, based on the analysis of existing products, stakeholder needs, laws, constraints, and other requirement sources.

Additional/altered features

10.1.2 Interrelation with Domain Design

The output of domain requirements engineering provided to domain design encompasses all defined domain requirements including commonality and variability as well as the definition of the product line variability in the orthogonal variability model (③ in Fig. 10-2). The variability model defines at least the external variability but may also specify part of the internal variability of the product line.

Requirements and variability

Highly interactive   The interrelation between domain requirements engineering and domain
process   design can be characterised by the *twin peaks model* of [Nuseibeh 2001]
                       presented in Fig. 10-3. The figure expresses the interrelation by a spiral
                       alternating between requirements (problem view) and architecture (solution
                       view) that at the same time progresses from coarse to detailed. While the
                       reference architecture increasingly takes shape, the need for more detailed
                       requirements arises as well. In addition, existing requirements may for
                       example turn out as too ambitious from the viewpoint of domain design,
                       which leads to change requests (④ in Fig. 10-2).

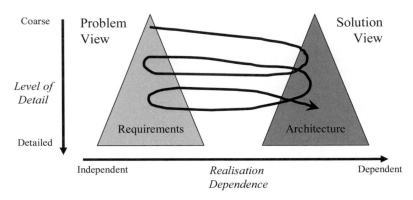

Fig. 10-3:   The twin peaks model describes the interrelation of requirements and architecture
                 (adapted from [Nuseibeh 2001])

10.1.3 Interrelation with Application Requirements Engineering

Reusable   Domain requirements engineering provides the predefined common and
requirements   variable requirements artefacts as well as the orthogonal variability model to
                 application requirements engineering (⑤ in Fig. 10-2). Consequently the
                 orthogonal variability model supports the communication of the product line
                 variability and thus the reuse of domain requirements artefacts. We elaborate
                 on the reuse of domain requirements artefacts in Chapter 15.

Future domain Application requirements engineering provides feedback to domain require-
requirements   ments engineering in terms of requests for additional and altered require-
                 ments (first bullet of ⑥ in Fig. 10-2) as well as application requirements
                 artefacts which may be incorporated in the domain artefacts (second bullet of
                 ⑥ in Fig. 10-2). This feedback may lead to an adaptation of the domain arte-
                 facts and thus to an evolution of the software product line. The decision on
                 whether the feedback from application engineering is incorporated in the
                 domain artefacts is made by product managers and other stakeholders who
                 decide on the evolution of the product line. However, the feedback can also
                 lead to an application-specific adaptation of the product line's capabilities,
                 i.e. it can lead to an application-specific change. The integration of applica-

tion-specific artefacts in the domain artefacts means that domain requirements engineers, domain architects, etc., must reengineer the application
artefacts and prepare them for reuse.

10.2 Traditional Requirements Engineering Activities

Before we elaborate on the details of requirements engineering for software
product lines, we give a brief overview of the major requirements engineering activities in single-system engineering [Pohl 1996; Pohl 1997].

- *Elicitation*: The goal of requirements elicitation is to understand the
  users' needs and constraints for the system. The elicitation process uncovers needs, requirements, and constraints from different sources, such
  as stakeholders (e.g. customers or domain experts), user documentation,
  legislation, and standards. Elicitation also involves the development of
  new and innovative requirements for the intended product (see e.g.
  [Carroll 1995; Gougen and Linde 1993; Hay and v. Halle 2002; Pohl
  1997; Weinberg 1988]).

  User needs, require-ments, constraints

- *Documentation*: The goal of the requirements documentation activity is
  the well-structured recording of the elicited requirements with all necessary information. The final requirements specification is the foundation
  for later development phases or changes in the product [Alexander and
  Stevens 2003; Kovitz 1999]. To address different stakeholders such as
  customers and designers, it is often necessary to document requirements
  using different representation formats (see e.g. [Pohl 1994]).

  Requirements specification

- *Negotiation*: The goal of requirements negotiation is to achieve a sufficient consensus among different stakeholders with respect to elicited
  and/or documented requirements. The requirements specification is
  more stable during further development phases, if sufficient agreement
  is obtained. Without an agreement on the requirements, the project is
  likely to fail, for instance by running out of time (see e.g. [Wiegers
  1999]).

  Agreement about requirements

- *Validation and verification*: The goal of requirements validation/veri-
  fication is to prove that the system requirements are clear, complete,
  correct, and understandable. Validation ensures that the right requirements are documented. Verification ensures that the documented requirements are correctly defined (see e.g. [Thayer and Dorfman 1997;
  Sommerville and Sawyer 1997]).

  Quality assurance

- *Management*: The goal of requirements management is to maintain the
  requirements continuously throughout the development and system life
  cycle and thus to ensure that a consistent and up-to-date requirements

  Continuous maintenance

specification is available at all times. This is supported by recording trace information between requirements, from requirements to their sources, and from requirements to their realisation. It is the responsibility of requirements management to enforce adherence to the defined requirements engineering process. An up-to-date requirements specification is a prerequisite for later releases, failure fixes, and requirements reuse (see e.g. [Thayer and Dorfman 1997; Hull et al. 2002]).

The goals of the requirements engineering process can be characterised based on the three dimensions of requirements engineering [Pohl 1994]:

Understanding of system requirements
- *Specification*: This dimension characterises the achieved level of understanding about the requirements for the system under consideration. Initially, the understanding is usually weak. The goal is to achieve as complete an understanding as possible of the system requirements.

Representation of requirements
- *Representation*: This dimension deals with different kinds of representations used to document requirements. At the beginning of the requirements engineering process, typically informal representations such as sketches or natural language statements are used. The goal is to arrive at a precise requirements specification documented using as formal a requirements modelling language as possible.

Agreement about requirements
- *Agreement*: This dimension deals with the reconciliation of conflicting opinions. Typically, at the beginning of the requirements engineering process, the individual stakeholders (managers, users, domain experts, etc.) have their own view of the goals and requirements of the system. The agreement dimension characterises the gradual integration of the different views by uncovering and negotiating conflicts. The goal is to arrive at a sufficient agreement on the requirements for the system.

10.3   Challenges of Domain Requirements Engineering

Domain requirements engineering has to take into account the variability of the product line. This implies additional tasks for the requirements engineer. In this section we present the tasks that are unique to requirements engineering in software product lines.

10.3.1 Specific Activities

Precise definition of variability
The explicit documentation of the proper common and variable requirements is essential for enabling the planned reuse of requirements in application engineering. The required variability has to be documented in the orthogonal variability model in order enable its communication to other sub-processes,

such as domain design or domain testing. In this chapter, we elaborate on the three following activities:

- *Commonality analysis*: The goal of commonality analysis is to identify which requirements are common to all applications of the software product line (Section 10.6).

  Common requirements

- *Variability analysis*: The goal of variability analysis is to identify which requirements differ among the applications, and to determine the differences precisely (Section 10.7).

  Variable requirements

- *Variability modelling*: This activity is concerned with modelling variation points, variants, and their relationships. It is closely related to modelling variable requirements (Section 10.8).

  Variation points and variants

The three activities are closely related to each other. This holds in particular for the commonality and variability analysis (for additional reading on commonality and variability analysis, see e.g. [Weiss and Lai 1999]).

Commonality and variability analysis

10.3.2 Variability in Different Views

In addition to the identification and modelling of variability, domain requirements engineering has to establish consistency across the different requirements artefacts and their documentations. The incorporation of different views facilitates the communication of the commonality and variability of the product line to different stakeholders. Examples of requirements artefacts are goals, features, scenarios, use cases, data models, behavioural models, functional models, and textual requirements (see Chapter 5 for a more detailed elaboration on the different requirements artefacts).

Consistent requirements artefacts

10.4   Overview of Major Steps

The requirements artefacts developed in domain requirements engineering encompass common and variable parts. The representation formats typically used for documenting common as well as variable requirements are explained in Chapter 5. In the following, we briefly characterise the basic steps for defining common and variable requirements.

10.4.1 Defining Common Requirements

Before any requirements can be defined as a commonality of the product line, a commonality analysis has to be performed in order to determine which requirements are actually common to all applications; see Section 10.6. Defining common requirements consists of two basic steps:

Commonality analysis first

Basic
steps

1. Identify a set of common requirements.
2. Document the common requirements in detail in a representation format (features, use cases, etc.) that is suitable for the considered view.

Iteration of
the steps

The steps are performed iteratively in the course of detailing and revising the domain requirements. Moreover, common and variable requirements are closely related and are therefore typically modelled together within the same artefacts.

There are at least two other important issues that have to be considered in defining common requirements:

High
quality

- Common requirements are the basis for all product line applications. The work of different stakeholders depends on the quality of these requirements. Typically, much effort has to be put into keeping the requirements artefacts up to date, consistent across different views (Section 10.3.2), and to ensure a high quality (e.g. comprehensibility). Reviews help to ensure a high quality for common requirements.

Change of
commonality and
variability over time

- Common requirements may change to variable requirements. For example, the evolution of the product line can cause a common requirement to become variable as a consequence of introducing new variability. Documenting the rationales and assumptions on why a requirement is common helps to understand why a requirement is common and thus avoid unnecessary changes of common requirements into variable requirements. It thus prevents ending up with a fully variable, yet overly complex requirements specification.

10.4.2 Defining Variable Requirements

Modelling
variability

Variable requirements are identified during variability analysis. Defining variable requirements involves modelling the variability of the product line in the variability model and documenting variable requirements in a suitable notation. Figure 10-4 illustrates the basic steps for modelling variable requirements. The four steps are:

Basic
steps

1. Identify an initial set of variable requirements.
2. Develop the orthogonal variability model.
3. Document the requirements in detail in a suitable notation.
4. Relate each variable elements of the developed requirements artefact (e.g. use cases, scenarios, or classes) to the corresponding variants in the orthogonal variability model.

Steps 3 and 4 are repeated until all required views have been considered.

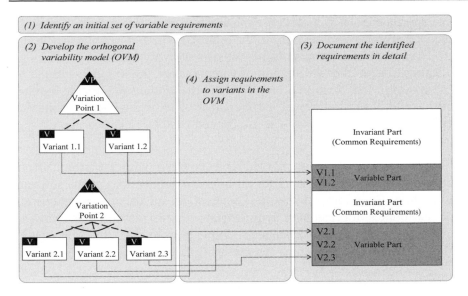

Fig. 10-4: Steps for modelling variable requirements

10.5 Requirements Sources

Domain requirements engineering incorporates different *requirements sources* such as stakeholders, existing products, failure reports, or competitors' products to define the common and variable requirements for the product line. These sources are used to detail the features defined by product management.

Stakeholders, existing products, etc.

To identify the domain requirements and their variability, domain requirements engineers can often make use of existing applications (see e.g. [Fantechi et al. 2003]). The development of a software product line rarely starts from scratch as product line engineering requires sophisticated domain experience (Section 1.4). Consequently different applications already exist that serve the markets and customer groups envisaged by the product line. These existing applications may be own applications or competitors' applications. When performing the commonality and variability analysis as explained in the following sections, requirements engineers should use, among other requirements sources, the existing applications in their domain.

Use of existing applications

10.6 Commonality Analysis

Along with the elicitation of requirements for the intended software product line applications, the commonality of the applications has to be defined.

As much commonality *as possible*

It is important to have as much commonality as possible, and thereby to reduce the amount of variability to the required minimum [Ardis and Weiss 1997]. Common requirements form the basis of every software product line application. The higher the amount of commonality, the less effort has to be spent in design for flexibility. Nevertheless, the amount of variable requirements should at least allow the development of individual applications that satisfy the goals and needs of the envisioned customers and/or market segments.

Exploration of *applications*

The identification of common requirements starts with the simultaneous exploration of the requirements for all foreseen applications of the software product line. Requirements that are identical for all these applications are good candidates for common requirements. There are different ways of identifying common requirements. A simple way to perform commonality analysis is to use an application–requirements matrix.

10.6.1 Application–Requirements Matrix

Contents of *the matrix*

The application–requirements matrix (see Table 10-1 for an example) gives an approximation of the commonality (and also of the variability) for a given set of software product line application requirements. The application–requirements matrix details the product roadmap, which typically defines common and variable features at a higher level of abstraction. The left column of the matrix lists the requirements of the considered applications. The applications themselves are listed in the top row. In the body of the matrix it is marked for which application a certain requirement is mandatory.

Table 10-1:   Structure of an application–requirements matrix for four applications

Application Requirements	App. 1	App. 2	App. 3	App. 4
R1	mandatory	mandatory	mandatory	mandatory
R2	-	-	mandatory	mandatory
R3	-	mandatory	-	-
…	…	…	…	…

In the application–requirements matrix presented in Table 10-1 the requirement 'R1' is mandatory for all applications and is thus a candidate to be defined as a common product line requirement. Requirement 'R2' is not available in 'App. 1' and 'App. 2'. Hence, it is not identified as a common requirement for the product line. The same holds for requirement 'R3'.

10.6.2 Priority-Based Analysis

A more sophisticated analysis of commonality can be obtained by applying the priority-based analysis scheme. Priority-based commonality analysis is based on set of requirements in which each requirement is rated by different stakeholders according to a certain scheme such as the classification proposed by Kano [Kano et al. 1996] (see Chapter 9 for more details on the Kano classification).

Prioritised requirements

Common requirements encompass at least the set of all *basic requirements* that every application for the envisioned domain must fulfil. Example 10-1 describes such a basic requirement.

Basic requirements

Another indicator for commonality is a requirement having a *high priority* for a large group of customers, and the other customers do not reject it. This case is illustrated in Example 10-2.

High-priority requirements

Furthermore, it is useful to define all requirements that might be of interest to many customers in the future as common requirements. We refer to this kind of requirements as *strategic commonalities*. Strategic commonalities are foreseeable basic needs that will appear in the product line's lifetime, and thus should be implemented as commonalities to attain a stable set of common artefacts. Such kinds of commonalities may be important to differentiate from competitors' products (Example 10-3).

Strategic commonality

Example 10-1: *Heating Control as a Basic Requirement*

The Kano classification reveals that the requirement "The home automation system shall be able to control the heating of the home" is a basic requirement. Hence, it is a good candidate to be included into the set of common requirements.

Example 10-2: *Access Control as a High-Priority Requirement*

The requirement "The home automation system shall be able to control access to the home" is rated with a high priority by most customers. There are no customers who rate this requirement negatively. Thus it is likely to be accepted as a common requirement.

Example 10-3: *Wireless Communication as a Strategic Commonality*

The requirement "The home automation system shall communicate via a wireless network" is going to become a basic need in the near future. Hence, it is defined as a commonality of the product line.

10.6.3 Checklist-Based Analysis

Requirements
categories

A more general approach than the priority-based identification of common requirements is the use of checklists. Each item on the checklist represents a category of requirements that should be considered as candidates for common requirements. The basic needs, high-priority requirements, and strategic commonalities described in Section 10.6.2 are examples of such categories. In addition the following general categories should be considered:

- Requirements that are prescribed by national or international laws and standards.

- Requirements that are prescribed by organisational standards.

- Requirements that only differ marginally.

- Requirements that do not conflict with each other.

- Requirements that are necessary for the technical support, like error handling, maintenance, communication, etc.

10.7 Variability Analysis

Defining variation
points and variants

The goal of variability analysis is to identify requirements variability and to define the variation points and their variants related to these requirements. In software product line engineering, there is no strict need to harmonise different requirements that for example originate from contrasting customer needs or from the necessity to support different legacy systems. Rather, requirements that differ from each other indicate a need to introduce variation points and variants. However, not for every difference a variation point is defined. Whether a variation point should be introduced needs careful consideration by the stakeholders involved, as the variation point may, for instance, have significant influence on the reference architecture. The following example illustrates the introduction of a variation point due to different customer needs:

Example 10-4: *Variability in the Home Security System due to Different Customer Needs*

The different requirements of customers with regard to the security system lead to the introduction of a variation point 'home security by' with the variants 'motion detection' and 'camera surveillance'. Each application of the product line can be customised to provide either motion detection or camera surveillance.

To extract the necessary variability information, the requirements analyst has to examine the requirements for all product line applications. The identification of variability starts with the analysis of high-level requirements. The analysis reveals those requirements that are unique to a subset of the applications and those that have different characteristics in different applications. As a result of variability analysis, variation points and variants are defined.

Examination of high-level requirements

10.7.1 Variability Analysis with the Application–Requirements Matrix

Variability analysis is based on the same techniques as commonality analysis. The application–requirements matrix helps to identify variable requirements. Requirements that are only mandatory for one or a small set of applications are definitively candidates for variable requirements.

Initial set of variable requirements

10.7.2 Priority-Based Variability Analysis

Requirements that have a high priority for some customers but a low priority for other customers are candidates for variable requirements. Example 10-5 illustrates the identification of a requirement with different prioritisations.

Different priorities

Example 10-5: *Variability due to Different Prioritisations*

A study reveals that the requirement "The system shall automatically inform the police in case of intrusion" is rated high by a significant group of customers but is of less importance for another group of customers. Hence, the requirements engineer defines this requirement as a variable requirement of the software product line.

Similarly, requirements that are rated positively by one group of customers but are rated negatively by another group of customers can lead to the introduction of variability.

Conflicting priorities

Example 10-6: *Conflicts in Home Security Requirements*

The requirement "the security system shall be equipped with a video storage system that records all surveillance video data" is appreciated by a significant group of customers. Yet the requirement "The system shall not record personal data" also has a high priority for many customers. Hence, the requirements engineer decides to define video storage as a variable requirement.

In addition, there may be requirements with high ratings, possibly from different customer groups, which cannot be realised within the same application as they are in conflict with each other. This may be due to a real, semantic

Conflicting high-priority requirements

conflict or due to technical incompatibility. This situation is illustrated in Example 10-6.

10.7.3 Checklist-Based Variability Analysis

Candidates for requirements variability

In general each difference in structure, functionality, behaviour, or quality between different applications is a candidate for requirements variability. A checklist helps in identifying requirements variability. Apart from the categories defined in Section 10.7.2, a checklist may contain, for example, the following items:

- Differences in functionality.
- Different quality attributes, e.g. with respect to safety, security, or dependability.
- Different interface requirements, in order to allow the exchange of information with different legacy systems (e.g. legacy heating control).
- Different requirements with respect to the system's user interface.
- Different design constraints, such as different databases, network types, COTS components, or operating systems.

10.8   Defining Requirements Variability

Orthogonal variability model

Defining the variability of domain requirements is a prerequisite for the sufficient understanding of, and the communication about, the variability of a product line. In Chapter 4, we introduce an orthogonal variability model for defining variability in different development artefacts. In Chapter 5, we outline how variability in various requirements artefacts should be documented using the orthogonal variability model.

Defining variability

To define the requirements variability of the indented software product line, the domain requirements engineer has to:

- Carefully define the right set of variation points and variants.
- Determine their dependencies.
- Define together with product managers which part of the product line variability is offered to the customer as external variability.

10.8.1 Variation Points and Variants

Related variability subjects

Initially it is often not clear which variant has to be related to which variation point. The documented requirements often do not state this explicitly. However, by considering the common variability subject of the variants, appropriate variation points can typically be identified. Example 10-7 illustrates this:

> **Example 10-7:** *Finding Correlated Variants*
>
> Application 'App. 1' has the requirement "The front door shall be secured with a keypad." whereas 'App. 2' has the requirement "The system shall provide fingerprint-based authorisation." These requirements refer to the same variability subject, namely the identification mechanism used. Hence, the variation point 'door lock identification mechanism' is defined with the two variants stated above. These variants are associated with the corresponding requirements artefacts.

After the variation point and the initial variants have been defined, additional variants have to be identified. Reasons for introducing additional variants can be the provision of an additional benefit for the customers or the differentiation of the software product line from competitors' products. Especially variants leading to high customer satisfaction should be taken into account in this step (we introduced the term "delighters" for requirements that lead to high customer satisfaction, see Chapter 9). The identification of additional variants can also be performed before the definition of the variation point. However, identifying additional variants after the definition of the variation point is usually better, since the variation point and the variants, which have already been identified, support the identification of additional variants.

Additional variants

10.8.2 Variability Dependencies

The types of the variability dependencies between a variation point and its variants and the defined alternative choices (Section 4.6) determine the permissible combinations of variants for each product line application. For some variants the appropriate variability dependency and/or alternative choice may be clear from the available requirements sources, such as product brochures (Example 10-7). If such information is not available directly, the requirements engineer has to involve the relevant stakeholders to identify the proper variability dependencies and alternative choices.

Mandatory, optional, and alternative choice

Again, by defining the variability dependencies, the requirements engineer should consider the fact that the variability can have a strong influence on the reference architecture. For example, designing a reference architecture which supports a wide range of optional variants that differ significantly in quality may be impossible. Consequently, among other stakeholders, architects should be involved in the definition of variability dependencies. Or, more generally, software architects must be involved in the definition of requirements variability.

Software architects involved in variability definition

> **Example 10-8:** *Identifying the Proper Variability Dependency*
>
> A product brochure for the home security system states that the system is always delivered with the feature "acoustic alarm". In addition, the customer may choose the "police information" feature, which enables the system to inform the police in the case of an attempted burglary. The variability model of the home security product line contains the variation point "alarm activation" with the mandatory variant "acoustic alarm" and the optional variant "police information".

First example application

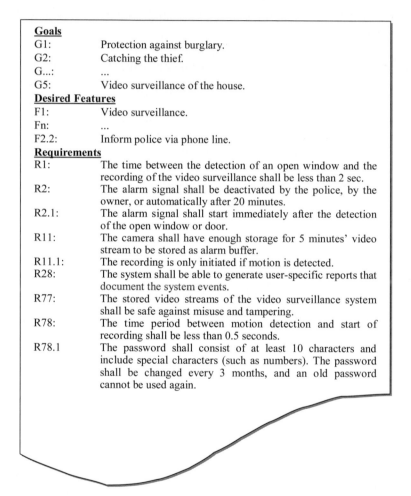

Goals
G1:   Protection against burglary.
G2:   Catching the thief.
G...:   ...
G5:   Video surveillance of the house.

Desired Features
F1:   Video surveillance.
Fn: ...
F2.2:   Inform police via phone line.

Requirements
R1:   The time between the detection of an open window and the recording of the video surveillance shall be less than 2 sec.
R2:   The alarm signal shall be deactivated by the police, by the owner, or automatically after 20 minutes.
R2.1:   The alarm signal shall start immediately after the detection of the open window or door.
R11:   The camera shall have enough storage for 5 minutes' video stream to be stored as alarm buffer.
R11.1:   The recording is only initiated if motion is detected.
R28:   The system shall be able to generate user-specific reports that document the system events.
R77:   The stored video streams of the video surveillance system shall be safe against misuse and tampering.
R78:   The time period between motion detection and start of recording shall be less than 0.5 seconds.
R78.1   The password shall consist of at least 10 characters and include special characters (such as numbers). The password shall be changed every 3 months, and an old password cannot be used again.

Fig. 10-5:   Example excerpt of a requirements specification for the first application

10.8.3 Constraint Dependencies

By defining constraint dependencies ("requires" and "excludes", see Section 4.6.5 for the definitions) the domain requirements engineer restricts and/or enforces the binding of variation points during application engineering. The requirements engineer has thus to determine the essential influences among the variants that exist at the requirements level. In other words, the domain requirements engineer must elicit and document the variant to variant, variant to variation point, and variation point to variation point "requires" and "excludes" dependencies stemming from domain requirements artefacts.

Restricting admissible combinations

10.8.4 Adaptation of Product Line Variability Based on Product Management Decisions

The final decisions on the variability in domain requirements artefacts are made by product management. In other words, product management decides:

Final decisions by product management

- If a variation point identified and defined in the domain requirements engineering sub-process should be part of the product line or not, or even if a new variation point should be added.

- If the variants identified and defined in the domain requirements engineering sub-process should be part of the product line or not, or even if a new variant should be added.

- If the variability constraints and dependencies defined in the domain requirement engineering sub-process are correct, or if they have to be adapted and how.

- Whether a variation point is categorised as external product line variability or as internal product line variability.

Domain requirements engineers have to adapt the requirements artefacts affected by changes or adaptations of the variability definitions in the orthogonal variability model made by product management.

Adaptation of requirements artefacts

10.9   Example

In this section, we provide an example of how to identify and document variable requirements for a software product line. We first provide a simple outline of the requirements for the first three foreseeable applications. Subsequently, we demonstrate the major steps performed during commonality analysis, variability analysis, and during the documentation of common and variable requirements artefacts. Figures 10-5 to 10-7 present excerpts of the requirements for each of the three software product line applications.

Three example applications

Second example
application

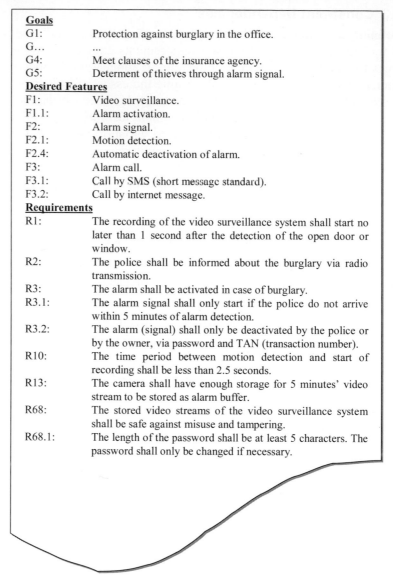

Goals
G1:   Protection against burglary in the office.
G…   …
G4:   Meet clauses of the insurance agency.
G5:   Determent of thieves through alarm signal.
Desired Features
F1:   Video surveillance.
F1.1:   Alarm activation.
F2:   Alarm signal.
F2.1:   Motion detection.
F2.4:   Automatic deactivation of alarm.
F3:   Alarm call.
F3.1:   Call by SMS (short message standard).
F3.2:   Call by internet message.
Requirements
R1:   The recording of the video surveillance system shall start no later than 1 second after the detection of the open door or window.
R2:   The police shall be informed about the burglary via radio transmission.
R3:   The alarm shall be activated in case of burglary.
R3.1:   The alarm signal shall only start if the police do not arrive within 5 minutes of alarm detection.
R3.2:   The alarm (signal) shall only be deactivated by the police or by the owner, via password and TAN (transaction number).
R10:   The time period between motion detection and start of recording shall be less than 2.5 seconds.
R13:   The camera shall have enough storage for 5 minutes' video stream to be stored as alarm buffer.
R68:   The stored video streams of the video surveillance system shall be safe against misuse and tampering.
R68.1:   The length of the password shall be at least 5 characters. The password shall only be changed if necessary.

Fig. 10-6:   Example excerpt of a requirements specification for the second application

10.9.1 Commonality Analysis

Requirements
matrix
The identification of common requirements is done top down from abstract requirements artefacts to detailed ones. We use the application–requirements matrix to document in which applications the requirements are mandatory. In Fig. 10-8 a set of common requirements is identified in the application–

requirements matrix. Those requirements that are mandatory for all applications constitute the commonality of the product line.

In a next step, the matrix is analysed for further commonalities between the applications. The requirements are analysed, for example, with regard to:

Detailed analysis

- The same content, represented in different words.
- Requirements that will become common in the near future.
- Requirements that only differ slightly from each other.
- Requirements that should be common from a strategic point of view.

Third example application

Goals

G1:	Safety against thieves.
G...:	...
G5:	Video surveillance of the flat.

Desired Features

F1:	Video surveillance.
F1.1:	Activation by motion detection.
F...:	...
F2.2:	Door and window sensor.
F2.3:	Manual deactivation of alarm (by owner, or police).

Requirements

R1:	The police shall be informed immediately after the detection of an open window or door.
R1.1:	The police shall be informed via internet message or SMS.
R2:	The alarm signal shall start immediately after the detection of the open window or door.
R2.1:	The alarm signal shall be deactivated by the police, by the owner, or automatically after 20 minutes.
R9:	The video surveillance shall be active as soon as activated by the user.
R9.1:	A recording is only initiated if motion is detected.
R9.2:	The camera shall have enough storage for 5 minutes' video stream to be stored as alarm buffer.
R10:	The time period between motion detection and start of recording shall be less than 0.5 seconds.
R11:	The video recording shall continue for 2 minutes after the last motion was detected.
R79:	The stored video streams of the video surveillance system shall be safe against misuse and tampering.

Fig. 10-7:   Example excerpt of a requirements specification for the third application

Requirements	App. 1	App. 2	App. 3
The police shall be informed immediately after the detection of an open window or door.			mandatory
The police shall be informed via internet message or SMS			mandatory
The alarm signal shall start immediately after the detection of the open window or door	mandatory		mandatory
The alarm signal shall only start if the police does not arrive within 5 minutes after alarm detection		mandatory	
The alarm signal shall be deactivated by the police, by the owner, or automatically after 20 minutes	mandatory		mandatory
The video surveillance is active as soon as activated by the user			mandatory
...	...	...	...
A recording is only initiated if a motion is detected.	mandatory		mandatory
The camera shall have storage for 5 minutes' video stream to be stored as alarm buffer	mandatory	mandatory	mandatory
The time period between motion detection and start of recording shall be less than 0.5 seconds	mandatory		mandatory
The time period between motion detection and start of recording shall be less than 2.5 seconds		mandatory	
The video recording shall continue 2 minutes after the last motion was detected			mandatory
The stored video streams of video surveillance system shall be safe against misuse and tampering	mandatory	mandatory	mandatory

Fig. 10-8:   Using the application requirements-matrix to identify variability

---

Example 10-9: *Identifying Similar Goals*

Application 1, G1: "protection against burglary"

Application 2, G1: "protection against burglary in the office"

Application 3, G1: "protection against thieves"

The three goals of the different applications can be described by one common goal: "protect against burglary".

In Example 10-9 we illustrate three different goal descriptions that can be summarised by a single goal "protection against burglary".

10.9.2 Variability Analysis

The application–requirements matrix presented in Fig. 10-8 is used to identify an initial set of variable aspects among the requirements of different applications. The candidates for variable requirements, which we focus on in the following, are highlighted in Fig. 10-8 by grey bars. The requirement "the alarm signal shall be deactivated…" is variable because it is only mandatory for applications "App. 1" and "App. 3". In addition, the requirement itself contains variable aspects; see Examples 10-10 and 10-11.

Identifying variable requirements

Example 10-10: *Variable Aspects Within a Requirement*

The requirement differentiates among the following variants: 'The alarm signal shall be …'

Variant 1: "…deactivated by the police"

Variant 2: "…deactivated by the owner"

Variant 3: "…deactivated automatically after 20 min."

Example 10-11: *Variants Among Different Applications*

For the authentication variant 'password authentication' the security requirements differ among the applications. App. 1 requires a high password quality, whereas App. 2 requires a low password quality.

Variant 1 'high password quality': Req-78.1, App. 1: "The password shall consist of at least 10 characters and include special characters (such as numbers). The password shall be changed every 3 months, and an old password cannot be used again."

Variant 2 'low password quality': Req-68.1, App. 2: "The password shall be at least 5 characters long. The password shall only be changed if necessary."

10.9.3 Defining Variation Points and Variants

The correct definition of variation points is essential, since a variation point provides the central location for binding the variability during application engineering. Typically, the variation subject is a good indicator for a variation point and its name. In Example 10-12, we define the variability subject by abstracting from related variants.

Determining the variability subject

Example 10-12: *Defining a Variation Point for a Set of Variants*

By abstracting from the requirements "the alarm signal shall be deactivated…" we define the variation point 'alarm deactivation'. Moreover, we define only two variants as manual deactivation can be done by any person authenticated by the system.

Hence, for the variation point 'alarm deactivation' the following variants are available:

Variant 1: "…manual deactivation by an authenticated person"

Variant 2: "…automatic deactivation after 20 minutes"

10.9.4 Defining Variability Dependencies

After determining the variation point and its variants, the required variability dependencies have to be defined. We illustrate this step in Fig. 10-9 for the variation point 'alarm deactivation' from Example 10-12.

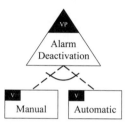

Fig. 10-9:   Example of a variation point with a an alternative choice of two variants

---

Example 10-13: *Definition of Variability Dependencies*

The variants 'manual' and 'automatic' shall be optional variants for deactivating the alarm. Exactly one of them must be selected for an application. Hence, we relate them to the variation point 'alarm deactivation' using optional variability dependencies and group the dependencies by an alternative choice with a range of [1..1]. As this is the default range we do not show it in Fig. 10-9.

10.9.5 Defining Constraint Dependencies

Variant to variation point constraint

In Example 10-14, we illustrate the use of a constraint dependency between a variant and a variation point. If the variant at the source end of the constraint dependency ('video surveillance') is selected, the variation point at the target end ('video surveillance quality') has to be bound by selecting the desired variants. The selection thus has to take into account the defined variability dependencies and alternative choices.

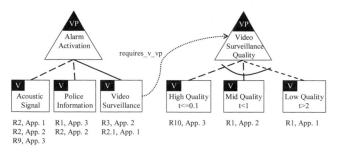

Fig. 10-10: "Requires" dependency between a variant and a variation point

---

Example 10-14: *Use of the "Requires" Constraint Dependency*

The 'requires_v_vp' dependency between the variant 'video surveillance' and the variation point 'video surveillance quality' (Fig. 10-10) means that the video surveillance system is available in different quality variants, such as required by the individual applications.

10.9.6 Documenting Domain Requirements

Variants in a use case scenario

Commonality and variability have to be defined in the various requirements artefacts and related to the corresponding concepts (variants and/or variation points) in the orthogonal variability model. Figure 10-11 illustrates an excerpt of a variable use case scenario, which is enriched by XML tags. These XML tags structure the textual scenario in different elements. Due to the definition of the elements in the scenario the variable parts (e.g. steps, preconditions, etc.) of the use case scenario can be related to the corresponding variants in the variability model.

10.10 Differences from Single-System Engineering

Identifying and defining commonality and variability

The main goal of domain requirements engineering is the prospective development of common and variable requirements artefacts for the product line in order to enable large-scale reuse in application engineering. Consequently, the requirements engineering activities (elicitation, documentation, negotiation, and validation/verification) do not deal with a single application but with the requirements of all envisioned product line applications. The requirements engineer has to involve a potentially large number of different stakeholders (product managers, architects, customer groups, maintenance staff, etc.) and different requirements sources (legacy systems, country laws, etc.) to be able to identify all relevant common and variable requirements.

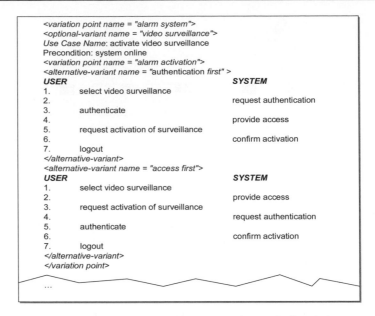

```
<variation point name = "alarm system">
<optional-variant name = "video surveillance">
Use Case Name: activate video surveillance
Precondition: system online
<variation point name = "alarm activation">
<alternative-variant name = "authentication first" >
USER                                           SYSTEM
1.          select video surveillance
2.                                             request authentication
3.          authenticate
4.                                             provide access
5.          request activation of surveillance
6.                                             confirm activation
7.          logout
</alternative-variant>
<alternative-variant name = "access first">
USER                                           SYSTEM
1.          select video surveillance
2.                                             provide access
3.          request activation of surveillance
4.                                             request authentication
5.          authenticate
6.                                             confirm activation
7.          logout
</alternative-variant>
</variation point>

...
```

Fig. 10-11: Example of a variable, textual scenario description

10.11 Summary

Identification of commonality and variability

Along with the elicitation of requirements from different sources, the domain requirements engineering sub-process has to identify which requirements are common to all applications, and which requirements differ among the applications. Hence, also during domain requirements engineering a commonality and variability analysis is performed. The application–requirements matrix provides a synopsis of the high-level requirements for several applications and can thus be used to support the identification of commonality and variability. A more sophisticated analysis can be performed on a set of prioritised requirements. In addition, checklists can be used to guide the identification of common and variable requirements.

Definition of variability

To support efficient communication and to enforce consistency of the variability of the software product line, the variability is defined in the orthogonal variability model. Variability modelling involves the identification and definition of variation points, variants, variability dependencies, and constraint dependencies. Variation points and variants are identified by abstracting from variable requirements and/or by grouping similar requirements artefacts. Architects have to be involved in the definition of product line variability as the variability has a strong influence on the reference architecture. External variability is defined together with product management.

Frank van der Linden

11

Domain Design

In this chapter you will learn:

- o *About the interrelations of the domain design sub-process with the domain requirements engineering, domain realisation, and application design sub-processes.*
- o *The key mechanisms to embed variability into a reference architecture.*
- o *About the consideration of quality requirements, in particular flexibility, evolvability, and maintainability, for the reference architecture.*

11.1   Introduction

Goals of domain design

The main goal of the domain design sub-process is to produce the reference architecture, defining the main software structure and the texture. The architect determines how requirements, including variability, are reflected in the architecture. The sub-processes and artefacts closely related to the domain design sub-process are highlighted in Fig. 11-1.

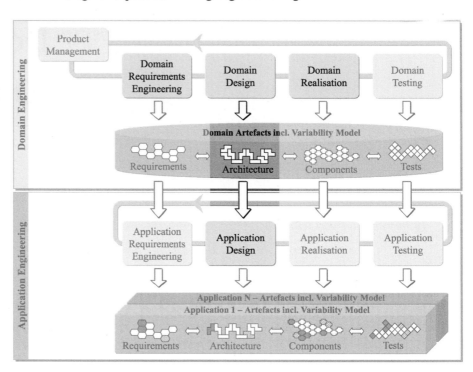

Fig. 11-1:   Sub-processes and artefacts related to domain design

The most important connections of domain design are the relations with domain requirements engineering, domain realisation, and application design; see Fig. 11-1. Domain design provides a reference architecture for the software product line to domain realisation and to application design. An important characteristic of this architecture is the ability to select and configure reusable software artefacts.

11.1.1 Interrelation with Domain Requirements Engineering

Requirement variability

Domain requirements engineering is responsible for providing common and variable requirements together with a variability model that defines the external variability of the product line but may also define internal variability (① in Fig. 11-2). The input from domain requirements engineering is used to determine the technical solutions that are chosen in the reference architecture. The variability model defines the basis for the variability in the reference architecture. It is adapted in domain design by resolving part of the variability and adding internal variability.

Domain requirements engineering and domain design are performed iteratively. Due to the decisions made in domain design and the additional insights gained, the need for detailed and for revised requirements arises (② in Fig. 11-2; Chapter 10 describes this interrelation in more detail). In the course of the interplay between domain requirements engineering and domain design, the stakeholders assign priorities to the requirements. The architects use the priorities to guide the design process.

Detailing and revision of requirements

11.1.2 Interrelation with Domain Realisation

Domain design provides the reference architecture to domain realisation (③ in Fig. 11-2). The reference architecture includes a variable structure that is the basis for the structures of all applications. Furthermore, the reference architecture provides the texture of reusable components and interfaces (we elaborate on the architectural structure and texture in Chapter 6). Along with the reference architecture, a selection of reusable domain artefacts that domain realisation must build is passed on. The selection of artefacts encompasses the reusable components and interfaces as well as their traceability to application-specific components and interfaces.

Reference architecture

The most important task of domain realisation is to build the reusable components and interfaces. Issues arising in realising domain artefacts, e.g. problem reports, are provided as feedback to domain design to improve subsequent design (④ in Fig. 11-2).

Feedback from realisation

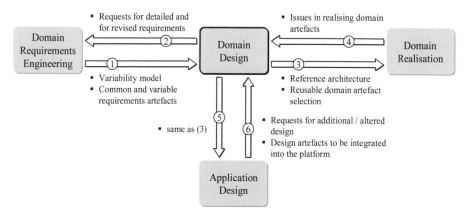

Fig. 11-2:   Information flows between domain design and other sub-processes

11.1.3 Interrelation with Application Design

Reuse of reference architecture

Domain design supplies the reference architecture to application design, which has to specialise the reference architecture for a single application (⑤ in Fig. 11-2). In doing so, application design has to obey the rules defined in the architectural texture. As the application developers must know what reusable software artefacts are available, the reusable software artefact selection is also passed on to the application design process.

Feedback from application design

Application design provides feedback to domain design in terms of requests for additional and altered design artefacts (first bullet of ⑥ in Fig. 11-2). For example, the application architect may find that the architectural structure is not sufficient for a particular kind of application. By providing this kind of feedback, the application architect initiates improvements in the reference architecture. Furthermore, application design may provide domain design with design artefacts to be integrated into the platform (second bullet of ⑥ in Fig. 11-2). Such artefacts are newly developed parts of the application architecture that are of interest for the product line. To integrate them into the reference architecture means initiating an evolution of the product line and investing additional effort for reengineering. The reengineering ensures flexibility and prepares the corresponding artefacts for reuse. The decision on whether the application artefacts are integrated into the product line is made by product managers and domain engineers.

11.2   Traditional Design Activities

Building an architecture

The most important single-system design activity is to define an architecture, which determines the way the system is going to be built. Requirements, including their variability, have to be mapped to technical solutions, to be used during the realisation of the system. The architecture determines the structuring of the software into parts and their relationships and the common rules to be applied. To support this, the architect performs the following supporting activities:

Complexity reduction

- *Abstracting*: This activity clusters information of the system in abstractions by considering certain aspects only. This reduces complexity of the design. Separate abstractions deal with different aspects of the systems.

Support for reasoning

- *Modelling*: This activity relates abstractions to each other in order to enable reasoning about them.

Model execution

- *Simulating*: This activity "executes" certain models in order to measure certain system aspects. There is often a software execution theory available that allows translating the measurement results into actual system properties.

- *Prototyping*: This activity produces fast implementations, covering important system aspects. The purpose is to execute the prototype to measure how actual systems behave.

  Fast partial implementation

- *Validating*: In addition to the design activities, the architect has a role in the validation of the realisation results. The validation considers whether the architecture is obeyed by the realisation sub-process.

  Enforcement of architecture rules

11.3 Quality Requirements

Many requirements do not deal with the functionality. Instead, they are related to the quality of the resulting systems, dealing with issues like performance, security, safety, and usability. The architect tries to localise these concerns by addressing them in specific parts of the structure or texture only. This may be done by having separate components and interfaces dealing with the requirement at hand, or the determination of certain aspects, giving rise to texture, which applies to all components.

Quality: driver for the architecture

In addition, requirements originating from the development organisation have an impact on the choice of the architecture. For instance, the organisation needs to do early integration and testing, which means that the architect has to make a system that can be developed incrementally. Whenever realisation has finished an increment, integration and testing can proceed in parallel with the realisation of the next increment.

Quality of development

Architecture evaluation is a means to assess the architecture according to certain selected quality requirements. The architecture is tested against a set of development scenarios [Kazman et al. 2000]. These scenarios deal with the quality issue at hand, such as preventing unauthorised intrusion into the system, or dealing with a user that does not act according to the manual.

Evaluation of architecture

Certain quality requirements arise just from doing software product line engineering. The most important ones are support for variability, flexibility, evolvability, and maintainability. Quality assurance also has to ensure that these qualities are met, for instance through reviews of the architectural design. Architecture reviews are fundamental to ensure a high quality of all products.

Product line quality requirements

Variability support is crucial for domain design. The architect determines which configuration mechanisms to use and where they should apply. The work of application design and realisation relies upon the choice of the right mechanism. Only when the adequate configuration mechanisms are chosen

Design for variability

can quality products be derived easily and is mass customisation supported (see Section 12.5 for a description of configuration mechanisms).

External and internal variability

Software developers have to be aided in finding easily the right way to build applications based upon variable requirements. Variability available in the requirements has to be designed into variability in the architecture. In addition, technical options may introduce additional internal variability, which has to be incorporated as well.

Design for flexibility

Flexibility is a quality of the architecture providing easy changes. As not all future applications can be envisioned, the architecture needs to have ways to cope with that, still keeping its high quality to remain usable for the product line. When new applications arise in the product line that have unexpected requirements, the architecture should be ready to accommodate such environments. It is important to distribute different, identifiable pieces of functionality over different components and interfaces. In this way, there can be independent solutions for each of these. In addition, variation points where unexpected variants may be introduced later are ways to separate them even further. Texture that allows late binding times in the realisation sub-process increases the flexibility, since variation points may be bound late in the realisation phase. For instance, the use of plug-in components and their specific properties is a decision involving the texture. Plug-in components have only few dependencies on the remainder of the system, and thus allow late binding.

Example 11-1: *Flexibility in Lock Control*

The architecture of the lock control has incorporated several means for flexibility. For instance, the separation of the functionalities of lock control, authentication, and user control enables adaptations to each of them, independent of the others. This is shown in Fig. 11-3. Improvements stay local, increasing the flexibility. In addition, the use of separate plug-in components for each of them improves flexibility further. By using the right plug-in components, all kinds of lock control are configured even at late binding times.

Design for evolvability

Evolvability is the quality of being able to evolve the architecture according to requirements changes that will possibly come in future. This quality goes further than flexibility, which only demands that new systems can be accommodated. Evolvability deals with changes to the architecture itself. The architecture has to evolve, since not all future needed solutions are incorporated now. However, existing applications in the product line still need to conform to the architecture. Otherwise, the product line cannot be managed well and the architecture may deteriorate to a low quality. Evolvability ensures that the architecture does not change drastically.

An important precondition for evolvability is a clear separation of concerns. Solutions for certain stable classes of quality requirements should be as independent as possible from solutions for less stable classes of quality requirements. Solutions for these latter ones should be as independent from each other as possible. Mechanisms that help in evolvability are the layering of the architecture to separate lower and higher level concerns. Other useful techniques are the use of separate frameworks for separate quality requirements, and the introduction of separate architecture views for them. Still, there is no simple way to measure the evolvability of architectural models. The degree of evolvability achieved depends on which kinds of adaptations will occur in the future.

Separation of concerns

Example 11-2: *Evolvability of Lock Control*

Evolvability of architectural models cannot be measured easily from the architectural models. It depends on an appropriate separation of concerns. Given the separation of concerns depicted in Fig. 11-3, for instance, the need may arise to separate user control for entering the building and user control for managing information, since both evolve differently. Yet, distinguishing too many separate concerns hampers evolvability, since each adaptation may affect many different concerns.

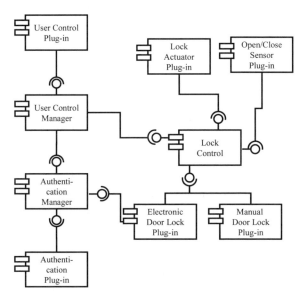

Fig. 11-3: Flexibility in lock control

Design for maintainability   Maintainability is the quality of being able to resolve changes in applications in the field. Maintainability is improved by the possibilities to use late-binding techniques that allow the uploading of new software and the removal of unwanted software. As the product line evolves, errors are fixed, and systems in the product line have to be adapted accordingly, resulting in a good quality for all products in the product line. As the product line grows, maintainability must be supported adequately. Many present-day commercial operating systems have a component infrastructure support to facilitate such update actions. Maintainability also deals with the ease of finding errors in running systems. The field support may use a separate field support framework to be able to inspect every running component, and/or to have debug reports available.

Example 11-3: *Maintainability of Lock Control*

Maintainability of lock control is related to the conformance to standards of the architectural texture and the availability of rules dealing with maintainability in the texture of the architecture. For instance, the texture may demand that each component provides a maintenance interface; see Fig. 11-4. This interface allows the internal state of the component to be read and adapted and to enable logging for actions with the component. Actual logging is performed by a different component. This enables the plug-in of different logging mechanisms for different purposes. Maintainability is improved if maintenance can be done remotely through Internet or phone connections. In addition, the maintainability is facilitated if components can be replaced on the fly with improved ones. The use of a separate initialisation and recovery interface for the component allows it to be reset and to initialise an updated version of it.

Architecture evaluation   Reference architecture evaluation is a quality assurance technique. It uses scenarios for the above-mentioned product-line-related quality requirements. Such a scenario is, for instance, the addition of a new application to the portfolio with more or less different requirements. For software product line engineering, an assessment of the reference architecture is crucial, at least for the product-line-related quality requirements. Only an architecture that supports the quality requirements sufficiently will survive long enough to be a reference architecture.

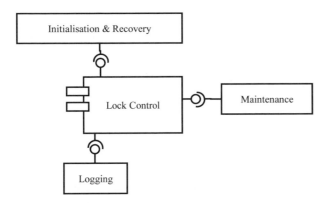

Fig. 11-4:   Maintenance support for the lock control component

---

Example 11-4: *Evaluation of the Home Automation Architecture*

Assessment of the home automation architecture uses the requirements in a systematic way to check the architecture. The software product line properties discussed above are part of the requirements. Use cases dealing with these topics have to be identified and prioritised. It is checked how the architecture behaves under the mentioned use cases. Such use cases are described in Examples 11-1 to 11-3. They deal with independent improvements of functionality, addition of new functionality, and maintenance scenarios.

11.4   Commonality and Variability in Design

A large part of the commonality and variability in the reference architecture originates from the commonality and variability in requirements. An essential issue for domain design is to take into account the requirements variability in the development of the reference architecture. As the reference architecture typically cannot realise all requirements to the same extent, a prioritisation of requirements is necessary. Moreover, domain design has to add variability for different reasons such as the preparation for future changes in requirements (see Section 9.7 and Chapter 10 respectively for details on commonality and variability analysis).

Realising requirements variability

In the following subsections, we elaborate on requirements prioritisation in software product lines and describe the resulting mapping between requirements and design. Finally, we deal with the basic rules for adding variability in design.

11.4.1 Requirements Prioritisation

High-priority requirements

Based on the requirements prioritisation established during domain requirements engineering, the architect prioritises the requirements and considers those with the highest priority first. In software product line engineering, the design for flexibility, evolvability, and maintainability typically has the highest priority. This usually results in common decomposition rules and patterns within the architecture [Buschmann et al. 1996]. For instance, the decision to use a layered component-based architecture is inspired by these requirements. When performance is an important common issue, it should result in common patterns for process creation and interaction, for example, and in common guidelines for resource usage. When usability is an important common requirement, then it is important to have specific subsystems dealing with the user interaction. Note that these common solutions are applicable if their issues are important for a large group of applications to be considered, even if the corresponding requirements involve variability. If possible, a single design covering low- and high-end requirements for a single issue improves the effort needed to develop and maintain the application.

Example 11-5: *Commonality in the Reference Architecture*

The home automation reference architecture is layered to differentiate between 'basic control', 'device control and management', 'home functions', and 'integrated functions'. The architecture is component based. For each of the layers, specific frameworks are present to fix the variation points and variation mechanisms. Figure 11-3 shows a framework within the 'home functions' layer. It defines a fixed configuration of the components 'user control', 'lock control', and 'authentication'. Each of the components has to be specialised by plug-in components for the different variants. The framework determines the presence of interfaces and the components carrying them for the required functionality.

Low-priority requirements

Lower priority requirements have to fit into the structure determined by the higher priority requirements. This often leads to the introduction of a framework following the already established rules. Consequently, satisfaction of a requirement is distributed over several places in the framework. For instance, the functionality is distributed over several layers. Often it is the case that both components and interfaces are needed for satisfying a given requirement. The initial requirements may have given rise to common, textural rules to determine the distribution of the requirements over several components.

11.4.2 Mapping Between Requirements and Design

There are several reasons why the traceability relationship between requirements and architecture is not a simple one-to-one mapping; see Fig. 11-5. There are even circumstances when a common requirement is related to a variable architecture asset and vice versa. However, a good architect lets the traceability relationship be a few-to-few mapping, where "few" is deliberately a vague word, and is certainly dependent on the circumstances. However, traceability is only usable when it is comprehensible. Reasons for deferring from a simple one-to-one mapping are:

Few-to-few mapping

- Interaction of the requirements.
- Product line requirements, like flexibility and adaptability.
- Technology options.
- Availability of development resources (people, tools, etc.).
- Preparation for the future.

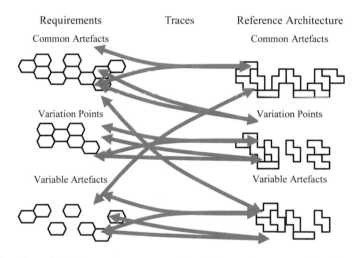

Fig. 11-5:   Traceability between common and variable requirements and architecture assets

Requirements variability is an important source of variability in the reference architecture. Variation in requirements often results in variation in design and/or realisation. The architect analyses the commonality of the variation first, reducing the variation to a minimum to ease flexibility and evolvability. Except for this external variability, originating from variability in requirements, the design also takes additional internal variability into account, which is introduced by the technical solution. Differences in quality requirements may lead to differences in hardware devices or basic software functionality such as used protocols or data base access. This results in variation at several places in the software. The commonality is captured in

Influence of requirements variability

the texture and in frameworks. The variation is captured in multiplicities and plug-in components.

Trace links

The trace links in Fig. 11-5 document the relation between requirements variability and variability in the reference architecture as well as between domain requirements and domain design artefacts. The links enable, for instance, the estimation of the impact of changes in the course of a change management process.

Distribution of variability

Because of the initial design choices on quality requirements, the remaining variability is often distributed, for instance because several subsystems and layers are involved. The architect has to avoid duplication of the same information as far as possible. It is not a good idea to have the parameters of a single variation point distributed over several places in the application. A possible solution is to store the parameters at a single place, and let other parts of the application access this place to get their information.

Example 11-6: *Duplication of Variability Information*

In the lock control software, several parts need to know the number of door actuators. The door lock control software needs to know how many of them are connected to a single door, and have to be actuated in case of opening it. The 'actuator control' component in the 'device control and maintenance' subsystem activates the actuators and regularly checks the correct functioning of them. It needs to know the number of all actuators and for each of them the port and address to use to submit opening and closing commands. It may even be the case that the actuators for both doors and windows are controlled by the same component. It is not a good idea to have the number of door actuators for each door stored in the 'lock actuator plug-in component', and independently have the number and addresses of all actuators stored in the 'actuator control' component. It is better to have a 'lock actuator configuration' component, storing the number of doors (and windows) and store the mapping of actuators and their addresses; see Fig. 11-6. The 'lock actuator configuration' component provides door opening functionality towards the 'lock actuator plug-in component' that is not interested in the exact number of actuators per door, only in the number of doors that can be opened. The 'actuator control' component needs the number and exact address information, but does not need the mapping towards actual doors and windows.

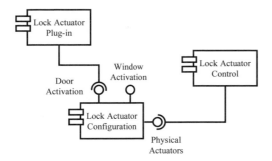

Fig. 11-6: Actuator configuration

11.4.3 Adding Variability in Design

Future changes in technology find their way into architecture variability. In many cases, it is known several years in advance that certain technology will become available or change. Often it is clear where the new technology should fit. The architect introduces variation points for future variants. The variants are designed only as soon as the technology becomes available.

Internal variability

Example 11-7: *Future Technology for Home Automation*

Introducing iris scan authentication affects the 'basic control' layer through the introduction of a new driver; see Fig. 11-7. The 'device control and management' layer and the layers above it are adapted at selected places, which deal with authentication. 'Integrated functions' may be unaffected, because they may abstract from the specific authentication method used.

A main concern of the architecture is to deal with unstable requirements. This means that it is known or expected that these requirements will change over time. In discussion with product management and requirements engineers, it should be made clear which new or adapted requirements can be expected in the shorter or longer term. The architecture has to support future adoption of these requirements as far as possible. Just as with normal requirements, the expected priority of the new requirement influences how much impact the requirement has on the architecture, and whether the architect should take measures at an early stage to deal with them. For instance, through the introduction of frameworks and the use of their plug-ins, the necessary changes are bound to specific locations. Nevertheless, late changes to the reference architecture cannot be avoided completely.

Unstable requirements

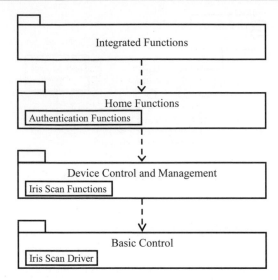

Fig. 11-7:   Incorporating iris scan authentication

Example 11-8: *Expected Requirements Changes in Authorisation*

Within the authorisation software, the present systems deal with key and card locks. It is expected that in future technology will become available that allows authorisation based upon fingerprints, iris scan or voice or face recognition. These latter ways of authorising have higher storage, processing, and bandwidth requirements than what is necessary for the present applications. The architecture may already introduce measures for dealing with this, e.g. separate authorisation variation points dealing with different algorithms and processing requirements; see Fig. 11-8.

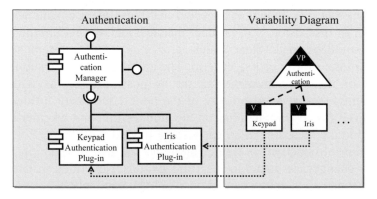

Fig. 11-8:   Expected future requirements on authentication

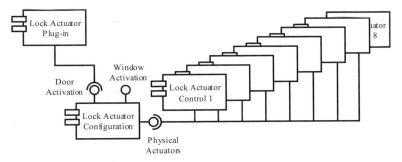

Fig. 11-9: Variability in lock actuator components

There may be several manufacturers producing a similar piece of equipment. However, they all differ more or less. The differences may be visible to the clients of the applications, because there are differences in behaviour of the equipment, which are related to behavioural variability of the application. However, some of these differences are not visible to the clients. They relate to the choice of the manufacturer to support a certain protocol, or have different approaches towards ensuring correct functioning, e.g. repeated triggering, or active fault management at the equipment side. It is not always a wise choice to reduce this supplier variability. This is part of the risk management of the home control systems provider. Being dependent on a single manufacturer for a specific piece of equipment can mean that the freedom to negotiate the price is diminished. Moreover, there is a risk that the manufacturer may go out of business, or redesign its own equipment in such a way that it becomes less useful. The architecture has to take into account this kind of variability.

Provider independence

Example 11-9: *Actuator Variability*

The home automation application developer uses eight types of actuators from five different manufacturers, supporting three protocols. They have four levels of robustness with regard to failure. Only the latter point is of relevance for the customers. They see this in the robustness and guaranteed speed of opening a door. The other variability is hidden in the 'device control and maintenance' subsystem, which has variants for all these kinds of actuators; see Fig. 11-9.

11.5 Designing the Reference Architecture

In this section, we elaborate on the major topics of designing the reference architecture that are related to variability. In particular, we deal with component frameworks, the use of application-specific components, the use of aspects, and the role of the architectural texture.

11.5.1 Use of Component Frameworks

Configurations
The reference architecture typically consists of a large number of components that can be connected through interfaces. Component frameworks (Definition 6-8) restrict the number of component configurations. If the configuration task is completely left up to application developers without any restrictions, configurations can be made that are unwanted since they lead to unusable or badly performing applications. The application developer may not find the right configuration within reasonable time, because the number of possibilities is too large.

Components and interfaces
Components and interfaces are important domain artefacts. A framework provides a common structure of components and interfaces. At predefined places, plug-in components may be added. Plug-in components may be application specific. In cases where many applications use a specific plug-in component, it may be designed as a reusable domain component as well.

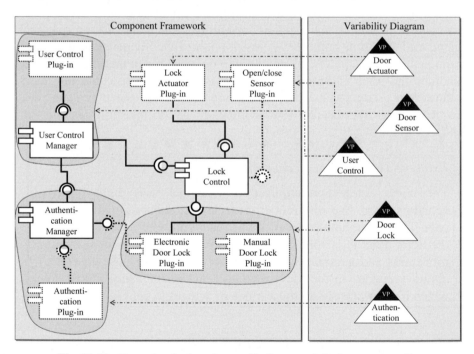

Fig. 11-10: Example of a domain-specific framework for home automation

The reference architecture determines many frameworks to support a diversity of quality requirements. After a framework is chosen, they guide further design. Each framework demands a number of plug-in components to be provided. Concerns related to the plug-in components can be designed independently. However, if in future a new independent concern arises, there is a need to adapt the framework, which may be hard to do. This is a drive to increase the number of plug-in components. On the other hand, if there is a group of plug-in components that always change together, it is not a good idea to separate them. Separate realisations cannot profit from each others' knowledge, which may lead to less development efficiency. This is a drive to fewer plug-in components.

Number of plug-in components

Example 11-10: *Framework Use*

Figure 11-10 shows a domain-specific framework for home automation. It contains a fixed configuration of 'lock control', 'user control manager', and 'authentication manager' components. In addition, several plug-in components are in the diagram to address separate concerns for 'door lock', 'authentication', 'user control', 'door actuator', and 'door sensor'. This enhances flexibility since realisation can provide independent solutions for each of these issues. However, it also restricts future adaptations of the application.

There may be different rules for the use of plug-in components. Although the 'authentication plug-in' component is optional, the 'user control plug-in component' has to be available. This means that it has to be provided even in cases, not yet conceived, where no user control is needed, e.g. because it is triggered by a clock, by weather conditions, or by something else in the environment. Of course, even in these cases, a solution can be found in a default 'user control plug-in component', or a mock-up simulation user control. An even larger problem occurs when a future design not only needs actuators and open/close sensors, but for instance also a sensor to measure a distance in which the door is open.[35] This needs a redesign of the framework, where also 'lock control' may need adaptation. Since such applications are not yet envisioned, the framework is not made that general, since that would hamper present-day realisation.

Not all frameworks are domain-specific. Many frameworks, for more or less basic functionality, can be acquired externally in the market; see for instance the collection of frameworks in J2EE [Alur et al. 2003]. An architect chooses to use such external frameworks in the reference architecture to

External frameworks

---

[35] This distance is measured in a certain way, e.g. an angle or an opening width.

solve common problems. The choice of such a framework speeds up design. However, it restricts the architecture much more than a domain-specific framework, since it cannot be adapted at all. Therefore, the use of an external framework supports the independent solution of certain concerns from each other, whereas for other concerns, no support is available, and the architect has to provide solutions.

11.5.2 Use of Application-Specific Plug-ins

Plug-in locations for application-specific variants

The reference architecture determines what reusable software assets are in the software product line. This covers not only the commonality over the applications, but also variants that are chosen often. By using many of these prepared variants, application engineering can be very efficient. However, there may be cases where reusable assets are not applicable, e.g. because of very specific requirements. In that case, the application architect defines application-specific variants at places where this is allowed by the reference architecture. The domain architect has to prepare for the possibility of such application-specific variants.

Example 11-11: *Domain- and Application-Specific Components*

The requirements have a variation point for the support of different kinds of door locks. Variants are the distinct door locks, both manual and different kinds of electronic locks. Consequently, the reference architecture for home automation also defines one or more variation points for door locks. If an electronic door lock is chosen, a terminal and a key database are necessary, each with its own variability. The simplest way to realise the variation point is to define an interface that the door lock software has to provide. In this case, the variants have to be developed for each application separately, and are not part of the reference architecture. This may put a lot of effort on application engineering, which hampers mass customisation. Therefore, the architect defines generic, reusable components that do not differentiate between the different types of locks. The generic terminal and database components are optional, but still generic and reusable. The variants of locks, terminals and databases can be designed independently as variant-specific components. By satisfying mass customisation requirements, the single variation point in the requirements is spread over different parts of the architecture.

11.5.3 Use of Aspects

Cross-cutting concerns

The domain architect introduces aspects [V.d. Linden and Müller 1995] to recurring problems of realisation, thereby both reducing the effort of realisation, and improving the commonality over the complete design. Aspects provide solutions for several architectural concerns, such as maintainability. The texture contains, for instance, realisation guidelines and the rule to separate aspects. The architect may require separate interfaces for certain aspects, to be provided or required by each component. Although this holds for any architectural concern, it certainly holds for rules regarding variability. A common treatment of variability eases subsequent application configuration, since only a few recognised variability-binding mechanisms are used.

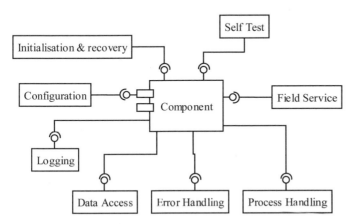

Fig. 11-11: A component decorated with aspect-related interfaces

---

Example 11-12: *Aspect-Related Interfaces in Home Automation*

The architecture requires the provision of interfaces for the following aspects: enabling a uniform treatment of 'initialisation & recovery', 'self test', 'configuration', and 'field service'. In addition, it is required that a component uses specified interfaces for certain other aspects, for 'logging', 'data access', 'error handling', and 'process handling'. In Fig. 11-11 a component is shown with its aspect interfaces.

11.5.4 Role of the Architectural Texture

The architectural texture consists of coding rules and general mechanisms such as styles [Shaw and Garlan 1996] and design patterns [Gamma et al. 1995] to deal with specific situations that may occur during design, realisation, and coding. Texture determines the common solution for high-priority requirements and decomposition rules for lower priority requirements. It is the main set of guidelines used for realisation.

General rules

Texture is part of the common platform

In the case of software product line engineering, the texture has to be present within all applications. In particular, this means that the texture is defined once for all applications, and thus it is a part of the commonality in the architecture. Textures are also used to provide a common way to deal with variability. We introduce some commonly used textures for variability.

Frameworks

A framework is part of the texture, since it restricts the variability to using plug-in components at predefined places. Inside the framework, there may be widespread use of certain patterns. For instance, in the framework we have a high-level controller surrounded with specific managers, each controlling a single type of hardware or software device. The specific device is implemented through a plug-in component. In addition, the use of registration of the plug-in components is part of the texture.

Example 11-13: *Textures for Home Automation*

Within the home automation example the texture contains the facade pattern [Gamma et al. 1995] for providing a single interface at subsystem level. It uses the observer pattern for decoupling user interface issues from the data. With regard to the quality requirements of flexibility, evolvability, and maintainability, the texture determines the use of layers and components, as well as the role of the layers and which piece of functionality has to be implemented in which layer. For instance, single-device control has to be done in the 'device control and management' layer; see Example 11-5. In addition, the texture requires the presence of certain common interfaces in each component, such as a maintenance interface, a debug interface, a reset interface, and an initialisation interface.

11.6 Architecture Validation

In this section, we describe the issues for architecture validation that arise from domain design. The reference architecture is an important asset that determines the design of many software assets. Because knowledge of the reference architecture is necessary for the validation, the architect is often involved in the validation of these assets. In particular, this holds for the application architectures and the results of domain realisation.

Validation of application architecture

In order to keep the application architecture consistent with the reference architecture, it has to be validated. This mainly involves checking the structure and the texture. Only after the application architecture is validated should it be used to build the application. In that case, ease of integration of domain assets can be guaranteed.

Example 11-14: *Application Architecture Check*

In the home automation case, the domain architect checks whether newly provided plug-in components meet the structural rules of the virtual plug-in components provided by the reference architecture. They should carry the right interfaces, and they should be present in the right subsystem. Other components should not call the plug-in components directly. Otherwise, it is difficult to replace the plug-in components with new ones.

After domain realisation has finished with the design of a component or interface, the design must be validated for conformance to the architecture. Both structure and texture should be checked. For instance, the following checks may be performed:

Validation of domain assets

- Do interfaces carry the right functionality to the right level of abstraction?
- Are components and interfaces produced according to texture?
- Does each component carry all its interfaces, and no more?
- Do components call only the required interfaces, and all of them?

If the asset does not conform to the architecture, problems may occur in future, both in maintaining the software and in fulfilling all kinds of dependability requirements. In that case, a redesign should be done.

Example 11-15: *The Architecture Review of 'Simple Lock Control'*

After the design of the 'basic lock control' component, the architect checks whether it carries all the interfaces it provides. As designed, these are the 'bind authentication' interface and all interfaces of 'lock control': 'bind lock', 'lock command', and 'bind lock actuator'; see Fig. 11-12. In addition, the component should carry all interfaces defined by the texture, e.g. for initialisation, field service, or self-test. Since the open/close sensor is designed later, the component should not carry related interfaces of 'lock control' such as a 'bind open close sensor' interface. Calls to interfaces that are not required should not be present. The only calls should be to the call-back interfaces of the plug-in components: 'lock authentication', 'lock actuation', and 'lock command'. Again, the calls to 'open close status' are designed later. In addition, the interface rules in the texture should be obeyed. It should call, for instance, the specified interfaces for error handling and logging. Finally, of course, the component is checked to perform the required functionality, i.e. performing the right actions on its plug-in components.

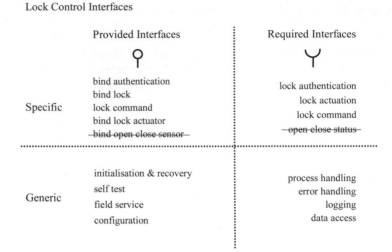

Fig. 11-12: Lock control component interfaces

Integration test validates architecture

Only when the architect has accepted the asset may implementation start. After implementation and unit testing the architect is involved in integration testing for the first set of applications using the asset. The first set of applications shows whether the asset indeed behaves as was planned. If this is not the case, the architect has to adapt the architecture, after which detailed domain design has to adapt the assets produced. This should be avoided as much as possible since it usually takes a lot of time and effort. This is another reason for a thorough acceptance check before implementation. However, it is often the case that several redesigns are necessary before a reusable software asset is stable and reusable in many contexts.

11.7 Differences from Single-System Engineering

Reference architecture

The domain architect has to provide a reference architecture for the software product line. This means that:

Mass customisation

- The reference architecture has to support mass customisation. It defines common parts of the product line and determines its variability in a technical sense.

Reusable parts

- The reference architecture determines which software parts are reusable. These parts are part of the platform and are reused in the development of applications.

Under-specification

- The reference architecture may be under-specified. Certain variants do not differ too much, so that it does not make sense to capture them completely in the reference architecture. The specifics of these variants can better be designed during application design.

- The domain requirements may conflict with each other, or have conflicting priorities to be satisfied for different applications. This is captured in variability of the requirements, and the architecture has to consider this variability.

  Variability

- The texture in the reference architecture not only captures the commonality within a single system, but also defines commonality that is present within all applications. It is defined once for all applications, and thus it is a part of the commonality in the architecture. Texture gets an additional role by providing common ways to deal with variability issues.

  Texture

- Even more than for normal development, an important task for the architect is to make the architecture robust and future proof. It should support the quality requirements of evolvability, flexibility, and maintainability. This provides, together with thorough design reviews, a high level of quality assurance.

  Quality

11.8 Summary

The architect has to map the domain requirements to technical solutions. The main result of domain design is the reference architecture, involving variation points, supporting platform and mass customisation. The reference architecture has to be flexible, evolvable, and maintainable. Its design incorporates the accommodation of future requirements and technology. In particular, the reference architecture changes over time. The domain architect has many interactions with neighbouring sub-processes, i.e. domain requirements engineering and realisation as well as application design.

Prospective design

External variability in the requirements has to be designed into variability in the architecture. In addition, technical options introduce internal variability, which has to be incorporated as well. The architects are stakeholders in the requirements engineering process. They provide feedback on what is easy and what is more difficult to vary. Similarly, developers providing the realisation inform the architect where adaptability is most needed.

Variability in design

With respect to normal single-system software development, the relationship to application design is different. Application architects use the reference architecture to prepare application development. This means that the domain and application architects together have to find a balance between what is better done at the domain level and what is done at the application level.

Balance between domain and application design

Over time, this balance changes, as solutions applicable for a single application may become useful for others as well.

Quality requirements   In addition to the normal architecture issues, variability and reuse have to be solved by the reference architecture. Moreover, the architecture should solve the quality requirements of variability, flexibility, evolvability, and maintainability. For many other quality requirements the architecture has to provide solutions that work for a group of applications, not all of which are envisioned.

Frank van der Linden

12

Domain
Realisation

In this chapter you will learn:

o *About the interrelations of the domain realisation sub-process with the domain design, domain testing, and application realisation sub-processes.*

o *About the role of interfaces of components for defining and realising commonality and variability.*

o *How to realise configurability of components.*

o *About different implementation mechanisms for variability.*

12.1   Introduction

*Goals of domain
realisation*

The goals of the domain realisation sub-process are to provide the detailed design and the implementation of reusable software assets, based on the reference architecture. The reusable software assets are mainly reusable components and interfaces. However, other artefacts like thread designs, database tables, protocols, and data streaming formats are also products of domain realisation. In addition, domain realisation incorporates configuration mechanisms that enable application realisation to select variants and build an application with the reusable components and interfaces. The sub-processes and artefacts closely related to the domain realisation sub-process are highlighted in Fig. 12-1.

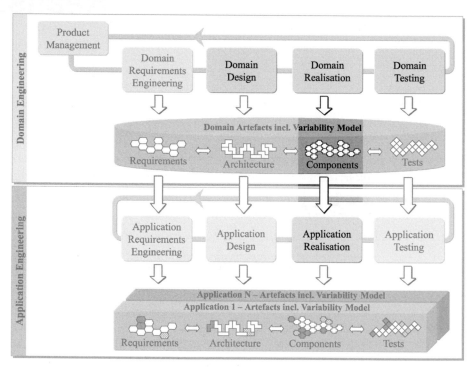

Fig. 12-1:   Sub-processes and artefacts related to domain realisation

*Interrelations with
other sub-processes*

The main relations of domain realisation are those with domain design, domain testing, and application realisation. In Fig. 12-2 the relationships with the most important neighbouring sub-processes are depicted. In the next sections, we briefly describe the relationships of domain realisation with these neighbouring sub-processes.

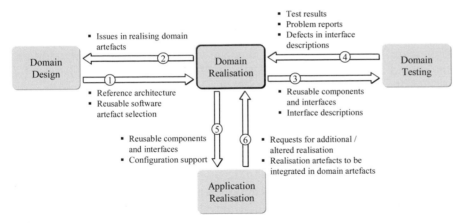

Fig. 12-2: Information flows between domain realisation and other sub-processes

12.1.1 Interrelation with Domain Design

Domain design provides the reference architecture, which determines the structure and texture of the complete software product line, and a selection of reusable software artefacts that determines which are the reusable parts in the structure (① in Fig. 12-2). Domain realisation designs and implements the corresponding reusable artefacts.

Defined structure and texture

Domain realisation provides domain design with issues in realising domain artefacts designed and implemented according to the architecture (② in Fig. 12-2). The issues include all kinds of problem reports.

Problem reports

12.1.2 Interrelation with Domain Testing

Domain realisation provides reusable components and interfaces ready for test to domain testing (③ in Fig. 12-2). In addition, domain realisation provides domain testing with interface descriptions, which serve as test references for the design of component tests.

Detailed design specifications

Domain testing reports back test results, which state whether the object under test has passed or failed a test, and problem reports that describe in which way the object under test has failed. If domain testing detects defects in interface descriptions, these defects are also reported back to domain realisation (④ in Fig. 12-2).

Test results

12.1.3 Interrelation with Application Realisation

Domain realisation passes the reusable components and interfaces designed, implemented, and ready for reuse (i.e. after having passed the tests performed in domain testing) on to application realisation. In addition, application realisation needs configuration support to assemble the specific

Reusable components and interfaces

applications (⑤ in Fig. 12-2). The configuration support may be automated, e.g. by providing a configuration management tool.

Evolution   Application realisation provides feedback through requests for additional and altered realisation (first bullet of ⑥ in Fig. 12-2). This involves functionality or quality that should be provided by the domain artefacts but is not realised sufficiently well or not realised at all by the reusable components. The feedback initiates an evolution of the software product line. The decision on whether the feedback from application realisation leads to an adaptation of the domain artefacts and thus to software evolution is made by domain architects and other stakeholders who decide on the evolution of the product line. Furthermore, application realisation provides domain realisation with realisation artefacts which may be incorporated into the product line (second bullet of ⑥ in Fig. 12-2). These are designs and implementations of application-specific components and interfaces which turn out to be actual needs of the domain. The integration of application artefacts into the product line usually involves some reengineering as the artefacts are not realised primarily with reuse in mind.

12.2 Traditional Realisation Activities

Detailed design and implementation   The most important realisation activity is to build a working system according to the reference architecture. This activity includes the detailed design and implementation of software artefacts and compiling, linking, and configuring them to executable code. In single-system engineering, the detailed design determines the internal structure of components and software packages before they are implemented. In addition, other artefacts like threads, database tables, protocols, and data streaming formats are the subject of realisation. However, the realisation of these artefacts does not differ much from the realisation of components. Therefore we do not treat such realisation activities separately.

Components and interfaces   The reference architecture determines the decomposition of an application into software artefacts, such as components and interfaces. Detailed design provides designs for each of them, and, after validation, they are implemented. In many cases, the realisation of different software artefacts is done by different groups of people, each taking care of some related artefacts. The following activities belong to realisation:

- *Interface design*: Interfaces are designed in close cooperation with all developers of components providing or requiring them. This design is a compromise between the abilities of the components that provide or use the interface functionality.

- *Component design:*[36] Components are designed to deliver functionality of the provided interfaces using the functionality of the required interfaces.

- *Interface implementation*: After interface design, its implementation is usually rather straightforward. Its elements have to be declared in a programming language file, to be included by the implementation of the components that provide and require the interface.

- *Component implementation*: After the design of the components, they are implemented in a programming language. Usually the component developer performs a unit test before the component is delivered and used for application configuration.

- *Compilation*: All components have to be compiled into object files. These object files are linked into working executables during application realisation.

12.3 Realising Interfaces

In this section, we elaborate on the detailed design of the interface of a variable component. The same interface is valid for a number of components. Hence, interfaces deal with common aspects of the components. Variability makes it necessary, on the one hand, to abstract from the differences in providing components and, on the other hand, to offer functions that expose certain information related to variability at the interface, e.g. to determine the required variant at run-time.

Effects of variability

12.3.1 Variable vs. Invariant Interfaces

An interface specifies functionality that is provided by certain components and required by others. As such, the interface is a contract between providing and requiring components. Variability is implicit through the independent abilities of having variability both at the providing component's side and at the requiring component's side. The interface itself is invariant, as both providing and requiring components have to interpret it in the same way. The requiring component can only rely on the presence of some variant of the providing component but without knowing which variant. The introduction of variants in the interface itself leads to variable choices by the providing and requiring components which may lead to incompatibilities.

Variability in interfaces

Interfaces may be used to access the variability realised in components. A provided interface may have functions that adapt internal variant selection.

Accessing variability

---

[36] And threads, database tables, protocols, streaming formats, etc.

This means that it is possible for the environment to adapt the variant at run-time. A required interface may be used by a component to enquire about variability-related information from the environment [V. Ommering et al. 2000].

12.3.2 Interface Elements

Level of interface detail

The interface provides elements that are abstractions of internal details of the providing components. These elements may be functions, constants, types, exceptions, events, and object classes to use or from which to inherit. However, the developer of the interface should be careful not to provide too many details of the component (Example 12-1). Otherwise, variation may be bound too early, ruling out different implementations. On the other hand, the requiring component needs at least a minimum level of detail before it can actually use the functionality.

Specific and abstract data types

The level of abstraction determines how generic or specific the information is that is shown at the interface (Example 12-2). If the level of abstraction is high, the interface can be used for many purposes, but the developers of the requiring components are in doubt about what is actually going on, and whether the provided functionality matches the required functionality. If the level of abstraction is too low, too much irrelevant information is exposed at the interface. This has to be matched exactly by the providing components.

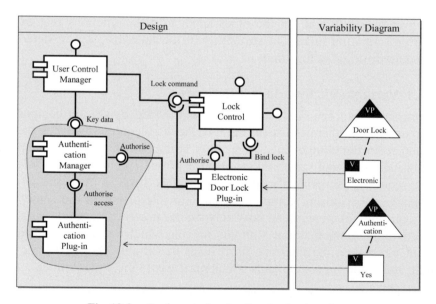

Fig. 12-3: Lock control and authentication interfaces

Example 12-1: *Interface Details*

In the home automation example, there are several components dealing with lock control and authentication; see Fig. 12-3. The 'lock control' component provides a 'lock command' interface to the user interface. This interface is meant to issue open/close commands. The commands are transferred to the 'door lock plug-in' via the 'authorise' interface to determine whether the open/close command is permitted. The 'door lock plug-in' requires a 'bind lock' interface at the 'lock control plug-in' to make its 'authorise' interface known. In case of authorisation, the door lock plug-in is an 'electronic door lock plug-in', which also uses the 'authorise' interface of the authentication manager as part of its own authorisation procedure. Authorisation key data information is passed directly from the 'user control manager' to the 'authentication manager', which is available before an authentication request is issued. The 'door lock plug-in' may also use the 'lock command' interface in case of a lock that has to be closed automatically after some period has elapsed. The interfaces carry the following information, and no more:

- 'Lock command' interface: open/close commands including information to determine the door to be opened or closed.
- 'Bind lock' interface: function for binding the 'authorise' interface of a specific door.
- 'Authorise' interface: function for getting permission to perform an (opening or closing) action.
- 'Key data' interface: function to pass through authentication key data.

In certain cases, a low level of abstraction cannot be avoided. Then, a simple data type such as a byte stream is transferred between two components. This may be the case if all kinds of objects are transferred, e.g. to and from an object-oriented database. This works if both sides of the interface have the same understanding of the meaning of the byte stream. They share the same data dictionary, and are thus able to interpret the information transferred in the byte stream. An exchange of such a data dictionary may be the first step before the actual data exchange is done. During the design of both components, it has to be clear which kinds of data dictionaries may be transferred. New dictionaries often result in new designs of the components using them, or they cannot produce or transcribe the received data completely.

Low-level abstractions

> **Example 12-2:** *Interface Abstraction*
>
> We reconsider the 'key data' interface from Example 12-1. The authentication information has to be passed through. This information is the kind of information provided by the user interface. Making it too precise in the interface, e.g. that it shall be an integer, is too low a level of abstraction, and may block future, perhaps more complex, authorisation algorithms that use a large amount of user data. Alternatively, the designer may give a lot of freedom by defining a byte stream as the type of an authorisation parameter. Such an interchange format is too high an abstraction level to be able to test adequately the components carrying the interface as all kinds of data can be represented as byte streams. To avoid both too high and too low levels of abstraction, it is better to use an authorisation information type or class that may be specialised for different cases of authorisation.

Interfaces for many components There may be interfaces that are provided by many components. This holds for instance for the aspect-related interfaces. Such an interface has to be very generic. Otherwise, it cannot be provided by each component. The types in these interfaces have to be at a low level of abstraction. Byte streams and data dictionaries may be necessary to transfer complex data. Similar restrictions on the level of detail hold for interfaces called by many components, e.g. an interface for logging actions.

12.4   Realising Variable Components

The variability of the product line eventually has to be realised in terms of reusable components. In order to enable reuse, domain realisation develops high-quality components that provide the required variability.

12.4.1 Quality of a Component

Robustness Reusable domain components are used in many applications. For their design, this means that special attention is given to their robustness. The usage context of a component is not known at development time. Thus, only assumptions can be made that are justified by the required and provided interfaces. Robustness means that the component interacts correctly in many circumstances, independent of resource usage and the order and timing between calls. This does not mean that a component must be designed to perform the called function under any circumstances. An appropriate error message may be returned in cases in which the component is not able to fulfil a request. However, this means that such behaviour is already declared in the interface.

The provided interfaces determine the functionality of a component. The functions, types, and classes are all provided in the way that is declared in the interface. No additional restrictions may be put on them, such as a calling order, or limiting re-entrance conditions. Parts of the provided interface typically also occur in the required interface of a component and thus can be used directly by the component. A component may only use external functionality that is made available through required interfaces.

Interfaces determine functionality

12.4.2 Distributing Variability over Components

Component design is constrained by the interfaces provided and required. The reference architecture determines most of the variability. Variability occurs mainly through different configurations. Domain realisation has to provide several variants for a single component having the same interfaces. In many cases, several variants of the component are realised, where each of them combines certain variants. A balance has to be found between the effort for building separate components and the ease of understanding of the variability internal to the components. The two extreme choices are usually avoided since both take too much effort to build:

Complexity and development effort

- A single component containing all variants may incorporate too much variability internally, which increases internal complexity and is therefore difficult to realise. This only works if the variability is limited.

All variants in one component

- Having a separate component for each variant introduces a large number of components, which require much development and maintenance effort. Again, this only works if the variability is limited.

A component for each variant

Example 12-3: *Variable Components for Home Automation*

In the home automation example, several 'door lock plug-in' components are needed. Each of them implements different door lock behaviour. Realisation decides to provide six variants, each with its internal variability; see Fig. 12-4. They are separated by having 'auto close' or not, and independent from this by having a lock that is 'manual', 'electronic without authentication', or 'electronic with authentication'. The plug-in components with authentication have variability related to the authentication functionality. Those with auto close have variability with respect to the parameters that are necessary to close the door automatically, such as delay times and speed. The product line may additionally contain more complex plug-in components, but these are designed to be application specific.

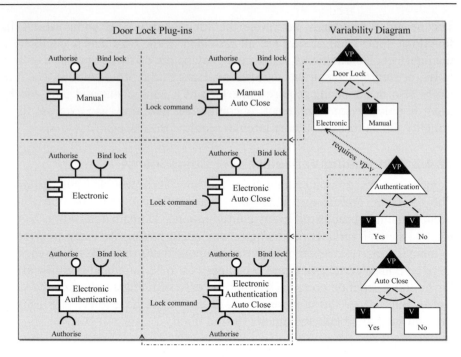

Fig. 12-4: Six reusable door lock plug-in components

12.5 Binding Time of Variability

Implementing variability

Implementation is the final step of domain realisation. In this step the actual coding is done, based on the design of the components and their interfaces. Architectural texture, e.g. coding standards, has to be obeyed. Since there are many ways of realising variability, it is important that the architecture provides clear guidelines on what to do under which circumstances. We provide a brief overview of the basic principles of implementing variability.

Configuration steps

The components and interfaces are implemented in program files. These files are configured and combined in applications in several steps:

- Compilation leads to object files.

- Linking leads to executables and DLLs (Dynamic-Link Libraries).

- Loading brings several executables and dynamic link libraries together in the same system.

For a more detailed description of the different options for the binding time, the consequences for flexibility, and other concerns, see [Coplien 1998].

Binding mechanisms

The realisation defines different binding times of variability. Different mechanisms are used to bind variants before, during, or after each step. Such mechanisms have to provide the appropriate means to locate variants and to determine which variants have to be bound. The choice of binding time and the supporting mechanism is independent of variability modelling. It is a consequence of decisions made during design and realisation. Demands for flexibility and the support of tools allow late binding times or even the use of variable binding times [V. Ommering 2004]. The exact technology at hand and the competing requests for comprehensibility and flexibility lead to specific choices of binding mechanisms. As a consequence, these are issues to be solved in design. The mechanisms that have to be used are dictated by the architectural texture. Some exemplary configuration mechanisms are those described in the following subsections.

12.5.1 Before Compilation

Automatic code generation is a technique that generates parts of the code automatically, based on some design model and/or on parameter lists. Part of the components is not programmed in the traditional way, but produced by a code generator. Variants are selected by giving values to the available parameters. Examples of such approaches are domain-specific languages [Batory et al. 2004], generative programming [Czarnecki and Eisenecker 2000], and model-driven architecture [Kleppe et al. 2003].

Code generation

Aspect-oriented programming is a technique where diffcrent views of the code, so-called aspects, get their own implementation [Kiczales et al. 1997]. Prior to the actual compilation the different aspects are weaved together into a single piece of code dealing with the different aspects. Each aspect may have its own variability. Choosing a variant for an aspect leads to a variant of weaved code.

Aspect-oriented programming

There are other realisation approaches that are well suited for product line engineering. Atkinson describes a method called KobrA which supports a model-driven UML-based representation of components and a product-line-based approach to their development and evolution [Atkinson 2001]. The representation is implementation independent and uses a simple and orthogonal feature set so that feature overload is avoided and the most appropriate kind of implementation method can be used.

Model-driven approaches

The "Software Factories" described in [Greenfield et al. 2004] are also an approach to model-driven development. They apply domain-specific languages and the Extensible Markup Language (XML) to describe their models.

12.5.2 At Compile Time

Pre-compiler macros

Before compilation, the compiler reads one or more files containing macro definitions. A macro can be any fragment of program code and thus be used to realise a variation point. The defined code fragments correspond to the variants of this variation point. The macros are expanded to their definition at every occurrence in the code. Moreover, IFDEF statements may guard certain pieces of code; depending on the presence of a definition of the macro, a piece of code will or will not be compiled. Thus, generation of code is dependent on the definition of the macro. It is a very generic mechanism, which may become very complex, since the IFDEF statement can govern any piece of code, and the consequences of using it cannot always be determined easily, especially when IFDEFs are nested. The advantage of using pre-compiler macros is the code efficiency obtained. Configuration takes place before actual compilation. Code that is not useful for a specific application is not present. The complexity can be managed if the macro usage is regulated by architecture rules, determining which macros are admissible, what their meaning is, and where and how they have to be applied in the code.

Conditional compilation

Conditional compilation is a similar mechanism to pre-compiler macros. In this case the macro definitions are not defined in a file, but given as parameters to the compiler command. The advantages and drawbacks are similar to the pre-compiler macros.

12.5.3 At Link Time

Makefiles

The makefile is an executable file that is able to perform a sequence of compilations and linkages. Depending on the makefile parameters, different sets of compilations and linkages are performed. Variation points can be realised by the parameters provided to the make command which executes the makefile. The selection of variants is realised by the different sequences of the makefile that are executed based on these parameters. For instance, depending on the makefile parameters, different compiler parameters are used, and/or different macro files are included. In this case configuration is performed before actual compilation. However, the mechanism can also be used to select different configurations of variable binary components. The makefile determines a sequence of dependencies, and is usually very difficult to read. Therefore, architecture rules are necessary to limit its use. Moreover, it is recommended to use makefile generator tools, to generate the makefiles from more comprehensible configuration notations.

12.5.4 At Load Time

A configuration file contains a list of files that have to be loaded together. *Configuration files* The set of files in the selection forms an executable system. The configuration file may have variable content in order to realise different variants of a variation point. The configuration file uses the run-time system to locate and initiate all files that should be loaded. This mechanism is useful for producing systems consisting of variable binary component configurations. Usually architecture rules are necessary to provide each executable with the right mechanisms to enable its localisation, initialisation, and linkage to the remainder of the system.

12.5.5 At Run-Time

The target machine may host a central registry, in which each compiled component registers its interfaces together with their access points within the component. If at run-time a certain component needs another component carrying a certain interface, it can be found through the registry. No separate configuration files are necessary, each component should just know which interfaces it needs, and from which kinds of components. After the binary components are loaded, an initialisation mechanism makes them known to the registry. Components carrying the same interface may realise variants of the same variation point. *Registry*

12.6 Realising Configurability

During application realisation, variability in components is bound. Domain realisation has to prepare for this. The component designer determines a collection of configuration parameters to be able to select the right component variant (Example 12-4). Many mechanisms can be used to deal with configuration parameters. Configuration mechanisms such as compiler parameters, macros, and parameter files are discussed in Section 12.5. Alternatively, certain languages enable components to be parameterised, either through a parameter list, or through a separate file with component parameters. Part or all of the parameters can be exposed over interfaces towards other components, which may use the parameter values to determine their internal variants, or alternatively may set them to certain values, depending on their own parameter values [V. Ommering et al. 2000]. *Configuration parameters*

Because there are many parameters that belong to a single application, the parameters must be related to the variation points and variants in the variability model. This is crucial for the selection of the right variants. A variation point may have an impact within several components, and the selection and configuration of components is based on the given variants. *Variability model*

Configuration independence

A component is configuration independent when it does not need much of its environment in order to work correctly. The level of configuration independence of a component or interface is dependent on the role it plays in the reference architecture. This means that it should be designed in such a way that it provides precisely the functionality specified in its provided interfaces and use precisely what is specified in its required interfaces. It should not put any additional restrictions on the functions that can be called through its provided interface. The component designer should not rely on presently available implementations of its required interfaces, e.g. that results are presently always sorted, while this is not specified in the interface itself. New implementations may not sort the results. Knowledge of the role of the component in the product line may reduce the effort to make a component more or less dependent on the configuration, while it still is robust.

Level of detail and abstraction

Two important aspects support configuration independence: level of detail and level of abstraction. The level of detail relates to the granularity of the functions exposed at the interface. The level of abstraction relates to the data types exposed at the interface; see Section 12.3.2.

Example 12-4: *Configuration Variability*

The selection of the door lock plug-in components of Fig. 12-4 is related to several parameters. First, there are parameters that select the right component to use:

- Bool: Door_lock_electronic
- Bool: Door_authentication
- Bool: Auto_close

Next, there are parameters that govern the internal variability of certain of these components:

- String: Authentication_algorithm, for selecting the authentication algorithm.
- Int: Auto_close_delay, for selecting the delay before auto close takes effect.

The five configuration parameters may also be necessary for selecting variants in other components as well. In particular, they are used by the 'lock control' component (Fig. 12-3). It is the case that all these components use the same parameters, and that their value is defined only once.

12.7   Differences from Single-System Engineering

Domain realisation provides a coherent collection of reusable software artefacts. This means that:

- Domain realisation does not provide a complete application. Therefore, *No executable*
  domain realisation is not able to build an executable. Instead, domain
  realisation provides mechanisms to application realisation in order to
  configure the domain realisation results with the results of application
  realisation into executables.

- Interfaces have to be designed carefully with the appropriate level of *Interface*
  detail and the appropriate level of abstraction to be usable in many *design*
  applications. Too much detail or too low a level of abstraction restricts
  the providing components too much. Too low a level of detail or too
  high a level of abstraction makes it too generic for the requiring components to do something useful.

- Configuration management is an activity that is more important for *Variability in*
  domain engineering than for single-system development. At any *time and space*
  moment, there are applications that use different versions of reusable
  components. For maintenance purposes, it is crucial to know which version of any component and interface is used in which application.

- Software artefacts have to incorporate variability. Software artefacts *Variable software*
  have variation points and variants. Domain realisation has to provide *artefacts*
  mechanisms to select the variants before the domain realisation results
  are integrated into an application.

- The components and interfaces are more robust than what is required *Quality*
  for single-system development. Reusable components have to be configuration independent to ensure that they can be used in different
  applications with different variability bindings.

12.8   Summary

Domain realisation deals with the design and implementation of reusable *Component and*
components and interfaces. In particular, the design of interfaces is crucial, *interface design*
since they are the basis for architectural variability based upon configuration
variants. As different components provide or require a single interface, there
may be many stakeholders in the component design, having their own interest in moving the level of abstraction. Reusable components should only use
functionality that is presented by their required interfaces and they should
provide exactly what is declared by their provided interfaces.

Realisation mechanisms for variability

The component developer has different mechanisms available to implement the variability of components. The choice is guided by the architectural texture, thus allowing a high degree of uniformity to be achieved in the implementation. The variability has to be presented to the application developer in order to enable the selection of the proper variants. For instance, this can be done by relating component parameters to the variability model.

Robustness and configuration independence

The components and interfaces have to be designed for robustness and configuration independence to be reusable. Interface adaptations have to be reduced to a minimum. Each such adaptation results in many component adaptations. Components do not always have to be designed from scratch. Often a component that was originally designed for a single application is promoted to a domain component. This involves redesign to remove the dependency of the component configuration in the specific application. In addition, variability has to be added in order to get the application-specific components as variants.

Klaus Pohl
Andreas Reuys

13

Domain Testing

In this chapter you will learn:

- o *About the interrelations of the domain testing sub-process with domain requirements engineering, design, and realisation as well as with application testing.*
- o *Strategies to accomplish testing in software product line engineering.*
- o *About the embedding of variability in domain test artefacts.*

13.1 Introduction

Goals of domain testing The goal of domain testing is to validate the output of the other domain engineering sub-processes. Our main focus is on the validation of the realisation artefacts. The derivation of test cases is based on the input from domain requirements engineering, domain design, and domain realisation. The goal of domain testing is to establish an efficient overall testing process. This involves testing early and often what can be tested within the domain engineering process and providing reusable test artefacts. Testing aspects have to be considered right from the beginning of the development, e.g. to ensure that requirements and design support testing. For instance, testing requires that the state of a component can be evaluated at run-time to be able to compare the expected results of an action with the actual results. Consequently, component interfaces need to be designed to enable the introspection into a component's state at run-time. The sub-processes and artefacts closely related to the domain testing sub-process are highlighted in Fig. 13-1.

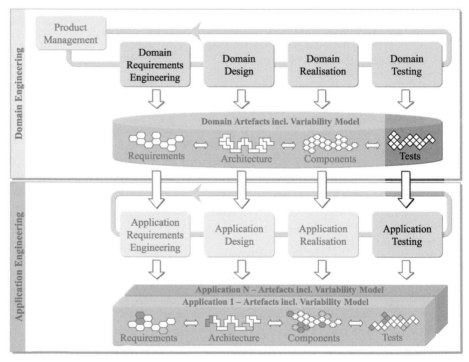

Fig. 13-1:   Sub-processes and artefacts related to domain testing

Variability The main challenge for domain testing is to deal adequately with both the separation between domain engineering and application engineering and the presence of variability. The variability of the product line and its relation to domain artefacts are documented in a variability model throughout domain engineering. In domain testing the variability model is used to derive test artefacts for the domain artefacts under test.

Variable artefacts pertaining to only one or a few applications are not realised in domain engineering. They are defined during application engineering. For example, plug-in components that are required only for one specific application are designed during application engineering (Section 11.5). We refer to variants for which no realisation is available in domain engineering as "absent variants" (Section 13.5). The absence of a variant complicates domain testing, as part of the component interactions cannot be tested easily.

Absence of realisation

In order to test the interactions between a common component and an absent variant, a stub can be used. The stub simulates the behaviour of the corresponding plug-in component during integration testing. Yet, stubs have three major shortcomings. First, the creation of stubs requires considerable effort. Second, a stub is often no adequate substitute for the plug-in component. The actual component's behaviour may be quite different from the stub's behaviour and thus may cause errors that do not occur in the integration test with the stub. Third, the stub itself is a source of errors and must be tested. Consequently, the interactions of common components with plug-in components cannot be regarded as sufficiently tested in domain engineering even if stubs are used.

Limited value of stubs

In order to achieve the goals of domain testing and avoid the problems related to the handling of variability, we employ specific software product line engineering test strategies. These strategies consider both the separation between domain testing and application testing and the presence of variability. The activities performed in domain and application testing strongly depend on the strategy pursued.

Product line test strategies

The essential interrelations between domain testing and the other domain engineering sub-processes are shown in Fig. 13-2. The results produced during domain requirements engineering are used as input for the domain system test. The architecture resulting from the domain design is required for the domain integration test, and the components produced during domain realisation are validated in the domain unit test. Moreover, the application that is finally delivered must be validated. Application testing reuses domain test artefacts to test specific applications. Test levels, i.e. system test, integration test, and unit test, are explained in more detail in Section 13.2 along with other test foundations.

Interrelations with other sub-processes

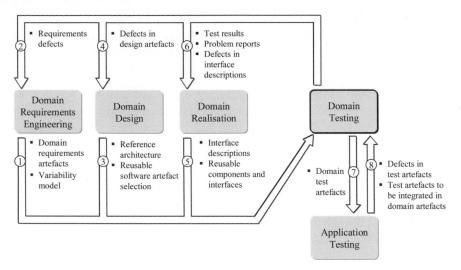

Fig. 13-2:   Information flows between domain testing and other sub-processes

13.1.1 Interrelation with Domain Requirements Engineering

Domain requirements artefacts and variability model

The input stemming from domain requirements engineering for domain testing consists of the domain requirements artefacts and the variability model (① in Fig. 13-2). The domain requirements artefacts contain the specifications of common and variable domain requirements. The variability model defines the variability of the software product line. Domain testing uses the domain requirements artefacts to develop system tests. As the platform merely contains a set of loosely coupled components but no complete applications, the test engineer can only perform system tests on the parts of the system that realise common requirements and are not affected by the variability of the software product line. Thus, strategies are necessary to deal with the lack of an executable application and the variability in requirements and components respectively. Part of such a strategy is the use of the variability model for developing test cases that contain variability themselves (Chapter 8).

Feedback about domain requirements

It may be the case that system tests cannot be derived from the requirements, because the requirements are not clearly stated or there are unwanted dependencies between the requirements that prevent the creation of tests. Such requirements defects are reported back to domain requirements engineering (② in Fig. 13-2) so that the defects in the requirements artefacts can be corrected. Consequently, domain testing contributes to the validation of domain requirements, and thus, to the overall quality assurance of the software product line.

13.1.2 Interrelation with Domain Design

The input from domain design consists of the reference architecture and the selection of reusable software artefacts (③ in Fig. 13-2). Integration tests use the reference architecture as a test reference for validating the interactions between components. Such interactions are, for example, evident from the architectural structure and, in particular, from the component frameworks (Definition 6-8), or from the use cases defined in the domain requirements engineering sub-process.

Reference architecture

Integration tests cannot validate all interactions between the components as there may be variable components that are not realised during domain engineering. The reusable artefact selection indicates which component realisations are part of the platform and sets the scope for the domain integration tests. As stated above, the interactions with components that are realised in application engineering cannot be sufficiently tested in the domain testing sub-process. However, it is possible to define reusable test artefacts for such interactions.

Absent components

The design of integration test artefacts leads to some kind of validation of the reference architecture. Defects in domain design artefacts such as incompleteness and ambiguity prevent the definition of test artefacts. They are reported back to the domain design sub-process (④ in Fig. 13-2).

Feedback on reference architecture

13.1.3 Interrelation with Domain Realisation

The input from domain realisation consists of interface descriptions and the reusable components and interfaces implemented and ready for test (⑤ in Fig. 13-2). Domain testing uses the interface descriptions as a test reference for the unit test. Again, testing can be performed only for the components that are implemented within the domain realisation sub-process.

Interfaces and components

Domain testing provides domain realisation with the test results including acceptance or rejection as well as the corresponding problem reports (⑥ in Fig. 13-2). Defects in interface descriptions detected in domain testing are reported back as well. The test results capture which test cases have been performed and whether the object under test passed or failed the test. The problem reports capture the observed deviations from the expected behaviour, which the object under test should possess according to the test reference. Defects in interface descriptions hamper test case design and must be corrected before testing can be completed.

Test results

13.1.4 Interrelation with Application Testing

Domain testing provides application testing with reusable test artefacts (⑦ in Fig. 13-2) such as test cases. As domain tests may have to be performed again in application testing, all test cases, including those already performed

Reusable test artefacts

in domain testing, are delivered to application testing. Like other domain artefacts, domain test cases may contain variability. Application testing binds the variability to obtain test cases for the specific application.

Feedback from application testing

Application testing returns defects in domain test artefacts as well as test artefacts to be integrated into the domain artefacts (⑧ in Fig. 13-2). Test artefacts are developed in application testing, for instance to test application-specific features. If application-specific features are integrated in the domain artefacts, the test artefacts, along with the design and realisation artefacts, have to be integrated as well.

13.2 Software Testing

In dealing with software testing, the notion of software defects and the notion of software test levels are essential.

Part of quality assurance

Software testing (Definition 13-1) allows the stakeholders to determine the quality of the software. It is an essential part of the quality assurance process, which also includes reviews of all requirements and design specifications, code reviews, acceptance procedures, etc.

Definition 13-1: *Software Testing*

Software testing is the process of uncovering evidence of defects in software systems and is a necessary part of any quality assurance process.

[McGregor and Sykes 2001]

Testing uncovers the evidence of defects

Examples 13-1 and 13-2 present two cases of software testing. Testing is performed before the delivery of an application. It does not include debugging and fixing bugs. The defects detected in testing are reported back to the development team in charge.

Example 13-1: *Software Testing – Positive Case (Release)*

Three software testers perform testing for a whole week and find three defects in the components of the "door & window management" subsystem. After the defects are corrected, the subsystem is released as the defects were hard to find and did not impede the use of the software components. The testing results give rise to the assumption that the components are free of serious defects.

> **Example 13-2:** *Software Testing - Negative Case (Further Testing)*
>
> Three software testers perform testing on the "security & safety management" subsystem for a week and each tester finds one defect per hour. The defects are recorded in a protocol and passed on to the domain realisation team that developed the components. The amount of defects makes further testing necessary after the detected defects have been corrected.

13.2.1 Defects

A *defect* (Definition 13-2) can be interpreted as a difference between a requirement, which defines the desired behaviour, and its realisation in the software.[37]

Defect

> **Definition 13-2:** *Defect*
>
> Defects occur when a software system does not behave as desired or specified.

> **Example 13-3:** *Defect in the User Interface*
>
> The specification of the smart home user interface requires that the icon for lighting control is always visible. Yet, in the implemented user interface components, there are some dialogs, in which the icon is hidden behind other elements. This behaviour is a defect as it does not fulfil the specification.

13.2.2 Test Levels

Techniques and methods for software testing typically distinguish between different test levels such as system testing, integration testing, and unit testing, see e.g. [Burnstein 2002; McGregor and Sykes 2001; Spillner and Linz 2004]. Before we elaborate on the different test levels, we define the term test level:

> **Definition 13-3:** *Test Level*
>
> A test level is defined by the granularity of the items to be tested (test items) and the requirements used as the test reference.

---

[37] We define the term defect in analogy to [IEEE 1990]. The definition in [IEEE 1990] additionally distinguishes between error, fault, failure, and defect. We only use the term defect in this book as our focus is on testing issues that are specific to software product line engineering.

Test, test item, and   The key terms and their relationships used in the definition are shown in Fig.
test requirement   13-3. A 'test' validates a 'test item' with respect to the test reference. The
test reference is called a 'requirement' in Fig. 13-3 but, in fact, can be any
kind of specification. For example, a signature (or interface description) can
be used as the test reference to validate a single component. This shows that
the requirement and the specified item are on the same level of development.
In the context of testing these two artefacts determine the test level.

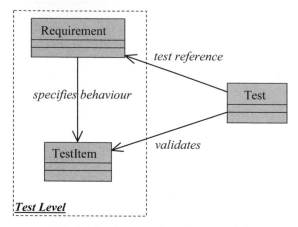

Fig. 13-3:   The test dependency model

Definition 13-4: *Unit Test*

The unit test validates the behaviour of a component, method, or class
against its input/output behaviour specified in the corresponding signature.

Example 13-4: *Unit Test Case*

A method of the LockActuator class, which is a part of the basic control subsystem, has the signature "bool unlock(Lock l, Authentication
auth)". The documentation of the method explains the parameters and
the return value and describes the method's behaviour. A test case for
the "unlock" method ensures that the initial state of the lock object is
"locked" and the authentication object contains valid authentication
data. Subsequently the test case calls the unlock method, and checks
whether the return value is "true", i.e. whether the method reports that
unlocking the door succeeded. Finally, the test case checks the internal
state of the lock object to verify that the lock is unlocked.

The unit test is a test level that is often performed by the programmer of the unit. The programmer tests each implemented method, procedure, or function. The test validates the behaviour of the implemented code against its specification.

Validation of isolated code units

> **Definition 13-5:** *Integration Test*
>
> The integration test validates the behaviour of two or more components that together form a configuration specified in the architecture.

The integration test is usually performed on units or components that have successfully passed the unit test. Therefore, one can assume that the units behave as specified. Nevertheless, the functionality of the configuration may deviate from the specified behaviour.

Validation of interactions

> **Example 13-5:** *Integration Test Case*
>
> An integration test case of the home security product line checks the interaction between the 'authentication plug-in', the 'authentication manager', and the 'electronic door lock' components (Section 6.4). The test case authenticates a test user against the 'authentication plug-in' component and checks the interaction with the 'authentication manager' component to ensure that the test user is authenticated properly. Subsequently, the test case requests the 'electronic door lock' component to unlock a door and checks the interaction between the 'electronic door lock' and the 'authentication manager' components to verify that the 'authentication manager' authorises the 'electronic door lock' component to unlock the door.

The system test is performed after the integration test has been successfully passed (at least partially).

> **Definition 13-6:** *System Test*
>
> The system test validates the behaviour of a whole system against its system requirements specification.

The internals of the system are usually not considered during a system test. The system requirements define the desired behaviour of the system. System tests validate the implemented system against the specification.

Validation of the behaviour of a system

> **Example 13-6:** *System Test Case*
>
> A system test case for the home security product line includes a scenario with the following steps: the user approaches the authentication terminal of the front door and inserts a magnetic card into the card reader. The terminal checks the data on the magnetic card against the list of authorised users, acknowledges that the user may enter the home, and unlocks the front door. The user opens the door, enters the home, and shuts the door. After 5 seconds the security system locks the door again.

Incremental testing

In practice[38] there are even more test levels. The architecture provides layers or subsystems that can be tested incrementally. Thus, there may be several incremental integration test levels. Incremental integration testing reduces complexity since earlier increments have already been tested and can thus be assumed to be correct during the test of the next increment. Incremental integration tests do not differ much from normal integration tests. We therefore do not consider incremental integration tests in the remainder of this chapter.

13.3   Domain Testing and Application Testing

Two test processes

Testing is performed in domain and application engineering. Domain testing deals with loosely coupled, reusable components, whereas application testing deals with complete applications. Both testing processes have to cooperate to reduce complexity and to establish synergies.

Defects in domain artefacts

Domain testing uncovers the evidence of defects in domain artefacts and creates reusable test artefacts for application testing (Example 13-7). Domain testing encompasses the same activities as single-system software testing but additionally has to deal with variability and the fact that there is no executable system.

> **Example 13-7:** *Domain Testing for Home Automation*
>
> In the home automation system, domain testing validates the door control functionality. The test encompasses functions such as checking the status of a door, opening, and closing a door.

Defects in applications

Application testing reuses domain test artefacts to uncover evidence of defects in the product line applications (Example 13-8). In spite of the tests

---

[38] See [V.d. Linden and Müller 1995] or [Reuys et al. 2004a] for case studies of industrial test approaches and intermediate test levels.

performed in domain testing, each application has to be tested extensively. Common artefacts may have interdependencies with variable artefacts, which have to be retested.

> **Example 13-8:** *Application Testing in Home Automation*
>
> An installed home automation system is tested for a correctly working door control. All installed doors are tested with respect to the requirements specification, which includes status information, open, close, and automatic close functionality.

Retesting domain artefacts during application testing has some commonalities with regression testing in single-system engineering. The goal of regression testing is to detect defects that are caused by modifications to the software. In regression testing, test cases of older versions of a software product are reused to test a new software version. Testing only the modified parts of the software is not sufficient as changes to one part of the software may cause errors in other parts. An impact analysis is used to determine the subset of test cases to be reexecuted depending on the changes made to the software. Although regression testing does not offer adequate means to deal with variability in space, the basic ideas of regression testing can be adapted to support application testing. For further reading on regression testing, see e.g. [Binder 1999].

Regression tests

13.4   Testing Variability at Different Test Levels

Variability has an impact on all test levels. Figure 13-4 below shows a part of the V-model [V-Model 1997; Dröschel and Wiemers 2000; V-Model XT], which is a commonly used development process in single-system engineering. The left branch of the "V" shows the different development steps. The test items, which are defined considering the development artefacts, are shown in the different test levels on the right branch of the "V". The grey bricks at each test level represent common software units or components. The white bricks indicate variability. The black ellipses indicate test cases that cover some parts of the specific test item. In the following, we discuss the impact of product line variability on the different test levels in more detail.

Variable test cases in the V-Model

13.4.1 Domain Unit Test

The techniques used for the domain unit test depend on the realisation of the variability. If the variability is realised, for example, by IFDEFS (Section 12.5), the unit under test has to be built with each defined variant once and

Local variability

each build is tested as in single-system engineering. The units to be tested can embed variability. Since this type of variability is local to the test object, there is typically no problem in performing the unit test during domain engineering.

Example 13-9: *Unit Test for the Electronic Door Locks*

The unit test for the electronic door locks tests each unit separately. One unit containing variability is the authorisation database. The test checks whether the component is capable of accepting and rejecting simulated inputs from magnetic card readers, fingerprint scanners, etc. Therefore, the methods for the variants, e.g. magnet card reader, must be linked to the unit at first. Second, the methods are tested with valid and invalid data to validate the unit's behaviour against its signature. The test is carried out for each variant separately.

13.4.2 Domain Integration Test

Test of common interactions

Variability influences components and component interactions in three ways. Variability may occur within a component, in the way components interact, or the component itself may realise a variant. Due to variability, it is typically impossible to test all component interactions during domain testing. One reason is that not all components that participate in these interactions are realised during domain realisation (Section 13.1). Even if all the components were available, there would still be many optional or alternative interactions. Testing all component pairs and all possible interactions is thus close to impossible. Existing product line test approaches therefore perform only the test cases for common interactions and those that contain few variable interactions with already realised components.

Example 13-10: *Integration Test for Electronic Door Locks*

During integration testing in domain engineering, the units are integrated in pairs. The server is connected to the fingerprint scanner, the keypad, or the magnetic card reader. More combinations between these units, e.g. one fingerprint scanner, one keypad, and the server for both of them, are possible, but in the foreseeable future there will not be an application with this configuration. Therefore, these combinations are not tested during domain testing.

13.4.3 Domain System Test

Test of sample configurations

The variability relevant for system tests is defined in domain requirements artefacts. They are the test references for system testing (Fig. 13-4). It is impossible to perform a complete system test in domain engineering due to the presence of variability, and due to the fact that domain engineering does not deliver a complete system. The variability poses similar problems for the system test as explained for the integration test. The part of the system tested by a system test case is typically much larger than the part of the system tested in an integration test. It is thus difficult to find test cases that do not include variability. Consequently, system tests cannot be performed on domain artefacts. To perform a system test a defined configuration of variants is required. This may be a fictive configuration or an application defined by product management. Without a configuration, system test case scenarios can be defined (e.g. with the means provided in Chapter 8), but not executed.

Example 13-11: *System Test for the Electronic Door Locks*

The system test for the electronic door locks can only be performed on a particular application. The system test requires one specific configuration of fingerprint scanners, keypads, card readers, and one or more control devices. This configuration is not available during domain testing. It is defined during application engineering.

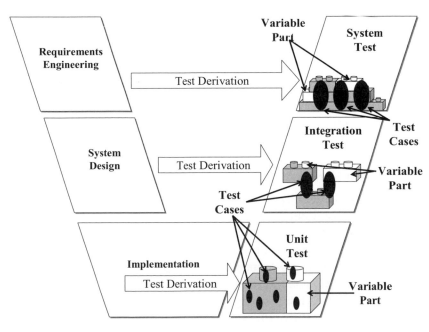

Fig. 13-4: Test levels and their increasing complexity due to variability

13.5   Criteria for Product Line Test Strategies

Impact of variability

The description of the three test levels in Section 13.4 shows that variability has a high impact on testing. While unit testing can be performed relatively well, higher test levels suffer from several problems related to variability. For example, either variants may be not fully implemented in domain engineering or there may be a huge number of configurations. Finally, there is no executable system to test.

This impact of variability on the integration and system test stresses the need for a software product line test strategy. Before we elaborate on possible strategies, we define five essential criteria for evaluating a product line test strategy.

13.5.1 Time to Create Test Artefacts

Overall effort

A large part of the testing effort is spent on the creation of test artefacts. Test artefacts, e.g. test cases, are created in domain engineering as well as in application engineering. The time to create test artefacts is influenced by the amount of test artefacts as well as by the difficulty of creating them. Variability in requirements makes the creation of domain test artefacts a complex task. This increases the time to create them, but reuse helps to compensate for the increase in development time. This holds particularly for the planned reuse of domain test artefacts in application testing.

First criterion

The *time to create test artefacts* criterion (see Definition 8-1 for the definition of "test artefacts") is the estimation of the overall time required for creating test artefacts in domain and application testing. The main questions related to this criterion concern how far the test strategy supports the reuse of test artefacts, and how far it accelerates the development of test artefacts.

13.5.2 Absent Variants

Workarounds for lacking realisation

During domain engineering, some variants might not be realised as they are developed on demand during application engineering. We call such variants absent variants since they are not available during domain testing. The ability to deal with the situation of absent variants is important in domain testing. If techniques or workarounds are defined, the test engineer is able to perform the integration and system test cases that involve variability at least partially. This enables the test engineer to test more than just the common parts during domain testing, which yields a high quality of the product line.

Second criterion

The *absent variants* criterion evaluates how well a test strategy copes with absent variants.

13.5.3 Early Validation

One important aspect to ensure a high quality of the product line is to perform an early validation of development artefacts (by performing reviews, tests, etc.). This helps to keep the costs for repairing defects low. The costs rise the later the defects are detected and repaired in the development life cycle [Davis 1993]. Therefore, the development artefacts, especially the domain artefacts, should be tested as soon as possible.

Early detection of defects

The *early validation* criterion is an indicator for the elapsed time between the finalisation of an artefact and its validation. The time should be low to ensure that defects are detected early, preferably in domain testing.

Third criterion

13.5.4 Learning Effort

The separation between domain and application engineering and the presence of variability lead to an adaptation of the testing process and testing products, e.g. test cases. A test engineer who is only familiar with single-system testing has to learn how the software product line test process works and how to deal with variability. A good strategy makes only few adaptations to the test process and test products, but enable the test engineers to perform their task in product line engineering.

Differences from single-system testing

The *learning effort* criterion assesses product line test strategies with regard to the time it takes until a software test engineer is able to perform the test activities associated with the considered test strategy.

Fourth criterion

13.5.5 Overhead

Overhead may be caused by producing the same artefact more than once or by performing additional activities which are not necessary, for instance for a single-system test process. Modelling variability can be overhead, and insufficient test artefact reuse can lead to overhead as well.

Effort caused by unnecessary activities

The *overhead* criterion evaluates the amount of activities performed and/or the amount of artefacts produced unnecessarily as the same result could be achieved with lower effort.

Fifth criterion

13.6 Product Line Test Strategies

In contrast to single-system engineering, testing activities in product line engineering have to consider product line variability as well as the differentiation between the two development processes, i.e. domain and application engineering. In this section, we define and evaluate four fundamental test strategies for testing product line artefacts.

13.6.1 Brute Force Strategy

Extensive test of all configurations

The goal of software product line testing is to assure a sufficient quality of domain artefacts as well as all product line applications. Therefore, a straightforward idea is to ensure the quality as early and as completely as possible, which is in line with the early validation criterion. The brute force strategy aims at assuring the quality of the product line by performing an extensive domain test for all possible applications (Definition 13-7). This includes tests at all test levels (unit test, integration test, and system test) for all possible configurations.

> **Definition 13-7:** *Brute Force Strategy (BFS)*
>
> Perform all test activities at all test levels and for all possible applications during domain testing.

BFS unusable in practice

As the BFS takes into account all possible applications, no application testing has to be done during application engineering (Fig. 13-5). The inability to deal with the absence of components implies a longer domain realisation process that includes the implementation of all components. As the early validation criterion is fulfilled, the strategy seems quite attractive.

All tests in domain testing

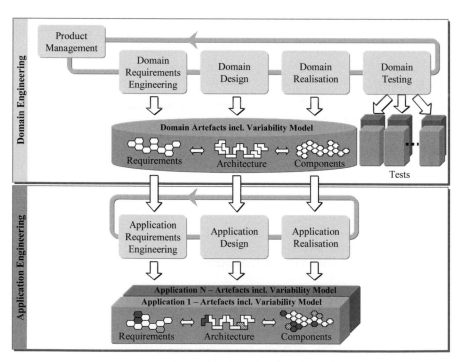

Fig. 13-5: Brute force strategy (BFS)

Nevertheless, it is not usable in practice. The number of possible configurations is by far too large. Example 13-12 shows this for a very small case. Industrial projects may involve a huge amount of variation points and variants. The respective number of possible applications prevents the application of the BFS.

Table 13-1 summarises the evaluation of the BFS. A "+" indicates that the strategy yields positive results for a criterion, a "-" indicates that the strategy yields negative results for a criterion, and a "0" indicates that advantages and disadvantages are almost balanced for a criterion. For the BFS, the time to create test artefacts criterion is rated with a "-" due to the large amount of test artefacts that must be created. The learning effort is rated with a "0" as the BFS requires learning how to deal with different configurations, but avoids having to learn how to deal with variability in test artefacts. The inability of the strategy to deal with absent variants leads to a "-" for the absent variants criterion. Early validation gets a "+" as all tests are performed in domain testing. The overhead is rated with a "-" as most configurations are tested unnecessarily.

Evaluation results

> **Example 13-12:** *Amount of Possible Configurations*
>
> Following the discussion in [Kolb and Muthig 2003], a product line with only ten variation points, each of which has three possible variants, leads to $3^{10} = 59,049$ possible configurations or applications.
>
> This is an artificial example with independent variation points and variants, where exactly one variant must be chosen per variation point. If the variants are optional and the application may be used without a variant or with up to three variants per variation point, eight possibilities exist per variation point, leading to $8^{10} = 1,073,741,824$ possible applications.

Table 13-1: Evaluation of the BFS

Evaluation of the Brute Force Strategy				
Time to create	Absent variants	Early validation	Learning effort	Overhead
-	-	+	0	-

13.6.2 Pure Application Strategy

The opposite strategy to BFS is to neglect domain testing, and to perform application testing only (Definition 13-8).

> **Definition 13-8:** *Pure Application Strategy (PAS)*
>
> Perform tests only in application engineering. Here, only application-specific tests are created and performed. No reusable domain test artefacts are created during domain testing.

No domain testing

PAS considers only the artefacts used in the actual application (Fig. 13-6). This approach resembles applying single-system software testing in software product line engineering. The defects found during application testing are forwarded to the application engineering team. The development team is responsible for determining whether a defect is application-specific or pertains to the domain artefacts.

High overhead

The pure application strategy is not suitable for application in practice either, as it performs poorly in two of the criteria. The first problem is the high overhead. The test artefacts for the applications are developed all over again for each application. Such a product line test strategy does not have an advantage over single-system testing. Consequently, the PAS causes a bottleneck in the software product line engineering process. Whereas all development stages are able to assemble the reusable artefacts, testing has to start from scratch for each application.

All tests in application testing

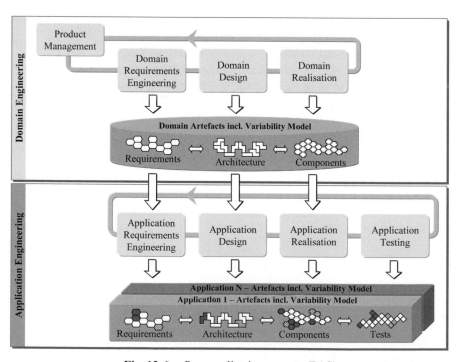

Fig. 13-6: Pure application strategy (PAS)

The second problem with the PAS is the lacking early validation. Nothing is tested until the first application is built. The stakeholders cannot trust the quality of the platform and it may take a lot of time and money to repair the defects.

No early validation

We summarise the evaluation results of the PAS in Table 13-2. The time to create test artefacts is rated with a "0" as it is roughly equal to the time needed in single-system engineering. As test engineers neither have to deal with absent variants nor with variability, the absent variants criterion and the learning effort are both rated with a "+". Early validation is rated with a "-" since no tests are performed in domain testing. The overhead is rated with a "-" since similar test cases have to be defined for each application.

Evaluation results

Table 13-2: Evaluation of the PAS

Evaluation of the Pure Application Strategy				
Time to create	Absent variants	Early validation	Learning effort	Overhead
0	+	-	+	-

13.6.3 Sample Application Strategy

The following strategy achieves an early validation at reasonable cost. Instead of testing all applications like in the BFS, in this strategy only one or a few sample applications[39] are assembled and tested (Definition 13-9).

> **Definition 13-9:** *Sample Application Strategy (SAS)*
>
> Use one or a few sample applications to test the domain artefacts. Application testing is still required for each application.

The SAS aims at ensuring a sufficient quality of the domain artefacts. With the sample application, a representative system is created that can be tested. This sample application has one particular configuration. All common components are tested in the context of the selected variants of the sample application(s). Furthermore, the selected variants themselves are tested. Since not all possible applications are tested, application testing has to be performed, too. This is depicted in the right part of Fig. 13-7. The application may reuse some test artefacts produced in domain testing.

Sample applications

---

[39] The sample applications may stem from product management or from development. The development team may choose a configuration that is easy to realise in order to speed up testing if product management does not define suitable samples.

Validation of common artefacts

One speciality of the SAS is that the sample application not only enables an early validation of the domain artefacts, but also enables the validation of the commonalities of the whole product line (Example 13-13). Moreover the definition of the sample applications ensures that the derivation of an application is possible and that the binding mechanisms work correctly.

Effort as in single-system engineering

The evaluation of the SAS regarding the criteria is as follows. The time to create test artefacts in domain engineering is as high as in single-system engineering as the sample application is tested in a single-system-like manner. However, it is possible to reuse test artefacts during application engineering, e.g. for the common parts or variants. This reuse reduces the time to create the test artefacts in application engineering. However, as the artefacts have been developed specifically for the sample application, they have to be adapted. The SAS thus gets an average rating for the time to create test artefacts criterion.

Absent variants, early validation

The ability to handle absent variants is not directly addressed by this strategy. The problem of absent variants is avoided by creating a sample application. This leads to a good evaluation result for the absent variant criterion. Early validation is achieved with this strategy, as the common parts and even some typical variants can be tested during domain engineering.

Test of sample applications

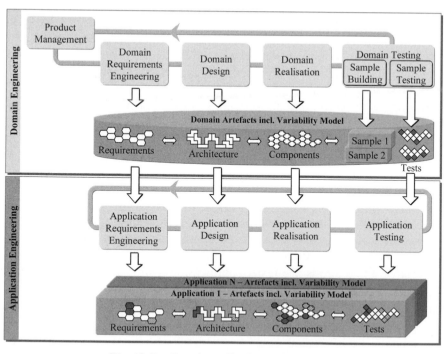

Fig. 13-7:   Sample application strategy (SAS)

The learning effort criterion is also positive for this strategy since the test products and activities are very similar to the products and activities in single-system engineering. Variability does not occur in the documents the test engineer receives for a sample application.

Low learning effort

The SAS has a negative evaluation for the overhead criterion. This is due to the fact that one or more complete applications have to be realised to enable testing. Nevertheless, realising the applications proves that applications can be derived from the platform. Therefore the overhead is costly, but may be worth doing.

High overhead

Table 13-3 depicts the evaluation results of the SAS. This is only a rough evaluation as the values depend on the detailed method that is used to realise the strategy, e.g. on the number of applications used as samples. If the number of applications is high, the time for creating the test artefacts increases, leading to a "-" for the time to create test artefacts criterion.

Evaluation results

Example 13-13: *SAS for the Home Automation System*

The sample application for the home automation system includes the following configuration of realised variants. The application is equipped with automatic window control, central heating control, and central air-conditioning control. For each room, camera surveillance is installed, and for each door, a lock secured by a magnetic card reader is present. Based on the configuration, the quality of the product line is validated. The sample application is tested at the different test levels. The domain integration test validates the interactions of the components. The domain system test validates the meaningful behaviour of the entire application.

Table 13-3:   Evaluation of the SAS

Evaluation of the Sample Application Strategy				
Time to create	Absent variants	Early validation	Learning effort	Overhead
0	+	+	+	-

13.6.4 Commonality and Reuse Strategy

The fourth strategy distributes test activities between domain engineering and application engineering and facilitates systematic reuse of test artefacts (Definition 13-10). Available domain artefacts are tested during domain engineering. This usually applies to common artefacts, as depicted by the left arrow in domain testing in Fig. 13-8.

Domain testing and application testing

> **Definition 13-10:** *Commonality and Reuse Strategy (CRS)*
>
> Domain testing aims at testing common parts and preparing test arte-facts for variable parts. Application testing aims at reusing the test artefacts for common parts and reusing the predefined, variable domain test artefacts to test specific applications.

Reusable test artefacts

In addition, domain testing prepares test artefacts for test items that contain variability. Consequently, the test artefacts themselves must include variability definitions. Test artefacts that contain variability are added to the domain artefacts (depicted by the right domain testing arrow in Fig. 13-8) thus establishing a test artefact repository.

Test artefact reuse in application testing

An application is defined during application engineering. At this stage, the configuration of variants for the application is known (Example 13-14). In application testing, the test of the common artefacts is conducted with the test artefacts created during domain testing. This ensures that the common parts work correctly for the specific application with its specific plug-ins. For the variable parts, the corresponding test artefacts from the test artefact repository are adapted according to the binding of the variability and then used to perform the tests.

Reuse of tests in application testing

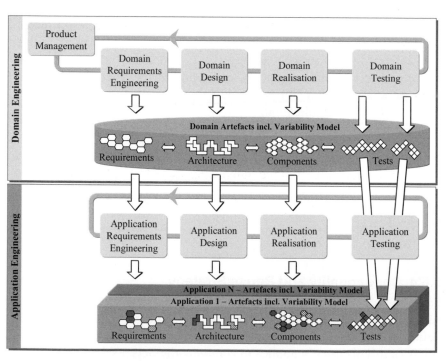

Fig. 13-8:   Commonality and reuse strategy (CRS)

The evaluation of the CRS with respect to the time to create test artefacts criterion is positive. The inclusion of variability in the test artefacts significantly reduces the amount of test cases that must be created from scratch in application testing. For instance, a domain test artefact may define how a variation point with all its variants has to be tested. In application testing, the test artefacts can be reused by binding the appropriate variants for the application artefacts under test.

Time to create test artefacts low

The handling of absent variants is excellent as variability is included in the test artefacts. The evaluation of this criterion is thus a "+". Concerning the early validation criterion, the CRS has a shortcoming since test cases can be executed only after the variability has been bound, i.e. in application engineering. However, test cases that affect only commonalities can be executed during domain testing. We rate the early validation criterion with a "0" as the development of reusable test artefacts involves at least a partial validation of the test references used (domain requirements, reference architecture, and interface descriptions).

Absent variants and early validation

The learning effort is higher than for the other three strategies as it takes some time to teach test engineers how to specify test artefacts that contain variability. Nevertheless, as test artefacts for variants preserve the variability, they can be reused in all applications. Therefore, no overhead is produced during domain engineering. Table 13-4 gives a rough summary of the strategy regarding the criteria.

Learning effort, low overhead

Example 13-14: *CRS for the Home Automation System*

During domain testing, tests are performed to ensure that the door locking hardware can interact with the server and that the windows can be opened and closed automatically. Reusable test cases are developed to enable the creation of application-specific test cases for the interaction of the three locking mechanisms in specific homes.

Application testing must perform tests to ensure that the home automation system has a sufficient quality. The home security subsystem must work correctly in the given configuration, i.e. it must not contain defects. When there are two fingerprint scanners and one keypad interacting with one server in a specific home automation system, application testing must test the interaction of these components in the given configuration.

Table 13-4: Evaluation of the CRS

Evaluation of the CRS strategy				
Time to create	Absent variants	Early validation	Learning effort	Overhead
+	+	0	-	+

13.6.5 Conclusions for Strategy Selection

BFS and PAS unusable

As two of the strategies have obvious shortcomings (BFS and PAS) we do not recommend their use. The two remaining strategies, namely the sample application strategy (SAS) and the commonality and reuse strategy (CRS) are reasonable approaches. This leads to the question of when to use which strategy.

Overhead reduction for the SAS

The SAS performs very well in all criteria except the time and the overhead criteria. The overall time to create test artefacts is unsatisfactory as the SAS does not produce variable test artefacts and does not establish a systematic reuse of domain artefacts. The overhead stems from the additional effort to create the sample application. When a software product line is initiated, in many cases, the management already has a market or one or more customers in mind. In this case, the intended applications for the market or the customers can be used as samples so that there actually is no overhead.

CRS preserves variability

The overhead is the main reason for using the CRS in any other case. No overhead is produced with this strategy. Furthermore, test artefacts for all possible combinations of variants can be derived from the test artefacts that include variability.

Composite strategy based on SAS/CRS

However, if one combines the two strategies, the strengths of both strategies can be retained. The composite strategy enforces the creation of reusable test artefacts in domain testing and the reuse of these artefacts in application testing. This leads to a good rating for the time criterion. In addition, an early validation is performed with fragments of a sample application. This means that no complete application is built, but only parts that are large enough to perform the tests. This indeed implies a minor overhead, but the overhead is significantly lower than the overhead of the SAS. We provide a summary of the strategies in Table 13-5.

Table 13-5: Strategy summary

	Time to create	Absent variants	Early validation	Learning effort	Overhead
(BFS)	-	-	+	0	-
(PAS)	0	+	-	+	-
SAS	0	+	+	+	-
CRS	+	+	0	-	+
Combined SAS/CRS	+	+	+	0	0

13.7 Domain Test Activities

The software test process typically consists of the five activities of test plan- *Software*
ning, test specification, test execution, test recording, and test completion, *test process*
see e.g. [Spillner and Linz 2004; British Standards 1998]. In domain testing,
these activities cannot be performed directly, since variability hampers testing, for instance due to the absence of variants.

The application of the SAS does not influence the traditional test process – it *CRS changes*
is just one execution of application engineering during domain testing. *test process*
However, the CRS results in a test process that includes the variability
defined in the orthogonal variability model in the test artefacts. Consequently, the CRS affects all activities dealing with the development of test artefacts for common and variable components. In the following, we briefly
explain the single-system test process and sketch the adaptations required to
realise the CRS.

13.7.1 Domain Test Planning

To perform the test planning activity, the test references, i.e. the specifica- *Test*
tions of the test items, must be available. For making a schedule it is import- *references*
ant to know when the specified items become available for testing.

In software product line engineering, test planning is based on domain arte- *Domain artefacts*
facts, i.e. on the domain requirements, the reference architecture, the detailed *as test references*
design artefacts, and, most notably, the variability model of the product line.
The product roadmap determines the schedule when the product line applications have to be finished. It is therefore relevant for the testing schedule.

In domain testing, there is no single, executable application to be tested. *Sample*
Following the SAS, test engineers may specify a sample application, e.g. one *application*

that can be realised with very few, simple application-specific plug-in components. Alternatively they may create an application that is specified in the product roadmap in order to enable testing. This typically requires more effort, i.e. the entire application engineering process has to be performed, but reduces the overhead as the created application is not a throwaway product. Only the sample applications are the testable configurations. Nevertheless, potentially many more other applications can be built from the common and variable parts of the platform.

Test strategy

The first step of test planning is to select the test strategy. This may be the SAS, the CRS, or a composite strategy. Depending on the selected strategy, the resources are allocated, and the test cases are defined (Example 13-15) and prioritised. To complete the test planning, the tool support should be defined.

Example 13-15: *Planning the Home Automation Domain Test*

The test engineers of a home automation product line plan to follow the CRS in combination with a small sample application. The unit test is performed on all components. Additional tests are performed on the common components. Moreover, a test application is set up to perform the remaining test cases, which are currently not accounted for by the test plan. A team is allocated to create reusable test cases.

13.7.2 Domain Test Specification

Test cases

The test specification activity aims at creating reusable test cases. The test cases are created in two steps. In the first step, logical test cases are created, which lack concrete details like data, GUI elements, etc. (Section 8.2). In the second step, the logical test cases are refined to detailed test cases, where the missing information is defined.

Generic test cases for variants

In domain testing, test cases are created for both common and variable domain artefacts. Detailed test cases are created only for common artefacts. The effort of creating detailed test cases (including test case scenarios) for each possible binding of the product line variability typically is significant and leads to a high overhead. Nevertheless, logical test cases and generic test case scenarios can be created that reflect the requirements and design variability defined in the variability model (we deal with the documentation of variability in test artefacts in Chapter 8). For details on the derivation of domain test case scenarios that contain variability, see [Kamsties et al. 2003a; Kamsties et al. 2003b] and [Reuys et al. 2003].

Traceability

For each test artefact, a traceability link is established to the corresponding test references. Traceability links between domain test artefacts and the underlying test references are required to support the reuse of test artefacts in application testing. For instance, when system test cases are derived from use cases, each system test case is related to the corresponding use case by a traceability link. If application test engineers know the requirements that have been reused for the considered application, they can easily identify the appropriate domain test cases by following the traceability links between domain requirements and domain test artefacts. In Chapter 18, we show in more detail how to exploit the established traceability links.

13.7.3 Domain Test Execution, Recording, and Completion

During test execution, the test cases are applied to the test items. A test protocol with the test results is created. The protocol includes the test case, the version number of the object under test, and the test result. Documenting the test execution in this way makes the tests repeatable and the test results verifiable. During test completion, the test record is analysed and the error classes and the origins of errors are determined. Finally, a test summary report (see Sections 8.2 and 8.3) is created.

Documenting test results

In domain testing, only the test cases for common domain artefacts and for the sample applications are executed. Only for those items are detailed test cases available. The tests not covered by domain test execution are the responsibility of application testing. Moreover, as stated in Section 13.3, test cases performed in domain testing may have to be repeated in application testing.

Common artefacts and sample applications

13.8 Differences from Single-System Engineering

There are two key differences between testing product lines in software product line engineering and testing applications in single-system engineering:

- Two test processes: domain testing and application testing
- The consideration of variability in domain and application testing

The main difficulty of domain testing is that there is no single, executable configuration of components that can be tested. Hence, appropriate strategies are necessary to ensure early validation of the product line as well as planned reuse of test artefacts by application engineering.

No executable system

Test activities are distributed between domain engineering and application engineering. To avoid creating test artefacts for each application from scratch, domain testing provides variable test artefacts. Variability in test artefacts originates from the variability introduced in requirements, design, and realisation, but may also take into account additional variability, e.g. in the execution environment.

Variability in test artefacts

13.9 Summary

In this chapter we establish the foundation for testing in software product line engineering. Domain testing is characterised by the need to provide an early validation of the product line, to avoid a bottleneck in the testing process, and to reduce the learning effort for test engineers.

Product line test strategies

Two strategies are recommended that can also be applied in combination. The first strategy, the SAS, involves building one or more sample applications. This enables an early validation of the software product line. In addition, testing can be performed in the same way as in single-system engineering. The second strategy, the CRS, performs tests for the common artefacts in domain engineering and provides variable test artefacts for reuse in application testing. The reuse of these artefacts reduces the effort during application testing. We elaborate on the effects of the strategies on application testing in more detail in Chapter 18.

Klaus Pohl
Nelufar Ulfat-Bunyadi

14

Selecting High-Level COTS Components

In this chapter you will learn:

- o *The key aspects that have to be considered when selecting a commercial off-the-shelf (COTS) component for a software product line.*
- o *How to select a COTS component for a software product line.*
- o *About the interrelation of the COTS-selection process with the other domain engineering sub-processes.*

14.1   Introduction

High- and low-level selection

In order to select a COTS component, candidate components that are available in the market or which exist in the organisation have to be evaluated and ranked according to defined criteria. We distinguish between high- and low-level component selection. The key discriminator is the fraction of functionality that a COTS component is supposed to provide with respect to the overall functionality of the software product line. Low-level components provide a minor part of the overall functionality and have little influence on the reference architecture. They are selected during domain realisation. The focus of this chapter is on the *high-level* components. Since they provide a significant fraction of the overall functionality they must be considered in the design right from the beginning. When we speak about COTS selection in this book, we refer to the high-level COTS selection process. The sub-processes and artefacts closely related to high-level COTS selection are highlighted in Fig. 14-1.

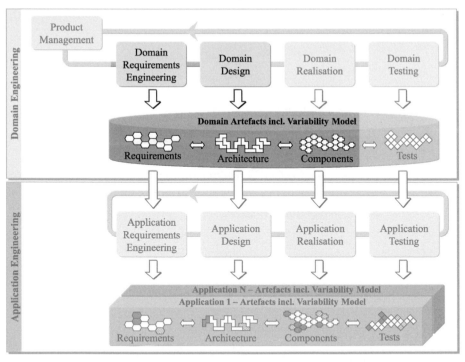

Fig. 14-1:   Sub-processes and artefacts related to COTS selection

A COTS component is evaluated and selected either during application engineering or during domain engineering. Evaluating the component in application engineering means to consider its integration into only one application of the software product line. This kind of evaluation resembles the single-system engineering case. More important for software product line engineering is the evaluation and selection of a COTS component within the domain engineering process. That is, to consider the integration of a COTS component as a domain artefact into the software product line. Such a component must fulfil domain requirements and be integratable into the reference architecture (Fig. 14-1). In addition, it has to provide variability in order to be adaptable to different applications.

COTS selection for a product line

The high-level COTS selection process is closely interrelated with domain requirements engineering and domain design. It takes requirements, architecture, and the variability model as input to find the best-fitting COTS component for use as a domain artefact in the product line. In addition to the identification of strengths and weaknesses of the examined components, COTS selection may also reveal necessary adaptations of requirements, architecture, and the variability model [Pohl and Reuys 2001]. Figure 14-2 depicts the main interrelations between the COTS selection process and the domain requirements engineering and domain design sub-processes.

High-level COTS process

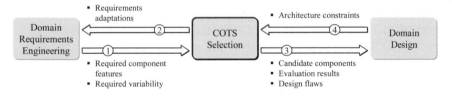

Fig. 14-2: Information flows between high-level COTS selection and other sub-processes

14.1.1 Interrelation with Domain Requirements Engineering

Domain requirements engineering defines the required component features (first bullet of ① in Fig. 14-2) which are considered during the COTS selection. They define the required functionality and quality that a component should offer. COTS components usually realise basic requirements or satisfiers and rarely provide delighters (Section 9.5.4 classifies requirements into indifferent requirements, basic requirements, satisfiers, and delighters).

Required features

In addition to the requirements artefacts, a component must match the variability desired for the software product line. Besides the requirements artefacts, the required variability is thus the second important input from the domain requirements engineering process (second bullet of ① in Fig. 14-2).

Required variability

Requirements
adaptation

As a result of a COTS selection process, adaptations of requirements can be required (② in Fig. 14-2). One reason for such an adaptation is the identification of functionality or quality offered by a COTS component that was not considered by the product line, but which will improve the product line and is thus added as a new feature. Another reason for an adaptation is the fact that it is quite unlikely for a COTS component to match all the desired requirements artefacts and/or to comply fully with the desired variability. Also in this case an adaptation of the requirements or the variability is required.

14.1.2 Interrelation with Domain Design

Candidate
components,
evaluation results

The output of COTS selection includes the identified candidate components (first bullet of ③ in Fig. 14-2). Typically, rankings of the components with regard to several criteria are provided. A detailed evaluation is conducted only for components that perform well in a preliminary screening activity. The evaluation results of each component (second bullet of ③ in Fig. 14-2) are passed on to domain design. In addition, the analysis of the candidate components may unearth design flaws (third bullet of ③ in Fig. 14-2) in the current reference architecture and thus initiate design adaptations.

Architecture
constraints

As the selected COTS has to become an integral part of the reference architecture, domain design imposes architecture constraints (④ in Fig. 14-2) to be considered during COTS selection, such as the architectural styles and patterns that the component must conform to, compatibility constraints, and constraints caused by the process structure of the reference architecture.

14.2   The CoVAR Process

Focus on
technical aspects

CoVAR (*C*omponent Selection considering *V*ariability, *A*rchitectural Concerns, and *R*equirements) is a process for selecting high-level COTS components during domain design [Pohl and Reuys 2001; Ulfat-Bunyadi et al. 2005]. CoVAR supports COTS component evaluation and the identification of the most suitable COTS component for a software product line from a technical point of view. In the final decision for or against some component, the stakeholders have to consider other aspects such as cost, ROI (Return On Investment), legal aspects, etc. Such aspects are considered and decided by product management. CoVAR focuses on the engineering and thus only on the technical aspects.

Required vs.
provided variability

Each COTS component has some built-in variability, its so-called *provided variability*. One goal of the component selection process is to determine the component that achieves an adequate fit between required variability and provided variability.

A selection process that has to take into account provided and required variability of a component differs from traditional COTS selection. In order to investigate a conventional component it is often sufficient to check the documentation and an evaluation copy of the executable component. When evaluating a component with regard to its provided variability, several problems occur that are specific to software product line engineering:

Problems during COTS evaluation

- Information regarding the variability provided by a COTS component is often hidden. In most cases, the documentation of a candidate component does not explicitly state all variation points as components today are usually not developed with the goal in mind that they should become part of a software product line. Despite this fact, designers and developers usually have envisioned different usage situations and prepared the component for them. Moreover, there is often a mismatch in terminology between a customer looking for a component and a supplier offering one.

Hidden information

- Conventional information sources are not sufficient. The issues arising from the insufficient documentation of a component require a deeper examination of the component itself. The variability implemented in the component has to be identified. Different mechanisms exist for implementing variability; see Section 12.5. This makes an evaluation difficult. Depending on the configuration mechanism used, variants are bound at different times (e.g. before compilation or during linking). These binding times make it necessary to investigate not only the executable component, but also its source code and its compiling and linking instructions. For example, if the binding time of a variation point is implementation time, then this variation point cannot be detected in an executable component. Instead, only the bound variant can be spotted. Moreover, because of the variability, not all features exist in parallel in one executable version of the investigated component. That is, several configurations of a component must be evaluated because the provided functionality and quality vary.

Binding time of variants

The bottom line is that the usual documentation, such as marketing material, is not sufficient, especially when variability is considered. Thus, besides the executable evaluation copy of the component, more artefacts such as configuration mechanisms and information must be evaluated. The evaluation is performed in two ways:

1. The artefacts must be checked for the existence of required features, required variation points, and required variants.

2. Configurations of the component must be checked for the functionality and quality they provide.

Three main activities

To cope with these problems, CoVAR defines three main activities: component screening, detailed component evaluation, and component selection (see Fig. 14-3). During the component screening activity, the most promising candidate components are identified on the basis of available documentation. The detailed component evaluation provides a detailed evaluation of the components on the basis of development artefacts and evaluation copies. An evaluation copy denotes an executable version of a component that is provided by the component vendor for evaluation purposes. The final component selection activity produces a ranked list of components so that the best-fitting component can be selected.

Interaction with domain requirements engineering

The interaction between domain requirements engineering and COTS selection described in Section 14.1.1 occurs mainly during the activities of component screening and detailed component evaluation. The following detailed descriptions of each activity show that interaction is supported and even promoted. Thus, the understanding of already specified requirements, variation points, and variants is increased and is then reflected in the respective artefacts.

Note that, although the sub-activities of each activity are explained in a sequential order, they may be iterated, if necessary, or performed in parallel.

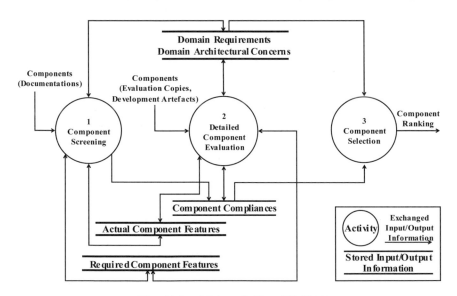

Fig. 14-3:   Main activities of CoVAR.

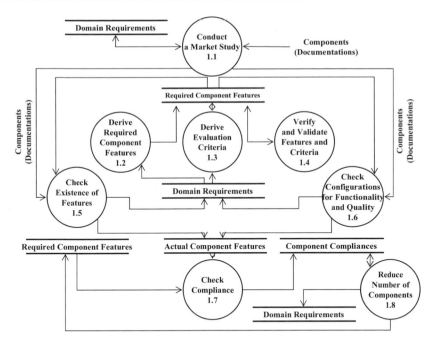

Fig. 14-4: Sub-activities of the component screening activity

14.2.1 Component Screening

During component screening, a first evaluation of candidate components is performed on the basis of available component documentations, e.g. marketing material, technical manuals, experience reports. The goal is to reduce the number of candidate components for the subsequent detailed evaluation to three to seven components and consequently reduce the time and effort needed for the whole evaluation. The components are mainly checked for providing the required basic functionality and quality. Only if too many candidate components pass this check are the requirements considered in the examination extended to additional functionality and quality in order to be able to exclude more candidates. Figure 14-4 provides an overview of the steps of the component screening activity.

Three to seven candidates

The steps of the component screening activity should be performed in the following way:

Screening steps

Step 1.1: *Conduct technical market study*. In order to identify candidate components, a market study is conducted on the basis of the domain requirements. Sources may be the public market or in-house. Available documentations about the candidates are collected. The result of this sub-activity is, thus, a set of potential candidates for reuse along with the infor-

Market study

mation that could be gathered about these components. The market study may lead to an update of domain requirements, e.g. if no components can be identified that satisfy them.

Common and variable
component features

Step 1.2: *Derive required component features*. Based on the domain requirements that address the whole software product line, required component features are derived that specifically describe what is expected from the COTS component. Variability is inherent in required component features just as it is in domain requirements. Thus, we distinguish between common and variable features. Variable features express two kinds of expectations:

1. Required variation points, which express the fact that certain variability subjects have to be accounted for.

2. Required variants, i.e. the choices that should be possible for variability subjects.

Documentation
of features

Required component features, just as, at a later stage, actual component features, and their dependencies (e.g. excludes or requires) should be documented to ensure traceability from the expected features defined at the beginning of the evaluation to the results of the evaluation. Features are often captured in feature models (Section 5.2). These models serve as a basis for discussions between stakeholders, i.e. the evaluation team consisting of the domain analysts, the domain designers, and the domain experts.

Attributes of
the features

In addition to the feature model containing the required component features, an accompanying textual description is provided for each feature. The textual description of a feature should contain the following information:

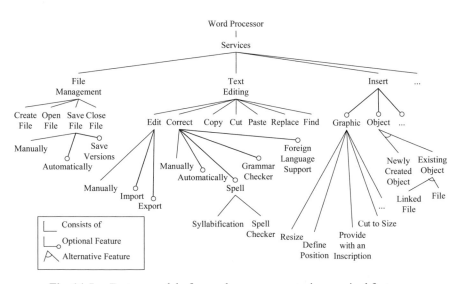

Fig. 14-5: Feature model of a word processor capturing required features

- *Name*: name of feature.

- *Description*: description of feature.

- *Class*: class of feature: basic | satisfier | delighter.

- *Constraint dependencies*: "excludes:" <list of feature names>, "requires:" <list of feature names>.

Example 14-1: *Required Component Features for a Word Processor*

The home automation system offers two variants: a standard and a professional variant. The standard variant is able to generate protocols and summary reports. The professional variant provides additional functionality: it comes with an integrated email program that allows, for example, the system to be called by phone and let one's mails to be read out via the phone. Furthermore, it provides the services of an integrated secretary such as dictating letters, etc. to the home automation system. For these purposes, both the standard and the professional variant require a word processor component. For the standard variant, the component is configured as a simple text editor whereas, for the professional variant, the component is configured as a more sophisticated word processor. An excerpt of the feature model with the required component features is depicted in Fig. 14-5.

Step 1.3: *Derive evaluation criteria.* A set of evaluation criteria is derived from the required component features. More precisely, an evaluation criterion is developed for each feature that represents a leaf of the feature model. When a feature is not fully refined by its child features, an evaluation criterion is developed for this feature and not for its child features. If a feature is not detailed enough for deriving an evaluation criterion from it, it is refined. The textual description of an evaluation criterion should contain the following information:

Documentation of evaluation criteria

- *Identifier*: a unique identifier for the evaluation criterion.

- *Definition*: the definition of the evaluation criterion.

- *Rationale*: a description of the rationale of the criterion and how it relates to required component features.

- *Scale*: the definition of the scale of measurement for the criterion.

- *Unit/classes*: the definition of the unit of measurement for the criterion.

- *Screening rule*: the definition of a possible threshold that is required for a component to be selected for detailed component evaluation (this attribute is used for documenting which criteria were used in the component screening activity).

- *Baseline*: the baseline represents the minimum required level of functionality and features that a component must satisfy when it is integrated into the software product line.

- *Qualitative description*: guidelines on how additional information gathered about the criterion should be documented.

- *Feature interaction*: a description of features that influence each other (e.g. efficiency and user-friendliness) and should therefore be evaluated in close relationship to ensure that an acceptable level of both can be reached at the same time.

- *Priority*: a description of how important the evaluation criterion is (possible classes are required, recommended, optional).

Quality assurance for features and criteria **Step 1.4**: *Verify and validate features and criteria*. Before features and evaluation criteria are used for evaluation, they are verified and validated with all relevant stakeholders.

Variability dependencies **Step 1.5**: *Check existence of features*. For each component, the documentation is analysed with regard to the existence of the required component features. The existence of variable features is checked independently of their variability dependency (Section 4.6). That is, features are considered from the viewpoint of the evaluator. A required optional feature, for example, is first checked for existence and second for the type of required variability dependency (optional in this case). If the feature does not exist, the evaluator documents this fact as – despite being optional – the feature is required for at least part of the product line applications. The same holds for a group of alternative features. This check for the existence of required features results finally in a feature model of the actual component features (see Example 14-2) and accompanying textual description of these features.

Possible configurations **Step 1.6**: *Check configurations for functionality and quality*. During the component screening activity, the candidate components are not part of the intended configurations. However, possibly information is available about configurations which are similar to the intended configurations. The available information is investigated with respect to the functionality and quality provided by the configuration. The results are recorded in an informal way in the accompanying textual description of the provided component features. The feature model may be extended during this step.

Step 1.7: *Check compliance*. For each component, the required and actual component features are compared, and a rough quantification is given such as "passed", "not passed", or "deferred". The result is a component compliance tuple for each component.

Step 1.8: *Reduce number of components*. Based on the component compliances, those components are screened out that received one or more "not passed".

Example 14-2: *Provided Component Features (from Documentation)*

TX Text Control from The Imaging Source Europe GmbH is an example of a word processor component. The analysis of its documentation leads to the feature model with provided component features shown in Fig. 14-6. Apparently, a lot of features that were required from the component in Example 14-1 are not supported.

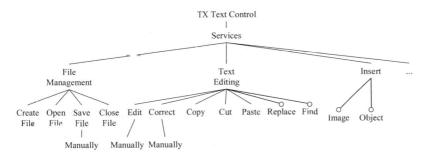

Fig. 14-6: Provided component features identified from documentation

14.2.2 Detailed Component Evaluation

During detailed component evaluation, evaluation scenarios are developed and performed on the candidate components. Figure 14-7 provides an overview of this activity. At the beginning of detailed component evaluation, a pilot component evaluation is conducted on a subset of two to three candidate components. The aim of the pilot component evaluation is to develop *evaluation scenarios* that are applicable to all candidate components that successfully passed component screening. That is, initial evaluation scenarios are developed, applied to the two to three candidates, reviewed, and possibly adapted. Next, the revised evaluation scenarios are used to evaluate the remaining components (see Fig. 14-7). If the changes to the scenarios invalidate the evaluation results made so far, the two to three candidate components used during the pilot evaluation must be evaluated again using the revised scenarios.

Evaluation scenarios

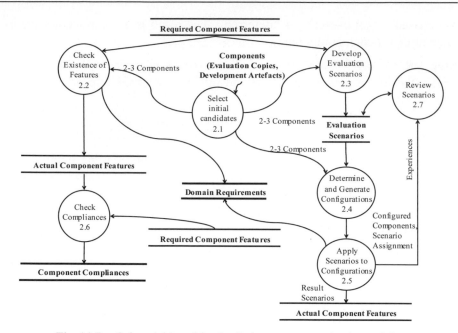

Fig. 14-7:   Sub-activities of the detailed component evaluation activity

Check of functionality and quality

Evaluation copies and other development artefacts of the candidate components are used for the detailed component evaluation. The components are checked for the fulfilment of the basic requirements and satisfiers, the quality, and the support of intended variation points and variants. The following steps are performed:

Initial candidates

Step 2.1: *Select initial candidates.* Two to three candidate components for the pilot component evaluation are selected. It is suggested to select the components with the largest differences in their realisation of requirements and variation points so that the resulting evaluation scenarios can be expected to hold for the other components as well.

Required and additional features

Step 2.2: *Check existence of features.* Using the evaluation copies and development artefacts of each component, the components are checked for the existence of the required component features. The feature model and feature descriptions developed during component screening are used as input. The first goal is to check if the required component features are actually provided by the component under evaluation. That is, all required component features (regarding basic functionality as well as satisfiers) are checked using the development artefacts and the evaluation copies. The second goal is to identify additional functionality, additional variation points, and additional variants of expected variation points.

Validating that required variation points are supported by a component, and identifying new variation points as well as new variants that belong to an already known variation point, require knowledge about how variation points are realised in the different development artefacts. Variation points can be implemented using different configuration mechanisms offering different binding times. The binding time allows categorisation of the variation points. For example, a variation point may have been realised in a component by using the IFDEF statement in its source code (written in the C/C++ programming language). In this case, variants are bound at compile time. In the cases when the support of a required variation point is validated or additional variants are identified, the region of the artefact to look at can be limited. In addition, identifying new variation points necessitates browsing through the whole artefact.

Binding mechanisms, binding time

Example 14-3: *Provided Component Features (from Evaluation)*

Figure 14-8 shows the feature model of the actual component features of the word processor component TX Text Control. It becomes apparent that the component actually supports significantly more features than could be found in the documentation.

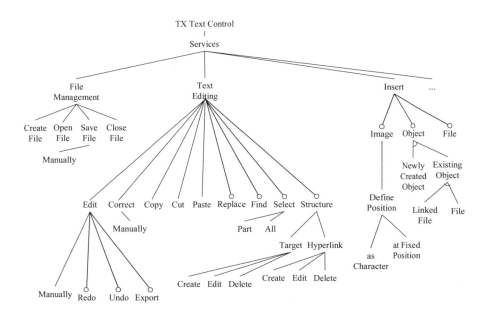

Fig. 14-8:   Feature model with provided features after component evaluation

Updated documentation

In this way, the feature model and the accompanying documentation of each component (resulting from component screening) are validated and completed. Thus, performing the step yields an updated feature model and updated textual description.

Evaluation scenario for each criterion

Step 2.3: *Develop evaluation scenarios.* For each evaluation criterion determined during component screening, an evaluation scenario for measuring it in a precise and repeatable fashion is developed. Sometimes, it is useful to cover several evaluation criteria using a single scenario, if the concerned features are closely related and interfere with each other. This case is indicated by the feature interaction attribute of the respective evaluation criteria. Evaluation scenarios are usually narrative scenarios that describe actor actions and desired component responses (see Example 14-4).

Ensuring objectivity

A traceable decision-making process is performed in parallel with the component evaluation. Therefore, for each evaluation scenario, measurement rules for ranking the component's behaviour are defined. Different levels of scenario fulfilment are distinguished. The overall goal is to define scenarios and evaluation criteria in such a way that component evaluations can be performed by different stakeholders. That is, to ensure as far as possible that:

1. Two evaluations of the same component by different people lead to almost the same result.

2. Two evaluations of different components by different stakeholders lead to comparable results.

Example 14-4: *Evaluation Scenario for the Word Processor*

Figure 14-9 illustrates an evaluation scenario that is developed for the criterion "inserting an existing file as OLE object". Since the developers of the evaluation scenario know that a word processor's stability may suffer from inserting OLE objects into a document, they evaluate the two criteria together.

Reducing evaluation effort

Step 2.4: *Determine and generate configurations.* During detailed component evaluation, configurations of the candidate components can be generated using evaluation copies. In most cases, it is impossible to check all features on all possible configurations of all investigated components. Even though only three to seven candidates are left for detailed evaluation, the effort might be unreasonably high. A more efficient solution is to check each common feature and each variable feature only once on a configuration of a candidate component. In order to minimise the number of configurations, the number of features that are checked on one configuration of a component is maximised.

Scenario for the Criterion 'Inserting an existing file as OLE object'

Primary goal: check criterion 'Inserting an existing file as OLE object'

Secondary goal: check criterion 'Stability of the Word Processor'

Actor: Evaluation team member

Scenario step sequence:

1. The evaluation team member edits a text comprising 150 pages manually into a newly created Word document.
2. Below the text, the team member inserts an OLE object created from an existing file.
3. The team member opens the OLE object within the Word application in its server application and makes some changes.
4. The team member closes the server application and returns to the Word application.
5. The team member checks if the OLE object in the Word application has been adapted to the changes made in the server application.
6. The team member saves the document.

Fig. 14-9:   Example of an evaluation scenario

Evaluating configurations

Another problem that may occur is that dependencies between variants cannot be identified by investigating the component. A component can be checked for required dependencies, but it must also be assured that a component under investigation does not restrict the combination of variants more than required. To this end, a number of foreseeable configurations are generated. This helps to ensure that there are no hidden dependencies among variants built into a component prohibiting certain configurations. As a result of this step, these foreseeable configurations of the candidate components are generated. Furthermore, each evaluation scenario is assigned to the configuration it is executed on.

Result scenarios

Step 2.5: *Apply scenarios to configurations*. As specified by scenario assignment, the evaluation scenarios are applied to the component configurations. The results are also captured in scenarios. These result scenarios describe the actual behaviour of the components and thus concretise the actual component features. Therefore, they should be related to the respective features of the feature model of the actual component features.

Quantitative results

Step 2.6: *Check compliance*. Required and actual component features are compared just as during component screening. But this time the compliance vector is supplemented by a detailed quantification for each feature covered by an evaluation scenario. The quantification results from applying the measurement rule that is assigned to each scenario.

Step 2.7: *Review scenarios*. Based on the experiences gained during steps 2.5 and 2.6, the evaluation scenarios and accompanying measurement rules are reviewed to ensure that they can be applied to all components. If necessary, they are adapted.

Evaluation
of remaining
components

Step 2.7 represents the final step of the pilot component evaluation. The revised evaluation scenarios can then be used for the evaluation of the remaining components. As stated above, if the changes to the scenarios invalidate the evaluation results for the two to three candidates used for the pilot evaluation, these components must be re-evaluated using the revised scenarios. For this subsequent evaluation, only steps 2.2 ("Check existence of features"), 2.4 ("Determine and generate configurations"), 2.5 ("Apply scenarios to configurations"), and 2.6 ("Check compliance") have to be performed with the components.

14.2.3 Component Selection

Multi-criteria
decision

Component selection is the final activity of the CoVAR process. During this activity, evaluation criteria are prioritised and a final ranking of the components is computed based on the component compliances. To determine the final ranking, an established multi-criteria decision-making process such as the AHP (Analytic Hierarchy Process, see e.g. [Saaty 1990]) may be used. In contrast to the other two main activities of CoVAR, the component selection activity typically does not lead to new insights about domain requirements and variability therein.

Ranking

The result of the component selection activity is a ranking of components from which the highest ranked component should be selected. All information that was gathered about the selected component is then used during further activities of software product line engineering, such as the integration of the component into the domain architecture.

14.3   Differences from Single-System Engineering

Variability

The main difference between the integration of a COTS component into a single system and its integration into a software product line as a domain artefact is variability. Since variability is inherent in domain requirements and architecture, it has to be taken into consideration as a third facet (besides requirements and architectural concerns). Considering variability during COTS component evaluation and selection in turn results in new problems that have to be solved:

Lacking
documentation

- Provided variation points and variants are often not specified explicitly in component documentations, although they are often present in order to allow the adaptation of a component to different modes of usage. This situation requires a closer examination of the component itself.

Evaluation
of code

- For investigation purposes, conventional information sources, such as documentation and evaluation copies, are not sufficient – a second problem that results from considering variability during evaluation. An evaluation copy is executable and, thus, contains bound variants. Consequently, depending on the binding time of variation points, more artefacts of a component must be investigated, such as source code and compiling and linking instructions.

- Because of the variability provided by a component, not all features exist in parallel in one executable version of the component. That is, a component's provided functionality and quality may vary from one configuration to another. This third problem requires an evaluation of component configurations with respect to the provided functionality and quality.

Different configurations

14.4 Summary

The CoVAR process supports an evaluation team in evaluating COTS components for a software product line. CoVAR consists mainly of two evaluation activities and a component selection activity.

CoVAR

During the first evaluation activity, the component screening, candidate components are evaluated on the basis of available documentations and the number of components is reduced to three to seven candidates.

Component screening

During the second evaluation activity, the detailed component evaluation, these candidates are evaluated on the basis of evaluation copies and development artefacts. In each evaluation activity, the components are checked in two ways. First, they are checked for the existence of required component features as well as required variation points and variants. Second, specific configurations of the components are checked for the functionality and quality they provide. Based on the results of the component screening and detailed component evaluation, a ranking of the examined components can be determined in order to select the component that fits best.

Scenario-based component evaluation

Part IV

Application Engineering

Part IV: Overview

The main goal of application engineering is to derive a software product line application by reusing as many domain artefacts as possible. This is achieved by exploiting the commonality and the variability of the product line established in domain engineering. In this part you will learn how the orthogonal variability model is used in the application engineering sub-processes highlighted in Fig. IV-1 to:

- *Consider the commonality and the variability of the product line when defining the requirements for a specific application.*

- *Document the selected variants.*

- *Bind the selected variants from requirements to the architecture, to the components, and to the test cases.*

- *Estimate the impacts originating from differences between application requirements and domain requirements on architecture, components, and tests.*

The orthogonal variability model supports the consistent reuse of the domain assets, i.e. the domain requirements, architecture, components, and test cases.

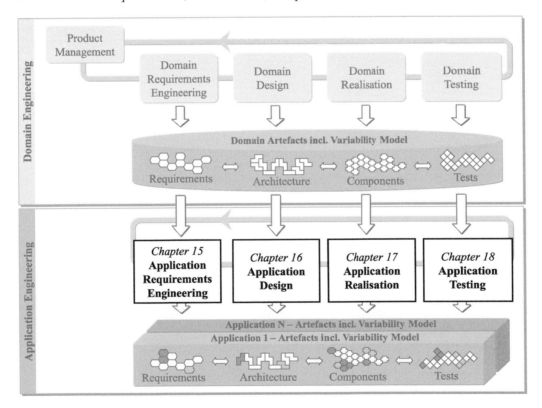

Fig. IV-1: Chapter overview of Part IV

Günter Halmans
Klaus Pohl

15

Application Requirements Engineering

In this chapter you will learn:

o *About the interrelations of the application requirements engineering sub-process with the product management, domain requirements engineering, and application design sub-processes.*

o *How to communicate the external variability and the commonalities of the product line to the stakeholders.*

o *How to identify deltas between stakeholder requirements and product line requirements.*

o *How to analyse and document changes such as adding new features or adapting product line features for a particular product line application.*

15.1   Introduction

Goal of application requirements engineering

The goal of application requirements engineering is to elicit and to document the requirements artefacts for a particular application and at the same time reuse, as much as possible, the domain requirements artefacts. The reuse of domain requirements artefacts for each application supports the overall goal of obtaining a high degree of domain artefact reuse.

Related sub-processes

The sub-processes and artefacts closely related to the application requirements engineering sub-process are highlighted in Fig. 15-1. Application requirements engineering is related to product management, domain requirements engineering, and application design. Product management defines the major features of the applications to be developed. Domain requirements engineering creates the domain requirements artefacts, which are reused for the application under consideration. The application requirements engineering sub-process reuses the domain requirements artefacts to define the application requirements artefacts. The application requirements artefacts serve as a basis for application design.

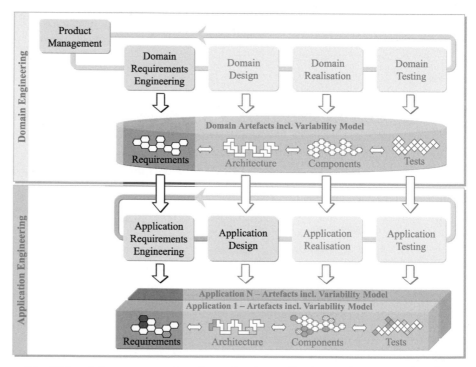

Fig. 15-1:   Sub-processes and artefacts related to application requirements engineering

An essential activity of application requirements engineering is the communication of the domain requirements artefacts to the stakeholders. Hence, product managers and customers are typically involved in the application requirements engineering process.

Communication with stakeholders

Product managers determine the major features of the applications in the product portfolio based on their market and product (line) strategy. Customers demand an application that satisfies their individual needs at an affordable price. In cases where customers are known to the organisation, application requirements engineering communicates the commonality and external variability of the software product line to them. In the more common case where the customers are not personally known, product managers and marketing experts represent the customer as stakeholder of the application requirements engineering sub-process.[40] The communication about domain requirements artefacts[41] enables customers, or their representatives, to evaluate the extent to which the software product line can satisfy their needs.

Product managers and customers

Software product line applications can be divided into two basic categories with respect to the degree of domain artefact reuse. The first category comprises applications which have only requirements artefacts that are a subset of the domain requirements artefacts. The second category comprises applications which have requirements artefacts that are not part of the domain requirements artefacts. For applications of the first category, the domain requirements artefacts are communicated to the stakeholders, and the appropriate requirements are selected and documented. The second category asks for more effort for application engineering. As the applications of the second category cannot be realised by reusing domain requirements artefacts exclusively, the differences or *deltas* between domain requirements artefacts and application requirements artefacts have to be detected and documented. Requirements deltas lead to adaptation effort in all application engineering sub-processes and thus increase the price of the application.

Two application categories

Figure 15-2 shows the interrelations between application engineering and its related sub-processes. In the following, we describe each interrelation in detail.

15.1.1 Interrelation with Product Management

Product management defines the major application features (① in Fig. 15-2) for all applications of the product line. The development of the applications

Application features

---

[40] A distinction can also be made between the derivation of individual applications and the derivation of mass-market applications [Halmans and Pohl 2002]. Here, we distinguish between customers and product managers as stakeholders of the application requirements engineering process, which largely correlates with the differentiation between individual applications and mass-market applications.

[41] In the following, we use the term requirements as a synonym for requirements artefacts (Definition 5-2).

is supported by the commonality and variability of the platform. Application requirements engineering reuses the common parts and chooses the variant parts that are suitable to match the features defined by product management for the application. Certain features are application specific, i.e. they only apply for a single application. As the corresponding application requirements artefacts do not yet exist, application requirements engineering has to define them.

Feedback to product management

Application requirements engineering leads to new insights about required features, e.g. by communicating with different stakeholders. Based on the new insights application requirements engineering makes suggestions for additional and altered features that might be incorporated in the software product line (② in Fig. 15-2).

15.1.2 Interrelation with Domain Requirements Engineering

Domain requirements artefacts and variability model

Domain requirements engineering provides application requirements engineering with common and variable requirements artefacts and the domain variability model (③ in Fig. 15-2). Application requirements engineering employs the variability model to determine the variants as well as the corresponding domain requirements artefacts that can be reused for the application.

Additional needs

Application requirements engineering passes on requests for additional and altered domain requirements artefacts to domain requirements engineering (first bullet of ④ in Fig. 15-2). The requests typically originate from insights and experiences gained in assembling a specific application. In addition, customer requirements should be evaluated if they also affect other product line applications (i.e. if they rather represent needs of the domain than of a single application). If so, the requirements are passed on to domain requirements engineering to be elaborated further.

Application-specific requirements

Product management designates application-specific features to be worked out during application requirements engineering, e.g. if a lead product strategy is followed. If application-specific requirements address actual needs of the domain, they might be integrated into the domain artefacts. For this purpose, the application requirements artefacts are passed on to domain requirements engineering (second bullet of ④ in Fig. 15-2). Before these artefacts can be integrated into the product line, a decision within the domain engineering process has to be made and, if the decision is to integrate them, the domain artefacts have to be adapted to incorporate the new requirements.

15.1.3 Interrelation with Application Design

The main output of application requirements engineering is the application requirements specification (⑤ in Fig. 15-2) which is a complete specification of the application. It includes the application variability model, which is derived from the domain variability model, the requirements artefacts that are reused from the domain artefacts, and the requirements deltas. Requirements deltas are determined by analysing the requirements posed by the customer or product manager and comparing them with domain requirements artefacts. The application requirements specification is described in more detail in Section 15.5. Based on the application requirements specification (and the reference architecture), application design derives the application architecture.

Application requirements specification

Application requirements engineering typically involves trade-off decisions with regard to the requirements posed by a customer or representative. The realisation effort for the requirements depends on the degree of reuse that can be achieved. Requirements deltas, such as performance requirements that are tighter than anticipated by the product line, may involve significant modifications of the architecture and the reusable components. As such modifications affect the development costs for the application, trade-off decisions are necessary on whether to accept a higher price or to abstain from the specific requirement that causes cost-intensive modifications. Application design has to support such decisions by providing an effort evaluation of requirements deltas (⑥ in Fig. 15-2).

Effort for deltas

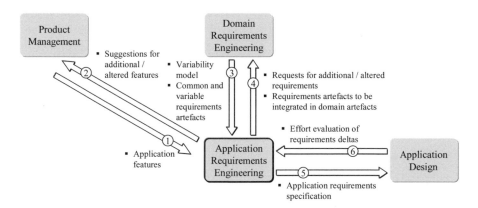

Fig. 15-2:   Information flows between application requirements engineering and other sub-processes

15.2   Application Requirements Engineering Activities

Stakeholder
requirements
In the following, we do not distinguish whether the need to develop application-specific requirements artefacts originates from product management, from customer needs, or from any other source. We treat the different cases similarly by the assumption that there are some stakeholders who pose requirements with respect to the considered application. We define these requirements as *stakeholder requirements*:

> **Definition 15-1:** *Stakeholder Requirements*
>
> Stakeholder requirements are requirements that stakeholders state for a particular application, i.e. requirements that the stakeholders expect to be fulfilled by the application.

Application
requirements
Due to trade-off decisions made in the application requirements engineering process, the initial stakeholder requirements are not necessarily identical with the resulting *application requirements*. We define application requirements as follows:

> **Definition 15-2:** *Application Requirements*
>
> Application requirements are requirements that completely specify a particular product line application.

Decision
options
The agreement about the application requirements is a result of the application requirements engineering process. The following options exist with regard to a particular stakeholder requirement:

- The stakeholder requirement can be completely fulfilled by an application requirement or set of application requirements.

- The stakeholder requirement can be partially fulfilled by an application requirement or set of application requirements.

- The stakeholder requirement cannot be fulfilled by any application requirement or set of application requirements.

The decisions about stakeholder requirements affect the interrelations between stakeholder requirements, application requirements artefacts, and domain requirements artefacts:

- *Interrelation between stakeholder requirements and application requirements artefacts*

Feasibility
    Normally, stakeholder requirements should be fulfilled by the application requirements artefacts. Yet, if the realisation of requirements deltas

leads to a significant effort, the stakeholders may decide that their requirement should only be partially fulfilled by the application or not fulfilled at all. We address this topic in Section 15.4.4.

- *Interrelation between stakeholder requirements and domain requirements artefacts*
  The requirements engineer maps stakeholder requirements to domain requirements artefacts with the goal to find domain requirements artefacts that satisfy the particular stakeholder requirement. In case a specific domain requirements artefact satisfies a particular stakeholder requirement, the domain requirements artefact can be reused. In case a particular stakeholder requirement cannot be fulfilled by domain artefacts, adaptation effort is necessary to satisfy the stakeholder requirement. Then, a trade-off decision is necessary on whether the application requirements artefacts must fully comply with the stakeholder requirement or may be adapted to eliminate the delta (or at least reduce the adaptation effort). In the latter case, the stakeholder requirement is not fulfilled (completely).

  Reuse

- *Interrelation between application and domain requirements artefacts*
  An application requirements artefact is identical to a domain requirements artefact if the domain requirements artefact satisfies a particular stakeholder requirement and thus can be completely reused. An application requirements artefact has a delta to a particular domain requirements artefact in case the stakeholder requirement cannot be completely satisfied by a domain requirements artefact.

  Requirements deltas

For the elicitation and documentation of application requirements, the following three activities are essential:

- *Communicating the commonality and external variability of the product line*[42]
  The goal of this activity is to make the stakeholder aware of the capabilities of the product line and to elicit application requirements. By considering the commonality and variability of the product line in application requirements engineering, the level of domain artefact reuse can be increased [Halmans and Pohl 2001]. The orthogonal variability model plays a central role in this activity as it enables the requirements engineer to communicate the relevant variation points, variants, and their dependencies to the stakeholder (① in Fig. 15-3). Additionally, the variability model and its traceability links to domain requirements artefacts enable the requirements engineer to describe the functionality and quality of a particular variant. The stakeholders survey the product line

  Awareness of product line capabilities

---

[42] Depending on the knowledge the stakeholder already has about the commonality and variability of the product, the steps of this activity are more or less distinct.

commonality and the external variability and communicate their requirements for the application to the requirements engineer (② in Fig. 15-3). The requirements engineer collects the domain requirements artefacts to be reused for the application. The result of the activity is a set of domain requirements artefacts, which may not completely fulfil the stakeholder requirements.

Estimation of realisation effort

- *Evaluating deltas between domain and application requirements*
Deltas between domain and application requirements occur when stakeholder requirements cannot be completely satisfied by domain requirements artefacts. These deltas have to be evaluated with respect to the required realisation effort. During the evaluation process, first, deltas to the domain variability model caused by the stakeholder requirements are analysed. Second, the impact of the variability model deltas on the corresponding domain requirements artefacts is analysed. The results of this analysis are variability model and requirements artefact deltas. They are communicated to the application architect who estimates the realisation effort based on the deltas. The feedback on the estimated realisation effort (③ in Fig. 15-3) allows the stakeholder to decide whether the requirements artefact deltas should be realised or not. The stakeholder communicates the decision to the requirements engineer (④ in Fig. 15-3). As a result of the delta evaluation activity, the application requirements, and the corresponding requirements artefact and variability model deltas, are defined.

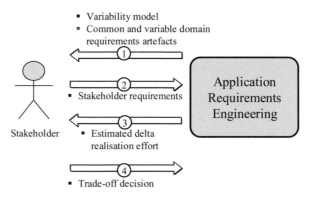

Fig. 15-3:   Information flows with respect to the stakeholder

Basis for later development phases

- *Documentation of application requirements*
The two activities described above result in a documentation that includes the application requirements artefacts, the deltas between application and domain requirements artefacts, and the traces between application requirements artefacts and the corresponding domain

requirements artefacts. In addition, the application variability model (which is the result of incorporating the variability model deltas) and the traceability links of application requirements to the application-specific variability model are documented. Moreover, the estimated realisation costs are related to the deltas to keep decisions about the deltas traceable. The resulting application requirements specification is the basis for the later development phases.

15.3 Communication of the Product Line Variability

This section focuses on the communication of external variability, using the orthogonal variability model, to the stakeholders. The variability model provides a coherent view of the variability of the product line. The requirements engineer navigates between the variability model and the different requirements artefacts to supply stakeholders with more detailed information, e.g. about the functionality and quality of the variants under consideration.

Requirements artefacts and variability

15.3.1 Variation Points and Variants

The communication of external variability based on the orthogonal variability model typically starts with the variation points that provide the topmost level of abstraction. Communicating a single variation point involves:

1. Communicating the variants related to the variation point as well as the variability dependencies and the alternative choices defined for the variation point.

2. Communicating dependent variation points and/or variants by following the existing constraint dependencies.

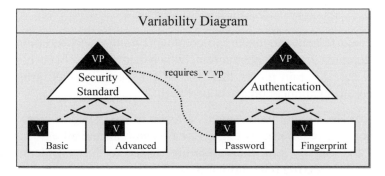

Fig. 15-4: Variation points 'security standard' and 'authentication'

Example 15-1 illustrates the communication of variation points and variants to a stakeholder. For a more detailed description of communicating the variability of the software product line, see [Halmans and Pohl 2003].

Example 15-1: *Communicating a Variation Point*

Figure 15-4 depicts an extract of an orthogonal variability model. It shows the two variation points 'security standard' and 'authentication'. The stakeholder is interested in the variation point 'authentication'. The following information can be communicated to the stakeholder:

- The product line provides two authentication mechanisms. Exactly one of these has to be selected: authentication via 'Password' or authentication via 'fingerprint'.

- In case of the variant 'password', additionally, the variation point 'security standard' has to be bound. The stakeholder has to select either 'basic' or 'advanced' security.

15.3.2 Domain Requirements Artefacts

Different views

To make a decision for or against a variant the stakeholder may need more detailed information concerning the functionality or quality associated with the variant. For instance, the features related to the variant under consideration are used to provide a management view. The related model-based requirements such as a class diagram provide a more detailed, solution-oriented view. Example 15-2 illustrates the communication of the domain requirements artefacts that are related to the variant 'password'.

Navigating the variability model

Having considered the domain requirements artefacts of a certain variant, different strategies can be followed to find the next variation point and variants to be considered. Two basic options are:

- The requirements engineer can communicate the next variation point at the topmost level of abstraction, which has not yet been considered. Thus the variation points that may affect coarse-grained properties of the resulting application are bound first.

- If a certain domain requirements artefact is associated to more than one variant, the requirements engineer can communicate all associated variants and thereby bind the variability related to the considered artefact before considering other artefacts.

Example 15-2: *Communicating the Details of a Variant*

The stakeholder is interested in more details about the variant 'password' depicted in Fig. 15-5 . By following the traceability link to the domain requirements artefacts, the requirements engineer finds the use case 'authentication by password'. By considering the use case description, the stakeholders get a more detailed idea of the benefits of this use case (the use case description is not depicted in Fig. 15-5).

The variant 'password' is interrelated with the variation point 'security standard'. Thus, to explain the considered variant 'password' in more detail, the requirements engineer shows the associated security requirements of the 'basic' variant and the 'advanced' variant to the stakeholder (see Fig. 15-5).

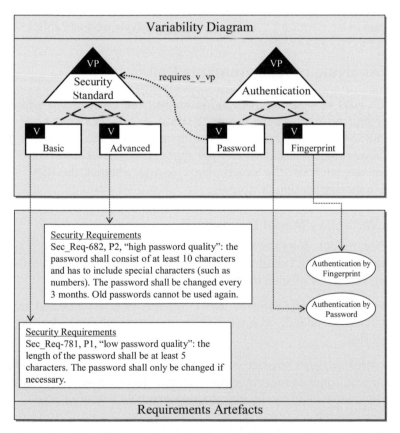

Fig. 15-5: Traceability links between variants and domain requirements artefacts

15.3.3 Result of the Communication Activity

The result of the communication activity is a classification of stakeholder requirements:

Reuse of domain artefacts

a) Stakeholder requirements that can be satisfied by binding variability defined in domain requirements artefacts.

  The domain requirements artefacts that satisfy these stakeholder requirements are documented as application requirements in a way that supports the reuse of domain artefacts in application engineering. We deal with this issue in Section 15.5.

Analysis of deltas

b) Stakeholder requirements that do not correspond to domain requirements artefacts.

  In this case, deltas between domain requirements artefacts and the application requirements artefacts that satisfy the stakeholder requirements exist. Section 15.4 deals with the analysis of these deltas.

15.4 Analysis of Requirements Deltas

Decision support

The main goal of delta analysis is to support the decision on whether the deltas should be realised for the application or not. We analyse the deltas caused by application requirements with respect to the variability model, domain requirements artefacts, and the application architecture. Based on the results of the analysis, the stakeholders decide whether the delta shall be realised in the application or not.

15.4.1 Variability Model Deltas

Variability model deltas are differences between the domain variability model (see Section 2.5) and the application variability model (Section 2.7). There are two types of such deltas:

- *Part of the existing external variability has to be modified*: A new variant must be added, or a variability or constraint dependency must be modified.

- *An invariant part must be turned into a variable part*: Part of the common requirements must be made variable. In this case, the external variability is extended by the introduction of a new variation point.

15.4.2 Impact on the Variability Model

Adding a new variant

In case the stakeholder requires, say, new functionality or quality with respect to a given variation point, a new variant must be included in the application variability model (Example 15-3). In case the stakeholder wishes to change the functionality or quality of an existing variant, a new variant (representing the changed variant) representing the changed functionality or quality is defined. Thus, the two variants (the original one and the changed one) are selectable.

The stakeholder may also demand modifications of the variability or constraint dependencies. For example, the following cases may occur:

Modification of dependencies

- The stakeholder rejects a mandatory variant.

- The stakeholder selects a different number of variants than the range of an alternative choice permits.

- The stakeholder selects two variants that are related by an "exclude" dependency.

- The stakeholder selects only one out of two variants that are related by a "requires" dependency.

Example 15-3: *Adding a New Variant*

The stakeholder might demand an additional notification mechanism that enables the home automation system to notify the owner of the home about alarms via SMS (Short Message Service). This delta can be realised by adding the new variant 'SMS information' (Fig. 15-6).

Modifications of variability and constraint dependencies often occur when the stakeholder uses the application as a component of a larger system, which itself is offered in different variants. Then, the permissible combinations of variants have to be aligned with the variability of the larger system. Example 15-4 illustrates the removal of an alternative choice.

Application as product line

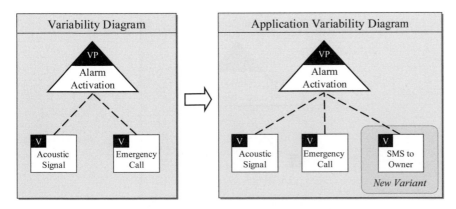

Fig. 15-6: Example of adding a new variant due to a requirements delta

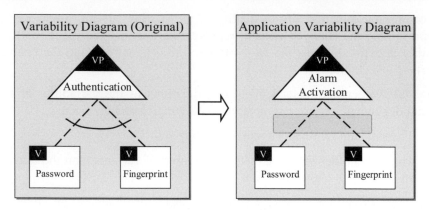

Fig. 15-7:   Example of a requirements delta realised by removing an alternative choice

Example 15-4: *Removing an Alternative Choice*

Figure 15-7 shows an alternative choice with two variants 'password' and 'fingerprint'. The stakeholder requires an application that can be configured to support any combination of variants, including no authentication. In order to satisfy these requirements, the alternative choice is removed resulting in two independent optional variability dependencies. Note that the same result could be achieved by defining the range [0..2] for the alternative choice.

Adding a new variation point   Stakeholder requirements may also require that a commonality is defined as variability in the application variability model. Making common parts variable is reflected in the variability model by adding a new variation point together with the required variants.

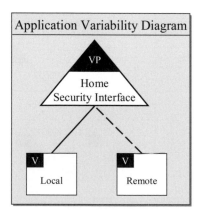

Fig. 15-8:   Example of adding a new variation point due to a requirements delta

---

Example 15-5: *Introduction of a New Variation Point*

A home security product line provides a common mechanism to set up the home security system via a local user interface. The stakeholder needs a home security system that also offers remote user interfaces. Hence, the stakeholder requires a variation point 'home security interface' with two variants 'local' and 'remote'. Local access must be available in each home automation system while the remote variant is optional. The corresponding excerpt of the variability model is shown in Fig. 15-8.

15.4.3 Impact on Requirements Artefacts

For each change to the variability model, the application requirements artefacts that are affected by the change have to be determined. The application requirements artefacts as well as the artefact dependencies to the variants may need to be adapted. In the following, we analyse the required changes of application requirements artefacts with respect to the different kinds of changes in the variability model.

The first type of requirements artefact deltas comprises changes caused by the introduction of new variants and/or new variation points. An example of such an adaptation is depicted in Fig. 15-5 and described in Example 15-6.

Changes in variation points and variants

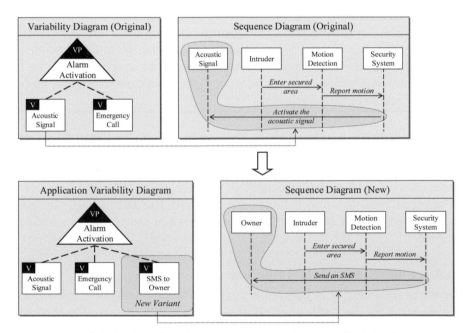

Fig. 15-9: Adaptation of a sequence diagram due to an adapted variant

> **Example 15-6:** *Introduction of a New Scenario*
>
> The upper half of Fig. 15-9 shows a variant 'acoustic signal' and its associated scenario. The scenario includes an actor 'acoustic signal' and an interaction that activates the acoustic signal. As the stakeholder requires an SMS notification, the variant 'SMS to owner' is introduced (lower half of Fig. 15-9). The variability model delta is incorporated into the new scenario by changing the scenario elements that deal with the acoustic signal in the original scenario.

Changes in dependencies

The second type of requirements artefact deltas comprises changes caused by adaptations to variability and constraint dependencies. Changes to variability dependencies may lead to restrictions on the permissible combinations of variants. Grouping a set of optional variability dependencies by an alternative choice with a range of [1..1] is an example of such a restriction. Some of the combinations of variants that were originally permitted become invalid. Requirements artefacts that describe such combinations have to be adapted. Changes to dependencies may also result in an extension of the possible combinations. This case is illustrated in Example 15-7.

> **Example 15-7:** *Impact of Variability Dependency Changes*
>
> In Example 15-4 the alternative choice for the two variants 'password' and 'fingerprint' is removed resulting in two independent optional variability dependencies. Consequently, requirements artefacts are needed that describe each combination of variants: no authentication, one kind of authentication, or both. For instance a scenario can be defined that describes unlocking a door using both password and fingerprint authentication together.

Impact on associated variants

Each requirements artefact may be associated with more than one variant. Hence, the requirements artefact delta to a particular application requirement may influence other associated variants. The requirements engineer stops the impact analysis when the influences of all changes in the variability model on the requirements artefacts have been analysed. For all changes, the stakeholders are involved to decide how the application requirements should be adapted.

15.4.4 Impact on the Architecture

Feedback about realisation effort

For the stakeholder, it is important to get feedback about the consequences of the deltas on the realisation effort. The realisation effort of a particular variability model delta and the respective requirements artefact deltas are evaluated with respect to:

- The adaptation effort for the product line architecture.

- The realisation effort for the components.

- The maintenance effort

The variability model delta and the associated requirements artefact deltas are provided to the application architect who maps them to the reference architecture using the traceability links established between domain requirements artefacts and domain design artefacts in the domain engineering process.[43] The adaptation effort for the reference architecture is roughly estimated by determining the category into which the architectural changes (e.g. changes of interfaces, the structure or the texture of the architecture) fall. For a more detailed estimation, the realisation effort for components has to be taken into account as well.

Categorisation of architecture changes

We distinguish between the following four categories of architectural adaptation:

- *Category A – No adaptation effort*: A particular variability model delta belongs to this category if no adaptation of the reference architecture is needed. In other words, the realisation of the delta has no impact on the architectural structure and texture.

No impact on architecture

- *Category B – Moderate adaptation effort*: A particular variability model delta is assigned to this category if only local architectural adaptations are required, e.g. changes to single components. Deltas that lead to slight adjustments of cross-cutting aspects belong to this category as well. This includes the adjustment of design quality requirements and simple changes of the architectural texture (but no significant change of architectural structure).

Local impact, slight adjustments

- *Category C – High adaptation effort:* Variability model deltas lead to a high adaptation effort if the reference architecture needs global changes. A change is considered to be global if, for example, a significant number of components and/or interfaces have to be changed.

Global impact

- *Category D – Too high adaptation effort*: A variability model delta that falls into this category means that no economically reasonable realisation of the delta is possible within the software product line. The developing company has to reject this delta unless the option exists to realise the desired application in a separate development project.

Out of product line scope

---

[43] The mapping of requirements to architecture ensures a consistent integration of changes. A scenario-based approach for mapping requirements to the architecture of a software product line is presented in [Pohl et al. 2001a].

Table 15-1:   Relation between deltas and architectural adaptation effort categories

Category\Delta	Category A — No adaptation effort	Category B — Moderate adaptation effort	Category C — High adaptation effort	Category D — Too high adaptation effort
1. New variant	X	X		
2. Adaptation of variability dependencies	X	X	X	
3. Adaptation of constraint dependencies		X	X	X
4. New variation point		X	X	X

Example 15-8: *Examples of Architectural Adaptation Effort*

- *Effort category B (delta 1)*: In case the stakeholder has special quality requirements with respect to a particular variant (e.g. performance requirements) this may lead to a moderate adaptation of the reference architecture.

- *Effort category A (delta 2)*: A change from "optional" to "alternative choice" may lead to essentially zero adaptation effort, because it is mainly a matter of configuration, i.e. configurations that include both variants have to be prohibited.

- *Effort category D (delta 3)*: The deletion of an "exclude" dependency might lead to a very large change in the architectural structure, e.g. if the dependency exists for technological reasons.

- *Effort category D (delta 4)*: A new variation point leads to too high an adaptation effort if the reference architecture is not able to support the required external variability. This may happen, for example, if the domain artefacts support sequential processing, yet to realise the delta, a variation point with the two alternative variants 'sequential processing' and 'parallel processing' is necessary. In this case all components would have to be reengineered to enable parallel access and synchronisation.

> **Example 15-9:** *Trade-off Decision*
>
> The stakeholder requires the following functionality: "The home owner shall be able to send a request about the door lock status via mobile phone." Yet, the product line provides the presentation of the door lock status only via the Internet. Now the stakeholder has the following alternatives:
>
> 1. Insisting on the mobile phone solution. Then the development organisation may realise the requirement as described above. This decision causes realisation effort that depends on the assignment to one of the described categories.
>
> 2. Accepting the Internet solution and giving up the requirement regarding the mobile phone. Then the stakeholder requirement is adapted (and is satisfied by the domain requirements artefact). The realisation effort will be very small because this stakeholder requirement can be fulfilled completely by reusing domain artefacts.

Table 15-1 shows the basic relations between the types of variability model deltas introduced above and the four categories of architectural adaptation effort. Variability deltas are depicted as rows in the table. Each column represents a category of architectural adaptations. A grey-filled table cell with an "X" indicates that the corresponding delta is likely to fall within the particular adaptation effort category.

Assignment of deltas to effort categories

When the stakeholders (and the application requirements engineer) get feedback from application design about the estimated realisation effort for a variability model delta and/or a requirements artefact delta, they have to decide between the following alternatives:

Decision about requirements

- The application variability model and/or the application requirements artefacts are adapted to fulfil the stakeholder requirement. In other words, the delta is realised.

Realisation of the delta

- The stakeholder adapts the requirement (which means the stakeholder might only get an 80% solution).[44] In this case no additional implementation is needed and the domain artefacts can be reused without changes.

Reuse of domain requirements artefacts

- The stakeholder requirement as well as the application variability model and/or the application requirements artefacts are adapted, i.e. the stakeholder requirement is partially fulfilled.

Partial realisation of the delta

---

[44] An 80% solution represents an application that fulfils most of the stakeholder's needs but involves certain compromises about stakeholder requirements on the one hand and realisation effort on the other hand.

Removed stakeholder
requirement

- The stakeholder decides that the requirement should not be realised due to the high adaptation effort (see the second alternative in Example 15-2).

Support of
trade-off decisions

In the case of a high adaptation effort, but also in other situations, the orthogonal variability model and the associated requirements artefacts provide assistance in finding an acceptable trade-off solution. The variability model presents options that can be chosen instead of realising the original stakeholder requirement. The stakeholder can select the best possible solution provided by the product line. Example 15-10 illustrates the support of a trade-off decision.

Example 15-10: *Support for Trade-off Decisions*

The variability model depicted in Fig. 15-10 contains the variation point 'home security by'. The stakeholder requirement under consideration demands outdoor intrusion detection via photo electric guard. The product line provides the feature 'outdoor motion detection'. Thus, a delta between the stakeholder requirement and the domain artefacts occurs. During the discussion with the stakeholder about the estimated realisation effort of this delta, the application requirements engineer uses the variability model to show the stakeholder possible alternatives. The engineer presents two alternatives with regard to home security: 'camera surveillance' and 'motion detection'. The description of the corresponding features may cause the stakeholder to resort to one of these alternatives.

15.5 Documentation of the Application Requirements

Contents of the
specification

The results of the activities described in Sections 15.3 and 15.4 have to be documented in the application requirements specification. The specification is the basis for the other application engineering sub-processes and defines all application requirements. The application requirements specification includes:

Reused
requirements

- *The application requirements artefacts that correspond to domain requirements artefacts including the traces to the respective domain requirements artefacts*
  This part of the documentation contains all application requirements artefacts that are reused without adaptations. It consists of the commonalities and the bound variation points, i.e. variation points that are bound to the selected variants.

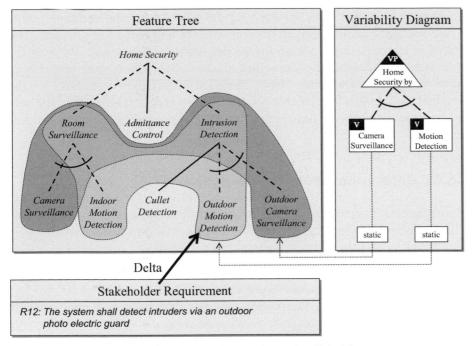

Fig. 15-10: Example of supporting trade-off decisions

- *The application variability model*
  This part of the documentation describes the application variability model with the selected variants, i.e. with the variability bindings.

  Application variability model

- *The variability model deltas including the traces to the original variability model elements*
  Variability model deltas are included in the application variability model.

  Application variability model deltas

- *The relation of the application requirements artefacts to the selected variants in the application variability model*
  This part of the documentation captures the traces between the requirements and the variants that are selected for the application.

  Traces to selected variants

- *The requirements deltas including the traces to the original domain requirements artefacts*
  This part of the documentation contains all requirements artefacts that are new or have been modified specifically for the application.

  Requirements deltas

The traces to domain requirements artefacts contained in the application requirements specification are an essential means to support the reuse of domain artefacts in application design, application realisation, and application testing. The bindings of the variability in the application requirements

Traceability

artefacts provide the basis for deriving the bindings for the variation points in the reference architecture, in the components, and in the test artefacts. The traces of changes to the variability model enable, for example, the application architect to refine the variability model deltas with respect to architectural variability. The traces from modified requirements artefacts to the original domain artefacts enable the application architect to identify the corresponding artefacts of the reference architecture and adapt them accordingly.

15.6   Differences from Single-System Engineering

Requirements engineering activities

Requirements engineering in single-system development encompasses the elicitation, validation, negotiation, and documentation of requirements (see e.g. [Pohl 1997]). In addition, continuous requirements management has to ensure that the specified requirements are always up to date.

Specific activities

The application requirements engineering sub-process in software product line engineering includes four major activities that differ from requirements engineering activities in single-system engineering:

Communication of variability

- *The communication of external variability to stakeholders*
  The goal of this activity is to communicate the variation points, variants, and associated requirements to the stakeholders. The results of this activity are a set of variants that have to be bound for the considered application and a set of deltas between the application requirements artefacts and domain requirements artefacts.

Deltas

- *The evaluation of the realisation effort for requirements deltas*
  The goal of this activity is to evaluate the impact of deltas on the variability model, the requirements artefacts, the reference architecture, etc. Based on the estimated effort, the stakeholder decides whether a delta should be realised or not.

Traceability

- *The documentation of application requirements*
  The goal of this activity is to define the application requirements and to record traceability links between the domain requirements artefacts and application requirements artefacts. The result of this activity is the application requirements specification.

Variability bindings

- *The documentation of variability bindings*
  The goal of this activity is to document the bindings of the variation points defined in the domain variability model. The result of this activity is the application variability model.

15.7 Summary

The goal of application requirements engineering is to elicit stakeholder requirements for the application and map the stakeholder requirements to common and variable domain requirements artefacts. Thereby domain requirements artefacts should be reused as much as possible. The reused common and variable domain requirements artefacts become part of the application requirements specification. The bindings of the variation points defined in the domain variability model are documented in the application variability model.

Reuse of domain requirements artefacts

If the stakeholder requirements for the application cannot be satisfied by reusing common or binding variable domain requirements artefacts, application-specific requirements artefacts may be introduced. Since these artefacts differ from the domain requirements artefacts, so-called requirements deltas arise. In addition, the application variability model may be adapted leading to deltas between the application variability model and the domain variability model. Application architects estimate the effort required for realising the application-specific requirements. This estimation is taken into account for deciding if the deltas are realised in the application or not. If it is decided to realise the deltas, the application requirements engineers adapt the application requirements artefacts and/or the application variability model to satisfy the stakeholder requirements.

Realising deltas

Frank van der Linden

16

Application Design

In this chapter you will learn:

- o *About the interrelations of the application design sub-process with the application requirements engineering, domain design, and application realisation sub-processes.*
- o *How to derive an application architecture from the product line reference architecture based on the application requirements.*
- o *How to bind variability in the reference architecture.*
- o *How to determine realisation costs of adaptations of the domain artefacts required for an application.*

16.1   Introduction

Goal of
application design

The main goal of the application design sub-process is to produce the application architecture. The application architecture is a specialisation of the reference architecture developed in domain design. Application architects bind the variability of the reference architecture and introduce application-specific changes according to the application requirements specification. The application architecture is passed on to application realisation where the reusable components and interfaces are assembled and where application-specific components and interfaces are developed. The sub-processes and artefacts closely related to the application design sub-process are highlighted in Fig. 16-1. The major information flows between application design and its related sub-processes are shown in more detail in Fig. 16-2.

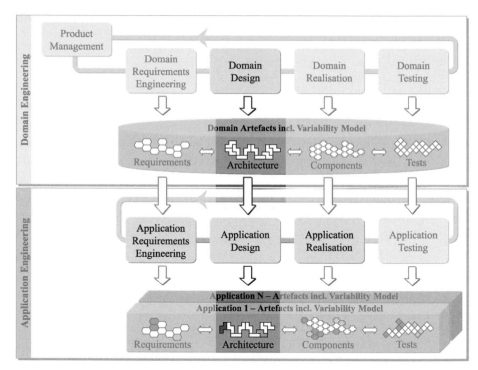

Fig. 16-1:   Sub-processes and artefacts related to application design

16.1.1 Interrelation with Application Requirements Engineering

Application
requirements

Application requirements engineering is responsible for developing the application requirements specification. The specification includes the application variability model as well as all application requirements, including the requirements reused from the domain artefacts and the application-specific requirements. It also contains traceability links to domain artefacts as well as the relation to selected variants in the variability model. The entire application requirements specification is passed on to application design (① in Fig. 16-2).

Application design supports trade-off decisions made in application requirements engineering by determining the estimated realisation effort (② in Fig. 16-2). The trade-off decisions about application-specific requirements are part of the negotiation with stakeholders in the application requirements engineering sub-process.

Realisation effort

16.1.2 Interrelation with Domain Design

Domain design develops the reference architecture, which is the basis for the application architecture. The application architect binds the architectural variability according to the bindings defined in the application variability model. The reusable domain artefact selection indicates the reusable domain artefacts (③ in Fig. 16-2).

Reference architecture

The application architect provides feedback through requests for additional and altered design (first bullet of ④ in Fig. 16-2) that may lead to an improvement of the reference architecture. Furthermore, application design delivers design artefacts, which have to be reengineered for flexibility and reusability and incorporated into the platform, to domain design (second bullet of ④ in Fig. 16-2).

Feedback from domain design

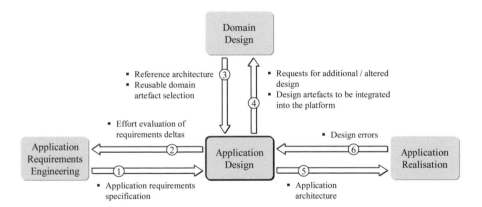

Fig. 16-2: Information flows between application design and other sub-processes

16.1.3 Interrelation with Application Realisation

Application architecture

Application realisation builds the application based on the application architecture (⑤ in Fig. 16-2). The application architecture determines the structure of the application to be built as well as the rules how to build it, which are contained in the texture. The application architecture also determines the configuration of reused domain components and interfaces that are part of the application as well as their interrelation with application-specific components and interfaces.

Design errors

Application realisation provides feedback on all kinds of design errors (⑥ in Fig. 16-2) that emerge during realisation and have to be solved by the architects. These include, amongst the normal design errors, components and interfaces that turn out not to be reusable, and configurations that do not work properly.

16.2   Development of the Application Architecture

Specialisation of the reference architecture

An application architect has similar responsibilities as a traditional architect. As such, abstraction, modelling, simulating, and prototyping are activities that are performed by the application architect. However, all those activities have to be performed only for the application-specific parts. The reference architecture includes a lot of decisions that can be reused in application engineering. The application architect starts with the reference architecture and specialises it towards the application architecture. The reference architecture models are specialised through the binding of variants according to the bindings in the application variability model and by adding application-specific parts.

Example 16-1: *Application-Specific Abstractions*

The home automation example employs domain abstractions for authentication such as "authentication key" and "authentication algorithm". A new application is planned that supports iris scan authentication, a feature that is not yet supported by any other product in the product line. Consequently, there are no abstractions available for iris scan authentication. The architect adds new abstractions such as "iris map" and "iris pattern" to support the new feature.

The platform provides abstractions to deal with quality features, such as safety, security, and performance. The new application needs preventive maintenance of hardware parts that fail frequently. The application architect thus provides abstractions dealing with maintenance, e.g. "error level" and "error rate".

16.2.1 Application-Specific Modelling

The application architect introduces abstractions that are necessary for the specific application at hand, i.e. the architect adds abstractions for application-specific aspects that are not covered by the domain artefacts. The additional abstractions are usually related to application-specific requirements. Especially when there are very strict quality requirements, new application abstractions have to be introduced. For instance, if performance requirements of the application are stricter than defined in the product line, the application architect adds abstractions for threads' synchronisation and communication. Also in the case where the application supports a feature that is not provided by the product line, abstractions related to the new feature are added (Examples 16-1 and 16-2). The abstractions of the application architecture have to be integrated with the abstractions defined in the reference architecture to obtain a consistent application architecture.

Application-specific abstractions

Example 16-2: *Lock Control Application Design Activities*

An application is planned for a mid-range system, including both a sliding door and an iris scan identification feature. Both are new features, and the application is the first one that has to support them. In addition, the application has a normal swinging door and the basic keypad commands for situations without iris scan. For instance, during the recognition phase of a specific iris the keypad is needed. The application architect provides the necessary abstractions of both new features and relates them to the abstractions in the reference architecture dealing with door control and authentication. The models get new elements related to the abstractions of the reference architecture. There are components or plug-ins for 'sliding door lock actuator', 'sliding door open/close sensor' and 'iris scan authentication'. A thread is added to perform the iris scan authentication. In order to ensure that this thread does not interfere with the other threads, an existing application is enriched with a mock-up iris scan algorithm that occupies the processor and the memory for one-half to three-quarters of a second and answers "no" or "yes" randomly. This system is used to simulate the additional thread.

The application-specific abstractions have connections to the concepts and models defined by the reference architecture. Application-specific models are built for establishing and dealing with these connections. Additional models are built to accommodate application-specific concerns, such as specific behaviour or specific quality requirements.

Application-specific models

Simulation and prototyping

As the application architecture is more concrete than the reference architecture, more realistic simulations can be performed. Application architects employ simulations to get an insight into the properties of a specific configuration and to evaluate application-specific variants (see Example 16-2). For example, performance simulations can be used to determine the configuration that satisfies the application-specific performance requirements best. As for simulation, prototyping can be more concrete at the application level, and relate to application-specific requirements.

16.2.2 Binding of Variants

Variants of reference architecture

The application architect has to bind the variants for the variation points of the reference architecture as defined in the application variability model. The quality of the reference architecture determines whether this is an easy job. It depends on:

- The way mass customisation is incorporated; this determines which styles, structures, and patterns are used to deal with variability.

- The abstractions used, determining which variation points and variants are available.

- The traceability between variability in domain requirements artefacts and the reference architecture.

Example 16-3: *New Variants in the Application Architecture*

The design of the door and window management subsystem for the considered application has to include additional functionality for sliding doors and for iris scan identification. The application architect reuses the keypad and swinging door functionality. For the new features, new components have to be made; see Fig. 16-3. For the sliding door feature, two application-specific plug-in components are needed: a 'sliding door lock actuator plug-in' component and a 'sliding door sensor plug-in' component. Note that the basic lock functionality does not need a door sensor. For the iris-scan feature, two plug-ins are needed: an 'iris control plug-in', which records the iris scan to initiate commands, and an 'iris authentication plug-in', which performs the actual authentication algorithm. Interfaces of the reference architecture are reused to connect the new components to the remainder of the door functionality. No new interfaces are needed, and no new patterns or frameworks either.

Reusable domain artefacts

To reduce the work of application realisation as much as possible, reusable domain artefacts have to be used whenever possible. The reference architecture determines common components and interfaces. By binding the variation points, the application architect selects additional domain design artefacts that can be reused. If no domain artefact is available, the application architect has to define an application-specific one to be realised during application realisation.

Certain variants have to be realised only for one single application. These variants may involve new components (Example 16-3) or interfaces, but sometimes also larger parts of the structure, such as configurations of components and interfaces, new patterns (Example 16-4), and even new component frameworks.

Design artefacts for new variants

> **Example 16-4:** *New Patterns*
>
> An application is specified that uses Bluetooth [Bluetooth 2004] to connect a wireless device for all kinds of user interaction. Since the product line does not yet have any wireless communication, several components have to be added to the application architecture. This also involves the introduction of new interfaces between them, and of corresponding patterns. For instance, there is a pattern involving generic Bluetooth functionality with plug-in components for several specific input devices. This pattern has to be integrated with the existing components dealing with user control.

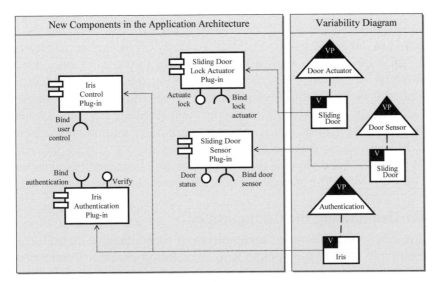

Fig. 16-3: New variants in lock control

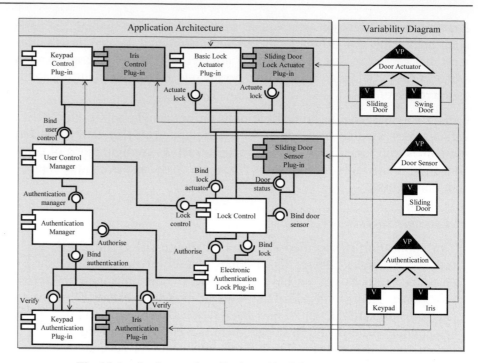

Fig. 16-4:   Lock control application with sliding doors and iris scan

Realisation effort

When designing the application-specific parts, the architect has to consider the additional effort in application realisation. Often, there are not enough personnel and time available to realise many specific components from scratch. The architect has to evaluate carefully what can be implemented specifically for a single application with regard to the available resources. The amount of available resources for realising the application has to be negotiated with application requirements engineering, the stakeholders, and product management. For normal application development, the amount of resources may be scarce, which means that not much additional work can be done. In applications that are of strategic relevance, e.g. if the application is a lead product, or the client is the most important client, additional resources may be allocated to the project. Section 16.4 treats this topic in more detail.

16.2.3 Determining the Configuration

Variants determine required components

The specific configuration of components in an application is the result of the binding of the variation points with the selected variants. Certain domain components are not required in the application and therefore are absent. If different variants that are realised in different plug-in components are simultaneously present in the application, more than one plug-in is needed. Application-specific components are designed as additional plug-ins, if possible.

In this case they are connected at the places that are planned for them in the reference architecture.

Example 16-5: *Lock Control Application Variants*

Figure 16-4 shows a part of the application architecture of the new application with both an additional sliding door and iris scan identification. Reusable domain components are depicted as white boxes. New application-specific components are depicted as grey boxes. These are the same as in Fig. 16-3. The configuration resembles the domain structure, but certain plug-in components are present twice, once for the basic functionality and once for the additional, new features. Moreover, the plug-in for manual door locks is absent. Basic functionality is provided by the standard, reusable domain plug-in components. The 'sliding door lock actuator plug-in' component is put in parallel[45] with the 'basic lock actuator plug-in' component. The 'sliding door sensor plug-in' component is the only door sensor plug-in since, for the basic lock functionality, a door sensor is optional and is not used in this application. The two plug-in components, 'iris control plug-in' and 'iris authentication plug-in', are put in parallel with the plug-in components for keypad authentication.

16.2.4 Consistent Selection of Component Variants

The application architect is in charge of deciding about the variants that have global consequences on the application. As the information about variants is distributed over the different components, care has to be taken to select a consistent configuration of component variants.

Global impact of variants

Part of the product line variability deals with the hardware specifics of the application, such as memory size and amount of peripheral hardware. Hardware-specific variations are either bound by selecting the appropriate components or by setting the configuration parameters of one or more components to the proper values.

Hardware-specific configuration

Example 16-6: *Hardware-Related Variability*

Each home automation system has a specific set of sensors and actuators in a specific configuration with other hardware, such as routers or switches. The application uses one of several pre-selected protocols, each suitable for a specific network configuration. Finally there is a limited memory size and bandwidth available.

---

[45] This means that it is connected to the same interfaces of other components, and both are present together.

> **Example 16-7:** *Consistency of Component Variants*
>
> The application with the sliding door and iris scan has a single sliding door and two swinging doors. Each swinging door needs one actuator. The sliding door needs two, one at the top and one at the bottom. Several variants are selected based on this hardware configuration:
>
> | Components | Variant |
> |-----------|---------|
> | Lock control | map of three doors to four door lock actuators |
> | Door lock plug-ins | three doors, their properties, and the identification of their authentication algorithms |
> | Actuator | activation and control of each of the four actuators separately |
>
> Application design uses one or more configuration files to keep such configuration information consistent. Application realisation has to use the information in these configuration files.

16.3   Feedback of Application Artefacts to the Domain

Application as test bed for the domain

Variants that are designed by the application architect may be usable for other applications as well. This also holds for other technical solutions provided by the application architect. The application architect is in discussion with the domain architect to identify such possible reusable artefacts, which may have a wider scope than the present application. In many cases the artefacts are first produced for a single application. This is a test bed for the domain architect. If everything works fine and product management decides that the new artefacts should be integrated into the domain artefacts, the domain architect takes over, and takes care of a redesign to make the artefacts reusable (Example 16-8).

> **Example 16-8:** *Integration of Application Artefacts into the Platform*
>
> Since the application with sliding doors and iris scan is a commercial success, the programme manager asks to allow the corresponding requirements to be reused in other applications. They are incorporated as variants of existing domain requirements artefacts for door control and authorisation. The domain architect takes over the application architecture for these parts, provides a redesign of the application design artefacts, and initiates adaptation during domain realisation.

After an application artefact has been successfully integrated into the platform, the application architect may decide to use the reusable artefact in new versions of the application instead of the non-reusable application-specific artefact which was originally built for this application. This reduces the amount of application-specific artefacts that have to be maintained.

Replacing non-reusable artefacts

16.4   Effort and Cost of Variants

The cost of selecting a variant for the application architecture depends on what has to be done to realise the variant in the application. If the variant is realised in the platform, the cost is small (category A, see Section 15.4.4). The main cost and effort are caused by determining the right parameters. In the case where application-specific components have to be developed, the costs are typically much higher. When the application-specific components provide and use only domain-specific interfaces, the development cost and effort are still moderate (category B, see Section 15.4.4). In many cases, application realisation can use other components as templates for the application-specific components. In the case where a large new part of the structure has to be provided, costs and effort are typically high (category C, see Section 15.4.4). In that case, new interfaces have to be provided, which have to be realised as well. In addition, simulation and validation have to be performed before the application architecture is finished. In cases where large parts of the architecture have to be added, e.g. the introduction of a new framework supporting a new (variant of a) feature, the changes may be very large, to such an extent that they cannot be realised using the reference architecture (category D, see Section 15.4.4).

Realisation cost

The following factors influence the required effort and costs:

Cost factors

- Number of new components to be realised.

- Number of interfaces to be realised.

- Number of small component and interface adaptations – care has to be taken that large component and interface adaptations cost almost the same as, or even more than, writing a new one.

- Simulations performed to verify the correct behaviour of adaptations and extensions – the need for simulation indeed depends on the kind of changes, but when new quality requirements are involved simulation is often inevitable.

- Adaptations to cross-cutting aspects – this may require adaptations to all, or many, components. It may require the addition of new interfaces to be provided or used by many components. Typically this also involves costs of simulations or other ways to verification.

- Tests to be performed on reused components and configurations.

- Tests to be performed on new components – this takes more effort, since new test cases have to be created.

Cost estimation

To estimate the effort and costs the organisation may have standard figures that apply for most situations. In specific situations, the organisation may have to adapt the standard costs, e.g. if a change does not differ much from another one, the costs may be smaller. If a complete, new design has to be introduced, costs may be estimated higher. The cost of introducing a new variant is communicated to the requirements engineers and other stakeholders, who, in the end, decide whether the costs are worth the value they bring. If the costs are too high, adaptations of the application requirements may lead to affordable development costs.

Cost amortisation for reusable features

In cases where the application is used as a test bed for a new feature, additional costs may be acceptable to the organisation since the new feature can also be reused within future applications of the product line.

16.5   Differences from Single-System Engineering

The application architect has to specialise the reference architecture to an application architecture for a single application. This means that:

Reuse of reference architecture

- A large part of the application architecture is determined by the reference architecture and does not have to be designed by the application architect. However, the reference architecture may be under-specified, meaning that application-specific artefacts have to be designed by the application architect.

- Variation points in the reference architecture are bound to application-specific variants according to the bindings of the variability defined in the application variability model. Thereby domain design artefacts are reused.

Traceable requirements

- Many application-specific requirements are specialisations of domain requirements. This gives a first indication of where the architecture has to be specialised.

Common rules from texture

- The texture in the reference architecture not only captures the commonality within a single system but also defines commonality that is present within all applications. The application architecture must conform to the texture. Texture has an additional role in providing common ways to deal with variability in the application architecture.

- Software product line engineering means that the activities of the application architect require less effort than in single-system software engineering. If no application-specific adaptations are required, the application architecture can be established by binding the defined variation points with predefined variants.

Reduced effort

16.6 Summary

Application design has the same role as single-system software design. The application architecture determines the overall structure of a particular application and must be capable of satisfying the application requirements. The application architect uses the reference architecture, which provides a design for many of the application requirements that the application architect must satisfy. Moreover, reusable components and interfaces, and configurations of them, are provided by the reference architecture. Therefore, application architects can focus their attention on the application-specific parts, thereby saving a lot of time.

Large-scale reuse

In discussion with the domain architect, certain solutions and application artefacts may become candidates for integration into the platform. Usually the integration takes place after the application is finished and the properties of the developed artefacts are validated. The application architect has the responsibility to provide the domain architect with information about such possible artefacts.

Source of future domain artefacts

Frank van der Linden

17

Application Realisation

In this chapter you will learn:

- o *About the interrelations of the application realisation sub-process with the application design, domain realisation, and application testing sub-processes.*
- o *How to bind the variability according to the application design and the application requirements.*
- o *How to derive application-specific components and interfaces from the application architecture and thereby guarantee a high degree of reuse.*
- o *How to realise a consistent application configuration.*

17.1   Introduction

Goal of application   The goal of application realisation is to develop applications that can be
realisation   tested and brought to the market after ensuring a sufficient quality. Application realisation provides the detailed design and implementation of application-specific components and configures them with the right variants of the
domain assets into applications. The main results of application realisation
are the application-specific components and interfaces, the selected variants
of reused components, and the application configuration. The sub-processes
and artefacts closely related to the application realisation sub-process are
highlighted in Fig. 17-1. The main information flows between application
realisation and its related sub-processes are depicted in Fig. 17-2.

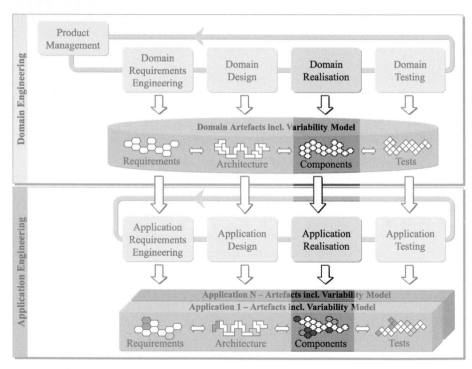

Fig. 17-1:   Sub-processes and artefacts related to application realisation

17.1.1 Interrelation with Application Design

Application   Application design provides the application architecture which determines
architecture   the configuration of components and interfaces, which are either reused from
the platform or designed specifically for the considered application (① in
Fig. 17-2).

Application realisation provides feedback with regard to all kinds of design errors (② in Fig. 17-2) that are uncovered during realisation and which have to be corrected by application design. An example of such an error is a configuration that does not work properly.

Design errors

17.1.2 Interrelation with Application Testing

Application realisation delivers a complete application (first bullet of ③ in Fig. 17-2), ready for testing. Application testing performs unit, integration, and system tests based on the application requirements, design, and realisation artefacts (i.e. the detailed design of components and interfaces). Application realisation supports application testing by providing the interface descriptions (second bullet of ③ in Fig. 17-2) required, for instance, for the unit test.

Executable application

As feedback, application realisation gets test results including the acceptance or rejection of the application and problem reports describing in which way the test item fails (④ in Fig. 17-2). The feedback is used to improve the application until acceptance is reached. Moreover, application testing reports defects in interface descriptions which are detected in application testing as they hamper the development of test cases.

Test results

17.1.3 Interrelation with Domain Realisation

The input for application realisation from domain realisation consists of reusable components and interfaces (⑤ in Fig. 17-2) designed, implemented, and ready for reuse. In order to be able to integrate these artefacts into an application, domain realisation additionally provides configuration support.

Reusable components and interfaces

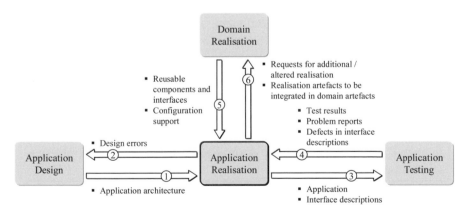

Fig. 17-2:   Information flows between application realisation and other sub-processes

Feedback to domain realisation

Application realisation provides feedback through requests for additional and altered realisation (first bullet of ⑥ in Fig. 17-2). The requests pertain to functionality or quality that should be provided by the platform. Furthermore, application realisation develops application-specific components and interfaces that may possibly be integrated into the domain artefacts (second bullet of ⑥ in Fig. 17-2).

17.2 Configuration

Domain realisation delivers components and interfaces for reuse by application realisation. Interfaces are reused without changes, but components often have internal variation points, which have to be bound.

Use of domain interfaces

Many interfaces between the components of an application are reusable domain interfaces. Most of the application components carry them as they are an important means to support the texture and to implement variation points. Different variants of a single component often require and provide the same interfaces. Plug-in components provide the interfaces required by a particular component framework. Moreover, the architectural texture may demand that each component provides aspect-specific interfaces (Section 11.5). Such interfaces are realised during domain engineering but are heavily used during application engineering.

Reusable component variants

Reusable domain components often have internal variation points. Domain realisation provides mechanisms to support variant selection. Variants within a component can be selected, for instance, by parameter bindings. Guided by the application architecture and the application variability model, application realisation selects the proper variants of the components to be part of the application. For each reusable component, application realisation determines the right choice of component parameters to bind the required variant.

> **Example 17-1:** *Lock Control Component Reuse*
>
> Suppose that the application has one sliding door with two actuators and one sensor, and two swinging doors, each with one actuator but no sensor. The 'lock control' component is reused. It has to be configured in such a way that each of the doors is controlled using the right sensors and actuators.

Parameter consistency

In many cases, several components need to know the same kind of information. This may result in a lot of redundancy in the set of parameters. Human error in providing the parameters may lead to inconsistencies. Application realisation has to keep track of the parameters and their relationships in order to keep the configuration of components consistent. The quality of the reference architecture and the resulting component designs determine whether it is a simple or a complex task to select component parameters consistently. To reduce the redundancy of parameters, domain design and realisation may introduce configuration components or employ tool support [V. Ommering et al. 2000].

Example 17-2: *Binding Variation Points in Components*

The application with sliding doors and iris scan reuses many platform components and interfaces, e.g. the 'user control manager', 'authentication manager', and 'lock control' components of the door control framework (Fig. 17-3). They have to be configured to be able to deal with the specific situation of having both keypad and iris scan, two swinging doors, and one sliding door. Domain realisation provides them in such a way that they get the necessary configuration information from plug-in components that are bound to them. The parameter information does not have to be provided twice. Certain plug-in components are reused as well:

- 'Keypad control plug-in' and 'keypad authentication plug-in' are reused by many applications. Their variants are chosen according to the authentication-key formats, e.g. four digits. Moreover, there may be variants that differ in the handling of situations when too few or too many keys are pressed. Since those components and key formats are already used by other applications, the configuration information can be reused.

- 'Electronic authentication lock plug-in' is one of the six kinds of reusable lock plug-in components defined in Example 12-3. It needs to be configured to be able to deal with two different authentication algorithms. The specific parameters of these algorithms are available in the respective components that deal with these algorithms. The main function of the component is to select the right algorithm in the right situation.

- 'Basic lock actuator plug-in' is reused in many applications with the same kind of swinging doors. For this component, configuration parameters like timing and speed have to be provided.

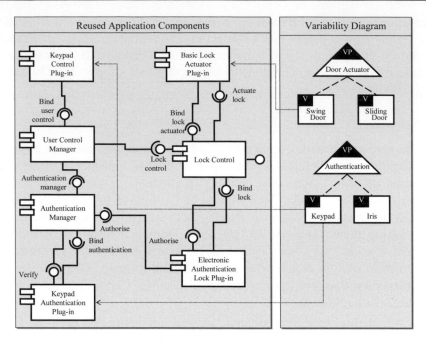

Fig. 17-3: Reused domain components and interfaces

17.3   Realisation of Application-Specific Components

Application-specific components are realised just as in single-system engineering. However, in many cases, domain interfaces can be reused for application-specific components. For instance, an application-specific plug-in component has to carry all interfaces that are determined by the domain architecture for such a plug-in.

Reusable component
adaptations
Application-specific components and interfaces are needed whenever there is no suitable reusable domain component available. Making application-specific components reusable is not of interest for the application developer whose focus is on a single application only. If the component has to be integrated into the domain artefacts, domain realisation takes over at an appropriate time, not disturbing application realisation. However, an application component may resemble already existing domain components. For instance, it may be the case that the application component and some reusable components are variants of a common variation point. In that case, it is a good idea to use the design of the existing variants as input for the design of the new variant.

Example 17-3: *Application-Specific Components for Lock Control*

The application architecture is available for an application that
includes both a sliding door and an iris scan identification feature.
Since there are no reusable components available for these features,
the application architect determines new components for 'sliding door
lock actuator plug-in', 'sliding door sensor plug-in', 'iris control plug-
in', and an 'iris authentication plug-in'; see Fig. 17-4. All these
components reuse existing interfaces:

- 'Bind user control'
- 'Bind lock actuator' and 'actuate lock'
- 'Bind door sensor' and 'door status'
- 'Bind authentication' and 'verify'

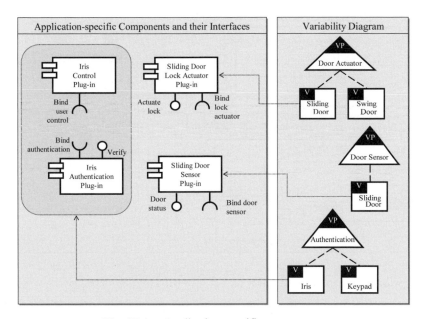

Fig. 17-4:   Application-specific components

17.4   Building the Application

The final task of application realisation is the realisation of the configuration
that is actually delivered as the application. Component variants have to be

compiled, linked, and deployed on the actual hardware. In all these steps variability may be bound, depending on the configuration mechanism used.[46]

Files for components and interfaces

A component variant is realised as a collection of files. The files encompass source code files, header files, and parameter definitions. Interfaces are usually realised in one or more header files. The header files for required interfaces are necessary to be able to compile the component variant. Note that the provided interfaces do not need to be included themselves. Linking combines the component variants to executables or dynamic link libraries. The application is made up of one or more executables and dynamic link libraries.

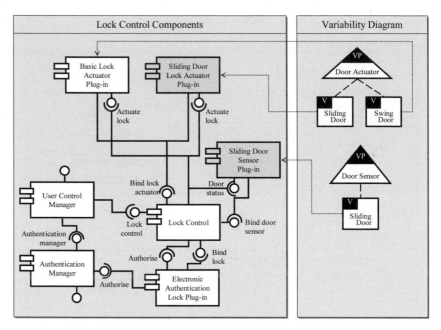

Fig. 17-5:   Lock control configuration

Versions and variants

As in single-system engineering, over time, each component and interface exists in several versions. New versions originate from maintenance as well as from the incorporation of new requirements. The latter situation occurs especially if a component is used for more than one application, which is the normal situation for platform assets. The selection of component variants also has to take into account the version to be used. A later version is often better with regard to the quality of the component. Yet, it is possible that a new version of a component cannot be introduced into an application as it is not able to interact with other components. This may be due to changes in

---

[46] For a list of possible configuration mechanisms, see Section 12.5.

functionality, changes in quality support, and changes in interfaces, for example. In addition, it may be the case that the application has a combination of components that has not yet been thoroughly tested yet.

Example 17-4: *Lock Control Configuration*

The application with the sliding door and iris scan is built from the compiled components that make up the configuration. Figure 17-5 shows the configuration around the 'lock control' component. The grey components are application specific and the white ones are reusable domain components. The plug-in components know statically to which component they have to connect, whereas the components that provide the connection facility do not know the plug-in components statically. Since only statically known connections can be linked off-line, they are the only ones that are bound before loading the software on the target machine. Thus the 'authorise' interface of the 'electronic authentication lock plug-in' component is bound on the target hardware at initialisation time to the 'lock control' through the 'bind lock' interface. The 'bind lock' interface is statically known to the 'electronic authentication lock plug-in' and already bound during linking. During initialisation, the 'electronic authentication lock plug-in' component announces its 'authorise' interface to the 'lock control' component using the 'bind lock' interface. If component support, such as COM, .NET, or Java Beans, is available on the target machine, part of the linking can be done based on that. But also in that case, the statically known connections are bound first, and the dynamic ones next.

During integration tests and during maintenance in the field, problem reports are issued. Application engineering is responsible for resolving the reported problems. When the problems are related to application-specific components and interfaces, it is the responsibility of application realisation to fix them. However, when the problem is related to domain artefacts, the problem report has to be taken over by domain engineering for fixing.

Responsibility for fixing errors

17.5 Differences from Single-System Engineering

Application realisation provides a working application that is ready for testing. The application is based on the application architecture and reuses domain components and interfaces. This reduces realisation effort significantly. This means that:

Working application

- The application developer selects variants of the reusable domain components.

- The reusable domain component variants should be consistent with each other and conform to the application architecture.

- The application is built by configuring application-specific and reusable components and interfaces.

17.6   Summary

Realisation and configuration

Application realisation deals with designing in detail, implementing, and configuring components to produce an executable application. Interfaces are reused from the platform without changes, but components often have internal variation points, which have to be bound, e.g. by providing values for parameters. Newly developed application-specific components and specialised reusable components are configured and connected by their interfaces to assemble the application. After assembly, the application can be tested and deployed on the target hardware.

Klaus Pohl
Andreas Reuys

18

Application Testing

In this chapter you will learn:

- o *About the interrelations of the application testing sub-process with the application requirements engineering, application design, application realisation, and the domain testing sub-processes.*

- o *How to reuse domain test artefacts for a particular application.*

- o *How traceability facilitates the reuse of domain test artefacts.*

- o *A systematic way for deriving application test cases from domain test cases based on application requirements, application design, and application realisation artefacts.*

- o *The principles of achieving sufficient test coverage in the system test.*

18.1   Introduction

Goal of application testing

The goal of the application testing sub-process is to achieve a sufficient quality of the application under test. Application testing thus complements the testing activities of domain testing.

Related sub-processes

The sub-processes and artefacts closely related to the application testing sub-process are highlighted in Fig. 18-1. Application testing reuses domain test artefacts. The unit test in application testing requires input from application realisation. The integration test requires input from application design, and the system test is performed on the basis of application requirements. The results of application testing are provided as feedback to the related sub-processes. Figure 18-2 shows the information flows between application testing and its related sub-processes.

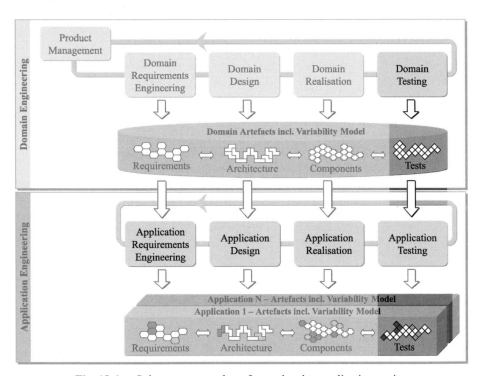

Fig. 18-1:   Sub-processes and artefacts related to application testing

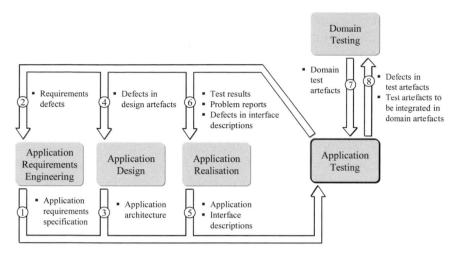

Fig. 18-2:   Information flows between application testing and other sub-processes

18.1.1 Interrelation with Application Requirements Engineering

Application system testing validates the created application against the application requirements specification (① in Fig. 18-2). The system test that is performed in application testing employs the application requirements as test references. The test must ensure that the application properly realises the application requirements and that no requirement has been omitted. Furthermore, the application variability model defines the variability bindings for the application, and thus the variants that have been selected for the specific application. Application testing binds the variation points in the domain test artefacts according to the variability bindings in the application variability model.

Application requirements

The creation of test cases is at the same time a validation of application requirements. Requirements defects such as ambiguous or incomplete requirements as well as errors in the configuration of variants are reported back to application requirements engineering (② in Fig. 18-2). Application requirements engineers must correct these defects before application testing can be completed.

Requirements defects

18.1.2 Interrelation with Application Design

Application design determines the architecture of the application including its static structure and its dynamic behaviour. The application architecture (③ in Fig. 18-2) is used as input for application integration testing. Due to the binding of the variation points, all components of the application are available for testing. The components that are part of the application can be separated into components that are reused from the domain artefacts and

Application architecture

application-specific components, which encompass modified domain components as well as newly developed application-specific components. For reused domain components, reusable test artefacts are available, e.g. if the CRS (see Chapter 13) is applied.

Defects in design artefacts   During application integration testing, the application design is validated. Test engineers must ensure that the variability in the design has been bound properly and that the application design is testable. Whenever the test engineer cannot fully determine the integration test cases and the data required for a test case, an incompleteness or ambiguity has been detected. Any defects in design artefacts (④ in Fig. 18-2) detected in application testing are reported back to application design.

18.1.3 Interrelation with Application Realisation

Executable application   Application realisation builds the application (⑤ in Fig. 18-2) and provides the interface descriptions to be used as the test references for the unit test. The application unit test validates the components, which have been newly developed or modified by application realisation, but also repeats tests already performed in domain testing. The different test levels and the corresponding tests are described in more detail in Section 18.4. In addition, application testing performs tests related to the binding of the variability as explained in Section 18.3.

Test results   Application testing reports all test results, together with problem reports as well as the uncovered defects in interface descriptions, back to application realisation (④ in Fig. 18-2). The test results capture which test cases have been performed and whether the object under test passed or failed the test. The problem reports capture the observed deviations from the expected behaviour, which the object under test should possess according to the test reference. Defects in interface descriptions hamper test case design and must be corrected before testing can be completed.

18.1.4 Interrelation with Domain Testing

Domain test artefacts   In order to avoid developing tests from scratch for each application, domain testing provides application testing with reusable test artefacts (⑦ in Fig. 18-2). In order to perform the tests, application test engineers must bind the variation points in the domain test designs according to the application variability model.

Feedback to domain testing   Any defects in the domain test artefacts themselves are reported back to domain testing (first bullet of ⑧ in Fig. 18-2). In addition, application-specific test artefacts (second bullet of ⑧ in Fig. 18-2) created during application testing may be passed on to domain testing. Domain testing may integrate application-specific test artefacts into the domain artefacts, for example if the application-specific test artefacts are relevant for more than one application.

18.2 Domain Test Artefact Reuse

The key idea of establishing test artefact reuse is to develop test artefacts once for the entire product line, include them in the domain artefacts, and reuse them for multiple applications. To achieve a sufficient degree of reuse, domain test artefacts must be reused for common as well as for variable parts of the application. Following the CRS (Definition 13-10), domain testing prepares test cases with explicit common and variable parts. Test cases for common parts can be reused as they are. For test cases that contain variability the variation points must be bound according to the application variability model before the test cases can be executed.

Implications of the CRS

If the SAS (Definition 13-9) is applied, the test cases developed for the sample application can be used as a basis for developing test cases for the application under test. It is quite likely that the test cases of the sample application have to be adapted. Therefore, the variants selected for the sample application are compared with the variants selected for the application under test. Based on the differences in the variability bindings, the required adaptations of the test artefacts can be determined. However, in case of large differences in the applications, significant rework might be required to create the application test artefacts. Note that additional test cases must be defined to validate application-specific requirements.

Implications of the SAS

In the following, we elaborate on two essential prerequisites for establishing an efficient reuse of test artefacts: dealing with variability and the use of traceability links. We thereby focus on system tests. However, the basic principles presented also hold for integration and unit tests.

Focus on system test

18.2.1 Dealing with Variability

The application test engineer has to understand the variation points and variants defined in the domain artefacts and know how to bind the variability defined in the domain test artefacts. Application test artefacts are built based on domain test artefacts. The test plans, test cases, and test case scenarios have to be adapted for the specific application. The application test engineer thus has to learn how to bind the variability defined in the domain test artefacts according to the application variability model. Example 18-1 illustrates the binding of variability in a domain test case scenario.

Binding variability

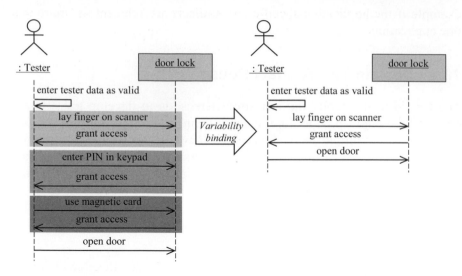

Fig. 18-3:   Example of variability binding in test case scenarios

---

Example 18-1: *Dealing with Variability in Application Testing*

The application test engineer of a home automation application considers the domain test case scenario depicted on the left side of Fig. 18-3 (this scenario is explained in more detail in Section 8.3). The domain test case scenario contains three variants: 'fingerprint scanner', 'keypad', and 'magnetic card reader'. According to the application variability model (not depicted in Fig. 18-3), the variant 'fingerprint scanner' has been bound for the application under test. In order to derive the application test case scenario, the test engineer binds this variant also in the domain test case scenario. The result is depicted on the right side of Fig. 18-3.

18.2.2 Use of Traceability Links

Retrieval of test artefacts

To allow for an efficient reuse of test artefacts it is necessary to support the retrieval of the applicable domain test cases. Figure 18-4 presents the basic idea. The trace information captured by application requirements engineering (Chapter 15) is used to detect the reused domain requirements artefacts. From domain testing, it is clear which test artefact relates to which requirement. Thus, based on the domain requirements, the reusable domain test artefacts can be retrieved. The domain test artefacts retrieved can be used to test the application requirements which correspond to the domain requirements related to the domain test artefacts.

Traceability is the first keystone for structured reuse. The second keystone is the requirements delta information that is contained in the application requirements specification. The deltas are the basis for determining whether a test case can be reused without changes, must be adapted, or created anew.

Requirements deltas

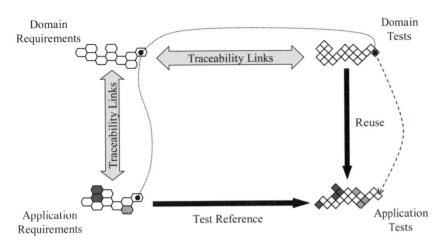

Fig. 18-4:   Traceability between requirements and system test artefacts

A detailed process description for application testing defines when to record and when to use trace information. Although we do not deal with trace information at this level of detail, clear rules for the recording and usage of trace information are required in industrial software product line engineering to facilitate the reuse of domain test artefacts.

Recording and using traces

Example 18-2: *Retrieving Domain Artefacts*

In Example 18-1, a trace exists between the requirements artefacts for electronic door locks and the test case scenario of Fig. 18-3. The dependency between the two artefacts is recorded by a traceability link, which we refer to as "DomainDoorLockTestTrace". Whenever one of the three door lock variants is incorporated into an application, the dependency between the domain and the corresponding application requirements artefact is recorded as well.

The "DomainDoorLockTestTrace" is used to identify the reusable domain test case. The domain test case is reused for a new application test case that validates the realisation of the corresponding application requirement.

18.3 Tests Related to Variability

Defect categories

The task of application testing is to validate that the application under test complies with the test references from domain engineering. This implies that the binding of variability and the configuration realised in the application are checked for correctness. More precisely, the application test engineer has to check if:

- Application engineers have bound variants for the application that should not be part of the application.

- Application engineers have omitted variants that should be bound for the application.

- Application engineers have configured the application in a way that violates the constraint and/or variability dependencies.

If the application contains variants that should not be part of it, different kinds of errors may occur. The usability of the application may be affected as the customer finds the variant impracticable or the variant consumes additional resources and thus affects system performance. If a variant that should bound for the application is omitted, the functionality and/or quality related to this variant is missing in the application. Furthermore, the violation of dependencies may lead to a malfunctioning application. For example, if a variant that is required by another variant or variation point is not included in the application, the components that require this variant may not work properly. If an "excludes" dependency is violated and thus a variant that is in conflict with another variant or variation point is included in the application, the conflicts between the different variants may lead to errors.

Tests

Specific tests are required to detect defects in the binding of variability and the configuration of an application since the proper functioning of an application may be affected by such defects. On the other hand, if a dependency that has strategical reasons is violated, this defect may be difficult to detect. Only a specific test can reveal this type of deviation from the application requirements specification. In the following, we thus introduce two types of tests for detecting defects in the variability bindings and the configuration of an application.

> **Definition 18-1:** *Variant Absence Test*
>
> The variant absence test ensures that an application does not include variants that were not defined to be included in the application.

Variant absence test

The variant absence test verifies that no more than the selected variants are incorporated into the application. To check whether a variant is present or not, the variant absence test may call a function that is provided by the variant and observe the reaction of the application. The variant absence test affects all test levels:

- The unit variant absence test verifies the absence of variants that influence code within a component. This kind of variability is often realised by compile time configuration mechanisms (e.g. IFDEF statements).

- The integration variant absence test verifies the absence of variants that influence entire components. This kind of variability is often realised by link time, load time, or run-time configuration mechanisms (e.g. registry).

- The system variant absence test verifies the absence of variants that have influence on major system features and may therefore be distributed over multiple components. This kind of variability is also realised by link time, load time, or run-time configuration mechanisms.

> **Definition 18-2:** *Application Dependency Test*
>
> The application dependency test checks if the application is in conformance with the constraint and variability dependencies specified in the domain and application variability models.

The application dependency test has to detect configurations of variants that are not allowed according to the domain and application variability models. This task can be subdivided into two sub-tasks:

Conformance to variability models

- Checking whether the presence of variants violates any restrictions imposed by variability and constraint dependencies (e.g. "excludes" constraint dependencies).

- Checking whether the absence of variants violates any restrictions (e.g. "mandatory" variability dependencies or the "[min..max]" range of an alternative choice).

> **Example 18-3:** *Application Dependency Test for Heating Control*
>
> The automatic heating control requires automatic windows to prevent the waste of energy. Once the home automation system detects that a room is too cold, the windows are closed and heating is turned on. The home automation system for a specific customer includes automatic heating control. Hence, the application dependency test checks whether the application also contains the automatic windows variant.

Similar to the variant absence test, the application dependency test affects all test levels. At each level those dependencies are tested that affect realisation artefacts at the corresponding level of granularity, i.e. code excerpts, components, or the entire application.

18.4   Testing Variability at Different Test Levels

In this section, we consider the influence of variability on the test levels in application testing.

18.4.1 Application Unit Test

Retesting due to variability

The goal of the application unit test is to validate single components against the component specifications. The application test engineers reuse the domain unit test cases for the common functionality of the unit. It is necessary to repeat unit tests even for common functionality as the specific configuration of the application may influence the test results (Section 13.3). The common parts of a component may not work properly due to a particular combination of variants or due to application-specific modifications.

Example 18-4: *Necessity to Reapply Domain Unit Test Cases*

The door sensor plug-in, which is a component of the door lock control subsystem, supports control devices to which up to eight door sensors can be connected. During domain testing the plug-in was tested with different configurations of sensors, and passed the test. The domain unit test cases are reexecuted during application testing, as it is still unclear whether the plug-in component behaves correctly for the particular configuration of sensors required for the application.

18.4.2 Application Integration Test

Test of component interactions

The goal of the application integration test is to validate the interactions between the components of the application. This includes the validation of the interactions between common components, bound variants of variable components, as well as application-specific components. During the application integration test, test cases that have already been performed in domain testing may have to be reexecuted to validate the interactions of all components in the specific context of the application (Section 13.3). The inputs for the application integration test are components that have passed the application unit test.

> **Example 18-5:** *Application Integration of the Home Security System*
>
> The domain integration test case for electronic door locks contains variability as there are three different variants (fingerprint scanner, keypad, and magnetic card reader). The application under test includes a door lock management component and three door control devices, each with a magnetic card reader and a lock actuator. The application integration test cases are created by reusing the domain integration test cases and by binding the variants defined in the application variability model. The test cases are used to validate the interactions between the three magnetic card locks and the server.

18.4.3 Application System Test

The goal of the application system test is to validate that the application satisfies the application requirements specification. Ideally, all requirements are tested to obtain a detailed assessment of the quality of the application. Most of the system test cases have to be performed during application system testing due to the absence of application-specific variants in domain engineering and the configurability of domain artefacts (see Chapter 13). If the commonality and reuse strategy is applied, application test engineers can reuse predefined domain system test artefacts by binding the variants defined in the application variability model.

Test of application features

> **Example 18-6:** *System Test of a Home Automation Application*
>
> A system test case for the home security part of the home automation application is the activation of the vacation mode. The test case scenario consists of the following steps. The user authenticates against the system, activates indoor and outdoor surveillance, and locks the doors. To create the application system test case, the test engineer reuses a domain system test case. As the domain system case includes different authentication mechanisms, different surveillance devices, etc., the test engineer binds the authentication variants, the surveillance variants, etc., as defined in the application variability model.

18.5 Application Test Coverage

In this subsection, we describe the different types of tests that have to be performed in application system testing. The different types are based on a classification of the application requirements:

Requirements coverage by category

- **Reused common requirements artefacts**: This category includes all application requirements that are reused common domain requirements.

- *Reused variable requirements*: This category includes all application requirements that are reused domain requirements with bound variability.

- *Adapted requirements*: This category includes all application requirements that are reused domain requirements containing application-specific adaptations.

- *New requirements*: This category includes all application requirements that are purely application-specific and are not derived from domain requirements.

18.5.1 Application Commonality Test

Retesting common requirements

The application commonality test covers the common parts of requirements models. It ensures that the common requirements of the product line are tested in the context of an application. Test cases for common requirements are developed and executed in domain testing. If, for instance, a common component is placed in the context of a specific application with its specific selection of variants, the component can fail even though it has not changed. Coupling mechanisms like shared variables or inheritance can cause such failures, even if the components have been tested extensively. Consequently, domain test cases for common requirements are reexecuted in application testing.

Example 18-7: *Testing Common Requirements*

One part of every application is the motion detection sensor. Test cases for the motion detection sensor are created during domain testing and executed on the sample application. The test case is reexecuted for each application to ensure correct behaviour.

18.5.2 Application Variant Test

Testing variants

The application variant test verifies that all selected variants are part of the application and ensures the correct behaviour of these variants. The test artefacts for the application variant test can be reused from domain test artefacts. Application test engineers bind the variants based on the application variability model.

Example 18-8: *Testing Variants*

The application under test contains exactly three magnetic door locks. The application variant test must ensure that there are three magnetic door locks and that each of them locks the specified door.

18.5.3 Application-specific Tests

The application-specific tests deal with testing new application requirements and adapted domain requirements.

The application modification test covers adapted requirements, i.e. the parts of application requirements models that are modified versions of domain requirements models. For this category of requirements it is not possible to reuse the domain test artefacts without adapting them.

Testing adapted requirements

> **Example 18-9:** *Testing Adapted Requirements*
>
> Another set of magnetic card locks from another provider has to be incorporated into an application. The test cases regarding the magnetic card locks must be adapted to cope with the new hardware, for instance, pull the card through a card reader instead of placing it on the card reader.

The application extension test covers parts of the application requirements models that were newly developed for a specific application. The test artefacts for this category of requirements have to be created from scratch. In addition, the newly implemented artefacts typically have a significantly higher defect density than reused artefacts.

Testing new requirements

> **Example 18-10:** *Testing New Application Requirements*
>
> An iris scanner lock is required for an application. Therefore, the application extension test must ensure that the requirements are realised within the application. New test cases have to be derived to validate this requirement.

18.6   Application Test Activities

The application test process description provides guidance for the entire application test process. It includes instructions on how to derive application test artefacts from domain test artefacts. The application test process consists of three main activities: application test planning, application test specification, and application test execution.

18.6.1 Application Test Planning

During application test planning the test engineers create an application test plan for the product line application. The test plan differs from application to application. For example, there may be some variants that have already been tested, or there may be new application-specific requirements, which require

Adaptation of the test plan

the definition of a new test plan. Consequently, the required effort for application testing also differs from application to application. The estimation of test effort can be based on a common scheme defined by domain testing. The test strategy and the tool support for executing the tests have already been determined during domain engineering. Only in exceptional cases are they adapted during application testing (e.g. in pilot projects for evaluating a new tool or a modified strategy). Such a case may be, for instance, an attempt to improve the efficiency of domain test artefact reuse.

Example 18-11: *Application Test Planning for the Home Automation System*

The differences between application and domain requirements artefacts and the previously performed tests are considered. If three magnetic door locks have to be built into the home, the interaction between three door locks and the server has to be tested in the application integration test. This validates that the application works with the three locks.

These test cases are identified on all test levels and for all types of application tests (e.g. variant absence tests). They are defined as part of the test plan. Resources are allocated to the test cases, e.g. one test engineer must perform the door lock interaction tests within two days.

18.6.2 Application Test Specification

Logical and detailed test cases

During application test specification, test engineers create logical test cases, detailed test cases, as well as the respective test case scenarios for the application. The effort for the specification activity depends on the achievable degree of domain test artefact reuse:

- For application commonality tests, logical and detailed test cases are available from domain testing and can be reused in application testing.

- For application variant tests and, to some degree, for application-specific tests (Section 8.3), logical test cases can be reused from domain test artefacts (Section 13.7). Detailed test cases have to be developed by the application test engineers.

- Application-specific tests must be developed from scratch (including the logical and detailed test cases) or obtained by adapting domain test artefacts.

> **Example 18-12:** *Application Test Specification for Electronic Door Locks*
>
> During the application test specification activity, test engineers create the detailed test cases for electronic door locks and adapt the test case scenarios for the selected authentication mechanism. As the application uses only magnetic sensors, the other two variants (keypad and fingerprint sensors) are omitted. Furthermore, the exact number of locks is incorporated into the detailed application test cases and application test case scenarios.

18.6.3 Application Test Execution

During application test execution, the application test engineers perform the specified test cases on the application. They record the results and complete the tests by determining the error classes. This also includes reporting the detected defects to the other sub-processes (see Section 18.1).

Perform test cases and record results

> **Example 18-13:** *Application Test Execution for the Electronic Door Locks*
>
> The test cases and test case scenarios for validating the three magnetic door locks and the interplay with the authentication server are executed. Defects in the 'electronic door lock control' component, in the interaction with the 'authentication' component, and in the entire application (e.g. failure during simultaneous access) are uncovered and reported to the developers.

18.7 Differences from Single-System Engineering

As for single-system testing, the goal of application testing in software product line engineering is to ensure a sufficient quality of an application by performing a set of tests that satisfies the chosen coverage criterion. In contrast to single-system engineering, the test engineers have to consider that the requirements as well as the application to be tested are created partly during domain engineering and partly during application engineering. Application requirements and components that are identical to domain artefacts are tested by repeating tests that have been created in domain testing. Application-specific artefacts are tested in a similar way as in single-system engineering since the test cases have to be newly developed or adapted.

Domain and application artefacts

Application test engineers must validate that the variability binding for the application complies with the application requirements specification, or, more precisely, with the application variability model. In addition, the appli-

Tests related to variability

cation must not violate any restrictions imposed by the domain variability model. In single-system engineering, there is usually no need to perform this kind of test.

Reuse　In the application testing sub-process in software product line engineering, the test process description as well as a large part of the required test artefacts do not have to be developed from scratch as they are both available from the domain artefacts, partly in a generic form. After binding the appropriate variants and adapting or concretising the artefacts, they can be employed in application testing (see Chapter 8 for more details on variability in test artefacts).

18.8　Summary

Extensive application test　During application testing a product line application is validated against its specification. For this purpose, a set of application test cases is defined that includes all test levels and fulfils a suitable coverage criterion. A thorough test, even of reused code, is necessary due to dependencies between reused and application-specific parts.

Efficient reuse　Many application test artefacts are reused domain test artefacts. To establish an efficient reuse process, for instance, application test engineers must be trained to deal with variable test artefacts. In addition, traceability links must be recorded in domain engineering as well as in application engineering activities that enable test engineers to locate easily the test artefacts for reuse.

Application test artefacts　The test cases performed together with the recorded test results indicate the level of quality achieved in an application. To ensure a traceable and repeatable application test process, the test documentation is recorded as an application artefact and interrelated with the other application artefacts, even if part of it is derived from domain artefacts. Just like other application-specific artefacts, test artefacts developed for a specific application might be included in the domain artefacts if they are of interest for other applications.

Part V

Organisation Aspects

Part V: Overview

For the successful introduction of the software product line engineering paradigm, organisation aspects are as important as the technical aspects. This part deals with organisation aspects which have to be considered when introducing a software product line engineering paradigm. In this part you will learn:

- *About the influence of the organisation structure on software product line engineering.*

- *How domain engineering tasks can be embedded in organisation structure.*

- *A cost model for determining the return on investment for software product lines.*

- *Transition strategies to be applied for introducing a software product line into an organisation.*

Günter Böckle

19

Organisation

In this chapter you will learn:

- o *About the influence of the structure of an organisation on software product line engineering.*
- o *How to realise software product line engineering in an organisation with a hierarchical structure.*
- o *How to realise software product line engineering in an organisation with a matrix structure.*

19.1 Introduction

In this chapter, we elaborate on the role of the organisation structure for software product line engineering. We establish properties of organisation structures that facilitate or hinder proper functioning of a software product line engineering process. Finally, several organisation structures are compared with respect to these properties.

The role of
organisation

In industry, many people have found that even with the best development technologies and skilled staff there may be little success. Problems may occur when the allocation of people to tasks is inadequate, or when decisions are delayed because the responsibilities are not clear and people cannot come to an agreement. Occasionally, departments may clash with each other over the power to make decisions. In all these cases, inadequate process and organisation structure significantly hinder successful development. This chapter discusses the effect of the organisation structure on software product line engineering, and how the structure can reduce the problems mentioned above.

19.2 Properties of Organisation Structures

Organisation structures may facilitate or hinder effective and efficient software product line engineering. First, we consider the negative effects that a chosen organisation structure may have on development work, and then determine which properties are needed to deal with the problems. The major problems caused by organisation structure are:

Problems due to
inadequate
organisation

- Decisions about the work are not clearly expressed, technologically comprehensible or economically sound.

- Decisions take too much time.

- People spend too much time aligning and coordinating their work and do not have enough time left for management and engineering work.

- Internal politics consume time and effort, and distract the employees' focus from product development.

- Employees are not encouraged and motivated to do good work.

- The staff focus more on perfecting the technology than on the customer.

Responsibilities
and roles

The process and other factors influence the severity of these problems, but the organisation is a major cause. Software product line engineering organisations encounter more problems than organisations producing single systems, because the former are usually larger[47] than the latter. More responsibilities are involved, for instance those for the domain and those for separate applications. In addition, special roles are needed to deal with the relationship between domain and application engineering.

Which structure is suited best for a company or organisation depends on many factors such as the market, company history, company culture and culture of the country, power distribution in the company, expertise and experience of the employees, practised development approaches, etc. These factors have to be considered together with the properties we develop here for selecting the most appropriate organisation. In the following, we consider several organisation aspects and discuss their properties with regard to the list of problems above:

Factors influencing organisation structure

- Responsibilities for decision making

- Overhead time

- Structure reflecting responsibilities

- Motivation

- Customer focus

Essential properties

The assignment of responsibilities has a big effect on the way the organisation behaves. The problem of unclear decisions and the long time to make decisions can be solved by a clear assignment of responsibilities for making certain decisions. Decisions internal to domain engineering are to be taken by those people who are involved in domain engineering, and similarly for application engineering. Specific responsibilities have to be assigned for overall coordination. For decisions that involve both domain and application engineering, coordinator roles are necessary. However, such decisions will only be effective if the people who are involved in domain and application engineering take part in them as well. In all cases, the number of people involved in decision making has to be small to be effective.

Responsibilities for decision-making

A major property of an organisation is the fraction of time that is spent on effective work versus overhead time. The overhead time we consider here encompasses time spent coordinating the work and coming to decisions about the work. The amount of overlap between the tasks of organisational units and how they influence each other contributes significantly to the overhead necessary to align and coordinate work. When overlaps and dependencies are minimised, the overhead is small. There are some necessary dependencies between the process phases of domain and application engineering that cannot be avoided. However, these dependencies are usually

Overhead time

---

[47] This does not necessarily mean that the companies involved are larger, but that larger parts of the same company are involved in the same development.

smaller than those internal to such a phase. The right organisation structures will consider this difference. The overhead time for decision making is also high when the responsibilities are not assigned clearly and when several interests conflict.

Structure reflects responsibilities

Responsibilities are only sustained if the distribution of responsibilities is reflected in the structure. This addresses the problem company policy. A certain position in the organisation implies certain tasks and responsibilities. If the assigned responsibilities are not the same as the implicit ones, managers try to increase their responsibility, which leads to power struggles. Therefore, it is crucial that the organisation structure reflects the presence of both domain and application engineering, and of coordination tasks.

Motivation

The way personnel are motivated and encouraged in their work influences the way they deliver the right value to the organisation. As both domain and application engineering are crucial for the organisation, this means that the work in domain and application engineering must be of equal value to the employees. In certain organisations, working in an application department is valued higher because the staff are making the final products that are sold to the customers and bring profit. In other organisations, the domain unit is esteemed higher. This difference in valuation decreases motivation in the lower esteemed group and thereby the effectiveness of their work.

Customer focus

Organisational units that have no direct customer contact are in danger of losing their customer focus. This reduces the effectiveness of their work. Especially large organisations encounter this problem as there are many people that are not in direct contact with the end-customer. This holds for instance in pure domain engineering units.

In the following, we consider some organisation structures for software product line engineering and show their strengths and weaknesses in relation to the properties described above.

19.3 Basic Hierarchical Organisation Structures

Managers and organisation units

In this section, we present different ways to map the different activities of software product line engineering in an organisation. We consider first hierarchical or line-oriented structures. These are typically organised along products or customers. Figure 19-1 shows a hierarchical structure with one manager at the top and four managers at the second level. These four managers each head an organisational unit (department, group, etc., shown in a dotted box) that represents, for instance, a particular product or project. In many organisations with such a hierarchical structure, there are strong product project units that are often rather autonomous and often have good contacts with their own customers. A leaf in the hierarchy tree in the figure may represent an individual, an unstructured set of people, or another hierarchy. The internal nodes represent managers.

There are only a few publications on hierarchical organisations in product line engineering. In [Jacobson et al. 1997] organisation structures for the "Reuse-Oriented Software Engineering Business" and the roles needed for a reuse organisation are presented. In [Weiss and Lai 1999] the use of the hierarchy as a starting point to distribute responsibility in the FAST process for product line engineering is discussed. And in [Bosch 2000a; Bosch 2000b] four basic types of structures are presented: namely, "development department", "business units", "domain engineering unit", and "hierarchical domain engineering units". The following descriptions of organisation structures consider, amongst others, these structures.

Hierarchies in product line engineering

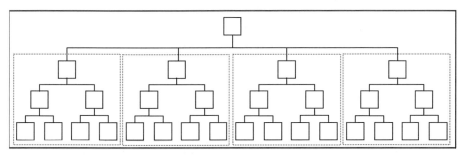

Hierarchical line organisation

Fig. 19-1: Basic hierarchical organisation with four projects

19.3.1 Development Department

In this case, there is only a single organisation unit dealing with the complete software product line engineering. Projects are created as needed within this unit. Responsibilities for certain tasks are often dynamically assigned when these tasks have to be performed. The strengths[48] of this kind of organisation are in motivation and customer focus:

A single development unit only

- Simplicity and ease of communication among the staff.

- Little organisational and administrative overhead.

- It is possible to adopt a product line approach without changing the existing organisation (because there is only one unit), which may simplify the adoption process.

The weaknesses are in responsibilities and structure:

- It is not scalable – there is a maximum size of a software development unit that can be managed.

---

[48] For details see [Bosch 2000a] and [Bosch 2000b].

- Often, either domain or application engineering has higher status and staff will prefer one and do the other insufficiently – if people have to switch too often between different tasks, one will be preferred.

- Often there is not a single responsible person, but responsibility switches with the temporary assignments.

- Maintenance may be forgotten when responsibilities switch.

- No one will press for usage of assets and no one will plan and support asset evolution, if there are no associated roles to do these tasks regularly.

This structure is applicable to small organisations with up to 30 software-related staff; more staff are not manageable without additional structuring.

19.3.2 Distributed Domain Engineering

Domain engineering in project groups

Figure 19-2 shows a (product) project-oriented organisation based on the hierarchical structure from Fig. 19-1. The dark squares indicate organisational units that do domain engineering. This is the same organisation as the "business units" in [Bosch 2000a] and [Bosch 2000b]. The four project units indicated by the dotted boxes in Fig. 19-2 typically develop single products (or product groups), each for a specific customer (group) or market segment. The task of domain engineering is distributed among these project units. Either there is a sub-unit for domain engineering inside each project unit or the domain engineering tasks and roles are mapped to roles in the original project structure, so that some people have double roles – one for domain and one for application engineering. An evaluation of this structure with respect to our properties yields the following results.

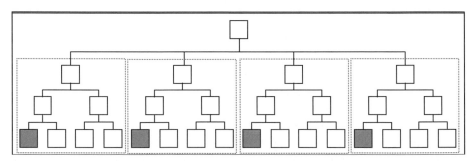

Fig. 19-2: Software product line engineering organisation with distributed domain engineering in four projects

The responsibility for the products stays with the project units and the responsibility for domain engineering is distributed. For decisions concerning domain engineering, the heads of the project units or their representatives have to come to a consensus. The primary focus of these managers will remain on their own product for their assigned customers, because that is where their money comes from. Consequently, decision making about common artefacts will be hard and time consuming because the managers will typically pursue their product-specific interests. Essentially, the organisation adapts to software product line engineering only at a low hierarchical level, while decision-making power is still focused on individual products. There is no single role with decision-making power for the platform that serves all products.

No clear responsibilities for decision making

The overhead time comes mostly from discussions about what artefacts should belong to the platform and which ones should be product specific. It comes also from discussions about adequate interfaces between artefacts. The partitioning of work over the domain engineering units of the different project units contributes to this overhead time, too, since the tasks may overlap and need synchronisation. Decisions about domain engineering topics in this organisation are not made by a single unit. Instead the project units have to come to a consensus. Therefore, there may be significant overhead involved for this.

Mostly high overhead time

The common tasks (for domain engineering) are mirrored somehow in the structure – but only at a low hierarchical level, inside the project units. For instance, the structure does not show the role that represents responsibility for the platform. Therefore, stakeholders who want to address platform interests have no one to talk to or have to talk to all project managers. Therefore, the mapping between responsibilities and structure is satisfactory only to a small degree.

Structure partially reflects responsibilities

Staff from the domain engineering unit inside a product project can easily be assigned tasks for product design when pressure is exerted to deliver a product. Such a reassignment may lead to neglecting the domain engineering tasks. This leaves people unsatisfied because they want to do their work properly. It also frequently occurs that domain engineering work is not as highly valued as project work, and this decreases motivation for doing it. However, since the domain engineering teams are part of the project units, the chances are high that they get the same compensation, which reinforces motivation. Thus, we have some aspects increasing motivation and some aspects decreasing it. Hence, we have only partial support for increasing the motivation.

Partial motivation support

The customer focus is strong in this organisation because of the integration of domain engineering into the project units with their strong customer

Good customer focus

focus. So, this property is fulfilled; actually, this is the major advantage of this organisation structure.

The organisation with distributed domain engineering is often selected when there are strong product projects with high decision authority. The managers of these projects would typically not allow another group to decide what kinds of platform assets will be built, who should use them, and how they should be used. They want to retain authority over domain engineering, only accepting cooperation among a set of equals, namely the other project units. The positive side of this is that people keep a customer focus.

The Owen project at Hewlett-Packard (Section 21.5) is an example of an organisation with distributed domain engineering; see [Douma and Schreuder 2002] and [Fafchamps 1994].

19.3.3 Centralised Domain Engineering

Another common organisation for software product line engineering is shown in Fig. 19-3. In [Bosch 2000a] and [Bosch 2000b] this type of organisation is referred to as "domain engineering unit".

This organisation has a separate unit for domain engineering, shown by the dark squares on the right hand side in Fig. 19-3. It is also indicated that the four project units get smaller when there is a domain engineering unit. The size of the domain engineering unit relative to the (product) project units may differ, depending on the relation of the efforts for domain and application engineering. In the uppermost hierarchical level, the domain engineering unit may be headed by the same manager as the project units or by a separate one. Jacobson describes the differences in these two cases of higher management assignment in [Jacobson et al. 1997]. An evaluation of this structure with respect to our properties yields the following results.

Separate domain-engineering unit

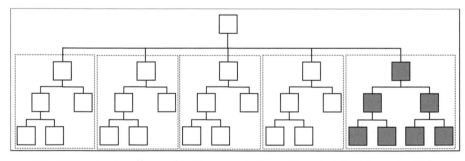

Fig. 19-3:   Product line engineering organisation with central domain engineering

The responsibility for domain engineering is clearly assigned to the unit represented by the hierarchy of dark squares in Fig. 19-3. Therefore, responsibilities for domain and application engineering are clearly separated.

Clear responsibilities for decision-making

The overall responsibility for domain engineering is assigned to one single role, the head of the domain engineering unit. The people from the domain engineering unit are responsible for the platform, the artefacts that are included and how these artefacts behave. Therefore, discussions on domain engineering topics can be short and fewer discussions are needed than in the organisation with distributed domain engineering. Thus, the overhead time for coordinating domain engineering work is low.

Low overhead time

The responsibility for domain engineering is clearly displayed in the structure by having a separate unit for domain engineering with its own manager.

Structure reflects responsibilities

In project units, there is often much pressure to finish products in time. To encourage this, people from project units may get a better remuneration than members of the domain engineering unit. Sometimes, domain engineering work is not valued as highly as application engineering work. Therefore, compensation and motivation are often problematic in organisations with central domain engineering. To support motivation, the respective work has to be given equal value and remuneration.

Partial motivation support

The members of the domain engineering unit often have no customer contact and do not work directly on the applications, so the customer focus may become lost.

Low customer focus

The organisation with centralised domain engineering in Fig. 19-3 has more of the required properties than the one with distributed domain engineering in Fig. 19-2. However, in cases in which a strong customer focus is important and there are strong project units with independent managers, the structure with distributed domain engineering may be adequate.

19.3.4 Several Domain Engineering Units

In big organisations, several domain engineering units may be required; they may be organised in a hierarchy. In [Bosch 2000a] and [Bosch 2000b] they are called "hierarchical domain engineering units". Typically, a considerable number of staff members, i.e. hundreds, are involved. This structure is an extension of the previous one.

Hierarchical domain engineering units

The strengths of this kind of organisation are in responsibilities and their mapping on structure:

- The structure can encompass large, complex product lines.

- It scales up to hundreds of software engineers.

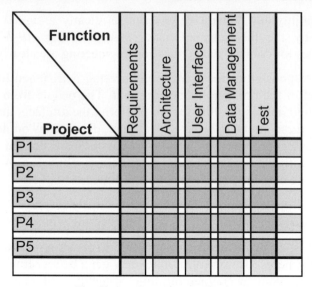

Fig. 19-4:   A matrix organisation

Weaknesses   The weaknesses are in the complexity of the structure, overhead, and customer support:

- There is considerable overhead involved for synchronisation because more units have to be synchronised.

- It is difficult to achieve agile reactions to changed market properties due to the increased number of stakeholders involved.

- A change in an artefact that is used by many applications may require considerable synchronisation effort because many stakeholders with different interests are involved.

19.4 Matrix Organisation Structures

Two or more   The hierarchical organisations described in Section 19.3 are often not suffi-
structuring criteria   cient for big organisations. Instead, they often use matrix organisations. The
most important reason for using a matrix structure is that there are two conflicting grouping criteria for an organisation. On the one hand, product-oriented units have a focus on the product and the customer to get products to the market in time and according to customer wishes. On the other hand, people are grouped according to functional knowledge in order to keep the knowledge up to date. Therefore, both groupings are combined in the two

dimensions of a matrix.[49] An example of a matrix organisation is shown in Fig. 19-4. Usually each of the dimensions has a hierarchy as well. This is not shown in the matrix. The product projects P1 to P5 are organised horizontally while major functions, like requirements engineering, architecture, user interface, data management, and test, are organised vertically. A problem with matrix structures is the decision-making power at the crossing points of the matrix. If this is not well determined, power struggles are inevitable and much time is spent coming to decisions. For product line engineering, domain engineering has to be added to the matrix. There are three possibilities: as a functional unit, as a project unit, or outside the matrix.

19.4.1 Matrix Organisation with Domain Engineering as Functional Unit

In Fig. 19-5 domain engineering is a functional unit; this is comparable to the structure in Fig. 19-2. This structure has the advantage that people in the domain engineering unit are close to the products and do not lose customer orientation. They may easily be assigned to product development tasks when there is time pressure. This is not a disadvantage if the domain engineering tasks are not neglected and people keep their customer focus. However, the balance between application and domain engineering tasks is not easy to maintain in case of time pressure for completing products. An evaluation of this structure with respect to our properties yields the following results.

Customer focus in domain engineering

Responsibilities are fully assigned in this structure, but the decision-making power must also be assigned; this depends on the actual situation. It must be clearly determined who has the power to make decisions at the crossing points of the matrix.

Assignment of power at crossing points

The overhead time depends on the unique assignment of decision-making power. If the decision-making power for all domain engineering tasks is assigned uniquely, preferably to the head of the domain engineering unit, and so is the power for the individual technical activities, e.g. domain requirements engineering, the overhead is low.

Overhead time mostly low

The responsibility of technical roles in domain engineering, e.g. for domain requirements engineering, is not represented in this structure. To deal with this property adequately, the technical roles in domain engineering have to be included in the structure.

Structure partially reflects responsibilities

---

[49] There are also multi-dimensional matrix organisations where more than two properties of organisation structures are captured in more dimensions. These are not considered here. Their extensions for product line engineering are similar to the ones described here.

Domain engineering distributed over projects

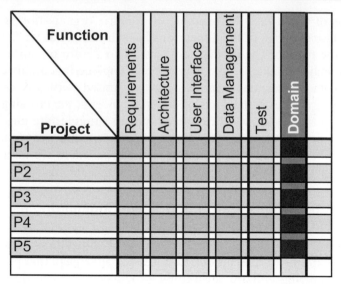

Fig. 19-5:   Matrix organisation with domain engineering as functional unit

Partial motivation support

Care has to be taken that the domain engineering unit has the same opportunities as the other units and that the staff are not reassigned to different tasks too often. Therefore, there is usually only partial motivation support.

Satisfactory customer focus

The domain engineering unit is also involved in projects. Therefore, there is a good chance that domain engineering staff have a good customer focus. The degree of customer focus depends on the actual assignments.

19.4.2 Matrix Organisation with Domain Engineering as Project Unit

Focus on domain engineering

Figure 19-6 shows a matrix organisation where domain engineering is assigned to a project unit. Here, the chances are high that people in the domain engineering unit can do their work without being assigned to application engineering work. However, this may reduce customer focus. This structure is well suited for dynamic platforms with many changes and a managed evolution because domain engineering staff can focus on their work, and decisions about changes can be made quickly, due to domain engineering roles with assigned responsibilities. An evaluation of this structure with respect to our properties yields the following results.

Adequate responsibilities for decision-making

The responsibilities for domain engineering are inside the domain engineering unit. Therefore, the assignment of responsibilities is clear. Care should be taken that the head of domain engineering unit has the same decision-making power as the project unit heads.

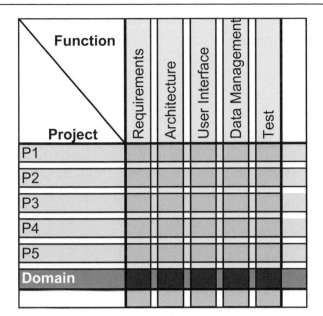

Fig. 19-6:   Matrix organisation with domain engineering as project unit

Domain engineering distributed over functions

The responsibilities for domain engineering are in the domain-engineering unit. So decisions can be made quickly, but they depend on the assignment of decision-making power at the crossing points of the matrix. Therefore, the overhead is mostly low.

Overhead time mostly low

The domain engineering tasks are clearly represented in the structure.

Domain engineering staff can focus on the platform and its evolution and they are in a project unit like the others. However, it must still be ensured that this unit is considered as equally important as the other units.

Good basis for motivation support

Customer focus depends on the integration of the domain engineering unit into the overall organisation.

Partial customer focus

19.4.3 Matrix Organisation with Separate Domain Engineering

Figure 19-7 shows a matrix organisation where the domain-engineering unit resides separately outside the matrix. This organisation can easily be extended to organisations with multiple product lines that use a common platform. Decisions about setting up and evolving the platform are easier than in the other structures, but usage of the platform may be harder because the projects are typically less involved in defining it (because the domain engineering unit is separate and not within the matrix). The use of platform assets for application engineering and its compensation has to be fixed specifically in the process to make this organisation effective.

Platform decoupled from projects

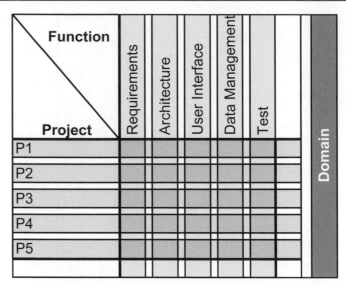

Fig. 19-7:   Matrix organisation with separate domain engineering unit

An evaluation of this structure with respect to our properties yields the following results.

Clear responsibilities   The assignment of responsibility supports simple and fast decision making
for decision making   because of the separate domain engineering unit.

Low   The domain engineering tasks and responsibilities are in a separate unit,
overhead   responsibilities for the domain engineering tasks reside there, and so decisions can be made quickly, yielding low overhead.

Structure   The structure mostly does not mirror functions like requirements engineering
partially reflects   inside the domain engineering unit, while common tasks are well shown by
responsibilities   the fact that there is a domain engineering unit. So, responsibilities are only partially mapped on the structure.

Partial motivation   Motivation and encouragement depend on the image of the domain engin-
support   eering unit and will be satisfactory if the platform and variability usage are clearly specified in the process. Equal valuation of domain engineering work and project work is necessary. So, there is only partial motivation support.

Low customer   This structure has the advantage that the people in this group may focus
focus   totally on domain engineering (even more so than in the previously described organisation). However, customer focus may easily become lost because the domain engineering staff are outside the matrix.

19.5 Detailed Structure

In application engineering organisation units, as in single-system engineering organisations, the coarse structures are based on products, projects, and functions like requirements engineering or architecture design. Below that coarse level there are more detailed structures, based, for example, on roles responsible for particular features. In domain engineering organisation units, typically functions form the main structuring criteria at a coarse level. The detailed structure, however, is different and often important for successful product line engineering. Here, roles that are responsible for the platform assets are defined. These roles have to deal with making the assets reusable for many products, with adequate quality, and with their evolution.

Role-based structures

19.6 Cross-Functional Teams

Cross-functional teams play an important role in the success of software product line engineering. These structures are often temporary and orthogonal to the primary structures that we have considered so far. For determining whether certain artefacts should be developed for the platform or not, someone from domain engineering is responsible. However, the decision making is often supported by a team consisting of product managers, requirements engineers, and domain and application architects. Therefore, the interests of the relevant stakeholders must be considered. For tasks that involve stakeholders from different units, e.g. from domain and application engineering, cross-functional teams are set up to express the interests of the different stakeholders and support decision making.

Secondary organisational structures

The domain engineering process and the application engineering processes have to be synchronised. Typically, application engineering waits for domain artefacts to be ready, but also domain engineering waits for application test results and other feedback from application engineering. Synchronisation of this is done by teams from both domain and application engineering. In the case of urgent problems, task force teams are set up, mostly comprising people from both domain and application engineering.

Synchronisation and task force teams

19.7 Organisation Theory

As mentioned earlier, many factors determine the effectiveness of an organisation. These factors have been analysed and described by different schools of organisation theory. Many books on organisation theory have been published; most cover aspects that are relevant to decisions about organisation structures for product line engineering, but none treats this topic specifically.

We provide a brief overview of the major schools and the factors they consider. Details can be found in the referenced literature.

Schools of organisation theory

For over a hundred years, from F. W. Taylor and Max Weber until today, organisation theory has analysed what factors determine organisations and their structures. Seven different schools of organisation theory are distinguished in [Morabito et al. 1999] (see also [Hill et al. 1992]). These schools and their major characteristics are as follows:

Tasks designed in detail

- *Scientific management*: Developed by Frederick Winslow Taylor in 1911 [Taylor 1911]. Characterised by detailed, scientific design of tasks, scientific selection and training of workers, separation of planning (management) and execution (labour). Another famous representative of this school is Henri Fayol; see [Fayol 1916].

Motivation and cooperation

- *Human relations*: This school sees an organisation as a cooperative system [Barnard 1938]. It is based on authority that does not flow from the top, but instead it is accorded to the manager by the employees; the role of the manager is to motivate the employees. Later, the human resources school was added and both were combined as the motivation-oriented approach. The Tavistock group represents this school.

Hierarchy and formal regulations

- *Bureaucracy*: According to Max Weber [Weber 1922], the ideal structure of an organisation is characterised by a division of labour, hierarchical decision making, a high degree of formal procedures and regulations, and impersonal relationships.

Focus on decision-making

- *Power, conflict, and decisions*: Other sources call this the decision-oriented approach, consisting of two major variants: first, the formal decision-theoretical approach that uses linear programming, game theory, and team theory; second, the behavioural approach (see for instance [Cyert and March 1963]). This school challenges the notion that organisations make rational decisions. Organisations are best understood by looking at power, conflict, and how decisions are actually made.

Manufacturing and knowledge technologies

- *Technology*: Mechanistic and organic forms of work are distinguished. In [Woodward 1965], Joan Woodward classified manufacturing technology into unit, mass, and process production and found a correlation between the type of technology employed and the structure chosen. Perrow looked at knowledge technology [Perrow 1970] and [Perrow 1972]; using the dimensions of task variability and problem analysability, four types of task technologies were identified: routine, craft, engineering, and non-routine. They are characterised by the control and coordination mechanisms employed.

- *Systems*: This school sees the organisation as an open system, e.g. Peter Senge's publications on learning organisations (see for instance [Senge 1990]). This school comprises two variants: the organisation-sociological approach and the systems-theoretical/cybernetic approach.

  Open systems

- *Institutional*: This school advocates the importance of culture, organisation history, and particular circumstances. It tries to encompass the other schools. Its approach is also called the interaction-oriented approach. It comprises three variants: the organisation-cultural approach, the micro-political approach, and the transaction-cost economical approach, see [Douma and Schreuder 2002].

  Interactions

There are also modern types of organisations that do not count as schools of their own (yet). These include lean organisations, fractal organisations, business process organisations, virtual organisations, and network-based organisations.

Modern organisation types

The schools of organisation theory help us to understand the factors that influence an organisation and that have to be considered when designing the structure for an organisation.

A method for structuring groups so that the interfaces between them are minimised, in order to reduce overhead, is presented in [McCord and Eppinger 1993]. For readers who wish to learn more about the role of motivation, the reports of Hackman and Oldman are recommended [Hackman and Oldham 1975; Hackman and Oldham 1976; Hackman et al. 1978; Hackman and Oldham 1980]. The role of organisation structure for the success of platforms in the automotive industry is presented in [Cusumano and Nobeoka 1998].

19.8 Differences from Single-System Engineering

In product line engineering the organisation structure has to provide for the integration of domain engineering and the assignment of the responsibility for the whole product line. There are various ways to achieve this, as shown in this chapter. The organisation can choose the most adequate structure depending on its current circumstances, such as market, customers, personnel structure, experience, culture, its experience in doing product line engineering, and its process maturity.

Integration of domain engineering

The detailed structure of an organisation is essential for its success in product line engineering. It should clearly assign the responsibilities for platform assets, and facilitate cross-functional teams who can bring different expertise together and thus support decision making.

High relevance of detailed structure

19.9 Summary

Situation-dependent selection

The organisations presented in this chapter all have their advantages and disadvantages. The selection of a structure depends on the actual situation of an organisation. Its markets, kinds of products, company culture, employees' skills, and many other factors determine the structure that fits best. Heuristics that support a decision about an adequate organisation can be found in [Boeckle et al. 2004b].

Small and medium-sized organisations

The basic hierarchical structures described in Section 19.3 are suitable for small and medium-sized organisations. For an organisation with strong project groups and with a need for a strong customer focus, the distributed domain engineering shown in Fig. 19-2 is suited best. In all other cases, central domain engineering is best, shown in Fig. 19-3. In all cases, the properties from Section 19.2 have to be considered.

Large organisations

For bigger organisations, matrix structures are best suited. To decide if domain engineering should be realised as a function unit, as a project unit, or as a separate unit, the current situation of the organisation has to be analysed on the basis of the properties from Section 19.2 and their evaluation for the different structures.

Günter Böckle

20

Transition

Process

In this chapter you will learn:

- o *How to initiate product line engineering in a company.*
- o *Different strategies for the transition process from single-system development to software product line engineering.*
- o *A cost model for estimating the costs of establishing a software product line.*
- o *The key steps of a transition process.*

20.1   Introduction

Goals of
a transition

An organisation that considers switching to product line engineering typically has products on the market and is under economic pressure. This pressure originates from the drive to produce the next products more efficiently or to get them to the market faster to stay competitive. Software product line engineering is a solution for both kinds of goals – increased efficiency and decreased time to market. However, a transition to software product line engineering is not easy. It requires investments that have to be determined carefully to get the desired benefits.

20.2   Motivation and Business Objectives

Triggers for the
transition

There are two major reasons for considering a move from the current way of development to software product line engineering. Often these reasons are related to each other; the first one is usually a trigger for the second one.

- *External pressure*: This comes from the market; customers ask, for instance for new features in the products and for a common look-and-feel. Alternatively, competition increases so that the organisation has to achieve a shorter time to market, cover more different markets, reduce production costs, or enhance quality. The product managers are those first affected by this pressure. This causes them to consider improving development so that time to market is decreased and more customer wishes can be realised in the products.

- *Internal pressure*: When time schedules cannot be met, project managers and architects are inclined to make the work more efficient. They try to improve development so that development time is decreased while retaining the quality.

Positive return
on investment

Improving the development means investing time and money. This must pay off, so the business objective is that the change must yield a positive return on investment (ROI). Product managers have to define the time frame: how long will it take from investing money until the ROI becomes positive. They also have to ensure that the ROI becomes positive for the organisation as a whole, not just for individual products. The basis for determining the ROI is a cost model; Section 20.4 presents such a cost model.

Reuse

To become more efficient, the amount of work has to be reduced or throughput increased. The business objective is to reuse what can be reused. Reuse was considered in big projects in the 1990s. Experience shows that reuse may entail more cost than benefit (see for instance [Schmidt 1999; McClure

1995]). Reuse has to be managed which leads to platforms (Definition 1-2). Reuse means two things: reusing existing artefacts and building new ones that can be reused for the applications. Thus, managed reuse leads to the introduction of two processes, one where the reusable artefacts are produced (domain engineering) and one where they are used to create the applications (application engineering); see Chapter 2.

To support the increased number of customer wishes and support more markets, the applications must be adaptable to these various wishes. Thus, the next business objective is to provide variety in features to satisfy customer wishes. This leads to the introduction of variability, and together with the required efficiency, to mass customisation.

Variety in features

To improve development, we need to improve the process, the development methods and technology, and the organisation. Therefore, the next business objective is that the transition to product line engineering improves the process, development methods and technology, and the organisation. In the past, the introduction of software product line engineering was often ad hoc (see for instance [Clements and Northrop 2001]). For a successful transition, we have to change all relevant aspects, not just some of them.

Process and technology improvement

A change of process and development methods can generate unrest in an organisation, and it can frustrate the staff if the changes are too drastic. In addition, current customers can get angry if the focus of the organisation changes too much towards new markets. The business objective is to consider the situation of the current and new markets, as well as that of the organisation for the transition.

Current and future situation

The business objectives listed above have to be considered to select the right transition strategy and to perform the right steps in that strategy, so that a positive ROI is achieved.

20.3 Transition Strategies

An important part of the transition process to software product line engineering is the determination of the transition strategy. The selection of this strategy has to take into account the business objectives stated above in Section 20.2. For a good introduction to fundamental transition strategies and their pros and cons, see [McGregor et al. 2002]. In the following, we present four major transition strategies (for details see [Boeckle et al. 2002]).

20.3.1 Incremental Introduction

The incremental introduction starts small and expands incrementally. Expansion may occur in two dimensions:

Expansion in two dimensions

- *Expanding organisational scope* starts with a single group doing software product line engineering and when that is successful, other groups are added incrementally.

- *Expanding investment* starts with a small investment for software product line engineering that is incrementally increased, depending on the success that has been achieved so far.

Expert group

For the first dimension, the initial group consists of experts who know the domain and have the necessary technical experience to assess new processes and new development methods.

Funding of activities

For the second dimension, a careful selection of the funded activities is performed at each increment. This has to guarantee a high ROI for each increment, fostering the acceptance of the succeeding increment. Activities funded in the increments often concentrate on creating reusable components or making existing components reusable. It is important that other specific activities are added in early increments, such as product planning in the product line context. Product planning gives the direction for the development efforts and makes the efforts measurable and predictable.

Recommendation for FAST process

Weiss and Lai recommend an incremental transition to their FAST process and provide some help to perform such a transition [Weiss and Lai 1999].

20.3.2 Tactical Approach

Driven by technical problems

The tactical approach is usually driven by problems with conventional engineering. For instance, these are problems with change management and configuration management for multiple related products (Example 20-1). Only specific sub-processes and methods are changed for introducing software product line engineering partially. The tactical transition may start informally. However, the product management sub-process and the planning of the further development have to be performed after a short initial phase so that the results can be made measurable and predictable. The tactical approach is often used as the transition strategy when architects and engineers drive the introduction of software product line engineering.

20.3.3 Pilot Project Strategy

Development of a new product

A pilot project involves the development of a new product in one of several alternative ways:

a) It is started as a potential first member of a software product line.

b) It is an extension of a series of related products.
   Often the goal is that the related products are going to be incorporated into the software product line.

c) It is realised as a toy product.

A toy-product project may be started when the risk or cost of creating a new product completely with a new approach is too high. The product of such a toy project must be sufficiently close to the organisation's products so that part of the results of the toy project can be reused when software product line engineering is later introduced for the "real" products.

d) It is realised by prototyping.

The engineering rules for prototyping are often less strict than for standard products; for instance, engineers get sufficient time to analyse and compare the new development approaches to their traditional ones.

The activities that are to be applied during the pilot project have to be planned and the process has to be determined accordingly. Measures have to be taken to find out if the pilot project is successful.

20.3.4 Big Bang Strategy

In the big bang strategy, software product line engineering is adopted for the new products of the organisation at once, in one "big bang". First, domain engineering is performed completely and the platform is built. When the platform assets are ready, application engineering starts and the applications are derived from the platform.

Complete platform first

Example 20-1: *Tactical Approach*

An organisation has a couple of individual home automation systems on the market. Each of those systems realises a user authentication. The applications use different techniques for identifying valid users, such as passwords, fingerprints, or iris-scan-based identification. Some of the applications even provide a combination of identification mechanisms. Even if they use different identification techniques, the applications share some commonalities, such as blocking the user account in case of three invalid accesses and sending a notification to the system operator, which have been implemented differently in each application. Error correction and technology adaptations have even led to more system versions. Configuration management gets more and more complex. New adaptations are hard to integrate. Chaos is growing, so the organisation decides to adopt a product line engineering approach. The development team creates a reference architecture that specifies the common parts and separates the variable parts for each possible identification technique. This results in a considerable reduction of the amount of work for the introduction of changes and of configuration management.

20.4   Benefits and Drawbacks of the Transition Strategies

Incremental strategy

The incremental strategy has the following advantages:

- The work on current products can go on as before since only a small group or small part of the money is devoted to the transition.

- The amount of money and time spent on the transition within any specific period is limited.

- The transition can be changed or stopped at any time if the measurement results determining the progress and the benefit of the activities are not satisfactory.

The incremental transition strategy has the following drawbacks:

- It takes a long time to build up the platform and introduce full product line engineering.

- The work on the current single products may change the conditions for the platform or variability model. Therefore, continuous adaptation of the artefacts built during the transition process is necessary.

- In case the current products are to be included in the product line, artefacts of the products built during the transition have also to be reworked for inclusion in the platform and for modelling variability.

- It takes longer to make the full profit from the product line, than in the big bang strategy.

Tactical strategy

The tactical strategy has the following advantages:

- It concentrates on the most urgent needs of the organisation.

- It can be started by a small group inside the organisation, e.g. by an engineering group.

- The cost of starting the transition is low.

The tactical strategy has the following drawbacks:

- Without integration into an overall transition plan, the start of the transition in only a small group of the organisation is likely to fail.

- The concentration on specific problems, for instance change and configuration management (see Example 20-1), may lead the effort in the wrong direction. Often the problems are caused at other places than where they occur. In this example they may have been caused by inadequate requirements engineering; without improving that, the improvement efforts will not be very effective.

- Without involving product management in the transition process, the effect of the transition is rather limited.

This approach may start informally; however, product managers have to get involved after a first starting phase, to plan the further development so that the results can be made measurable and predictable.

The pilot project transition strategy has the following advantages:

Pilot project

- The work on current products can go on as before.

- A prototype or toy product is available to check development effort and necessary process and technology changes before involving the rest of the organisation.

- The amount of money and time spent on the transition within any specific period is limited.

- The transition can be changed or stopped after the pilot project if the results are not satisfactory.

The pilot project transition strategy has the following drawbacks:

- The amount of money and time spent is mostly higher than in the incremental introduction.

- The prototype and the core assets built during the pilot project may have to be thrown away.

- It takes longer to make the full profit from the product line than in the big bang strategy.

The big bang strategy has the following advantages:

Big bang strategy

- It uses a comprehensive, all-encompassing transition plan so that the interdependencies between parts of the processes and the organisation can be considered from the beginning.

- The overall investment is lowest (until the full product line engineering development process is installed).

- The platform contains the right assets earlier than in the other strategies.

The big bang strategy has the following drawbacks:

- The investment is concentrated over a smaller time frame than for the other transition strategies. A large amount of money is needed at the beginning as an up-front investment. This strategy is only feasible if the organisation has enough money available during this time frame.

- The organisation is very much occupied with the transition and cannot work fully on the production of products. This may have a significant impact and customers may switch to competitors.

- If it turns out that product line engineering is not the right approach, it is hard to undo the transition and the loss of money and effort is substantial.

Management commitment

The big bang transition can be used in cases where the management of an organisation is convinced of the advantages of a software product line engineering approach and where it is essential for the business to achieve the benefits of this approach in a particular time frame. This approach needs significant investments and it takes some time for the first product to come to the market (the time for full domain engineering plus application engineering for it), but the succeeding products of the product line can be developed and brought to the market very fast.

Strategy selection based on ROI

To select the appropriate transition strategy, several factors have to be considered, the most important one being the ROI. The estimation of the ROI is based on a cost model. The next section presents a cost model that can be used to determine the ROI.

20.5 Cost Model

COCOMO

Cost models exist at various levels of detail. There is for instance the COCOMO II model from B. Boehm [Boehm et al. 2000]. It is used to make rather detailed cost estimations, but they take a lot of time. Other cost models determine the cost and the ROI at an abstract level, as in [Boeckle et al. 2004a] (see also [Cohen 2003]). Such models are less accurate but their advantage is that results can be determined much faster than with COCOMO II. They can be used to decide on the switching to software product line engineering in a fast go/no-go decision. In addition, when the data for using COCOMO II is not available, such models may still give results.

Our cost model (from [Boeckle et al. 2004a]) determines the general cost C for establishing a software product line of n products p_i according to the following formula:

Central cost formula

$$C = C_{org} + C_{cab} + \sum_{i=1}^{n}(C_{unique}(p_i) + C_{reuse}(p_i))$$

The cost model is based on a divide-and-conquer algorithm. The model decomposes the problem into relatively simple components, enabling experiments about cost scenarios. The constituents of the cost model are depicted in Fig. 20-1 and explained below.

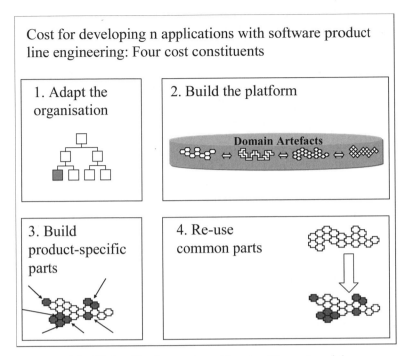

Fig. 20-1:   The four cost constituents of the cost model

The cost constituents are:

- C_{org}: This is the cost of adopting the software product line engineering approach for an organisation ("org" stands for "organisation"). Such costs include reorganisation, process improvement, training, and whatever other organisational actions are necessary. This cost depends on the actual situation of the organisation: the cost for process improvement depends on the process that is actually being used and the cost for training depends on the number of people affected and their knowledge. Example 20-2 illustrates how C_{org} can be determined.

- C_{cab}: This is the cost to develop a core asset base for the software product line ("cab" stands for "core asset base"). It includes costs for activities like the creation of the product portfolio for the product line, commonality and variability analysis, building a reference architecture, developing the common software and its supporting designs, documentation, and test infrastructure. The cost depends on the transition strategy chosen and the actual situation of the organisation, like the number of people assigned for domain engineering, commonalities in existing assets, etc. Case studies on software product lines or improved reuse metrics [Wayne 1996; Poulin 1997] can be used to determine the actual values. Experienced architects are best suited to estimate this value since they usually know how long it takes to perform these tasks. Example 20-3 illustrates how C_{cab} can be determined.

Costs for application-specific artefacts

- C_{unique}: This is the cost of developing unique pieces of software that are not based on the platform. This concerns those parts of the applications that have to be built individually in the application engineering process. C_{unique} is usually determined from the experience of the staff – this is standard software development effort estimation. In addition, COCOMO II may be applied here, see [Boehm et al. 2000].

Costs for reusing domain artefacts

- C_{reuse}: This is the cost of reusing core assets in a core asset base. This includes the cost of locating and checking out a core asset, binding variants, tailoring the core asset for use in the intended application (if necessary), and performing the extra integration and system tests associated with reusing core assets.

The resulting sum is C, the cost of developing n applications with software product line engineering.

Example 20-2: *Determining C_{org}*

The organisation makes an assessment to identify the process changes that are necessary for a transition. Twenty people take part in this assessment, for two hours each (including preparation). The assessment cost is then C_1 for the assessors plus the costs for 40 hours' work of the personnel. Then the 20 people need one week training courses each, plus three days to get used to the new process and engineering methods. Thus, C_{org} is C_1 plus the cost for 1,320 person hours (5 plus 3 days, 8 hours per day for 20 persons, plus 40 hours).

20.6 Application of the Cost Model to the Transition Strategies

ROI for tactical approach

We apply the cost model to the transition strategies by creating scenarios that help determine the constituents of the formula. For the tactical approach there is usually no ROI determined at the beginning, but as soon as product managers and upper-level managers become involved, the same kind of calculation has to be performed as for the incremental introduction. So, this case is not considered separately here.

20.6.1 Cost and ROI for the Incremental Transition Strategy

Scenario

We assume that the organisation has a set of n products in the marketplace that were developed more or less independently. Moreover, we assume that the core asset base is built on the basis of these products and that s of these products are rebuilt from the core asset base, using a software product line engineering approach. We determine first how much it costs to create the whole asset base and build the s old products anew, using the core asset base. Our cost formula gives the cost as:

$$C_1 = C_{org} + C_{cab} + \sum_{i=1}^{s} C_{unique}(p_i) + \sum_{i=1}^{s} C_{reuse}(p_i)$$

Cost for asset base and rebuild

C_{org} comprises mostly the cost to set up the group for domain engineering and to define and synchronise the increments of the incremental transition (including the cost for training the personnel added in the increments). C_{unique} depends on the amount of unique parts that can be reused from the s old products. C_{reuse} is the cost of reusing the core assets (Section 20.5).

Example 20-3: *Determining C_{cab}*

A group of product managers and requirements engineers is assigned to build a new product portfolio and enhance the existing requirements documentation. This needs four people working for six weeks, altogether 960 hours. Harmonizing the terminology requires the setup of a common glossary, needing another two person weeks (80 hours). A team of architects and other specialists (a requirements engineer and a designer) is set up to determine the new reference architecture. On average, five people work for four weeks to create the new reference architecture and link it to the requirements and components. Altogether this takes 800 hours. The setup of new design rules ("texture") and testing rules takes another 80 hours; the creation of the new system test specification (based on the existing ones) requires a test engineer to work for three weeks (120 hours). No new components are built for the platform, but existing ones are made reusable as domain assets. The overhead for creating a component so that it can be reused as a domain asset is, according to experience in companies, between 50% and 200%. So it takes between 1.5 and 3 times as long to create a domain component than a single-use component. We assume that designers involved in writing the original components are assigned to the job and need the same time for making the components reusable as they did for the original development of these components. Altogether, the development of the domain artefacts takes 960+80+ 800+80+120=2040 person hours plus the time that was needed to create the original assets that will belong to the platform.

We assume that the organisation brings k other products to the market, based on the asset base developed so far. For this, the application of our cost model gives the cost C_2 as:

Cost for new products

$$C_2 = C_{org} + C_{cab} + \sum_{i=1}^{k} C_{unique}(p_i) + \sum_{i=1}^{k} C_{reuse}(p_i)$$

C_{org} is mostly the cost for training the personnel added in the increments. C_{cab} is mostly zero; it may be greater than zero if new assets are added to the platform when the k new products are built. C_{reuse} is the same as before, the cost to reuse the core assets.

Total cost

The complete cost is $C = C_1 + C_2$. The effect of the scenario above is that we have a core asset base, s old products built anew, and k new products built from the core asset base.

For building the k new products in the conventional way we have a cost of:

Single-system development cost

$$C_{conv} = k \times C_{unique}$$

The ROI is then the cost to build the k new products in the conventional way minus the cost C of doing it with product line engineering, divided by the investment C:

Return on investment

$$ROI = (C_{conv} - C)/C$$

Boeckle et al. show how the ROI is created and for what values of k we actually get a positive ROI [Boeckle et al. 2004a]. For increments where the s products are rebuilt, the management needs to know what kinds of increments will bring the highest ROI. To determine that, we vary the value of s. The first step, creating the core asset base, is done incrementally in m steps with s_i products in each step, so that $s_1 + s_2 + ... + s_m = n$, for our n products that the organisation already has on the market. Several scenarios with varying values for s_i must be determined and compared to select the best increments.

20.6.2 Cost and ROI for the Pilot Project Transition Strategy

Scenario

The cost involved is determined in the same way as for the incremental introduction. We assume a scenario where, first, the core asset base is built from existing products and, next, a prototype is built from the core asset base. Again, we separate the total cost into two parts, C_1 and C_2; these are not the same as for the previous strategy. The application of our cost model delivers the cost C_1 to build the initial core asset base and the prototype p:

Cost for asset base and prototype

$$C_1 = C_{org} + C_{cab} + C_{unique}(p) + C_{reuse}(p)$$

C_{org} is rather small because only a small group is set up for the pilot project. C_{cab} determines the cost of setting up an initial core asset base that is sufficient for the pilot project. C_{unique} is the cost of creating the product-specific parts of the product created during the pilot project and C_{reuse} the cost of reusing parts from the asset base for this product.

We assume that the organisation decides to introduce software product line engineering for rebuilding other k_1 products, using the initial asset base and building k_2 new products. The application of our cost model delivers the cost C_2 for that:

$$C_2 = C_{org} + C_{cab} + \sum_{i=1}^{k_1+k_2} C_{unique}(p_i) + \sum_{i=1}^{k_1+k_2} C_{reuse}(p_i)$$

Cost for rebuilding old plus building new products

Here, C_{org} is the cost to adopt a product line organisation structure for the rest of the organisation. C_{cab} is the cost of increasing the core asset base for the additional $k_1 + k_2$ products. The value of k_1 is 0 if no existing products are rebuilt. The pilot or toy product p may be thrown away or extended to a real product. Then it is included in these k_2 new products.

The full cost of this scenario is then:

$$C = C_1 + C_2$$

Total cost

For building the k_2 new products the conventional way we have a cost of

$$C_{conv} = k_2 \times C_{unique}$$

Single-system development cost

The ROI is then, as before, the cost of creating the k_2 new products in the conventional way minus the investment C (the cost of introducing product line engineering plus creating the platform and k_1+k_2 products in the product line), divided by the investment C:

$$ROI = (C_{conv} - C)/C$$

Return on investment

20.6.3 Cost and ROI for the Big Bang Transition Strategy

In this strategy, software product line engineering is adopted for the new products of the organisation at once, in one "big bang". The scenario for this case assumes that the asset base is first built completely and that the applications are then derived from it.

Scenario

The cost for doing this, assuming that k applications are built, is:

$$C = C_{org} + C_{cab} + \sum_{i=1}^{k} C_{unique}(p_i) + \sum_{i=1}^{k} C_{reuse}(p_i)$$

Total cost

Here, C_{org} is the cost to set up the organisation for software product line engineering completely and C_{cab} is the cost of building the full core asset base from scratch.

Single-system development cost

For building the k new products in the conventional way we have a cost of:

$$C_{conv} = k \times C_{unique}$$

The ROI is then:

Return on investment

$$ROI = (C_{conv} - C)/C$$

With these formulae, the ROI for the different strategies can be determined and used to choose the best strategy for the situation of the organisation. ROI is just one of the factors for selecting a strategy – other factors are market pressure to deliver products to customers, for instance, which determines the number of people that can be assigned for the transition, and the available money for the investment.

20.7   Major Steps of a Transition Process

In this section, we examine the transition process itself. Many different aspects (e.g. business, architecture, technology, process, and organisation) have to be considered, and many changes have to be performed for such a transition. A description of a transition can be found in [Boeckle et al. 2002].

Five major steps

The major steps of the transition process are:

1. Identifying relevant stakeholders.
2. Determining the stakeholders' goals.
3. Creating business cases for all stakeholders.
4. Creating an adoption plan.
5. Launching and institutionalising software product line engineering.

20.7.1 Step 1: Identifying Stakeholders

For this transition process step, all roles in the current development process have to be considered as input and those roles that are affected by the transition and the new development process are identified as output.

Project staff and pilot customers

The most important stakeholders to be considered are those from the organisation's projects that are to be included in the new product line and potential pilot customers, namely:

- Product managers
- Managers

- Project managers
- Architects
- Engineers
- Quality assurance people
- Pilot customers

Some organisations may include only part of these stakeholders. Organisations who know their customers personally may inform some of them about the transition and ask for their opinions. But usually, the transition is not communicated to customers before it is completed.

20.7.2 Step 2: Determining the Stakeholders' Goals

As input for this transition process step the stakeholder roles from the previous step and the role descriptions of the development process are used. The output is a list of goals for each stakeholder role.

The goals of product managers encompass increasing revenue, profit, and market coverage, higher quality, as well as decreasing time to market. They define product strategy and product portfolio. Often they are involved in the assignment of budgets and the definition of organisation strategy. Their interest is in marketing, customer analysis, and product definition.

Product managers

The goals of managers are reducing cost and increasing efficiency; they also have to care for their staff and motivate them. They decide on budgeting and staffing. The goals of project managers are to get marketable products on time. Their tasks encompass project planning, measuring progress, and risk analysis. Managers will ask for their opinion about the approach.

Managers and project managers

Architects' and engineers' goals are in developing the products according to the requirements and with reasonable effort. These people must be convinced that the approach is technologically feasible and that it can make their work more efficient. Managers and project managers will ask for their opinion about the approach.

Architects and engineers

Quality assurance staff have the goal to reach the necessary quality as specified by the requirements and general rules. They, too, may be asked by management for their opinion about the approach.

Quality assurance staff

20.7.3 Step 3: Creating Business Cases

The input to this transition process step comprises the output of the two previous steps, stakeholder roles and their goals. The cost model from Section 20.4 and its application to transition strategies from Section 20.6 are used, too. The output is a set of business cases.

Goal achievement metrics

For each of the stakeholder roles a business case has to be developed that shows how software product line engineering helps them to achieve their goals. The business case comprises the adoption plan. It also contains metrics that are relevant for the stakeholders addressed in the business case to achieve their goals. These metrics measure how the goals described above for the stakeholder roles are reached, such as revenues and profits, costs and ROI. The metrics compare product development as single systems with software product line engineering, targeted to the envisaged markets.

We do not go into details of business cases here; more information can be found in [Business Case 2004; PL-Framework 2004]. Some examples of business cases for switching to software product line engineering are presented in [Clements and Northrop 2001].

20.7.4 Step 4: Creating an Adoption Plan

The input to this transition process step comprises information about the state of the organisation, including its development process and its structure. The output is the adoption plan, as described below.

Who does it

The persons creating the adoption plan are mostly product managers and architects. The structure of the adoption plan shows three major parts:

Three major parts

- Characterisation of the current state.
- Characterisation of the desired state.
- Strategies, objectives, and activities to get from the current to the desired state.

The adoption plan describes the change in process and organisation structure and is thus part of standard change management.

Current state

The state of the organisation is characterised by its process, the staff and their expertise, the organisation structure, the project management methods, the engineering methods, and many other business parameters. To characterise the current state, the maturity of the organisation has to be analysed and described. Such an assessment may be similar to a CMMI assessment; however, its purpose is not to obtain a number to compare the organisation with other organisations (as is often the case for CMMI levels). This assessment determines the strengths and weaknesses of the organisation for software product line engineering and the points where special care has to be taken for the adoption.

Desired state

To determine the desired state, each of the topics listed in the preceding paragraph has to be considered and its desired state has to be defined. This is specific to the process and the organisation structure chosen for software product line engineering. The process chosen will mostly be based on a core process like our software product line engineering framework.

The third step in the adoption plan is to determine a strategy for getting from the current state to the desired state. These strategies have been described in Section 20.3. The adoption plan has to characterise and prioritise them, and suggest the best-suited strategy for the transition to software product line engineering. The prioritisation depends on the values of the metrics for each strategy (like ROI), but also on the people involved.

Path from current to desired state

Whatever the strategy for the adoption, it is always necessary to introduce review points in the transition process where the current state of the adoption is evaluated and the results of the new approach are compared to the conventional approach. This requires introducing measurements during the transition process that can be used for the evaluations. These reviews have to adjust the transition process – they may even lead to a change in the adoption strategy. For the selected strategy, the adoption plan has to include a list of the risks that are involved, together with risk mitigation strategies.

Measuring progress

20.7.5 Step 5: Launching and Institutionalising the Transition

When the adoption plan with the three parts (current state, desired state, strategy to get from the current to the desired state) is ready, the best-suited strategy is chosen, depending on the estimations of the metrics described in the business cases. After that, the software product line engineering approach can be launched. Whatever strategy is chosen, as part of the launch the following must be specified:

- The stakeholders, their interests, needs, biases, culture, and motivation. This includes the original list of stakeholders and their goals, plus new roles that are defined in the adoption plan.
- The new organisation structure.
- The tasks and responsibilities of the new roles.
- A migration path from the old organisation structure to the new one.
- A software product line engineering process for the organisation, considering the products, skills, environment, etc. Our software product line engineering framework can be used as a basis for such a process.
- The production process (this includes packaging, for example).
- Plans for funding.
- Plans for staffing, including consultants and providers.
- Champions and angels for important activities.

Specifying the launch

Champion and angels

Champions are staff members who are convinced of a new idea like software product line engineering and are able to convince other staff members. They support others in applying the approach, present practical tips and support proliferation of the idea. Angels are members of management or senior engineers who have influence due to their role in the hierarchy or due to their experience and expertise. They give the necessary weight to the launch of software product line engineering.

Just launching software product line engineering is not sufficient. It has to be institutionalised by senior management and process managers so that the involved managers and staff consider it as part of their working culture.

Funding strategies

An organisation unit that develops a product and sells it to customers will be funded eventually by selling its products. But a domain engineering unit that develops the platform for software product line engineering requires an up-front investment that needs to be financed somehow, and therefore a funding strategy is necessary. Several strategies may be used for funding the domain engineering activities. For instance, the money may come from a kind of tax imposed on all affected application engineering units or from a corporate fund that may be assigned to these activities. When the products of a software product line are sold in the market, a certain percentage of the money paid by the customers may be assigned to domain engineering.

Merging and splitting product lines

Besides the transition from developing single systems, there are also other changes in the process and engineering approach in the context of software product line engineering. One scenario that has to be considered is an organisation having several product lines that overlap. Does it make sense to merge them or is it better to drop one of them completely? The cost model can help to determine the costs involved, see [Boeckle et al. 2004a]. For the start of a new product line in this scenario, it has to be considered if the software product line should be based on the existing ones or if it is better to build a new platform and develop a new, independent product line.

20.8 Summary

Planning of transition process

For software product line engineering to be successful, both engineering aspects and business aspects have to be considered thoroughly. The transition process for achieving fully working software product line engineering has to be planned and performed carefully. It should be based on metrics (such as ROI) and estimations, and use common process change management methods. The strategy for such a transition needs to be selected carefully, depending on the situation of the organisation.

Part VI

Experience and Future Research

Christian Dinnus
Klaus Pohl

21

Experiences with Software Product Line Engineering

This chapter:

o *Summarises 15 cases of applying the software product line engineering paradigm in industry.*

o *Reports on examples of cost reduction, shorter development times, and quality improvement achieved by introducing the software product line engineering paradigm in industry.*

o *Provides annotated references for further reading about the success stories, obstacles faced, and experience gained.*

21.1 ABB

Company background: Asea Brown Boveri (ABB) is a leading global technology company and has two main business areas, the power and automation technology for utility and industry customers [ABB 2004].

Power and automation technology

Products: ABB's power technology comprises, for instance, high- and medium-voltage products, transformers, and utility automation products. The automation technology branch comprises products such as control systems and robotics [ABB 2004].

Platform: ABB gained plenty of experience with different software product lines. The first example is the ABB Gas Turbine Family, which covers the power range of 35 to 270 MW with five basic turbine types varying in size, combustion technologies, and equipment [Ganz and Layes 1998]. The second example is the Semantic Graphics Framework. It supports the development of graphical applications that realise special requirements in the engineering domain [Rösel 1998]. The third example is ABB's train control product line which is an embedded real-time software system for controlling train movement [Eixelsberger and Beckman 2000].

Several year of use

Shorter development time

Quality improvements

Experience: The experiences of ABB with the software product line approach are positive. The Semantic Graphics Framework has been in use for several years in different business units. More than ten industrial applications have been derived from it [Rösel 1998]. The reference architecture of the turbine control system for the ABB Gas Turbine Family led to shorter development time, higher code quality, and eased the exchange of modules [Ganz and Layes 1998]. For the train control product line, ABB expected significant quality improvements and savings when developing additional product line members [Eixelsberger and Beckman 2000].

Annotated References

C. Ganz and M. Layes; "Modular Turbine Control Software: A Control Software Architecture for the ABB Gas Turbine Family", In: Proceedings of the Second International ESPRIT ARES Workshop, Las Palmas de Gran Canaria, Springer LNCS 1429, 1998, pp. 32–38.

This paper describes the object-oriented design principles of the control architecture of the gas turbine software product line. These principles are for example the use of object hierarchies and data encapsulation.

A. Rösel; "Experiences with the Evolution of an Application Family Architecture", In: Proceedings of the Second International ESPRIT ARES Workshop, Las Palmas de Gran Canaria, Springer LNCS 1429, 1998, pp. 39–48.

This paper shows the evolution of the Semantic Graphics Framework from a prototype to a software product line for different industrial applications. Three different perspectives are covered: architecture, documentation, and organisational issues.

W. Eixelsberger and H. Beckman; "The TCS Experience with the Recovery of Family Architecture", In: M. Jazayeri, A. Ran, and F. van der Linden (eds.), Software Architecture for Product Families – Principles and Practice, Addison-Wesley, 2000, pp. 209–231.

This report explains the experience with the development of a reference architecture based on the architectures of several existing train control systems. It describes the methods used for the architectural recovery in detail, such as the analysis of different views of the input architecture or the recovery itself.

21.2 Boeing Company

Company background: The Boeing Company is one of the leading manufacturers of commercial jetliners, military aircraft, satellites, missile defence, human space flight, and launch systems [Boeing 2004].

Products: The Bold Stroke software product line was originally initiated in 1995 at McDonnell-Douglas which, in the meantime, merged with the Boeing Company. The purpose of the product line was to avail reuse potentials in the operational flight program (OFP) software across multiple fighter aircraft platforms [Sharp 2000]. OFPs are mission-critical, distributed, real-time embedded applications supporting the avionics as well as the cockpit functions for the pilot [Hall of Fame 2004].

Operational flight program software

Platform: The first step of introducing Bold Stroke included the definition and of a reference architecture and its proof of concept, including hardware, software, standards, and practices. The main challenge when defining the reference architecture was to harmonise the differences in the avionics subsystems, mission computing hardware, and system requirements [Doerr and Sharp 2000]. The software architecture consists of reusable components. Hardware independence is achieved by layering and the use of a medium-grained abstraction level [Sharp 2000].

Experience: The success of the Bold Stroke software product line is based on the reduction of dependencies between components and the dependency on platform-specific hardware. The software design facilitates the modification of components and maximises the reuse in different OFPs [Doerr and Sharp 2000]. The Bold Stroke software product line was flight tested successfully on several different aircraft platforms hosted on different hardware configurations [Sharp 2000]. It is the foundation for different production and research programmes, e.g. performed by the Defense Advanced Research Projects Agency (DARPA) [Hall of Fame 2004].

OFP reference architecture

Annotated References

B.S. Doerr and D.C. Sharp; "Freeing Product Line Architectures from Execution Dependencies", In: Proceedings of the First Software Product Lines Conference (SPLC-1), Denver, Kluwer, 2000, pp. 313–329.

> This paper shows different ways of designing physical architectures for a software product line without introducing volatility into the application architecture, e.g. to remove platform-specific hardware dependencies.

D.C. Sharp; "Component Based Product Line Development of Avionics Software", In: Proceedings of the First Software Product Lines Conference (SPLC-1), Denver, Kluwer, 2000, pp. 353–369.

> This paper presents the Bold Stroke software product line architecture, which results from an object-oriented analysis and consists of reusable software components. Due to layering and the use of medium-grained abstraction levels the architecture is independent of the hardware.

SPLC2 – Product Line Hall of Fame, 2004, www.sei.cmu.edu/SPLC2/SPLC2_hof.html

> The Hall of Fame website contains an abstract of the software product line experiences at the Boeing Company and presents some technical issues, e.g. about the reference architecture.

21.3   CelsiusTech Systems AB

Company background: CelsiusTech Systems AB originally was a department of Philips, later became an independent company, and finally became an affiliated company of the Saab Group, Sweden, operating under SaabTech AB. SaabTech AB is a leading supplier of avionics and electronic warfare systems [SaabTech 2004].

Naval control software

Products: In the mid 1980s, CelsiusTech simultaneously obtained two contracts to build naval control systems. The systems had to be hard real time, fault tolerant, and highly distributed. They had to interface with radars and other sensors, missile and torpedo launchers.

Platform: Due to its prior experiences CelsiusTech could estimate the complexity and came to the conclusion that it could not realise these contracts by two separate teams. CelsiusTech recognised that the two systems had more similarities than differences, even though they had to serve ships of different classes in different navies. With its extensive background in the domain, CelsiusTech started one of the first software product lines, which is still running today, under the name ShipSystem 2000 [Clements and Northrop 2001; Brownsword and Clements 1996].

Experience: The ability to react quickly to customer needs in a hard-fought market, with strong competitors and only a few customers, gives a strong competitive advantage. CelsiusTech could quickly enter the new market of avionic systems because it reused 40% of its code directly from Ship System 2000. The general reuse rate is about 80% in the normal naval scope of the product line. CelsiusTech has also inverted its software/hardware costs ratio from 65:35 to 20:80 [Clements and Northrop 2001; Brownsword and Clements 1996].

Reuse rate of 80%

Annotated References

P. Clements and L. Northrop; Software Product Lines – Practices and Patterns, Addison-Wesley, 2001.

> The example of CelsiusTech Systems AB is used several times in this book because the software product line at CelsiusTech was one of the first case studies in successful software product line engineering.

L. Brownsword and P. Clements; "A Case Study in Successful Product Line Development", Technical Report no. CMU/SEI-96-TR-016, Carnegie–Mellon Software Engineering Institute, 1996.

> This paper describes in detail the changes that CelsiusTech had to make to its software, organisation, and process structures due to the software product line engineering paradigm, e.g. that marketers have to negotiate the desired product features based on the possibilities of the software product line.

SPLC2 – Product Line Hall of Fame, 2004, www.sei.cmu.edu/SPLC2/SPLC2_hof.html

> The Hall of Fame website describes briefly the success and complexity of the software product line at CelsiusTech, e.g. that the system comprises 1–1.5 Million SLOC (Source Lines of Code) in Ada and that more than 50 applications have been derived from the software product line.

21.4 Cummins Inc.

Company background: Cummins Inc. is a global leader in developing, distributing, and servicing engines and related technologies, including fuel systems, controls, air handling, filtration, emission solutions, and electrical power generation systems [Cummins 2004].

Products: Software is becoming ever more important for controlling the operation of an engine, e.g. electronics control the ignition and the fuel delivery. The software must be robust and highly reliable. In late 1993 six

Engine control software

critical engine software projects were underway, with another twelve planned [Dager 2000].

Platform: Every developer team worked autonomously and with different standards; for example, there was no common programming language and no reference architecture defined. Being anxious about the quality of the resulting applications, the project leader stopped all projects and established a focus group to develop core assets that all the applications could use. Furthermore, he defined common software development processes [Clements and Northrop 2001]. The first software product line at Cummins Inc. was therefore born.

Productivity improvement of 3.6

Experience: The experience of Cummins Inc. with the software product line approach is consistently positive. Cummins Inc. is able to build over 1000 different products based on the software product line. A wide variety of different functionality is integrated into the software product line: nine basic engine types ranging over 4–18 cylinders and 4–164 litres of displacement, with 12 kinds of electronic control modules, 5 kinds of processors, and 10 kinds of fuel systems. Cummins estimated that it would take more than 360 software engineers to produce these software systems separately instead of the 100 software engineers actually needed due to the software product line approach. This is an estimated productivity improvement of 3.6. Cummins also estimated an ROI (Return On Investment) of 10:1. Furthermore, Cummins can quickly access new markets, from rock crushers to ski lifts [Clements and Northrop 2001; Hall of Fame 2004].

ROI of 10:1

Annotated References

P. Clements and L. Northrop; Software Product Lines – Practices and Patterns, Addison-Wesley, 2001, pp. 417–442.

> This report deals with the experience gained at Cummins Inc. with introducing the engine control software product line. The initial problem situation is drafted and the way to launch the software product line is described including the necessary organisational restructuring.

J.C. Dager; "Cummins's Experience in Developing a Software Product Line Architecture for Real-time Embedded Diesel Engine Controls", In: Proceedings of the First Software Product Lines Conference (SPLC-1), Denver, Kluwer, 2000, pp. 23–46.

> This paper reports on the experience of introducing the engine control software product line, especially domain analysis and architectural views, as well as the architectural development process and the organisational challenges.

SPLC2 – Product Line Hall of Fame, 2004, www.sei.cmu.edu/SPLC2/SPLC2_hof.html

> The Hall of Fame website contains different qualitative statements about the success of the software product line at Cummins Inc., e.g. that 20 basic software builds have been parlayed into well over 1000 separate products.

21.5 Hewlett-Packard

Company background: HP is one of the world's leading IT companies with many different business areas, reaching from consumer handheld devices to powerful supercomputer installations [Hewlett-Packard 2004].

Products: One important business area is the manufacturing of printing technology. HP must maintain a wide range of different firmware of different products for printing, copying, scanning, and faxing [Hall of Fame 2004].

Firmware for printing, scanning, etc.

Platform: HP initiated the Owen Firmware Cooperative to install a software product line approach. Several product teams build a community to provide the product line in a cooperative way. Every product team adopts ownership of newly produced or significantly changed core assets, so everyone feels responsible for the quality of the platform. A small platform team ensures the robustness of the core assets and guides the product teams in using the core assets [Toft et al. 2000].

Experience: The software product line approach yields a reuse rate of about 70% for new products. About 20% of the application assets are based on slightly modified core assets and only 10% require writing new code. The reuse of the core assets leads to significant business advantages. Compared with the development of earlier products, the development of new firmware takes only 25% of the staff resources. In spite of the reduction of staff, the development takes only 33% of the time. This productivity improvement goes hand in hand with a qualitative advancement. The software product line approach leads to 96% fewer defects compared with earlier products [Hall of Fame 2004; SoftwareProductLines 2004].

Development time reduced by 67%

96% fewer defects

Annotated References

P. Toft, D. Coleman, and J. Ohta; "A Cooperative Model for Cross-Divisional Product Development for a Software Product Line", In: Proceedings of the First Software Product Lines Conference (SPLC-1), Denver, Kluwer, 2000, pp. 111–132.

> This paper describes the model of the cooperative organisation at HP for introducing and extending the software product line for printing devices, e.g. how product teams are organised and which key roles are necessary.

Another aspect is a short description of the component-based architecture.

D. Fafchamps; "Organizational Factors and Reuse", IEEE Software, vol. 11, no. 5, 1994, pp. 31–41.

This article presents the results of an empirical study conducted at Hewlett-Packard. The goal of this study was to find out why people sometimes resist reuse and which organisational models encourage reuse more than others. The experience of subsequent reuse programs showed that the relationship between producers and consumers of reuse components and services is a crucial factor. Based on the experiences gained in the study the article identifies and evaluates four different organisational models of producer–consumer relationships.

S. Douma and H. Schreuder; Economic Approaches to Organizations, 3rd edition, Prentice Hall, 2002.

The box on p. 43 briefly describes Hewlett-Packard's business principles, known as the "HP way". It also summarises the past strategic decisions that were necessary to retain the company's success, such as the introduction of a service-centred culture.

SPLC2 – Product Line Hall of Fame, 2004, www.sei.cmu.edu/SPLC2/SPLC2_hof.html

The Hall of Fame website briefly describes the cooperative organisation model of the software product line for printing devices at HP. Some qualitative statements about the success of the software product line are given, like the reduction of staff resources for developing new firmware up to 75%.

Software Product Lines, 2004, www.softwareproductlines.com

A report of the experience gained at HP with the software product line for printing devices can be found on this website. Three key success factors are given: the firmware architecture, the development approach, and the cooperative organisation.

21.6   LG Industrial Systems Co., Ltd.

Company background: LG Industrial Systems Co., Ltd (LGIS) is a Korean manufacturer of electric power equipment including industrial electric equipment, distribution, automation, and control systems [LGIS 2004].

Elevator control software

Products: A business area of LGIS is the development of elevator control systems (ECS). This embedded control software has a high diversity of customer needs and therefore rapidly changing market requirements. The competitive market of ECS demands a high flexibility in the products to retain a significant market share [Lee et al. 2000].

Platform: Doing it the old way, LGIS developed all its ECS separately, so LGIS had to modify the software frequently. Changes were often unmanaged and the software became error-prone. To improve the situation, LGIS decided to start a software product line for ECS. The product line engineering process was separated into two parts, namely domain and application engineering. Several phases ware passed through during domain engineering, e.g. the context analysis to set the scope of the domain or feature modelling to detect the commonalities and differences in the domain. The application engineering dealt with the configuration process of the software product line at LGIS, e.g. with the selection of features [Lee et al. 2000].

Experience: A result of the software product line is the decreasing complexity of the core assets. In the old version the system consisted of 51 modules with 603 functions, which were in part redundant. The re-engineered core assets for the software product line have a reduced size and complexity of 48 modules with 295 functions. One example of the reduced complexity is the number of functions, which had to be modified because of changes to a serial port. In the old system, 20 functions had to be modified and in the reengineered core assets only 8. The reduction of complexity also led to reduced maintenance costs [Lee et al. 2000].

Complexity reduced by 50%

Annotated References

K. Lee, K.C. Kang, E. Koh, W. Chae, B. Kim, and B.W. Choi; "Domain-Oriented Engineering of Elevator Control Software", In: Proceedings of the First Software Product Lines Conference (SPLC-1), Denver, Kluwer, 2000, pp. 3–22.

This paper describes the way from domain analysis to the component-based reference architecture for the elevator control. Several modelling techniques such as feature modelling and message sequence charts are used to model different architecture views.

21.7 Lucent Technologies

Company background: Lucent Technologies designs and delivers the systems, services, and software that drive next-generation communications networks, like telephony or data communication [Lucent 2004].

Products: Most of the telephone connections in the USA are established by the 5ESS switch from Lucent. The 5ESS switch has been in use since 1982. It has been advanced to accommodate emerging requirements, e.g. the Internet [Hall of Fame 2004; Ardis et al. 2000].

Telephone switching configuration software

Platform: In 1994 Lucent launched the Domain Engineered Configuration Control (DECC) project to standardise the configuration control software and to establish a software product line. The configuration control software monitors the run-time configuration of hardware components and maintains their status. For example, before removing one of the hardware components, the configuration control software has to check if there is a backup component. Furthermore the DECC developed a configuration process and tool for generating new software based on the core assets. The idea was to translate new specifications automatically into working code driven by a tool with a graphical user interface [Ardis et al. 2000].

Productivity improved by factors 3 to 5

Experience: In 1996 the DECC team started a trial use in comparison to a traditional project. The software product line had comparable run-time performances. Because of this experience, the DECC team invested a small amount of reengineering effort and started the first successful real project only a few months later [Ardis et al. 2000]. The switch maintenance domain showed productivity improvements by factors of 3 to 5 as a result of introducing product line engineering [Hall of Fame 2004].

Annotated References

M. Ardis, P. Dudak, L. Dor, W.-J. Leu, L. Nakatani, B. Olsen, and P. Pontrelli; "Domain-Engineered Configuration Control", In: Proceedings of the First Software Product Lines Conference (SPLC-1), Denver, Kluwer, 2000, pp. 479–493.

> This paper deals with the experiences of reengineering the configuration control software for the 5ESS switch according to the software product line engineering paradigm. The reengineering project was accomplished in three phases: discovery, design, and deployment.

SPLC2 – Product Line Hall of Fame, 2004, www.sei.cmu.edu/SPLC2/SPLC2_hof.html

> The Hall of Fame website describes the complexity of the software product line for the 5ESS switch by the statement, that any particular switch in the product line is operated by approximately 10 MLOC (Millions Lines Of Code). The transfer of the 5ESS switch control software to a software product line is one of the first applications of domain engineering to a large, complex system.

21.8   MARKET MAKER Software AG

Company background: MARKET MAKER Software AG develops and provides Europe's most popular stock market software that helps private and professional users to keep track of the stock market [Market Maker 2004].

Products: In 1999 MARKET MAKER decided to enter the new market of Internet services. The small development team was faced with different customer needs. Different operating platforms had to integrate different databases and content-producing software. The product had to be able to serve different requirements, such as showing different information in different representation formats based on different customer needs [Hall of Fame 2004].

Stock tracking software

Platform: The variety in the online version of the product led to the decision to apply the software product line engineering paradigm. By reusing the desktop version of the stock information system as a common core, a small team of six developers realised the additional software product line requirements for the online market in 36 person months. An additional requirement, for example, was that products of the software product line had to be integrated into different customer environments, which was achieved by separating the data and the application layers [Clements and Northrop 2001].

Experience: Each instance of the software product line must be built in accordance with customer requirements, installed, and tested on the customer's own platform. This takes as little as three days [Clements and Northrop 2001]. During the boom time of the New Economy in the late 1990s, MARKET MAKER could realise a short time to market as a major advantage over its competitors. After the end of the boom time, MARKET MAKER survived because of its small, efficient team required for maintaining the running systems [Hall of Fame 2004]. The development time for creating a new product is reduced by more than 50% and costs are reduced by roughly 70% [SoftwareProductLines 2004].

Three days to set up a new system

Cost reduction of 70%

Annotated References

P. Clements and L. Northrop; Software Product Lines – Practices and Patterns, Addison-Wesley, 2001, pp. 485–512.

> The detailed report of the case study at MARKET MAKER describes the experience of introducing a software product line into a small-sized company, beginning with the history of the company and a detailed problem statement. The different practices, like architecture definition or component development, for setting up the software product line are given.

K. Schmid; "A Comprehensive Product Line Scoping Approach and Its Validation", In: Proceedings of the 24th International Conference on Software Engineering (ICSE 2002), Orlando, Florida, ACM Press, 2002, pp. 593–603.

> This paper deals with aspects of scoping in the context of software product lines. Scoping means to set the focus of reuse on the functionality that promises an optimal return on investment. The chosen scoping

approach Pulse-Eco V2.0 is validated by the case study at MARKET MAKER.

O. Flege and T. Kiesgen; "Börseninformationssysteme bei der Market Maker AG" (in German), In: G. Böckle, P. Knauber, K. Pohl, and K. Schmid (eds.), Software-Produktfamilien – Methoden, Einführung und Praxis, dpunkt, 2004, pp. 207–220.

The architecture of the software product line is presented from different views, e.g. the logical view, the data structure, the component model, and the process view. XML files are used to configure the component-based architecture.

SPLC2 – Product Line Hall of Fame, 2004, www.sei.cmu.edu/SPLC2/SPLC2_hof.html

The Hall of Fame website describes the complexity of the software product line at MARKET MAKER. Every product has to be tailored to the customer's requirements which are, for example, the integration of the customer's database or enabling the operation on the customer's computing platform.

Software Product Lines, 2004, www.softwareproductlines.com

This online experience report explains the major points in introducing a software product line at a small-sized company like MARKET MAKER. Thinking into the future, paying attention to quality, taking care with the architecture, building an efficient team, and focusing on a domain are the keystones.

21.9 Philips

Company background: Royal Philips Electronics of the Netherlands is one of the world's biggest electronics companies and the largest in Europe. Its products vary from professional medical systems to lighting, consumer electronics, and domestic appliances [Philips 2004].

Products: Philips provides several product lines, mainly for consumer electronics and for medical systems. Furthermore, Philips is one of the leading commercial European researchers in the field of software product lines. The software product lines of consumer electronics and medical imaging systems are only some of the successful examples.

21.9.1 Philips Consumer Electronics

Company background: Philips' portfolio of consumer electronics systems includes audio–video equipment, like TV-sets, radio receivers, CD and DVD players and recorders, as well as set-top boxes [Philips 2004].

Products: Philips Consumer Electronics provides software product lines for audio–video equipment, such as TV sets [V. Ommering et al. 2000]. The customers have high demands with respect to performance. Because of the mass-market nature, the cheapest memory and processor chips are used. The products have to be very reliable as they are offered in the mass market. Hence, repairing them after delivery is very costly.

Consumer electronics

Platform: Philips Consumer Electronics has chosen to use a composition paradigm in the production of the product lines. The methodology is named *Koala* [V. Ommering 2002]. This means that the architecture has enough flexibility to allow many different configurations of the same basic components. The whole set of products is referred to as *product populations*, with many differences and many commonalities, but few commonalities that spread over all products. Components are combined to build more complex components. Interfaces that do not match are connected through glue code. Certain pieces of glue code are standard, and only need some parameters to instantiate.

Experience: By 2002, all mid- and high-range TV sets, and many other products as well, were produced in the population [V. Ommering 2004]. Surprisingly, the architecture did not need many adaptations after its first conception in 1996. For some experiences with interactive set-top boxes, see [De Lange and Jansen 2001].

Stable reference architecture

21.9.2 Philips Medical Systems

Company background: Philips' portfolio of medical systems includes products like X-ray, ultrasonic or computed tomography and services like training, business consultancy, or financial services [Philips 2004].

Products: Philips Medical Systems provides a software product line for medical imaging systems, which is motivated by an increasing complexity and diversity in this domain [Wijnstra 2002]. The customers have high demands on safety and reliability as the products may have a crucial impact on the health of the patients, e.g. the produced radiation can be dangerous [America and Van Wijgerden 2000].

Medical systems

Platform: Philips Medical Systems has decided to employ a sophisticated software product line approach. A medical middleware platform serves as the basis for other software product lines in the company. Thus the platform is a software product line in itself, which leads to additional variability requirements for the platform. The component-based reference architecture reuses existing software components that are transformed step by step into domain artefacts [SoftwareProductLines 2004].

Increasing number of products based on the platform

Experience: Since 2001, the number of products that use the platform has increased. Today, ten product groups are based on the platform. A product group is responsible for creating products and for maintaining several product lines. It takes about 1.6 times as many people to build a platform component as was necessary to do it the old way. Yet every product group that uses the platform saves significant time as most of the components do not have to be developed again [SoftwareProductLines 2004].

Annotated References

F.J. van der Linden and J.K. Müller; "Creating Architectures with Building Blocks" IEEE Software, November 1995, pp. 51–60.

For Philips, this was a report on the first successes of applying product line technology in industry. It reported on a product line for telecommunication switches in a niche market. These experiences have formed the basis for all work on product lines within Philips ever since. The basic ideas are used almost unchanged in all successful product lines.

R. van Ommering; Building Product Populations with Software Components, Ph.D. Thesis, University of Groningen, December 2004.

This Ph.D. thesis gives an overview of all work on Koala in the consumer electronics domain. It explains the compositional approach and how dedicated tools keep variability selection local and at the same time keep the resource consumption low.

F. de Lange and T. Jansen; "The Philips-OpenTV product family architecture for interactive set-top boxes", In: Proceedings of the 4th International Product Family Engineering Workshop (PFE-4), Bilbao, Springer LNCS 2290, 2001, pp. 187–206.

This paper describes the Philips-OpenTV product line architecture, which is used by different set-top box products. The design principles of the architecture are explained, such as separation of concerns, layering, and strict interfaces.

J.G. Wijnstra; "Component Frameworks for a Medical Imaging Product Family", In: Proceedings of Software Architectures for Product Families (IW-SAPF-3), Las Palmas de Gran Canaria, Springer LNCS 1951, 2000, pp. 4–18.

This paper describes the experiences of Philips Medical Systems with product line architectures in the medical imaging domain. Two different component frameworks build the architecture. The first component framework is the high-level product line architecture, which groups components to subsystems and defines their interfaces. The second component framework defines the different services of the components that are provided via an interface.

P. America and J. van Wijgerden; "Requirements Modeling for Families of Complex Systems", In: Proceedings of Software Architectures for Product Families (IW-SAPF-3), Las Palmas de Gran Canaria, Springer LNCS 1951, 2000, pp. 199–209.

This paper deals with the specification of a software product line for medical imaging systems using use cases and a requirements object model expressed in the UML. A process is presented for this approach, which has been validated in the medical imaging domain.

Software Product Lines, 2004, www.softwareproductlines.com

This report deals with the experience gained with the middleware platform for the medical imaging domain. The motivation for applying the software product line engineering paradigm is stated as well as technical details, e.g. of the component-based architecture. Furthermore, some qualitative statements about the success of the medical middleware platform are given, like its successful use in ten different product groups.

SPLC2 – Product Line Hall of Fame, 2004, www.sei.cmu.edu/SPLC2/SPLC2_hof.html

This report briefly describes the telecom case, which constitutes Philips' original experience with software product lines.

21.10 Robert Bosch GmbH

Company background: Robert Bosch GmbH is a leading supplier of the automotive industry and produces many different systems, such as micro-electronic sensor and control devices [Bosch 2004].

Products: This case study covers the example of driver assistance systems, which supervise the periphery of a car to assist the driver. A parking pilot is a typical example of a driver assistance system [Hein et al. 2000].

Driver assistance systems

Platform: The automotive domain is characterised by only a few car manufacturers, whose market power forces the suppliers to deliver systems adjusted to the individual needs of the car manufacturer with high quality at low prices. The concept of software product lines helps to attain these requirements [Hein et al. 2004]. Robert Bosch GmbH has dealt with development methods for software product lines in the automotive domain in the ITEA-Project CAFÉ [CAFÉ 2004]. The main goal of Robert Bosch GmbH was to establish a reference architecture for driver assistance systems, which had to be configurable, integratable, and highly performing [Hein et al. 2004].

Experience: Robert Bosch GmbH has reached the goals for its architecture. The architecture is configurable due to a reduction of the dependencies between different components. Integratability is reached by using the automotive standard CAN for the system interfaces. High performance is achieved

Reusable high-performance architecture

by parallel data processing. Therefore the software product line for driver assistance systems can be used in different contexts for different car manufacturers [Hein et al. 2004].

Annotated References

A. Hein, T. Fischer, and S. Thiel; "Fahrerassistenzsysteme bei der Robert Bosch GmbH" (in German), In: G. Böckle, P. Knauber, K. Pohl, and K. Schmid (eds.), Software-Produktfamilien – Methoden, Einführung und Praxis, dpunkt, 2004, pp. 193–205.

> This report presents the experience gained in developing a reference architecture of a software product line for the driver assistance domain. The different steps for introducing the software product line are presented in detail, like the explicit modelling of variability or the product configuration, which consists of the feature and architecture configurations.

A. Hein, M. Schlick, and R. Vinga-Martins; "Applying Feature Models in Industrial Settings", In: Proceedings of the First Software Product Lines Conference (SPLC-1), Denver, Kluwer, 2000, pp. 47–70.

> This paper presents an approach to model the variability of a software product line with feature-oriented domain analysis (FODA), which was validated in the car periphery supervision domain. An extension is introduced to enable FODA to model cross-links between features.

S. Thiel and A. Hein; "Systematic Integration of Variability into Product Line Architecture Design", In: Proceedings of the 2nd International Conference on Software Product Lines (SPLC-2), San Diego, USA, Springer LNCS 2379, 2002, pp. 130–153.

> This paper deals with the systematic integration of variability into the reference architecture of a software product line. The architecture design framework "QUASAR" is presented, which is applied successfully in the car periphery supervision product line.

CAFÉ – From Concept to Application in System-Family Engineering, 2004, www.esi.es/en/Projects/Cafe/cafe.html

> This website presents an overview of the purpose, partners and tasks of CAFÉ, which means "From Concept to Application in System-Family Engineering". The purpose of the CAFÉ project is the development of practices and methods for the application of software product lines in the development of software-intensive systems.

21.11 Salion Inc.

Company background: Salion Inc. is a software company specialising in software solutions for Supplier Customer Relationship Management (sCRM). The software is used by suppliers such as the automotive supplier industry which serves only a handful of global customers [Salion 2004].

Products: Salion implemented a system intended to serve the target customer base with an effort of 190 engineer months. The product implements typical requirements of the supplier domain, e.g. the process of acceptance of a bid. As Salion approached the market, the need for a software product line became clear because of different customer needs [Buhrdorf et al. 2003].

Supplier CRM software

Platform: A small company like Salion Inc. could not afford to implement a software product line from scratch (proactive approach), for which an effort of up to 570 engineer months was estimated. So, Salion decided to take the first product as the asset base (reactive approach) and invested two engineer months to establish a new configuration management tool and techniques to allow multiple product variations. Since the product line has been in use, Salion has enhanced and reengineered the asset base in reaction to new requirements [Buhrdorf et al. 2003].

Experience: The reactive approach significantly reduced the up-front investment for the platform from an estimated 570 engineer months to 2 engineer months. The continuous enhancement of the platform enables Salion to adapt its software product line to serve new customers. The effort for implementing new product variants ranges from 5% to 10% of the effort required for the baseline product. This is a productivity improvement of 10 to 20 [Krueger 2002].

Productivity improved by factors 10 to 20

Annotated References

R. Buhrdorf, D. Churchett, and C.W. Krueger; "Salion's Experience with a Reactive Software Product Line Approach", In: Proceedings of the 5th International Workshop on Software Product-Family Engineering (PFE-5), Siena, Italy, Springer LNCS 3014, 2003, pp. 317–322.

> This paper explains the initial situation at Salion Inc. before initiating the software product line, i.e. being a software start-up with no experience in building software in the target domain. The motivation for initiating a software product line with the reactive approach is explained: Salion Inc. cannot afford a long time to market because of its limited financial strength.

P. Clements and L.M. Northrop; Salion, Inc.: "A Software Product Line Case Study", Technical Report no. CMU/SEI-2002-TR-038, Carnegie–Mellon Software Engineering Institute, 2002.

> This report tells the story of introducing software product line engineering at Salion Inc. The main part explains how Salion built the platform assets and presents details like the process or architecture definition.

C.W. Krueger; "Data from Salion's Software Product Line Initiative", Technical Report no. 2002-07-08-1, BigLever Software, Inc., 2002.

> This report presents a well-founded statistical analysis of the resulting benefits of introducing the software product line at Salion Inc., e.g. the calculation of the ROI.

Software Product Lines, 2004, www.softwareproductlines.com

> This website deals with the motivation for selecting the reactive approach for initialising the software product line at Salion Inc., e.g. the reactive approach promises the shortest path to an operational software product line. Furthermore, several benefits achieved by the software product line approach are presented, e.g. a productivity improvement of 10 to 20.

21.12 Siemens AG Medical Solutions HS IM

Company background: Siemens Medical Solutions provides hospital applications from X-ray tubes and magnetic resonance and CT scanners to complete infrastructure support in hardware and software for hospitals and all other medical practitioners [Siemens 2004].

Radiology software

Products: One of the business areas of Siemens Medical Solutions is the development of software for the radiology domain that supports the process of radiology. The task of the radiologist starts with patient registration and ends after several activities with reporting and archiving of the images in the report repository.

Platform: The software product line at Siemens Medical Solutions provides qualitative variability, such as support for high-end and low-end hardware, as well as functional variability, e.g. different features during image post-processing. The system test of the different resulting products requires a systematic procedure. Siemens Medical Solutions uses the ScenTED method for testing the software product line. The ScenTED method was developed by the Software Systems Engineering group at the University of Duisburg-Essen. The ScenTED method supports the creation of domain test cases based on use cases that contain variability and the reuse of domain test cases in application testing (see e.g. [Reuys et al. 2004b; Reuys et al. 2005]).

57% reuse of test cases

Experience: The adaptation of the ScenTED method led to two major improvements in the test process at Siemens Medical Solutions. The first improvement is a reuse of test cases with a ratio of 57%, realised by enriching use case scenarios with variable and invariable scenario steps. The reuse led to a cost reduction for testing different products derived from the software product line. The second improvement from introducing the ScenTED method is a better traceability achieved by a systematic derivation of test cases. The results have been affirmed by a survey at Siemens Medical Solutions [Reuys et al. 2004b].

Annotated References

A. Reuys, H. Götz, J. Neumann, and J. Weingärtner; "Medizintechnik bei Siemens AG Medical Solutions HS IM" (in German), In: G. Böckle, P. Knauber, K. Pohl, and K. Schmid (eds.), Software-Produktfamilien – Methoden, Einführung und Praxis, dpunkt, 2004, pp. 247–259.

> This report presents the experience gained in testing a software product line with the ScenTED method at Siemens Medical Solutions. The survey provides the results conducted at Siemens Medical Solutions, which affirm, for example, that the ScenTED method improves test case reuse and traceability.

E. Kamsties, K. Pohl, S. Reis, and A. Reuys; "Testing Variabilities in Use Case Model", In: Proceedings of the 5th International Workshop on Software Product-Family Engineering (PFE-5), Siena, Italy, Springer LNCS 3014, 2003, pp. 6–18.

> Details of the ScenTED method for software product line testing can be found in this paper. To avoid a combinatorial explosion of the number of test cases, the variability of the product line is included in domain test cases. Segmentation and fragmentation techniques are proposed to preserve the variability of use cases. Furthermore, the different possibilities for variability to occur in use case scenarios are mapped to the UML sequence diagram.

21.13 Testo AG

Company background: Testo AG is one of the leading suppliers of portable electronic measuring instruments, e.g. for the measurement of temperature, pressure or humidity [Testo 2004].

Products: The market conditions for portable measuring instruments demand short time to market, so the development of new products took only about half a year to one-and-a-half years. Testo AG practised only opportunistic reuse; therefore the products have been redeveloped nearly completely, including hardware and software [Schmid et al. 2004a].

Portable measurement instruments

Platform: In 2001, the completion of an ambitious product development suggested that there was potential for reuse as essential commonalities in different products were recognised. Testo AG initiated a project to analyse the possible benefits of introducing a software product line in 2001. This project identified several tasks, such as the training of employees, the definition of a common reference architecture, the support of different views, a configuration management concept, and the development of the core assets [Schmid et al. 2004a].

Changed practices due to reference architecture

Experience: Testo AG has taken these steps and expanded established practices only to some degree in order not to overstrain its employees. For example, the development tools already in use were retained. The common reference architecture for the software product line is based on the architecture of already existing products [Schmid et al. 2004a]. It was necessary to introduce a new process for developing new products based on the software product line, so the developers had to use the architecture and the predefined interfaces. An example of the implemented variability is a printing component that includes 20 variation points [Schmid et al. 2004b]. The first products of the software product line were expected at the end of 2004 [Schmid et al. 2004a].

Annotated References

K. Schmid, I. John, R. Kolb, and G. Meier; "Eingebettete Systeme bei der Testo AG" (in German), In: G. Böckle, P. Knauber, K. Pohl, and K. Schmid (eds.), Software-Produktfamilien – Methoden, Einführung und Praxis, dpunkt, 2004, pp. 221–231.

In this report, the experience of introducing a software product line at Testo AG is presented. The stepwise development of the reference architecture is explained in detail, e.g. the documentation of the already existing architectures, the design of the reference architecture or the evaluation of the reference architecture.

K. Schmid, I. John, R. Kolb, and G. Meier; "Introducing the PuLSE Approach to an Embedded System Population at Testo AG", Technical Report no. 015.04/E, Fraunhofer IESE, 2004.

This technical report describes the application of the PuLSE approach at Testo AG. The PuLSE approach supports the development of a product line in a systematic way and focuses on technical and economic aspects.

21.14 The National Reconnaissance Office

Institution Background: The National Reconnaissance Office (NRO) designs, builds, and operates reconnaissance satellites for US governmental institutions such as the Central Intelligence Agency (CIA) or the Department of Defense (DoD) [NRO 2004].

Satellite control software

Products: The NRO plays a leading role in achieving information superiority for the US Government and armed forces. The satellites are used to guide weapons, pinpoint the enemy, navigate, communicate, and eavesdrop. Because of shrinking budgets, the NRO began to look for further customers and explored partnerships with industry [Clements and Northrop 2001].

Platform: The NRO decided to develop a software platform for its ground-based spacecraft command and control software as the applications in this domain have a large amount of commonality. The resulting software product line was named Control Channel Toolkit (CCT). Several assets have been produced during the engineering of the core assets. These were, for example, the CCT Domain Definition to define the system boundaries and the Generalized Requirements Specification to capture common capabilities of the CCT software product line. Further examples are the CCT System Test Architecture to describe a test system architecture used to verify CCT functionality or the CCT Reuse Guide to describe the steps necessary to build a product line application from the CCT core assets. The CCT Reuse Guide is of special importance as the CCT crosses organisational boundaries: the NRO delivers the platform, and the users of the platform build the needed products on their own [Clements and Northrop 2001].

Experience: In December 1999, the CCT was completed on schedule and within budget. During the development period, the costs were consequently higher than developing a single system. But the additional investments are expected to be compensated due to large-scale reuse. The development savings are anticipated at 18.2%. The first product of CCT could realise 50% reduction in overall cost and schedule, and nearly ten-fold reductions in development personnel and defects [Clements and Northrop 2001].

50% reduction in overall costs

Annotated References

P. Clements and L. Northrop; Software Product Lines – Practices and Patterns, Addison-Wesley, 2001.

> This study describes the whole story of introducing a software product line at the NRO. It begins with the institution background and the motivation for introducing a software product line. Technical details are shown as well as the management effort of the software product line. Finally the benefits of the software product line are presented.

21.15 The Naval Undersea Warfare Center

Institution Background: The Naval Undersea Warfare Center (NUWC) is the US Navy's research, development, test and evaluation, engineering, and fleet support centre for undersea warfare technology [NUWC 2004].

Products: The NUWC develops and supports different range facilities, including those to test and evaluate systems for the military forces of the USA. The facilities can be used as well for maximising force readiness by training ranges. A range is composed of a set of resources and the physical

Range facilities

assets required to conduct a specific test or training exercise [Cohen et al. 2002].

Platform: In the past, these range facilities were built for specific categories of weapon systems and missions, but these systems have become more and more complex. Nevertheless the systems share some commonalities, e.g. sensors are needed to acquire data, which must be logged and presented in various ways. The NUWC started a software product line called RangeWare to manage the commonality and complexity of the range facilities. The RangeWare software product line is structured by a reference architecture intended to cover the complete set of range operations. Using the reference architecture for building range systems, some assets have to be tailored for range-unique capabilities [Cohen et al. 2002].

Five to six new platform applications per year

Experience: In the year 2004, the software product line included seven systems already installed, with five to six new projects per year [Cohen et al. 2004]. The cost of producing new software for ranges is at least 50% lower using RangeWare. The development time has been reduced from years to months. At the same time, staff resources are cut by up to 75%. The increasing customer satisfaction and flexibility in starting new projects as well as the high reliability and predictability yield significant competitive benefits [Cohen et al. 2002].

Annotated References

S. Cohen, E. Dunn, and A. Soule; "Successful Product Line Development and Sustainment: A DoD Case Study", Technical Report no. CMU/SEI-2002-TN-018, Carnegie–Mellon Software Engineering Institute, 2002.

> This report presents the motivation of the NUWC for initiating a software product line and technical details for implementing the asset base. Different product line practice areas are explained, such as structuring the organisation or software system integration.

S. Cohen, D. Zubrow, and E. Dunn; "Case Study: A Measurement Program for Product Lines", Technical Report CMU/SEI-2004-TN-023, Carnegie–Mellon Software Engineering Institute, 2004.

> This report shows the experience of the NUWC in controlling the software product line effort and reaching defined goals. The measurement programme is explained in detail. For example, the arrangement of the measurement team, the goals of the measurement programme, and the final results, as well as the next steps, are shown.

Günter Böckle
Klaus Pohl
Frank van der Linden

22

Future
Research

In this chapter we briefly outline the key challenges for future research.

22.1   Domain Specialisation

Standardised abstractions

This book extensively introduced a comprehensive framework for software product line engineering. A major challenge for future research is to specialise this framework for a given application domain such as automotive systems or medical systems. Amongst others, such a specialisation would result in a set of well-defined types for modelling domain-specific variation points, variants, variability dependencies, and constraint dependencies. Such a specialisation will increase the semantics of the models – an essential foundation for offering improved tool support and for handling the enormous complexity of the variability more effectively. For example, standardised levels of abstraction and mechanisms for mapping the concepts and the variability defined at one level to another level in a consistent manner should be the results of a domain specialisation. To gain the full benefit of a domain specialisation, it should – or better, must – include the definition of domain-specific modelling languages for defining the software development artefacts.

22.2   Quality Assurance

We introduced a technique for defining and adapting system test cases in software product line engineering. There are, of course, other test techniques than system testing as well as other quality assurance techniques which have proven to improve significantly the quality of the software if used appropriately during software development.

Integration and regression tests

A key challenge in this area is the adaptation of integration test techniques and regression test techniques to the specifics of software product line engineering, i.e. the effective consideration of variability in integration and regression test techniques as well as their seamless integration in the domain and application testing processes.

Review techniques

Another key challenge is the adaptation of inspections, reviews, and walkthrough techniques for their use in domain and application engineering. For example, the results of inspections, reviews, and walkthroughs, obtained in domain engineering, should be effectively reused in application engineering.

22.3   Model-Driven Development

Coherent model-driven technique

Due to the separation of domain and application engineering, software product line engineering is an ideal candidate for employing model-driven development. There are attempts to introduce model-driven development in soft-

ware product line engineering, especially to support the model-driven derivation of product line applications. However, establishing a coherent,
effective, and easy to use model-driven development technique for software
product line engineering is still a key research challenge.

22.4 Evolution

Even in the case of the development of single software systems, managing   *Managing variability*
the evolution of the development artefacts is a challenge. In software product   *and evolution*
line engineering developers are faced not only with the evolution over time,
but also with the existence of different variants at the same time (variability
in space). Managing the evolution of software product line artefacts over
time and ensuring the consistent integration of the changes in all affected
product line applications are thus key research challenges. Developing and
validating a comprehensive technique that supports both the management of
the evolution of product line artefacts over time and the management of the
variability within the artefacts is also an open research issue.

22.5 Multiple Product Lines

In several domains the need to manage variability across different product   *Variability across*
lines arises. Solutions for defining and managing variability across different   *product lines*
product lines and across all software development artefacts are still imma-
ture. Managing variability across product lines is even more challenging if
the product lines are owned by different companies.

22.6 Tool Support

The engineering of high-quality software in an industrial setting needs ade-   *Managing*
quate tool support. However, for most of the aspects of software product line   *traceability*
engineering, sufficient tool support is missing. For example, tool support
offered today for managing variability across all development artefacts, or
for managing the interrelations between the product line applications and the
domain artefacts, is very weak. Establishing seamless tool support for managing variability and the development artefacts in the domain and the application engineering processes is a key challenge for future research (see e.g.
[PRIME 2005]).

22.7 Process Improvement and Assessment

Adaptation of assessments There are investigations and results for establishing process improvement frameworks and assessment methods for software product line engineering. Further research is, however, needed to fully adapt existing software maturity models such as CMMI as well as software development assessment techniques to software product line engineering. For example, adaptations are needed for assessing the specifics of the two development processes as well as for synchronising the activities between them. In addition, significant validation effort is required to prove that the adaptations have the desired effects.

22.8 Economics

Prediction of economic impact Predictive economic models, which help us to answer questions like "when should I invest in a product line?" or "when does the investment in a product line pay off?" have been proposed. Yet, they must be extended to include factors like maintenance costs, time to market, product quality, or customer satisfaction, in the prediction of economic impact.

Detailed models for ROI ROI (Return On Investment) models are needed that operate on a more detailed level. For example, ROI models are needed that predict the ROI of a certain feature or even the ROI of a certain variant within a feature.

The Authors

Prof. Dr. Klaus Pohl holds a full professorship at the University of Duisburg-Essen and leads the Software Systems Engineering research group. He received his Ph.D. and his habilitation in computer science from RWTH Aachen, Germany. He is involved in various technology transfer projects as well as major research projects which focus on different aspects of software product line engineering. Klaus Pohl is (co-)author of over 90 refereed publications. He has served as programme chair for several international and national conferences, such as the IEEE International Requirements Engineering Conference (RE'02), the Experience Track of the 27th International Conference on Software Engineering (ICSE 2005), the German Software Engineering Conference (SE 2005), the 9th International Software Product Line Conference (SPCL Europe 2005), and the 18th International Conference on Advanced Information Systems Engineering (CAiSE 2006).

Contact: pohl@sse.uni-essen.de

Dr. Günter Böckle works at Siemens Corporate Technology as a project manager. He received his Ph.D. in mathematics in 1976 from the University of Stuttgart. Since 1999 he has led several projects on software product line engineering. Before that he worked in the fields of simulation, modelling, system evaluation, processor architecture and design, parallelisation, software engineering, and systems engineering. He has published several papers and books and is a member of INCOSE (International Council on Systems Engineering).

Contact: guenter.boeckle@siemens.com

Dr. Frank van der Linden has worked at Philips Medical Systems since 1999. He is project manager for the series of ITEA projects ESAPS, CAFÉ, and FAMILIES. Before this he was involved in the EU ESPRIT project ARES, which provided basic architectural knowledge for product line engineering. Frank van der Linden received his Ph.D. in mathematics in 1984 from the University of Amsterdam. He worked at Philips Research between 1984 and 1999 on several topics in the field of software engineering, including component based software architecture. He was program chair of a series of five workshops on product line engineering (PFE) and is a member of the steering committee of the SPLC conferences.

Contact: frank.van.der.linden@philips.com

Stan Bühne is a research assistant in the Software Systems Engineering group at the University of Duisburg-Essen. He received his diploma in business information technology in 2002 from the University of Essen. He has experience in product line engineering from research projects and industrial projects with the automotive industry. His research interests are variability management and requirements engineering for software product lines.

Christian Dinnus is a research assistant in the Software Systems Engineering group at the University of Duisburg-Essen. Prior to this, he worked for four years as an independent software engineer. He received his diploma in business information technology in 2004. In his thesis, he analysed the variability of use case scenarios in the context of software product lines. His research interest is requirements engineering for software product lines.

Günter Halmans is a research assistant in the Software Systems Engineering group at the University of Duisburg-Essen. His research area includes requirements engineering for software product lines. Before joining the University of Duisburg-Essen, Günter Halmans worked for more than eight years as a product manager and requirements engineer in industry. He received a degree in computer science from the University of Dortmund in 1992.

Kim Lauenroth is a research assistant in the Software Systems Engineering group at the University of Duisburg-Essen. He received his diploma in computer science in 2003 from the University of Dortmund. He has experience in software product lines and variability management from several industrial collaborations. His research interests are the definition and management of variability.

Elisabeth Niehaus has been a research assistant in the Software Systems Engineering group at the University of Duisburg-Essen since 2003. She received a diploma in computer science in 2003 and a diploma in economics in 2001 from the University of Oldenburg. Her research focuses on economic models for software product line engineering.

Andreas Reuys is a research assistant in the Software Systems Engineering group at the University of Duisburg-Essen. He received his diploma in computer science in 1998 from the University of Dortmund. He has been involved in product line development projects since 1999. His research interest is the definition of methods for system test in product line engineering and their application in industry.

Ernst Sikora is a research assistant in the Software Systems Engineering group at the University of Duisburg-Essen. He received his diploma in applied computer science from the University of Dortmund. His research focuses on goal- and scenario-based requirements engineering for embedded systems. Amongst others, he has been involved in industrial projects in the automotive supplier industry.

Nelufar Ulfat-Bunyadi is a research assistant in the Software Systems Engineering group at the University of Duisburg-Essen. She received her diploma in business information technology in 2003. Her research areas include methods for COTS component selection and the extension of CMMI for software product line engineering.

Thorsten Weyer received his diploma with distinction in applied computer science from the University of Koblenz. He is a research assistant in the Software Systems Engineering Group at the University of Duisburg-Essen. Prior to this, he worked for several years as a consultant for national and international companies. His current research focuses on requirements engineering for software product lines and on variability management.

References

[ABB 2004] ABB Group; 2004, www.abb.com

[Akao 1990] Y. Akao; *Quality Function Deployment*, Productivity Press, Portland, Oregon, 1990.

[Alexander and Stevens 2003] I. Alexander and R. Stevens; *Writing Better Requirements*, Addison-Wesley, Reading, Massachusetts, 2002.

[Alur et al. 2003] D. Alur, D. Malks, and J. Crupi; *Core J2EE Patterns: Best Practices and Design Strategies*, 2nd edition, Prentice Hall, Englewood Cliffs, New Jersey, 2003.

[America and Van Wijgerden 2000] P. America and J. van Wijgerden; "Requirements Modeling for Families of Complex Systems", In: *Proceedings of Software Architectures for Product Families, IW-SAPF-3, Las Palmas de Gran Canaria*, Springer, Berlin Heidelberg New York, LNCS 1951, 2000, pp. 199–209.

[Ardis and Weiss 1997] M.A. Ardis and D.M. Weiss; "Defining Families: The Commonality Analysis", In: *Proceedings of the 19th International Conference on Software Engineering (ICSE '97), Boston, Massachusetts, 7–23 May*, 1997.

[Ardis et al. 2000] M. Ardis, P. Dudak, L. Dor, W.-J. Leu, L. Nakatani, B. Olsen, and P. Pontrelli; "Domain-Engineered Configuration Control", In: *Proceedings of the 1st Software Product Line Conference (SPLC-1), Denver, Colorado, August 28–31*, Kluwer, Dordrecht, 2000, pp. 479–493.

[Atkinson 2001] C. Atkinson; *Component-based Product Line Engineering with UML*, Addison-Wesley, Reading, Massachusetts, 2001.

[Bachmann et al. 2003] F. Bachmann, M. Goedicke, J. Leite, R. Nord, K. Pohl, B. Ramesh, and A. Vilbig; "A Meta-Model for Representing Variability in Product Family Development", In: *Proceedings of the 5th International Workshop on Product Family Engineering (PFE-5), Siena, Italy*, 2003, pp. 66–80.

[Baeten et al. 1990] J.C.M. Baeten, W.P. Weijland, and C.J van Rijsbergen; *Process Algebra*, Cambridge University Press, 1990.

[Barnard 1938] C. Barnard; *The Function of the Executive*, 1938; 30th Anniversary edition, Harvard University Press, Cambridge, Massachusetts, 1968.

[Batory et al. 2004] D. Batory, V. Singhal, J. Thomas, S. Dasari, B. Geraci, and M. Sirkin; "The GenVoca Model of Software-System Generators", IEEE Software, vol. 11, no. 5, September, 1994, pp. 89–94.

[Belina et al. 1991] F. Belina, D. Hogrefe, and A. Sarma; *SDL with Applications from Protocol Specification*, The BCS Practitioner Series, Prentice Hall, Harlow, Essex, 1991.

[Bergstra and Klop 1984] J.A. Bergstra and J.W. Klop; "Process Algebra for Synchronous Communication", *Information & Control*, vol. 60, no. 1/3, 1984, pp. 109–137.

[Binder 1999] R.V. Binder; *Testing Object-Oriented Systems – Models, Patterns, and Tools*, Addison-Wesley, Reading, Massachusetts, 1999.

[Bluetooth 2004] The Official Bluetooth Website, 2004, www.bluetooth.com/

[Boeckle et al. 2002] G. Boeckle, J. Bermejo, P. Knauber, C. Krueger, J. Leite, F. van der Linden, L. Northrop, M. Stark, and D. Weiss; "Adopting and Institutionalizing a Product Line Culture", In: *Proceedings of the 2nd International Conference on Software Product Lines (SPLC-2), San Diego, USA*, Springer, Berlin Heidelberg New York, LNCS 2379, 2002, pp. 48–59.

[Boeckle et al. 2004a] G. Boeckle, P. Clements, J. D. McGregor, D. Muthig, and K. Schmid; "Calculating ROI for Software Product Lines", *IEEE Software*, vol. 21, no. 3, 2004.

[Boeckle et al. 2004b] G. Boeckle, P. Knauber, K. Pohl, and K. Schmid (eds.); *Software-Produktlinien – Methoden, Einführung und Praxis* (in German), dpunkt, Heidelberg, 2004.

[Boehm 1988] B. Boehm; *A Spiral Model of Software Development and Enhancement*, IEEE Computer, vol. 21, no. 5, May, 1988, pp .61–72.

[Boehm et al. 2000] B. Boehm, E. Horowitz, R. Madachy, D. Reifer, B. Clark, B. Steece, A.W. Brown, S. Chulani, and C. Abts; *Software Cost Estimation with Cocomo II*, Prentice Hall, Englewood Cliffs, New Jersey, 2000.

[Boeing 2004] The Boeing Company Website, 2004, www.boeing.com

[Booch et al. 1999] G. Booch, J. Rumbaugh, and I. Jacobson; *The Unified Modelling Language User Guide*, Addison-Wesley, Reading, Massachusetts, 1999.

[Bosch 2000a] J. Bosch; "Organizing for Software Product Lines", In: *Proceedings of the 3rd International Workshop on Software Architectures for Product Families (IWSAPF-3), Las Palmas de Gran Canaria, Spain, March 15–17*, Springer, Berlin Heidelberg New York, LNCS 1951, 2000.

[Bosch 2000b] J. Bosch; *Design and Use of Software Architectures: Adopting and Evolving a Product-Line Approach*, Addison-Wesley, Reading, Massachusetts, 2000.

[Bosch 2004] Robert Bosch GmbH Website, 2004, www.bosch.com

[Bosch et al. 2002] J. Bosch, G. Florijn, D. Greefhorst, J. Kuusela, H. Obbink, and K. Pohl; "Variability Issues in Software Product Lines" In: *Proceedings of the 4th International Workshop on Product Family Engineering (PFE-4), Bilbao, Spain, October 3–5, 2001*, Springer, Berlin Heidelberg New York, LNCS 2290, 2002, pp. 13–21.

[Bræk and Haugen 1993] R. Bræk and Ø. Haugen; *Engineering Real Time Systems*, BCS Practitioner Series, Prentice Hall, Harlow, Essex, 1993.

[Brinksma 1988] E. Brinksma; *On the Design of Extended LOTOS – A Specification Language for Open Distributed Systems*, PhD thesis, University of Twente, 1988.

[British Standards 1998] British Standards; *Software Testing, Part 2: Software Component Testing, Standard 7925-2*, 1998.

[Brockhoff 1999] K. Brockhoff; *Produktpolitik* (in German), 4th edition, Lucius & Lucius, Stuttgart, 1999.

[Brownsword and Clements 1996] L. Brownsword and P. Clements; "A Case Study in Successful Product Line Development", Technical Report no. CMU/SEI-96-TR-016, Carnegie–Mellon Software Engineering Institute, 1996.

[Bühne et al. 2003] S. Bühne, G. Halmans, and K. Pohl; "Modeling Dependencies between Variation Points in Use Case Diagrams", In: *Proceedings of the 9th International Workshop on Requirements Engineering – Foundation for Software Quality (REFSQ'03), Klagenfurt/Velden, Österreich, June*, 2003.

[Bühne et al. 2004a] S. Bühne, G. Halmans, K. Pohl, M. Weber, H. Kleinwechter, and T. Wierczoch; "Defining Requirements at Different Levels of Abstraction", In: *Proceedings of the International Requirements Engineering Conference 2004 (RE'04), Kyoto, Japan*, IEEE Computer Society, 2004.

[Bühne et al. 2004b] S. Bühne, K. Lauenroth, and K. Pohl; "Why is it not Sufficient to Model Requirements Variability with Feature Models?", In: *Proceedings of the Workshop: Automotive Requirements Engineering (AURE'04), co-located at RE'04, Nagoya, Japan*, 2004.

[Bühne et al. 2004c] S. Bühne, K. Lauenroth, K. Pohl, and M. Weber; Modelling Features for Multi-Criteria Product-Lines in the Automotive Industry. In: *Proceedings of the Workshop on Software Engineering for Automotive Systems (SEAS), co-located at ICSE 2004, Edinburgh, UK*, 2004.

[Bühne et al. 2005] S. Bühne, K. Lauenroth, and K. Pohl; "Modelling Requirements Variability across Product Lines", In: *Proceedings of the 13th IEEE International Conference on Requirements Engineering (RE'05), Paris*, IEEE Computer Society, 2005.

[Buhrdorf et al. 2003] R. Buhrdorf, D. Churchett, and C.W. Krueger; "Salion's Experience with a Reactive Software Product Line Approach", In: *Proceedings of the 5th International Workshop on Software Product-Family Engineering (PFE-5), Siena, Italy*, Springer, Berlin Heidelberg New York, LNCS 3014, 2003, pp. 317–322.

[Burnstein 2002] I. Burnstein; *Practical Software Testing: A Process-oriented Approach*, Springer, Berlin Heidelberg New York, 2002.

[Buschmann et al. 1996] F. Buschman, R. Meunier, H. Rohnert, P. Sommerlad, and M. Stal; *Pattern-oriented Software Architecture – A System of Patterns*, Wiley, Chichester, 1996.

[Business Case 2004] The Business Case Web Site, 2004, at www.solutionmatrix.com/

[CAFÉ 2004] CAFÉ – From Concepts to Application in System-Family Engineering, The Official Homepage of the CAFÉ Project, 2004, www.esi.es/Cafe/

[Carroll 1995] J.M. Carroll; *Scenario-Based Design: Envisioning Work and Technology in System Development*, Wiley, New York, 1995.

[Carroll 2000] J.M. Carroll; *Making Use: Scenario-Based Design of Human-Computer Interactions*, MIT Press, Cambridge, Massachusetts, 2000.

[Chen 1976] P. Chen; "The Entity-Relationship Model – Towards a Unified View of Data", *ACM Transactions on Database Systems*, vol. 1, no. 1, March 1976. pp. 9–36.

[Clark and Wheelwright 1995] K. Clark and S. Wheelwright; *Leading Product Development*, Free Press, New York, 1995.

[Clements and Northrop 2001] P. Clements and L. Northrop; *Software Product Lines: Practices and Patterns*, Addison-Wesley, Reading, Massachusetts, 2001.

[Cockburn 2000] A. Cockburn; Writing Effective Use Cases, Addison-Wesley, Boston, Massachusetts, 2000.

[Cohen 2003] S. Cohen; *Predicting When Product Line Investment Pays*, SEI Technical Note no. CMU/SEI-2003-TN-017, 2003.

[Cohen et al. 2002] S. Cohen, E. Dunn, and A. Soule; *Successful Product Line Development and Sustainment: A DoD Case Study*, Technical Report no. CMU/SEI-2002-TN-018, Carnegie–Mellon Software Engineering Institute, 2002.

[Cohen et al. 2004] S. Cohen, D. Zubrow, and E. Dunn; *Case Study: A Measurement Program for Product Lines*, Technical Report no. CMU/SEI-2004-TN-023, Carnegie–Mellon Software Engineering Institute, 2004.

[Condon 2002] D. Condon; *Software Product Management*, Aspatore, Boston, Massachusetts, 2002.

[Cooper 2001] R. Cooper; *Winning at new products*, 3rd edition, Perseus Publishing, Philadelphia, 2001.

[Cooper et al. 2001] R. Cooper, S. Edgett, and E. Kleinschmidt; *Portfolio Management for new Products*, 2nd edition, Perseus Publishing, Philadelphia, 2001.

[Coplien 1998] J. Coplien; *Multi-Paradigm Design for C++*, Addison-Wesley, Boston, Massachusetts, 1998.

[Coplien et al. 1998] J. Coplien, D. Hoffmann, and D. Weiss; "Commonality and Variability in Software Engineering", *IEEE Software*, vol. 15, no. 6, 1998, pp. 37–45.

[Cummins 2004] Cummins Inc. Website, 2004, www.cummins.com

[Cusumano and Nobeoka 1998] M.A. Cusumano and K. Nobeoka; *Thinking Beyond Lean – How Multi-Project Management is Transforming Product Development at Toyota and Other Companies*, Free Press, New York, 1998.

[Cusumano and Selby 1998] M.A. Cusumano and R. Selby; *Microsoft Secrets*, Touchstone, New York, 1998.

[Cyert and March 1963] R.M. Cyert and J.G. March; *A Behavioral Theory of the Firm*, Prentice Hall, Englewood Cliffs, New Jersey, 1963.

[Czarnecki and Eisenecker 2000] K. Czarnecki and U.W. Eisenecker; *Generative Programming: Methods, Tools, and Applications*, Addison-Wesley, Reading, Massachusetts, 2000.

[Dager 2000] J.C. Dager; "Cummins's Experience in Developing a Software Product Line Architecture for Real-time Embedded Diesel Engine Controls", In: *Proceedings of the 1st Software Product Line Conference (SPLC-1), Denver*, Kluwer, Dordrecht, 2000, pp. 23–46.

[Davis 1987] S.M. Davis; *Future Perfect*, Addison-Wesley, Boston, Massachusetts, 1987.

[Davis 1993] A.M. Davis; *Software Requirements: Objects, Functions, & States*, 2nd edition, Prentice Hall, Englewood Cliffs, New Jersey, 1993.

[DeBaud and Schmid 1999] J. DeBaud and K. Schmid; "A Systematic Approach to Derive the Scope of Software Product Lines", In: *Proceedings of the 21st International Conference on Software Engineering (ICSE'99), Los Angeles, California, May 16–22*, IEEE Computer Society Press, Los Alamitos, 1999, pp. 34–43.

[De Lange and Jansen 2001] F. de Lange and T. Jansen; "The Philips-OpenTV Product Family Architecture for Interactive Set-Top Boxes", In: *Proceedings of the 4th International Product Family Engineering Workshop (PFE-4), Bilbao*, Springer, Berlin Heidelberg New York, LNCS 2290, 2001, pp. 187–206.

[DeMarco 1979] T. DeMarco; *Structured Analysis and System Specification*, Prentice Hall, Englewood Cliffs, New Jersey, 1979.

[Dijkstra 1972] E. Dijkstra; "Notes on Structured Programming", In: O. Dahl, E. Dijkstra, and C. Hoare (eds.); *Structured Programming*, Academic Press, New York, 1972.

[Doerr and Sharp 2000] B.S. Doerr and D.C. Sharp; "Freeing Product Line Architectures from Execution Dependencies", In: *Proceedings of the 1st Software Product Line Conference (SPLC-1), Denver*, Kluwer, Dordrecht, 2000, pp. 313–329.

[Douma and Schreuder 2002] S. Douma and H. Schreuder; *Economic Approaches to Organizations*, 3rd edition, Prentice Hall, Englewood Cliffs, New Jersey, 2002.

[Dröschel and Wiemers 2000] W. Dröschel and M. Wiemers; *Das V-Modell 97* (in German), Oldenbourg, München, 2000.

[Echelon 1999] Echelon Corporation; *Introduction to the LonWorks System*, 1999, www.echelon.com

[EIBA 2004] European Installation Bus Association, 2004, www.eiba.com

[Eixelsberger and Beckman 2000] W. Eixelsberger and H. Beckman; "The TCS Experience with the Recovery of Family Architecture", In: M. Jazayeri, A. Ran, and F. van der Linden (eds.), *Software Architecture for Product Families – Principles and Practice*, Addison-Wesley, Reading, Massachusetts, 2000, pp. 209–231.

[Erichson 2000] B. Erichson; "Prüfung von Produktideen und –konzepten" (in German), In: S. Albers and A. Herrmann (eds.), *Handbuch Produktmanagement*, Gabler, Wiesbaden, 2000, pp. 385–410.

[Fafchamps 1994] D. Fafchamps; "Organizational Factors and Reuse", *IEEE Software*, vol. 11, no. 5, 1994, pp. 31–41.

[Fagan 1976] M.E. Fagan; "Design and Code Inspections to Reduce Errors in Program Development", *IBM Systems Journal*, vol. 15, no. 3, 1976, pp 182–211.

[Fagan 1986] M.E. Fagan; "Advances in Software Inspections", *IEEE Transactions on Software Engineering*, vol. 12, no. 7, 1986, pp. 744–751.

[Fantechi et al. 2003] A. Fantechi, S. Gnesi, I. John, G. Lami, and J. Dörr; "Elicitation of Use Cases for Product Lines", In: *Proceedings of the 5th International Workshop on Software Product-Family Engineering (PFE-5), Siena, Italy*, Springer, Berlin Heidelberg New York, LNCS 3014, 2003, pp. 152–167.

[Fayol 1916] H. Fayol; *Administration Industrielle et Generale (in French)*, Paris, 1916.

[Feijs et al. 1994] L.M.G Feijs, H.B.M. Jonkers, and C.A. Middelburg; *Notations for Software Design*, FACIT series, Springer, Berlin Heidelberg New York, 1994.

[Fey et al. 2002] D. Fey, R. Fajta, and A. Boros; "Feature Modeling - A Meta-Model to Enhance Usability and Usefulness"; In: *Proceedings of the 2nd International Conference on Software Product Lines (SPLC-2), San Diego, USA*, Springer, Berlin Heidelberg New York, LNCS 2379, 2002, pp. 198–216.

[Firesmith 1994] D.G. Firesmith; "Inheritance Diagrams: Which Way is Up?", *Journal of Object-Oriented Programming*, vol. 7, no. 1, 1994, pp. 10–16.

[Freedman and Weinberg 1990] D.P. Freedman and G.M. Weinberg; *Handbook of Walkthroughs, Inspections, and Technical Reviews: Evaluating Programs, Projects, and Products*, 3rd edition, Dorset House, New York, 1990.

[Gamma et al. 1995] E. Gamma, R. Helm, R. Johnson, and J. Vlissides; *Design Patterns: Elements of Reusable Object-Oriented Software*, Addison-Wesley, Reading, Massachusetts, 1995.

[Ganz and Layes 1998] C. Ganz and M. Layes; "Modular Turbine Control Software: A Control Software Architecture for the ABB Gas Turbine Family", In: *Proceedings of the 2nd International ESPRIT ARES Workshop, Las Palmas de Gran Canaria*, Springer, Berlin Heidelberg New York, LNCS 1429, 1998, pp. 32–38.

[Geyer and Becker 2002] L. Geyer and M. Becker; "On the Influence of Variabilities on the Application-Engineering Process of a Product Family", In: *Proceedings of the 2nd International Conference on Software Lines (SPLC-2), San Diego, USA*, Springer, Berlin Heidelberg New York, LNCS 2379, 2002, pp. 1–14.

[Gilb and Graham 1993] T. Gilb and D. Graham, *Software Inspection*, 5th edition, Addison-Wesley, Boston, Massachusetts, 1993.

[Gougen and Linde 1993] J.A. Gougen and C. Linde; "Techniques for Requirements Elicitation", In: *Proceedings of the IEEE International Symposium on Requirements Engineering*, January 4–6, 1993, San Diego, California, IEEE Computer Society Press, Silver Spring, Maryland, 1993, pp. 152–164.

[Greenfield et al. 2004] J. Greenfield, K. Short, S. Cook, S. Kent, and J. Crupi; *Software Factories: Assembling Applications with Patterns, Models, Frameworks, and Tools*, Wiley, New York, 2004.

[Griffin and Hauser 1993] A. Griffin and J.R. Hauser; "The Voice of the Customer", *Marketing Science*, vol. 12, no. 1, 1993, pp. 1–27.

[Hackman and Oldham 1975] J.R. Hackman and G.R. Oldham; "Development of the Job Diagnostic Survey", *Journal of Applied Psychology*, vol. 60, 1975, pp. 150–170.

[Hackman and Oldham 1976] J.R. Hackman and G.R. Oldham; "Motivation through the Design of Work: Test of a Theory"; *Organizational Behavior and Human Performance*, vol. 16, 1976, pp. 250–279.

[Hackman and Oldham 1980] J.R. Hackman and G.R. Oldham; *Work Redesign*, Addison-Wesley, Reading, Massachusetts, 1980.

[Hackman et al. 1978] J.R. Hackman, J.L. Pearce, and J.C. Wolfe; "Effects of Changes in Job Characteristics on Work Attitudes and Behaviors: A Naturally Occurring Quasi Experiment"; *OBHPD*, vol. 21, 1978, pp. 289–304.

[Hall of Fame 2004] SPLC2 – Product Line Hall of Fame, 2004, http://www.sei.cmu.edu/SPLC2 /SPLC2_hof.html

[Halmans and Pohl 2001] G. Halmans and K. Pohl; "Considering Product Family Assets when Defining Customer Requirements", In: *Proceedings of the International Workshop on Product Line Engineering – The Early Steps – Planning, Modeling and Managing (PLEE'01), Erfurt, Fraunhofer IESE*, 2001, pp. 37–42.

[Halmans and Pohl 2002] G. Halmans and K. Pohl; "Software Product Family Variability: Essential Capabilities and Realization Aspects", In: *Proceedings of ICSE 2002 Workshop – 3rd International Workshop on Software Product Lines – Economics, Architectures, and Implications*, 2002.

[Halmans and Pohl 2003] G. Halmans and K. Pohl; "Communicating the Variability of a Software Product Family to Customers", *Software and Systems Modeling*, vol. 2, no. 1, March 2003, pp. 15–36.

[Harel 1987] D. Harel; "A Visual Formalism for Complex Systems", *Science of Computer Programming*, vol. 8, 1987, pp. 231–274.

[Haumer et al. 1999] P. Haumer, P. Heymans, M. Jarke, and K. Pohl; "Bridging the Gap Between Past and Future in Requirements Engineering – A Scenario-Based Approach", In: *Proceedings of 4th IEEE International Symposium on Requirements Engineering (RE'99), Los Alamitos*, IEEE Computer Society Press, 1999.

[Hay and v. Halle 2002] D. Hay and B. von Halle; *Requirements Analysis*, Prentice Hall, Harlow, Essex, 2002.

[Hein et al. 2000] A. Hein, M. Schlick, and R. Vinga-Martins; "Applying Feature Models in Industrial Settings", In: *Proceedings of the 1st Software Product Line Conference (SPLC-1), Denver*, P. Donohoe (ed.), Kluwer, Dordrecht, 2000, pp. 47–70.

[Hein et al. 2004] A. Hein, T. Fischer, and S. Thiel; "Fahrerassistenzsysteme bei der Robert Bosch GmbH" (in German), In: G. Böckle, P. Knauber, K. Pohl, and K. Schmid (eds.), *Software-Produktfamilien – Methoden, Einführung und Praxis*, dpunkt, Heidelberg, 2004, pp. 193–205.

[Herrmann 1998] A. Hermann; *Produktmanagement* (in German), Vahlen, München, 1998.

[Herrmann and Seilheimer 2000] A. Herrmann and C. Seilheimer; "Variantenmanagement" (in German), In: S. Albers and A. Herrmann (eds.), *Handbuch Produktmanagement*, Gabler, Wiesbaden, 2000, pp. 607–637.

[Hewlett-Packard 2004] Hewlett-Packard Website, 2004, www.hp.com

[Hill et al. 1992] W. Hill, R. Fehlbaum, and P. Ulrich; *Organisationslehre 2 – Theoretische Ansätze und praktische Methoden der Organisation sozialer Systeme (in German)*, 4th edition, Paul Haupt, Berne, 1992.

[Hoare 1985] C.A.R. Hoare; *Communicating Sequential Processes*, Prentice Hall, Harlow, Essex, 1985.

[Huber and Kopsch 2000] F. Huber and A. Kopsch; "Produktbündelung", In: S. Albers and A. Herrmann (eds.), *Handbuch Produktmanagement (in German)*, Gabler, Wiesbaden, 2000, p. 575–606.

[Hull et al. 2002] E. Hull, K. Jackson, and J. Dick; *Requirements Engineering*, Springer, Berlin Heidelberg New York, 2002.

[IEEE 1990] IEEE; *IEEE Standard Glossary of Software Engineering Terminology (IEEE Std 610.12-1990)*, IEEE Computer Society, 1990.

[IEEE 1998] IEEE Computer Society; *IEEE Standard for Software Test Documentation*, IEEE STD 829-1998, IEEE Press, IEEE Computer Society, Los Alamitos, 1998.

[InHouse 2004] Innovation Center Intelligent House Duisburg, 2004, www.inhaus-duisburg.de

[Jacobson et al. 1997] I. Jacobson, M. Griss, and P. Jonsson; *Software Reuse: Architecture, Process and Organisation for Business Success*, Addison-Wesley, Reading, Massachusetts, 1997.

[Jazayeri et al. 2000] M. Jazayeri, A. Ran, and F.J. van der Linden; *Software Architecture for Product Families*, Addison-Wesley, Reading, Massachusetts, 2000.

[John and Muthig 2002] I. John and D. Muthig; "Modeling Variability with Use Cases", Technical Report no. 063.02/E, IESE, Kaiserslautern, 2002.

[Kamsties et al. 2003a] E. Kamsties, K. Pohl, S. Reis, and A. Reuys; "Testing Variabilities in Use Case Models", In: *Proceedings of 5th International Workshop on Software Product-Family Engineering (PFE-5), Siena, Italy*, Springer, Berlin Heidelberg New York, LNCS 3014, 2003, pp. 6–18.

[Kamsties et al. 2003b] E. Kamsties, K. Pohl, and A. Reuys; "Supporting Test Case Derivation in Domain Engineering", In: *Proceedings of 7th World Conference on Integrated Design and Process Technology (IDPT 2003), Austin, USA*, December 2003.

[Kang et al. 1990] K. Kang, S. Cohen, J.A. Hess, W.E. Novak, and S.A. Peterson; *Feature-Oriented Domain Analysis (FODA) Feasibility Study*, Technical Report, Software Engineering Institute, Carnegie–Mellon University, 1990.

[Kang et al. 2002] K. Kang, J. Lee, and P. Donohoe; "Feature-Oriented Product Line Engineering", *IEEE Software*, vol. 19, no. 4, 2002, pp. 58–65.

[Kano 1984] N. Kano; "Attractive Quality and Must-be Quality", *Hinshitsu: The Journal of the Japanese Society for Quality Control*, vol. 14, no. 2, 1984, pp. 39–48.

[Kano et al. 1996] N. Kano, N. Seraku, F. Takahashi, and S. Tsuji; "Attractive Quality and Must-be Quality", In: J.D. Hromi (ed.), *The Best on Quality*, vol. 7, Quality Press, Milwaukee, Wisconsin, 1996.

[Kay and Houser 2001] E. Key and A. Houser; *XML Weekend Crash Course*, Wiley, New York, 2001.

[Kazman et al. 2000] R. Kazman, M. Klein, and P. Clements; "ATAM: Method for Architecture Evaluation", Technical Report CMU/SEI-2000-TR-004, Software Engineering Institute, Carnegie–Mellon University, 2000.

[Kiczales et al. 1997] G. Kiczales, J. Lamping, A. Menhdhekar, C. Maeda, C. Lopes, J.-M. Loingtier, and J. Irwin; "Aspect-Oriented Programming", In: *Proceedings European Conference on Object-Oriented Programming*, Springer, Berlin Heidelberg New York, LNCS 1241, 1997, pp. 220–242.

[Kleinaltenkamp and Plinke 1999] M. Kleinaltenkamp and W. Plinke; *Markt und Produktmanagement- Die Instrumente des technischen Vertriebs* (in German), Springer, Berlin Heidelberg New York, 1999.

[Kleppe et al. 2003] A. Kleppe, J. Warmer, and W. Bast; *MDA Explained: The Model Driven Architecture – Practice and Promise*, Addison-Wesley, Reading, Massachusetts, 2003.

[Kolb and Muthig 2003] R. Kolb and D. Muthig; "Challenges in Testing Software Product Lines" (in German), In: *Arbeitskreis Software-Qualität Franken e.V.: CONQUEST 2003, 7th Conference on Quality Engineering in Software Technology, Proceedings: EuroMotive 2003*, Automotive Software Technology, Nürnberg, 2003, pp.103–113.

[Kovitz 1999] B.L. Kovitz; *Practical Software Requirements: A Manual of Content and Style*, Manning, 1999.

[Kruchten 1995] P.B. Kruchten; "The 4+1 View Model of Architecture", *IEEE Software*, November 1995, pp. 42–50.

[Kruchten 2000] P. Kruchten; *The Rational Unified Process*, Addison-Wesley, Reading, Massachusetts, 2000.

[Krueger 2002] C.W. Krueger; "Data from Salion's Software Product Line Initiative", Technical Report no. 2002-07-08-1, BigLever Software, 2002.

[Kulak and Guiney 2003] D. Kulak and E. Guiney; *Use Cases: Requirements in Context*, 2nd edition, Addison-Wesley, Reading, Massachusetts, 2003.

[Larman 2002] C. Larman; *Applying UML and Patterns – An Introduction to Object-Oriented Analysis and Design and the Unified Process*, Prentice Hall, Englewood Cliffs, New Jersey, 2002.

[Laurent and Cerami 1999] S.S. Laurent and E. Cerami; *Building XML Applications*, McGraw-Hill, New York, 1999.

[Lee et al. 2000] K. Lee, K.C. Kang, E. Koh, W. Chae, B. Kim, and B.W. Choi; "Domain-Oriented Engineering of Elevator Control Software", In: *Proceedings of the 1st Software Product Line Conference (SPLC-1), Denver, Patrick Donohoe (ed.)*, Kluwer, Dordrecht, 2000, pp. 3–22.

[LGIS 2004] LG Industrial Systems Co., Ltd Website, 2004, www.lgis.com

[LonMark 2004] LonMark Interoperability Association, 2004, www.lonmark.org

[Lucent 2004] Lucent Technologies Website, 2004, www.lucent.com

[Market Maker 2004] Market Maker Software AG Website, 2004, www.market-maker.de

[McClure 1995] C. McClure; *Experiences in Organizing for Software Reuse*, Extended Intelligence, Inc., 1995.

[McCord and Eppinger 1993] K.R. McCord and S.D. Eppinger; "Managing the Integration Problem in Concurrent Engineering", MIT, Sloan School of Management, Report no. 10-48-93, 1993.

[McGregor and Sykes 2001] J.D. McGregor and D.A. Sykes; *A Practical Guide to Testing Object Oriented Software*, Addison-Wesley, Reading, Massachusetts, 2001.

[McGregor et al. 2002] J.D. McGregor, S. Jarrad, L.M. Northrop, and K. Pohl; "Initiating Software Product Lines", *IEEE Software*, vol. 19, no. 4, July 2002, pp.24–27.

[McMenamin and Palmer 1984] S.M. McMenamin and J.F. Palmer; *Essential Systems Analysis*, Yourdon Press, Upper Saddle River, New Jersey, 1984.

[Meyer and Lehnerd 1997] M. Meyer and A. Lehnerd; *The Power of Product Platforms*, Free Press, New York, 1997.

[Milner 1980] R. Milner; *A Calculus of Communicating Systems*, Springer, Berlin Heidelberg New York, LNCS 92, 1980.

[Morabito et al. 1999] J. Morabito, I. Sack, and A. Bhate; *Organization Modeling - Innovative Architectures for the 21st Century*, Prentice Hall, Englewood Cliffs, New Jersey, 1999.

[Muthig and Atkinson 2002] D. Muthig and C. Atkinson; "Model-Driven Product Line Architectures", In: *Proceedings of the 2nd International Conference on Software Product Lines (SPLC-2), San Diego, USA*, Springer, Berlin Heidelberg New York, LNCS 2379, 2002, pp. 110–129.

[Muthig and Patzke 2003] D. Muthig and T. Patzke; "Generic Implementation of Product Line Components", In: *Objects, Components, Architectures, Services, and Applications for a Networked World, International Conference NetObjectDays (NODe 2002), Erfurt, Germany*, Springer, Berlin Heidelberg New York, LNCS 2591, 2003, pp. 313–329.

[NRO 2004] The National Reconnaissance Office Website, 2004, www.nro.gov

[Nuseibeh 2001] B. Nuseibeh; Weaving the Software Development Process Between Requirements and Architecture, In: *From Software Requirements to Architectures (STRAW '01), 23rd International Conference on Software Engineering (ICSE 2001), Toronto, Ontario, Canada, 12–19 May*, 2001.

[NUWC 2004] The Naval Undersea Warfare Center Website, 2004, www.nuwc.navy.mil

[Obbink et al. 2000] J.H. Obbink, J. Müller, P. America, R. van Ommering, G. Muller, W. van der Sterren, and J.G. Wijnstra; *COPA: A Component-Oriented Platform Architecting Method for Families of Software-Intensive Electronic Products, Tutorial at SPLC-1, Denver, August*, 2000, www.extra.research.philips.com/SAE/COPA /COPA_Tutorial.pdf

[OMG 2003] Object Management Group; *Unified Modeling Language Specification, Version 2.0 (Final Adopted Specification, ptc/03-02-08)*, 2003, www.omg.org/cgi-bin/doc?ptc/2003-08-02

[OSGi 2003] The Open Services Gateway Initiative; *OSGi Service Platform Release 3*, March 2003, www.osgi.org

[Parnas 1976] D. Parnas; "On the Design and Development of Program Families", *Transactions on Software Engineering*, vol. SE-2, no. 1, March 1976, pp. 1–9.

[Pepels 2003] W. Pepels; *Produktmanagement* (in German), 4th edition, Oldenbourg, München, 2003.

[Perrow 1970] C. Perrow; *Organizational Analysis: A Sociological View*, Wadsworth, Monterey, California, 1970.

[Perrow 1972] C. Perrow; *Complex Organizations: A Critical Essay*, 1st edition 1972, 3rd edition, Random House, New York, 1986.

[Peterson 1981] J.L. Peterson; *Petri Net Theory and the Modeling of Systems*, Prentice Hall, Harlow, Essex, 1981.

[Philips 2004] Philips Website, 2004, www.philips.com

[PL-Framework 2004] SEI; A Framework for Software Product Line Practice, 2004, http://www.sei.cmu.edu/plp/framework.html

[Plinke 2002] W. Plinke; "Unternehmensstrategie" (in German), In: M. Kleinaltenkamp and W. Plinke (eds.), *Strategisches Business-to-business-Marketing*, 2nd edition, Springer, Berlin Heidelberg New York, 2002, pp. 1–55.

[Pohl 1994] K. Pohl; "The Three Dimensions of Requirements Engineering: A Framework and its Applications", *Information Systems, Special Issue on Computer Supported Information System Development*, vol. 19, no. 3, 1994.

[Pohl 1996] K. Pohl; *Process-Centered Requirements Engineering*, Research Studies Press, Wiley, Taunton, Somerset, 1996.

[Pohl 1997] K. Pohl; "Requirements Engineering", In: A. Kent, J. Williams, and C.M. Hall (eds.), *Encyclopedia of Computer Science and Technology*, M. Dekker, New York, vol. 36, 1997, pp. 345–386.

[Pohl and Haumer 1997] K. Pohl, and P. Haumer; "Modelling Contextual Information about Scenarios", In: *Proceedings of the 3rd International Workshop on Requirements Engineering – Foundation for Software Quality (REFSQ'97), Barcelona, Spain*, University Press Namur, Namur, 1997, pp. 187–204.

[Pohl and Reuys 2001] K. Pohl and A. Reuys; "Considering Variabilities during Component Selection in Product Family Development", In: *Proceedings 4th International Workshop on Product Family Engineering (PFE-4), Bilbao*, 2001.

[Pohl and Sikora 2005] K. Pohl and E. Sikora; "Requirements Engineering für eingebettete Software" (in German), In: P. Liggesmeyer and D. Rombach (eds.), *Software Engineering eingebetteter Systeme: Grundlagen – Methodik – Anwendungen*, Elsevier, Heidelberg, 2005, pp. 101–140.

[Pohl et al. 2001a] K. Pohl, M. Brandenburg, and A. Gülich; "Scenario-based Change Integration in Product Family Development", In: *Proceedings of the 2nd ICSE Workshop on Software Product Lines – Economics, Architectures, and Implications, Toronto, Canada, Fraunhofer IESE*, 2001.

[Pohl et al. 2001b] K. Pohl, G. Böckle, P. Clements, H. Obbink, and D. Rombach (eds.); *Proceedings Dagstuhl Seminar Product Family Development, University of Essen, Germany*, 2001.

[Poulin 1997] J. Poulin; *Measuring Software Reuse*, Addison-Wesley, Reading, Massachusetts, 1997.

[PRIME 2005] PRIME – Process Integrated Modelling Environments, SEGOS-VM Tool Website, 2005, www.software-productline.com/SEGOS-VM-Tool/

[PRTM 2004] PRTM Management Consultants, 2004, www.prtm.com/pressreleases/2000/08.21.asp

[Reisig 1985] W. Reisig; *Petri Nets – An Introduction*, EATCS Monographs on Theoretical Computer Science 4, Springer, Berlin Heidelberg New York, 1985.

[Reuys et al. 2003] A. Reuys, S. Reis, E. Kamsties, K. Pohl; "Derivation of Domain Test Scenarios from Activity Diagrams", In: *Proceedings of the International Workshop on Product Line Engineering – The Early Steps – Planning, Modeling and Managing (PLEES'03), Fraunhofer IESE, Erfurt, September*, 2003.

[Reuys et al. 2004a] A. Reuys, E. Kamsties, K. Pohl, H. Götz, J. Neumann, and J. Weingärtner; "Testen von Software-Produktvarianten – Ein Erfahrungsbericht" (in German), In: *Tagungsband zur Multikonferenz Wirtschaftsinformatik (MKWI)*, Akademische Verlagsgesellschaft, Mannheim, 2004, pp. 244–259.

[Reuys et al. 2004b] A. Reuys, H. Götz, J. Neumann, and J. Weingärtner; "Medizintechnik bei Siemens AG Medical Solutions HS IM" (in German), In: G. Böckle, P. Knauber, K. Pohl, and K. Schmid (eds.), *Software-Produktfamilien – Methoden, Einführung und Praxis*, dpunkt, Heidelberg, 2004, pp. 247–259.

[Reuys et al. 2005] A. Reuys, E. Kamsties, K. Pohl, S. Reis; "Model-based System Testing of Software Product Families", In: *Proceedings of the 17th Conference on Advanced Information Systems Engineering (CAiSE'05). Porto, Portugal, June*, 2005, pp. 519–534.

[Robertson and Ulrich 1999] D. Robertson and K. Ulrich; "Produktplattformen: Was sie leisten, was sie erfordern" (in German), *Harvard Business Manager*, 4/1999, pp. 75-85.

[Roever 1994] M. Roever; "Fokussierte Produkt- und Programmgestaltung zur Komplexitätsreduzierung" (in German), In: H. Corsten (ed.), *Handbuch Produktionsmanagement*, Gabler, Wiesbaden, 1994, pp. 115–129.

[Rolland et al. 1998] C. Rolland, C. Souveyet, and C. Ben Achour; "Guiding Goal Modeling Using Scenarios", *IEEE Transactions on Software Engineering*, vol. 24, no. 12, December, 1998, pp. 1055–1071.

[Rösel 1998] A. Rösel; "Experiences with the Evolution of an Application Family Architecture", In: *Proceedings of Development and Evolution of Software Architectures for Product Families, 2nd International ESPRIT ARES Workshop, Las Palmas de Gran Canaria*, Springer, Berlin Heidelberg New York, LNCS 1429, 1998, pp. 39–48.

[Rumbaugh et al. 2003] J. Rumbaugh, I. Jacobson, and G. Booch; *The Unified Modeling Language Reference Manual*, 2nd edition, Addison-Wesley, Reading, Massachusetts, 2003.

[SaabTech 2004] SaabTech Website, 2004, www.saabtech.se

[Saaty 1990] T.L. Saaty; "How to Make a Decision: The Analytic Hierarchy Process", *European Journal of Operational Research*, vol. 48, no. 1, 1990, pp. 9–26.

[Sabisch 1996] H. Sabisch; "Produkte und Produktgestaltung" (in German), In: W. Kern, H.-H. Schröder, and J. Weber (eds.), *Handwörterbuch der Produktionswirtschaft*, Schäffer-Poeschel, Stuttgart, 1996, pp. 1439–1450.

[Salion 2004] Salion Inc. Website, 2004, www.salion.com

[Sauerwein 2000] E. Sauerwein; *Das Kano-Modell der Kundenzufriedenheit* (in German), Deutscher Universitäts-Verlag, Wiesbaden, 2000.

[Schewe 2000] G. Schewe; "Produktimitation" (in German), In: S. Albers and A. Herrmann (eds.), *Handbuch Produktmanagement*, Gabler, Wiesbaden, 2000, pp. 55–74.

[Schmid 2002] K. Schmid; "A Comprehensive Product Line Scoping Approach and Its Validation", In: *Proceedings of the 24th International Conference on Software Engineering (ICSE 2002), Orlando, Florida*, ACM Press, 2002, pp. 593–603.

[Schmid et al. 2004a] K. Schmid, I. John, R. Kolb, and G. Meier; "Eingebettete Systeme bei der Testo AG" (in German), In: G. Böckle, P. Knauber, K. Pohl, and K. Schmid (eds.), *Software-Produktfamilien – Methoden, Einführung und Praxis*, dpunkt, Heidelberg, 2004, pp. 221–231.

[Schmid et al. 2004b] K. Schmid, I. John, R. Kolb, and G. Meier; "Introducing the PuLSE Approach to an Embedded System Population at Testo AG", Technical Report no. 015.04/E, Fraunhofer IESE, 2004.

[Schmidt 1999] D.C. Schmidt; "Why Software Reuse has Failed and How to Make It Work for You", *C++ Report*, SIGS, vol. 11, no. 1, January, 1999.

[Schneider and Winters 2001] G. Schneider and J.P. Winters; *Applying Use Cases: A Practical Guide*, 2nd edition, Addison-Wesley, Reading, Massachusetts, 2001.

[Schröder and Zenz 1996] H.-H. Schröder and A. Zenz; "QFD" (in German), In: W. Kern, H.-H. Schröder, and J. Weber (eds.), *Handwörterbuch der Produktionswirtschaft*, 2nd edition, Schäffer-Poeschel, Stuttgart, 1996, col. 1697–1711.

[Senge 1990] P.M. Senge; *The Fifth Discipline. The art and practice of the learning organization*, Random House, New York, 1990.

[Sharp 2000] D.C. Sharp; "Component Based Product Line Development of Avionics Software", In: *Proceedings of the 1st Software Product Line Conference (SPLC-1), Denver*, Kluwer, Dordrecht, 2000, pp. 353–369.

[Shaw and Garlan 1996] M. Shaw and D. Garlan; *Software Architecture: Perspectives on an Emerging Discipline*, Prentice Hall, Englewood Cliffs, New Jersey, 1996.

[Siemens 2004] Siemens AG Medical Solutions, 2004, www.smed.com

[SoftwareProductLines 2004] Software Product Lines Website, 2004, www.softwareproductlines.com

[Sommerville and Sawyer 1997] I. Sommerville and P. Sawyer; *Requirements Engineering*, Wiley, Chichester, 1997.

[Soni et al. 1995] D. Soni, R. Nord, and C. Hofmeister; "Software Architecture in Industrial Applications", In: *Proceedings ICSE'95*, 1995, pp. 196–207.

[Spillner and Linz 2004] A. Spillner and T. Linz; *Basiswissen Softwaretest* (in German), 2nd edition, dpunkt, Heidelberg, 2004.

[Standish Group 1995] The Standish Group; *The CHAOS Report*, 1995, www.standishgroup.com/sample_research /chaos_1994_1.php

[Svahnberg et al. 2001] M. Svahnberg, J. v. Gurp, and Jan Bosch; "On the Notion of Variability in Software Product Lines", In: *Proceedings of the Working IEEE/IFIP Conference on Software Architecture (WICSA 2001), Amsterdam, The Netherlands*, 2001, pp. 45–55.

[Szyperski 1997] C. Szyperski; *Component Software – Beyond Object-oriented Programming*, Addison-Wesley, Reading, Massachusetts, 1997.

[Taylor 1911] F.W. Taylor; *The Principles of Scientific Management*, New York, 1911; New edition: Dover, New York, 1998.

[TechTarget 2004] TechTarget – SearchCIO.com Definitions, 2004, whatis.techtarget.com

[Testo 2004] Testo AG Website, 2004, www.testo.com

[Thayer and Dorfman 1997] R.H. Thayer and M. Dorfman; *Software Requirements Engineering*, IEEE Press, Piscataway, New Jersey, 2000.

[Toft et al. 2000] P. Toft, D. Coleman, and J. Ohta; "A Cooperative Model for Cross-Divisional Product Development for a Software Product Line", In: *Proceedings of the 1st Software Product Line Conference (SPLC-1), Denver*, Kluwer, Dordrecht, 2000, pp. 111–132.

[Tomczak et al. 2000] T. Tomczak, S. Reinecke, and P. Kaetzke; "Konzept zur Gestaltung und zum Controlling existierender Leistungen" (in German), In: S. Albers and A. Herrmann (eds.), *Handbuch Produktmanagement*, Gabler, Wiesbaden, 2000, pp. 443–459.

[Ulfat-Bunyadi et al. 2005] N. Ulfat-Bunyadi, E. Kamsties, and K. Pohl "Considering Variability in a System Family's Architecture during COTS Evaluation", In: *Proceedings of the 4th International Conference on COTS-Based Software Systems (ICCBSS 2005), Bilbao, Spain*, Springer, Berlin Heidelberg New York, LNCS 3412, 2005.

[V. Lamsweerde 2001] A. van Lamsweerde; "Goal-Oriented Requirements Engineering: A Guided Tour", In: *Proceedings of the 5th International Symposium on Requirements Engineering, Toronto, August*, 2001, pp. 249–263.

[V. Ommering 2002] R. van Ommering; "Building Product Populations with Software Components", In: *Proceedings of the 24th International Conference on Software Engineering (ICSE 2002), Orlando, Florida,* ACM Press, 2002, pp. 255–265.

[V. Ommering 2004] R. van Ommering; *Building Product Populations with Software Components,* PhD. Thesis, University of Groningen, 2004.

[V. Ommering et al. 2000] R. van Ommering, F. van der Linden, J. Kramer, and J. Magee; "The Koala Component Model for Consumer Electronics Software", *IEEE Computer,* March 2000, pp. 78–85.

[V.d. Linden 2002] F. van der Linden; "Software Product Families in Europe: The ESAPS and CAFÉ Projects", *IEEE Software,* vol. 19, no. 4, July/August 2002, pp. 41–49.

[V.d. Linden and Müller 1995] F. van der Linden and J.K. Müller; "Creating Architectures with Building Blocks", *IEEE Software,* vol. 12, no. 6, November 1995, pp. 51–60.

[V.d. Maßen and Lichter 2002] T. von der Maßen and H. Lichter; "Modeling Variability by UML Use Case Diagrams", In: *Proceedings of the International Workshop on Requirements Engineering for Product Lines (REPL'02),* 2002, pp. 19–25.

[V-Model 1997] V-Model, Development Standard for IT Systems of the Federal Republic of Germany, 1997, www.v-modell.iabg.de

[V-Model XT] V-Model XT, Federal Republic of Germany, 2004, www.v-modell-xt.de

[Wayne 1996] L. Wayne; "Reuse Economics: A Comparison of Seventeen Models and Directions for Future Research", In: *Proceedings of the 4th International Conference on Software Reuse (ICSR),* IEEE Computer Society Press, Silver Spring, Maryland, 1996, pp. 41–50.

[Weber 1922] M. Weber; *Wirtschaft und Gesellschaft* (in German), Tübingen, 1921/1922

[Weidenhaupt et al. 1998] K. Weidenhaupt, K. Pohl, M. Jarke, and P. Haumer; "Scenarios in System Development – Current Practice", *IEEE Software,* vol. 15, no. 2, 1998, pp. 34–45.

[Weinberg 1988] G. Weinberg; *Rethinking Systems Analysis and Design,* Dorset House, New York, 1988.

[Weiss 1998] D. Weiss; "Commonality Analysis: A Systematic Process for Defining Families", In: *Proceedings Development and Evolution of Software Architectures for Product Families, 2nd International ESPRIT ARES Workshop, Las Palmas de Gran Canaria,* Springer, Berlin Heidelberg New York, LNCS 1429, 1998, pp. 214–222.

[Weiss and Lai 1999] D.M. Weiss and C.T.R. Lai; *Software Product-Line Engineering – A Family-Based Software Development Process,* Addison-Wesley, Reading, Massachusetts, 1999.

[Welge and Al-Laham 1999] M. Welge and A. Al-Laham; *Strategisches Management* (in German), 2nd edition, Gabler, Wiesbaden, 1999.

[Wiegers 1999] K.E. Wiegers; *Software Requirements,* Microsoft Press, 1999.

[Wieringa 1996] R.J. Wieringa; *Requirements Engineering: Frameworks for Understanding,* Wiley, New York, 1996.

[Wijnstra 2002] J.G. Wijnstra; "Component Frameworks for a Medical Imaging Product Family", In: *Proceedings of Software Architectures for Product Families (IW-SAPF-3), Las Palmas de Gran Canaria,* Springer, Berlin Heidelberg New York, LNCS 1951, 2000, pp. 4–18.

[Woodward 1965] J. Woodward; *Industrial Organisation: Theory and Practice,* Oxford University Press, New York, 1965.

[Yourdon 1989] E. Yourdon, *Structured Walkthroughs,* 4th edition, Yourdon Press, Upper Saddle River, New Jersey, 1989.

Glossary

Application Artefacts are the *development artefacts* of specific product line applications (Definition 2-5 on p. 23).

Application Design is the sub-process of *application engineering* where the *reference architecture* is specialised into the application architecture.

Application Engineering is the process of software product line engineering in which the applications of the product line are built by reusing *domain artefacts* and exploiting the product line variability (Definition 2-2 on p. 21).

Application Realisation is the sub-process of *application engineering* where a single application is realised according to the application architecture by reusing domain realisation artefacts.

Application Requirements Engineering is the sub-process of *application engineering* dealing with the elicitation of stakeholder requirements, the creation of the application requirements specification, and the management of application requirements.

Application Testing is the sub-process of *application engineering* where domain test artefacts are reused to uncover evidence of defects in the application.

Architecture, see *software architecture.*

Architectural Structure is the decomposition of a software system into parts and relationships (Definition 6-1 on p. 117).

Architectural Texture is the collection of common development rules for realising the applications of a software product line (Definition 6-2 on p. 117).

Asset, see *development artefact.*

Component is a unit of composition with contractually specified *component interfaces* and explicit context dependencies only; it can be deployed independently and is subject to composition by third parties.

Component Framework is a structure of *components*, or object classes, where plug-in components or object classes may be added at specified plug-in locations. To fit, each plug-in has to obey rules defined by the framework (Definition 6-8 on p. 128).

Component Interface provides a connector between *components*. A required interface of a component has to be connected to a provided interface of another one.

COTS is the acronym of "Commercial Off-The-Shelf". This term subsumes *components* from different sources with different degrees of modification possibilities. Sources may vary from in-house, through nuances of non-developmental, to commercial.

Development Artefact is the output of a sub-process of *domain* or *application engineering*. Development artefacts encompass requirements, architecture, components, and tests (Definition 2-3 on p. 23).

Domain is an area of process or knowledge driven by business requirements and characterised by a set of concepts and terminology understood by stakeholders in that area. The problem domain and the solution domain are two kinds of domains.

Domain Artefacts are reusable *development artefacts* created in the sub-processes of *domain engineering*. A synonym is *product line artefacts* (Definition 2-4 on p. 23).

Domain Design is the sub-process of *domain engineering* where a *reference architecture* for the entire software product line is developed.

Domain Engineering is the process of *software product line engineering* in which the commonality and the variability of the product line are defined and realised (Definition 2-1 on p. 21).

Domain Realisation is the sub-process of *domain engineering* where the set of reusable *components* and interfaces of the product line is developed.

Domain Requirements Engineering is the sub-process of *domain engineering* where the common and variable *requirements* of the product line are defined, documented in reusable *requirements artefacts*, and continuously managed.

Domain Testing is the sub-process of *domain engineering* where evidence of defects in domain artefacts is uncovered and where reusable test artefacts for *application testing* are created.

External Variability is the variability of *domain artefacts* that is visible to customers; see also *internal variability* (Definition 4-7 on p. 68).

Feature is an end-user visible characteristic of a system (Definition 5-4 on p. 92).

Goal is an objective the system under consideration should achieve (Definition 5-3 on p. 92).

Internal Variability is variability of *domain artefacts* that is hidden from customers; see also *external variability* (Definition 4-8 on p. 68).

Mass Customisation is the large-scale production of goods tailored to individual customers' needs (Definition 1-1 on p. 4).

Orthogonal Variability Model is a model that defines the variability of a software product line. It relates the variability defined to other software development models such as feature models, use case models, design models, component models, and test models (Definition 4-9 on p. 75).

Platform, see *software platform*.

Product Line Artefacts, see *domain artefacts*.

Product Line Engineering, see *software product line engineering*.

Product Management is the process of controlling the development, production, and marketing of the software product line and its applications (Definition 9-3 on p. 167).

Reference Architecture is a core *software architecture* that captures the high-level design of a software product line.

Requirement is (1) a condition or capability needed by a user to solve a problem or achieve an objective. (2) A condition or capability that must be met or possessed by a system or system component to satisfy a contract, standard, specification, or other formally imposed document. (3) A documented representation of a condition or capability as in (1) or (2) (IEEE Std 610.12-1990) (Definition 5-1 on p. 91).

Requirements Artefacts are products of the requirements engineering process specified using natural language and/or requirements models (Definition 5-2 on p. 92).

Scenario is a concrete description of system usage, which provides a clear benefit for the actor of the system (Definition 5-5 on p. 93).

Software Architecture is the set of the main guiding development principles for one or more software applications. The principles are the solution of one or more architectural concerns dealing with quality. There are other, more instrumental, definitions in the literature.

Software Platform is a set of software subsystems and interfaces that form a common structure from which a set of derivative products can be efficiently developed and produced (Definition 1-4 on p. 15).

Software Product Line Engineering is a paradigm to develop software applications (software-intensive systems and software products) using *software platforms* and *mass customisation* (Definition 1-3 on p. 14).

Software Product Line Engineering Framework is an abstract representation of the two core processes for *software product line engineering* and the *assets* produced.

Test Artefacts are products of the test process containing plans, specifications, and test results (Definition 8-1 on p. 151).

Use Case is a description of system behaviour in terms of scenarios illustrating different ways to succeed or fail in attaining one or more *goals* (Definition 5-6 on p. 94).

Variability in Space is the existence of an artefact in different shapes at the same time (Definition 4-6 on p. 66).

Variability in Time is the existence of different versions of an artefact that are valid at different times (Definition 4-5 on p. 65).

Variability Object is a particular instance of a *variability subject* (Definition 4-2 on p. 60).

Variability Subject is a variable item of the real world or a variable property of such an item (Definition 4-1 on p. 60).

Variant is a representation of a *variability object* within *domain artefacts* (Definition 4-4 on p. 62).

Variation Point is a representation of a *variability subject* within *domain artefacts* enriched by contextual information (Definition 4-3 on p. 62).

Index